Jews in Twentieth-Century Ireland

Refugees, Anti-Semitism and the Holocaust

Dermot Keogh

CORK UNIVERSITY PRESS

First published in 1998 by
Cork University Press
University College
Cork
Ireland

© Dermot Keogh 1998
Reprinted with corrections 1998

British Library Cataloguing in Publication Data
A CIP catalogue record for this book is available from
the British Library

ISBN   1 85918 149 X   hardcover
         1 85918 150 3   paperback

Typeset by Tower Books, Ballincollig, Co. Cork
Printed by ColourBooks, Baldoyle, Co. Dublin

This book is dedicated to
my mother, Maureen Keogh,
to Ann, Eoin, Niall, Aoife and Clare,
to Jim Kemmy,
to Fr Gearóid Ó Súilleabháin,
to Sheila and Gerald Goldberg,
and
to the Jewish community in Ireland

Jer 29:7 But seek the welfare of the city where I have sent you into exile, and pray to the Lord on its behalf, for in its welfare you will find your welfare.

Jer 29:7

וְדִרְשׁוּ אֶת־שְׁלוֹם הָעִיר אֲשֶׁר הִגְלֵיתִי אֶתְכֶם שָׁמָּה
וְהִתְפַּלְלוּ בַעֲדָהּ אֶל־יְהוָה
כִּי בִשְׁלוֹמָהּ יִהְיֶה לָכֶם שָׁלוֹם :

Contents

Foreword

The story of Irish Jewry over the years is a fascinating one. The first serious attempt to record that story was made by the late Louis Hyman in his book *The Jews of Ireland*. It is important that Professor Keogh takes up the story and unravels it before us. It is the story of the struggle and achievement of a small Jewish community which produced a fighter for Irish freedom like Bobby Briscoe, later Lord Mayor of Dublin, and indeed produced Lord Mayors of the three principal cities: Dublin, Belfast and Cork.

The quality and involvement of the community can best be gauged by the fact that this very small group of people has produced representatives in the Dáil representing the three major parties in Ireland, one of whom achieved a ministerial appointment in the Irish government.

The story of Irish Jewry is a thrilling and a moving one, which became an intimate part of the Irish story from the early days. Even James Joyce had recourse to the community, from which he produced many composite characters for his great work *Ulysses*. His most dominant character was from the Jewish ghetto of Dublin.

This is a story worthy of being recorded.

Chaim Herzog
President of Israel, 1983–93

Illustrations

Acknowledgements

This book could not have been written without the academic support, the kindness, the generosity and the hospitality of a large number of institutions and people in Ireland and abroad who helped me over the past six years to undertake the research for the project. I received generous financial support from the research fund set up at University College Cork by President Michael Mortell. I was also awarded a grant from the arts faculty research fund to work on the Jewish community in Limerick in 1904.

I owe a debt of gratitude to University College Cork and to all my academic and secretarial colleagues in the History Department. My thanks, in particular, to Professor Joe Lee, Liz Steiner Scott, Gabriel Doherty, Ken Nicholls, Geoff Roberts and Dave Edwards. Professor Matthew and Madelaine MacNamara answered many questions and provided important references on anti-Semitism and French culture and society. Professor MacNamara also translated diplomatic reports from German and French which I have cited in the text. Professor Edward Cahill and his wife Angela were very supportive of my efforts and constantly challenged me in our long conversations in Eyeries and other locations to continue with the work. The late Professor Brian Murphy guided me to a number of legal sources which proved to be very valuable. My thanks to Norma Buckley, Veronica Fraser, Charlotte Holland, Deirdre O'Sullivan, Suzanne Buckley, Jane O'Driscoll, and Margaret Clayton. The UCC press and information officer, Ruth MacDonnell, and Louise Tobin helped at various phases in the preparation of this volume. Donal Kingston resolved my computer problems with professionalism and calm.

The text was written, for the most part, while I was a senior fellow at the Institute of Irish Studies, Queen's University Belfast, during the academic year 1995/6. My thanks to the director, Professor Brian Walker, and to my many friends and colleagues in that fine institution. Professor Paul Bew, of the Department of Politics at Queen's University Belfast, generously pointed me towards a number of valuable sources, as did his colleague, Dr Patrick Maume.

Dr Caroline Windrum gave me extensive help in researching the Jewish community in Northern Ireland. My attention was drawn to important manuscript material in the National Library of Ireland by Dr Mary Harris, who also helped me secure archives covering the reception of Jewish refugee children in Ireland in 1948. I am grateful to both for their friendship, their help and their encouragement.

Dr Gordon Gillespie sent me copies of important documents which he had discovered in the Public Record Office, Belfast. Professors Terence Brown and Declan Kiberd gave me valuable references to works on James Joyce and Samuel Beckett. My thanks also to Deirdre McMahon, Katie Kahn-Carl, and Maureen and Tom Brady. Cian Ó hÉigeartaigh supplied important references to documents on the contacts between Joyce and the Department of External Affairs, and Seán Ó Mordha also helped with references on Joyce. Professor George Boyce gave me a number of valuable references. My thanks to Ann Gallagher for allowing me to consult and quote from her father's papers in Trinity College Dublin, and to Ramelle Irish who drew my attention to sources in twentieth-century European poetry.

I have been very fortunate to supervise a number of postgraduates who have been generous and helpful to me in the writing of this book. Ciaran Madden drew my attention to important files relating to Jewish refugees and helped with the research on the nineteenth-century section of the study. Colette Cotter uncovered valuable archival material in her excellent MPhil thesis. Tadhg O'Sullivan helped me to find material on the part played in the reception of Jewish refugees by the Society of Friends in the 1930s. Daisy Swanton and other members of the Society of Friends were very generous with their time and knowledge. My thanks also to Drs Aengus Nolan, Mervyn Samuel O'Driscoll, Finín O'Driscoll and Donal Ó Drisceoil, who have each produced pioneering theses in the fields of Irish foreign policy and in Irish cultural and religious history, as have Orlagh O'Callaghan, Maurice Fitzgerald and Nuala O'Shea. Susan Brennan and Robert MacNamara read and made useful comments on the text. Paula Wylie Bower, a former doctoral student working under my direction, also read the manuscript and gave me very helpful advice. Sandra McAvoy supplied me with some important references on the Jewish community in the 1930s. Helen Callanan was very supportive.

The former Minister for Justice, Nora Owen, granted me access to a number of very important records which proved to be of great value for this study. My thanks to her, to Gerry O'Connell and Brian Ingoldsby and to the staff of that department for their generous help. The former Minister for Foreign Affairs, Dick Spring, gave me access to many important files relating to refugees and aliens. Bernadette Chambers, the archivist in the Department of Foreign Affairs, was very supportive and helpful. Catriona Crowe, Tom Quinlan, Ken Robinson and Eamonn Mullally of the National Archives provided a professional service of great efficiency in the location and the copying of relevant documents. I remain in their debt. My thanks also to Commandant Peter Young, director of the Irish Military Archives in Dublin, his colleague, Commandant Victor Lang and staff, who helped answer my many obscure research queries and drew my attention to relevant files in an archive run to the highest international standards.

I am grateful to Archbishop Desmond Connell who gave me access to the Edward Byrne papers and to sections of the John Charles McQuaid papers. Archivist David Sheehy helped me to locate relevant documents in the Dublin Archdiocesan Archives, as did also Fr Ignatius in the Eamon de Valera papers, Franciscan Archives, Killiney, Co. Dublin.

I wish to thank the provincial of the Redemptorists in Ireland, Fr Brendan Callanan, and the then rector of the Redemptorist house in Limerick, Fr Tony Flannery, for giving me access to all relevant documents in the order regarding events in Limerick in 1904. The archivist of the Redemptorist Irish province, Fr Brendan Mc Convery, allowed me to read his manuscript on the history of the province. He also very kindly located further information about Fr John Creagh, who was at the centre of the 1904 conflict, and helped me select an appropriate quotation in Hebrew which forms the book's epigraph. The Redemptorists' openness to academic research is in keeping with that order's capacity to change to meet the needs of the times.

The Holy Ghost order were equally open and I was given access to the Fr Denis Fahey papers. My thanks to Frs Leo Leydon, Michael O'Carroll and Seán Farragher. The Jesuit order allowed me to consult the papers of Fr Edward Cahill. My gratitude also to Fr Tom Morrissey who made very useful comments about the work of Fr Thomas Finlay in particular. I would also like to record my thanks to the archivists in the diocese of Limerick, to the Irish College in Rome, and to other members of the Catholic clergy who drew many relevant sources to my attention.

Both Sr Katherine Butler and Manus O'Riordan, who have written extensively on the Jewish community in Ireland, sent me relevant articles. I am grateful to the late Jim Kemmy for his help and encouragement in the researching of this project. My thanks also to Denis Leonard, director of the Limerick Civic Trust, and to Sr Carmel Niland, secretary of the Irish Council of Christians and Jews.

The friendship and warmth shown to me while researching this book by leading members of the Jewish community in Ireland will remain an abiding memory of the past six years. I was given access to the history of many families and to their personal archives, letters and scrapbooks. In Cork, Dr Gerald Goldberg was most gracious, hospitable and generous with his knowledge and his time. He also gave me access to a number of important documents and manuscripts in his unique library on Irish and Jewish history. The head of the Jewish community in Cork, Frederick Rosehill, was most helpful, and he also gave me access to material relating to the history of the Jews in Cork. In Dublin, the families of Joe Briscoe and Ben Briscoe TD gave me access to valuable archives and granted me long interviews. Maurice Abrahamson made available to me important scrapbooks covering the life of the Nurock and Abrahamson families over three generations. Judge Hubert Wine gave me access to valuable personal archival material. He also read the manuscript and made many helpful comments and corrections. The historian of the community, Asher Benson, gave me copies of a number of important articles from his own archives. Michael Solomons provided me with information about his family and gave me access to family photographs.

The former Minister for Equality and Law Reform, Mervyn Taylor, gave me an extensive interview and introductions to many members of the Jewish community in Dublin. The Fine Gael TD, Alan Shatter, also gave me a long interview and offered to allow me to consult his archives. The chairman of the Ireland–Israel Friendship League, Brian Quinn, invited me to speak on a number of occasions to that organisation. He has been kind enough to give me access to his own writings on Irish–Israeli relations, and also introduced me to many leading members of the Jewish community.

The director of the Jewish Museum in Dublin, Raphael Siev, has given me every assistance in my research. I worked extensively on the valuable collection of archives held in the museum, where the volunteer staff, and Suzanne Collins in particular, gave me help and co-operation. Raphael Siev also secured for me a number of the illustrations reproduced in this book. His personal work in helping to record the history of Irish Jews deserves the fullest recognition. The Jewish Representative Council, which was founded in 1938, sought to locate their minutes books and archives for me. Unfortunately, they were unsuccessful in their extensive searches.

The late Chaim Herzog, Irishman and President of Israel, wrote a foreword for this volume. His untimely death meant that I never had an opportunity to interview him. However, his memoirs help to fill a gap in our knowledge about the Jewish community in Ireland during the 1920s and 1930s. My thanks also to Professor Shulamit Eliash, Professor Gordon Weiner and Rabbi Theodore Lewis who helped me with specific aspects of my research.

Many friends in the United States provided me with advice and archives. Dr David Kranzler, who I met at a conference in Oxford in the 1980s, sent me copies of a valuable collection of archives relating to Agudas contacts with de Valera during the war years concerning the rescue of Jews. I learned much while writing an article for Professor David Wyman's *The World Reacts to the Holocaust*. My thanks to the editor of the volume, Anne Adamus. My gratitude to Walter and Sandy La Feber in Cornell, Ithaca. In Washington, Bill Connolly of the Holocaust Memorial Museum helped me to answer many queries on two research trips in 1996 and 1997. At the Woodrow Wilson Center for Scholars, Dr Michael Lacey shared with me his deep knowledge of ethnicity. Both Michael and Kath also gave me a home, hospitality and the use of an excellent library on my regular research trips. Susan Nugent helped me to trace many obscure references at the Library of Congress and in other US libraries. I am grateful to her and to our mutual friend Charlotte Thompson for their practical help and friendship over the past ten years.

Tom and Mary Coghlan-Mason provided a refuge in West Cork to write in a telephone-free environment.

I am grateful to Helen Lewis and Han Hogerzeil, both of whom witnessed the barbarism of the Holocaust and its aftermath, for allowing me to interview them.

The illustrations for the book were kindly provided by the *Examiner*, Limerick Civic Trust, Maurice Abrahamson, John Behan, Ben Briscoe,

Gerald Goldberg, Terese and Jim Gorry, Jim Kemmy, Brian Kennedy, Jane and Tony O'Malley, Raphael Siev of the Jewish Museum, and Michael Solomons.

My thanks to Frs Gearóid Ó Súilleabháin, Brian Murphy and Kevin Kennedy for their continuous help over the years.

The UCC library staff, John Fitzgerald, Edward Fahey, Helen Davis, Pat Connolly, Teresina Flynn, Jill Lucey, Phil O'Sullivan, Joe Stynes, Valerie Fletcher, Joe Murphy and Trudy Ahern, met my many queries and requests for obscure texts with efficiency and professionalism.

My former postgraduate student and friend, Finbarr O'Shea, edited and proofread the text with professionalism. To him, too, I owe my gratitude.

My gratitude also to Brendan and Mary Keogh, Fiona, James, Gráinne and Colm O'Rourke for their hospitality.

I could not have written this study without the intellectual support, the love, the companionship and the good humour of Ann, Eoin, Niall, Aoife and Clare. I am in their debt.

Ireland

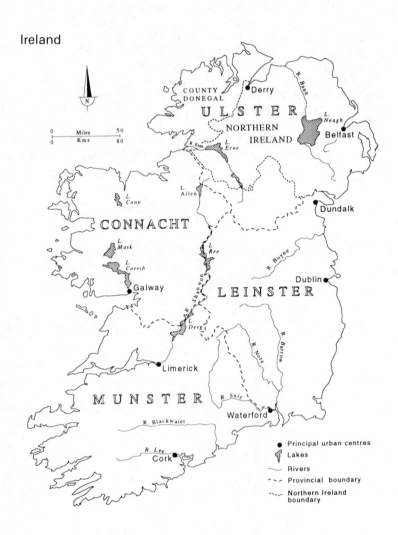

COUNTY
DONEGAL

ULSTER

Derry

R. Bann

NORTHERN
IRELAND

L.
Neagh

Belfast

R. Erne

L.
Erne

L. Allen

CONNACHT

L.
Conn

Dundalk

L.
Mask

L.
Ree

R. Boyne

L.
Corrib

Galway

LEINSTER

Dublin

R. Shannon

L.
Derg

R. Nore

R. Barrow

Limerick

MUNSTER

R. Suir

R. Blackwater

Waterford

R. Lee

Cork

● Principal urban centres
Lakes
Rivers
Provincial boundary
Northern Ireland boundary

Miles   50
0
Kms   80
0

N

Introduction

At a glance, it looked like an ink smudge on her arm. But it wasn't. A survivor of Auschwitz, Helen Lewis was pouring a cup of tea in her home in Belfast, and what I had glimpsed was her concentration camp number, BA677 to be precise. A Czech from the town of Trutnov, she had been in Northern Ireland since 1947. While a student of dance and philosophy in Prague, she married in 1938. Together with her husband Paul, she was taken in 1942 to the Jewish ghetto at Terezin and then to Auschwitz. Unlike her husband, she survived the camp and a winter death march. Helen Lewis only learned of his death following the liberation and her return to Prague. There, by chance, she met again an old Czech friend who had moved before the war to the family business in Belfast. They married in Prague soon afterwards and went to live in Northern Ireland.

Helen Lewis has told her story in *A Time to Speak*.[1] In September 1996, while I was a visiting scholar at the Institute of Irish Studies, Queen's University Belfast, I went to interview her about the Holocaust. But instead, we talked about Belfast, the Orange Order, and how a liberal Jew from Prague struggled to understand the politics and society of her adopted country. Since the late 1940s, Helen Lewis has made a strong contribution to the cultural and humanistic formation of young people from 'both' communities through her work in the world of modern dance and the theatre. Her contribution to the world of the arts in Ireland is testimony to a life spent enriching the culture of her adopted country. In a broader sense, her life is a witness to what might have been, had the refugee policies of Ireland, North and South, been more liberal and allowed greater numbers of Holocaust survivors to make their homes on the island.

Though I interviewed Helen Lewis after I had largely completed my research, I had her very much in mind while I wrote the text. This book is, in fine, prompted by a desire to explain to Helen Lewis and the wider international community Ireland's record during the Holocaust. It is also an effort

1

to answer the larger humanitarian questions on refugee policy raised by being a neutral during the Second World War. An archival fragment I found in the old Public Record Office in Dublin – before the implementation of the National Archives Act in the early 1990s – revealed the qualified opposition of the Department of Justice to the admission of Jewish refugees during the Second World War. This brought to my mind the issue of Irish refugee policy in general, and the attitude towards Jewish refugees in particular. How did the Irish record compare with other countries? How was Irish refugee policy perceived by international Jewish organisations during the 1930s, the war and its aftermath? When working on diplomatic history in other archives abroad in the following years, I accumulated further documentation on that topic. The initial findings revealed a very illiberal attitude towards the admission of Jews into the country in the 1930s and 1940s. As there were no previous studies available on the subject, it was a question of starting from the beginning and reconstructing the evolution of policy insofar as the records would permit.

One historical event in particular coloured international perceptions of Irish attitudes towards the Holocaust. Academic colleagues in Europe and in the United States had repeatedly drawn my attention to the visit of the Taoiseach (Prime Minister), Eamon de Valera, to the German envoy in Dublin on 2 May 1945 to express his condolences on the death of Hitler. If many academics were completely innocent of a knowledge of any other event in modern Irish history, a surprisingly large number were aware of this incident, and it was viewed, as might be expected, with puzzlement, incomprehension and outright hostility. The challenge I faced, therefore, was not merely to set de Valera's visit in its immediate historical context but to examine de Valera's attitude, and that of his government, towards the Irish Jewish community and to trace the origins of the country's refugee policy in a comparative, international context.

My earlier work on Catholicism in Irish society constantly obliged me to question how the struggle for independence and the early decades of the state's existence were viewed by a religous minority like the Jewish community. My work on the history of the Catholic Church in twentieth-century Ireland had also brought to light the prevalence of anti-Semitic ideas in the writings of a number of priests. There was, on the other hand, documentation demonstrating the strong friendship between leading members of the local Jewish community and prominent figures in the Irish political establishment, especially Eamon de Valera. The question which remained unanswered was the extent, if any, of the influence of anti-Semitic ideas on the development of Irish policy in domestic and foreign affairs since independence. But that could be best understood by tracing the existence of anti-Semitism in Ireland from the 1880s and 1890s when a large number of Jewish immigrants came to the country. From another perspective, my general study of Ireland's relationship with Europe during the Second World War and the Cold War had drawn my attention to the influence of ultra right-wing and fascist ideas in the country during this period. This became a particularly rich historical vein.

Encouraged by academics and friends in Ireland and abroad to write a monograph on the Jewish community's relationship with the Irish state during the 1930s and 1940s, I found it necessary to cast my work in a much broader context. The literature on the history of the Jews in twentieth-century Ireland is not extensive. Two books by Louis Hyman and Bernard Shillman stand out as the distinctive published scholarly contributions in the field.[2] While Hyman's study ends in 1910, Shillman's more condensed work covers the first half of the twentieth century. Unlike when Hyman and Shillman were writing their books, however, valuable new material has become available to scholars in recent years through the operation of the National Archives Act. I have studied hundreds of official files in the National Archives, Dublin, in the Public Record Office, Belfast, in the Public Record Office, London, and in the National Archives and the Holocaust Museum in Washington DC. I was also fortunate to gain access to a large number of papers in private collections. Much of this primary source material has never been published before.

In chapter 1, I deal with the large influx of Jews to Ireland following the Russian pogroms of the 1880s and 1890s. How did the new immigrants make their living? How were they received in Belfast, Dublin, Cork and Limerick by the small community of Jews already living in those cities? How did Irish people in general react to the influx? How prevalent was anti-Semitism? In chapter 2, I focus attention on the city of Limerick in 1904, where two anti-Semitic sermons by a Redemptorist priest, Fr John Creagh, set in train widespread intimidation of the local Jewish community and inspired the imposition of a boycott against Jewish traders. The chapter provides a comprehensive account of those events based on a range of new archival material.

Chapter 3 examines the history of the Jewish community in Ireland from the early twentieth century, through the period of revolutionary nationalism and the founding of two states on the island, to the arrival of Eamon de Valera in power in 1932. What success did the children of the late nineteenth-century immigrants have in business, in higher education and in entering the professions? Were members of the community politicised by the rise of nationalism in the south of the country and of radical unionism in the north? How did Jews react to the establishment of the Irish Free State and the state of Northern Ireland in the early 1920s? What was the relationship between the chief rabbi of the Irish Free State, Dr Isaac Herzog, and the political leaders of the new state, William T. Cosgrave and Eamon de Valera? These were among the questions to which I sought answers in official and private archives in Ireland, Britain, Israel and the United States.

The narrative in chapter 3 was helped greatly by the kindness of Maurice Abrahamson who allowed me to make extensive use of scrapbooks kept by the Nurock and Abrahamson families. The scrapbooks trace the families' history from the Russian pogroms in the late nineteenth century to their arrival and new lives in Ireland. Family photos, records of births, marriages and deaths, school and university examination reports, all help piece together the assimilation of two Jewish immigrant families in the Ireland of the early twentieth century.

Irish state archives provided me with most of the material used in the writing of chapters 4 and 5, which cover the period 1932–39. Chapter 4 examines the impact on Irish society of the rise of fascism and radical anti-Semitism in continental Europe. The radicalisation of Catholic thought is also examined, as is the role of Chief Rabbi Isaac Herzog in combating overt anti-Semitism. Chapter 5 focuses on the complexities and shadings of Ireland's response to pleas for help from Jewish asylum seekers in the late 1930s. In researching this chapter, I was fortunate to meet a number of people who knew about, or had been involved in, work with refugees.

Directed by his daughter Ann towards the Frank Gallagher papers in Trinity College Dublin, I read of the successful efforts of the Gallagher family to rescue a Jewish couple, the Wortsmanns, in 1939. Erna Wortsmann had been taught by Cecilia Saunders in Germany in 1912. There had been no contact afterwards between teacher and pupil until, remarkably, a letter written by Erna's husband Hugo out of desperation to the lord mayor of Cork in 1938 helped trace Cecilia who, by then, was living in Dublin and married to Frank Gallagher, the director of the Irish Government Information Bureau. The intervention of the Gallaghers saved the lives of that Jewish couple.

Chapter 6 deals with the war years and is based heavily on official archives in Dublin, London and Washington. I also received significant help from Gerald Goldberg, the distinguished former lord mayor of Cork, who gave me an insight into what it was like for a Jewish family confronted by the possibility of imminent German invasion in 1939 and 1940. Ben and Joe Briscoe also provided me with information about their own experiences and with documentation about their father, the Fianna Fáil TD Robert Briscoe. The books of Dr Robert Collis, who had served as a doctor during the liberation of the death camps, proved very helpful. His widow Dr Han Hogerzeil, who had served as an interpreter at Buchenwald, recalled for me the experience of being there. (Robert and Han adopted two Buchenwald children who now live in Ireland.) Two images in particular from that conversation remain with me. Han Hogerzeil spoke paradoxically of Buchenwald as a place where there was an awful lot of love. She also described the blackness of the smoke which hung over the camp the day the huts were burned down. She has small box camera photos recording the end of that chapter of infamy.

By an extraordinary coincidence, K. C. Condon arrived in my office in autumn 1996 with a box of documents and photographs belonging to his brother-in-law, Major Charles Peters, who had served in the British forces at the Battle of the Bulge. He was also one of the officers who took part in the liberation of Buchenwald. Among the items in the box were a dozen or so photographs, personal and uncensored images of those first days in the liberated death camp. One showed the listless, striped-clad figures sitting on their bunks. In another, two ex-prisoners displayed their concentration camp numbers on the outside of their left arms. These photos came to me by mere chance at a time when I was formulating the chapter on the Holocaust, and brought home to me in a vivid way the horror of the death camps.

Chapter 7 begins with an examination of the most controversial act in de Valera's long political career – his visit to the German minister to express his condolences on the death of Hitler. It goes on to analyse the development of Ireland's post-war refugee policy with particular reference to Jewish refugees. The conflict within the Irish administration over refugee policy is described in detail. In researching this chapter I located Department of Justice files relating to over a hundred Jewish children who were brought to Ireland from central Europe by Rabbi Solomon Schonfeld in 1948. A black-and-white photo of the head and shoulders of each child was attached to a personal file. They were the expressionless faces of children who had lived through the horrors of Nazi occupation and who must have been terrified by the sight of a camera. But they had survived and had reached Ireland. Helped by the local Jewish community, they were nursed back to good health in Ireland before moving on to new lives in Canada, the United States, Britain and Israel.

The arrival of these Jewish refugee children in 1948, and of other refugees who were allowed in before and during the war, points to a generosity of spirit among various church and voluntary bodies set up expressly to respond to the humanitarian crisis in Europe. That generosity of spirit was always evident among the many people who came forward to lend support and, in some cases, provide foster homes for orphaned children.

The epilogue sketches the history of the Jewish community in Ireland from the 1950s to the present day. It traces the decline of the Jewish community in both the North and the South, and reviews the overall contribution of Jews to Irish politics, culture and society – a contribution out of all proportion to the size of the community. Finally, the epilogue focuses on the visit of President Mary Robinson to Auschwitz in 1994 and on the manner in which the Irish state, responding to the fiftieth anniversary of the Holocaust, acknowledged how ungenerous had been the country's wartime refugee policy.

This book is not a history of the Jewish community in Ireland. It is, rather, an examination of the relationship between the Jewish community and the two Irish states with emphasis on the situation in the South. I hope it contributes to a better understanding of the historical role of the Jewish community in Ireland during the twentieth century.

1

The Russian pogroms and the growth of the Jewish community in Ireland

Between 1800 and 1880 the Jews who came to Ireland were, almost without exception, Ashkenazi, or those who came from northern or eastern Europe. The Sephardi, or the descendants of the Jews expelled from Spain in 1492, formed the majority of the minuscule community in Ireland before the nineteenth century.[1] Most of the arrivals up to the 1880s settled in Dublin. The Jews of Dublin between 1820 and 1880 were, according to the historian Louis Hyman, divided into three distinct classes. There were 'the natives', two families of German or Polish origin who remained from the eighteenth-century community. The second group comprised Jews from England, Holland, France, Germany, Poland, Galicia, Russia and Morocco who settled in the period 1820 to 1875. Finally, there was a group of twenty-five young Jews from Lithuania who arrived in the late 1870s.[2]

In the 1820s the tiny Dublin community came together to found a synagogue at 40 Stafford Street (now Wolfe Tone Street).[3] In 1835 the synagogue moved to Mary's Abbey.[4] That was to remain a place of worship until 1892.[5] The community in Dublin grew slowly. The register of births of the Jewish congregation records that, between 25 November 1838 and 7 May 1879, there were 308 births. The register of deaths records 140 deaths between 5 January 1842 and 8 February 1879. Up to 1880 there were never more than 350 Jews in Dublin.[6] Among them were craftsmen – gold and silver-smiths, brassworkers, picture-frame carvers, watchmakers, jewellers and grocers.[7] For the most part, they lived and traded in the inner city along the banks of the River Liffey.

On arriving in Ireland during the earlier part of the nineteenth century, many Jews found a common bond with the Catholic population, as both communities had certain areas of public life closed to them on religious grounds. In England and Ireland the leaders of both communities shared ideas on how to further the common cause of emancipation. When Daniel O'Connell was elected to the House of Commons for the Clare constituency in July 1828, the leader of the Jewish emancipation movement in Britain, Isaac Goldsmid, sent an envoy to Ireland to secure the support of 'the Liberator' for the introduction of a Bill for the removal of Jewish civil disabilities. O'Connell replied warmly thanking him and his 'amiable family' for the hospitality which he and his son had enjoyed at their home in London.[8] Supporting Goldsmid in his call for Jewish emancipation, he added: 'Ireland has claims on your ancient race, as it is the only Christian Country that I know of unsullied by any act of persecution against the Jews.'[9] O'Connell agreed entirely with Goldsmid on the principle of freedom of conscience, 'and no man can admit the sacred principle without extending it to the Jew as to the Christian'. Every day, according to O'Connell, was a day of injustice until that civil right was attained by Jews.[10] O'Connell supported the Bill, which passed the House of Commons only to be rejected by the Lords in 1831.[11] At the further instigation of O'Connell, the law requiring Jews to wear special dress was repealed in 1846.[12] But it was not until 1858 that Jews won the provisional right to sit in the House of Commons, a right that was made permanent in 1866.[13]

Irish Jews and Catholics were also brought together by a sense of common adversity. The Jewish community was quick to respond to the needs of those affected by the Great Famine of 1845–47.[14] The common bond of humanity led Dublin's Jews, numbering about twenty-five families in 1847, to give practical assistance in relieving famine distress.[15] Like their Catholic counterparts, Jews sought to overcome religious and social discrimination through entering the professions. Some were successful in gaining entry to Trinity College Dublin to study law and medicine.[16] Jews also made a significant contribution to the cultural life of Dublin in music and the arts.[17]

The Wormser Harris family was one of the best-known Jewish families in nineteenth-century Dublin. Lewis Harris, who was born in Germany, became a member of the Dublin merchant class. He made history in 1874 by becoming the first Jew to be elected to Dublin Corporation as alderman for the South Dock Ward. He died on 1 August 1876 just before he was to be appointed lord mayor of Dublin. Three of his six sons remained in Dublin where they played an active part in community affairs. His eldest son, Alfred Wormser Harris, also became an alderman.[18] Other prominent members of the Jewish community in Dublin included Myer Erlich, a jeweller and silversmith, who was vice-president of the Jewish congregation from 1866 to 1869. Morris Cohen had held that position from 1856 to 1858 and from 1862 to 1863. Marinus de Groot, a native of Rotterdam, was president of the congregation from 1876 until 1901.[19] The colourful Morris (Moses) Harris, who became an antique dealer at 30 Nassau Street, was vice-president from 1876 to 1878. He had been charged, according to Hyman, 'with as many sins as are levelled against Leopold Bloom in *Ulysses* and against Humphrey Chimpden Earwicker in *Finnegans Wake*'.[20] One of Harris's daughters married a Protestant, John Sinclair. Her twin sons, William and Henry, were raised as Jews and inherited their grandfather's business. In 1937, Henry successfully sued the author and surgeon Oliver St John Gogarty for libelling his grandfather.[21]

Turning to Belfast, the historian Bernard Shillman records that there were no Jews in that city prior to 1814.[22] By 1891, however, there were 282 Jews in what is now Northern Ireland, 164 male and 118 female. The majority, 205, lived in Belfast. The rest were dispersed as follows: 33 (19 male and 14 female) in Armagh, 33 (21 male and 12 female) in Down, 5 (4 male and 1 female) in Antrim, 5 in Derry, 1 in Tyrone and none in Fermanagh.[23]

Credit for the founding of the Belfast congregation went to Daniel Joseph Jaffe. The grandson of Mordechai Jaffe, president of the ecclesiastical court of Mecklenburg, he was born on 19 August 1809. He developed a very large mercantile business in Hamburg and his interests took him to Belfast in 1845. Martin, his eldest son, ran the Belfast branch of the business. The first Jewish service held in Ulster in the nineteenth century took place in 1864 in the Holywood home of Martin Jaffe. On 7 July 1871, the foundation stone was laid in Great Victoria Street for a synagogue, a Hebrew school and a residence for a minister. There were by then fifty-five Jews in the city. The undertaking was paid for by Daniel Jaffe, who died in Nice on 21 January 1874 and was buried in Belfast.[24]

Otto Jaffe, born in Hamburg on 13 August 1846, was Daniel's most distinguished son. He gained a reputation of being one of Belfast's most shrewd businessmen. Elected a city councillor in 1894, he was a member of the Belfast Harbour Board, governor of the Royal Hospital and German consul. In 1899 and again in 1904, he was elected lord mayor of Belfast. A strong supporter of education reform, he was particularly interested in primary education and was a pioneer in the advocacy of technical education. He was given an honorary LLD by the Royal University of Ireland.[25] Otto Jaffe was a life-president of the Belfast congregation.

Russian pogroms and new Jewish immigrants

Tsar Alexander II, the emancipator of the serfs, was assassinated by revolutionaries in March 1881. Russia's anti-Semitic press made scapegoats of the Jews and rioting spread through the south of Russia and into Poland.[26] Repressive legislation dating back to 1804 was strengthened by further anti-Semitic provisions in 1882 and again in 1891.[27] Between 1880 and 1914, an estimated two million Russian Jews emigrated. Most left for the United States, while some settled in Palestine, Canada, South Africa, Britain and Ireland.[28] Between 1881 and 1906, 150,000 eastern European Jews arrived in Britain. Many who came to settle in Ireland were from the province of Kovno Gubernia in Lithuania, the capital of which was Kovno. According to Len Yodaiken, whose family settled in Dublin, the founders of the Irish communities were usually referring to 'one of the Shtetls [villages] in that province when they said they were from Kovno'.[29] The core of the Dublin and Cork communities came from 'a rather derelict place called Akmijan'.[30] (This is Akmian in Yiddish and its current name is Akmene.) According to Yodaiken, 'in the old days, in Dublin, if you did not have an ancestor from Akmijan, you did not belong to the "Club"'. Written on his great-grandmother's

tombstone in the Jewish cemetery at Dolphin's Barn in Dublin is the following: 'Hanna Jackson a Good Woman of Akmijan'.[31]

Jewish immigrants also came from Zhager (today called Zagare), Klikul
(Klykoliai), Vexna or Svexna, Papiljan, Kurshjan (Kursenai) and Shavli
(Siaulia).[32] Between 1881 and 1901, the good people of Akmijan and from
these other Lithuanian villages came to Ireland in their hundreds. The
following table, drawn from census returns, shows the growth of the Jewish
community from the mid-nineteenth century to the mid-twentieth century
in what was to become the Irish Free State (twenty-six counties).

Year	Total population	Number of Jews	% Increase/Decrease
1861	4,402,111	341	–
1871	4,053,187	230	–32·6
1881	3,870,020	394	+71·3
1891	3,468,694	1,506	+282·2
1901	3,221,823	3,006	+99·6
1911	3,139,688	3,805	+26·6
1926	2,971,992	3,686	–3·6
1936	2,968,420	3,749	+1·7
1946	2,955,107	3,907	+4·2

Dublin Castle, the centre of the British administrative system in Ireland,
estimated the Jewish population as follows based on a reading of the 1891
and 1901 census returns.[33]

Provinces and counties	Number of Jews	
	1891	1901
Leinster		
Carlow County	5	9
Dublin City	971	2,048
Dublin County	86	121
Kildare County	15	8
Kilkenny County	1	2
Kilkenny City	11	–
King's County	6	9
Longford County	–	3
Louth Co. (including Drogheda)	7	54
Meath County	3	13
Queen's County	9	3
Westmeath County	1	3
Wexford County	2	8
Wicklow County	18	15
Total of province	1,135	2,296

Provinces and counties	Number of Jews 1891	1901
Munster		
Clare County	1	–
Cork County	62	88
Cork City	155	359
Kerry County	13	8
Limerick County	–	–
Limerick City	93	171
Tipperary County	11	20
Waterford County	4	–
Waterford City	15	42
Total of province	354	688
Ulster		
Antrim County	2	37
Armagh County	33	44
Belfast City	205	708
Cavan County	2	1
Donegal County	–	–
Down County	26	34
Fermanagh County	–	3
Londonderry City	5	58
Londonderry County	–	6
Monaghan County	7	6
Tyrone County	2	2
Total of province	282	899
Connaught		
Galway County	–	1
Leitrim County	2	–
Mayo County	2	–
Roscommon County	1	–
Sligo County	3	14
Total of province	8	15
Total of Ireland	1,779	3,898

Dublin, by the turn of the century, had a Jewish population of 2,048, Belfast 708, Cork 359 and Limerick 171. Among those who fled the pogroms was the grandfather of Harry Rosehill, the doyen of commercial travellers in the Munster region during the early decades of the new Irish state.[34] His story was typical of many who came at that time. Fearing the spread of the pogroms in the Kovno area, he travelled for two days from Nevelskaya to consult a rabbi about the rise of anti-Semitism and the future safety of his family in the region; he was advised to leave immediately. He had a brother living in Cork who ran a music shop on Patrick Street. He made the journey to Ireland, via Hull, left his two children with his brother and returned immediately to Akmijan, where he perished in the pogroms.[35]

Other families that came to Ireland in the wake of the pogroms and who were later to be prominent in the Jewish community included the Abrahamson, Briscoe, Goldberg, Good, Marcus, Nurock, Siev and Wine families. The large influx of 'foreign' Jews created for the first time Jewish quarters in the two largest cities, Dublin and Belfast, as well as in Limerick and Cork.

Jews in Limerick and Cork

According to the census returns, there was one Jew living in Limerick in 1861, two in 1871 and four in 1881. The number rose from 35 in 1888 to 90 in 1892 and 130 in 1896. About twenty-five families of Lithuanian Jews had settled in Limerick by 1900, mainly in the poor section around Edward Street.[36] Among these immigrants was Louis Goldberg; the oral evidence of his son, the distinguished Cork solicitor Gerald,[37] and the unpublished memoir of his daughter, Fanny, mother of the novelist David Marcus, provide a vivid portrait of the early years of the Jewish community in Limerick. One of a large family, Louis Goldberg was conscripted into the Russian army at the age of fourteen. But before he could serve as a soldier, the pogroms which followed the assassination of the Tsar forced him to flee his home in the Lithuanian village of Akmijan. He made the hazardous journey to Riga, where the authorities turned back a number of other boys in his group seeking to emigrate to the United States. Possibly because of his fair colouring, he was allowed to proceed and he found passage on a timber ship sailing to Ireland. This was supposed to be the first leg of his journey to the United States. He had never seen a map until he came to Ireland. Therefore, he did not know how far Ireland was from the United States. The year was 1882.

Put ashore at Cobh, he had the good fortune to be met by another Lithuanian Jew, Isaac Marcus, who regularly went to the docks to offer help to newly arrived co-religionists. He was taken to the home of the Sandlers, who also had come to Ireland from Akmijan. There Goldberg first met Rachel, who was to become his wife in 1891; she had arrived in Cork with her family from Lithuania in 1875 as a one-year-old child. The Sandlers kindly allowed him to rest for a few days in their home, where he became familiar with members of the small but growing Jewish community in Cork, his lifelong friend Zalman Clein among them. Louis set out on foot for Dublin – a distance of 158 miles – within weeks of his arrival. There he met a co-religionist named Jackson, who loaned him ten shillings with which he purchased a pedlar's licence and a small stock of holy pictures of Roman Catholic saints and popes. He returned to Cork on foot, selling his merchandise on the way.

Because he had family friends from Akmijan in Limerick, Goldberg moved there in 1883 and was taken in by his relatives, the Greenfields. The Wein-ronks, who had arrived from Akmijan in the 1870s, were his cousins. The two families remained very close during their Limerick sojourn. Goldberg was most probably related on his father's side to the Barrons, another Jewish family in Limerick. Louis Goldberg continued in the same line of work, travelling in the city and around the countryside. His daughter, Fanny, born in 1893, recalled in her memoirs the harsh life of her father. She remembered seeing the pedlars walking through the streets of Limerick laden with their goods strapped on their shoulders and, sometimes, with picture frames hanging on their arms: 'Rain and cold didn't cry halt. They had their families to keep', she stated. They were often known to their customers as 'tally men'. Working on the weekly payments system, the debt was marked down in a book and the 'tally' added up. With their broken English, the word 'weekly' became 'vickla'. In certain Jewish communities, that was the only word used to describe their business as 'tally men'. As they went about their work, Fanny also recalled that children in the streets of Limerick used to run after the 'tally men', with their backs bent with their packs, shouting 'a pitchie [picture] man, a tally man, a Jew, Jew, Jew'. 'I wonder often how they lived', she reminisced. The 'weeklies' also worked on foot in the countryside, returning to the cities at the weekend in time for the Sabbath.

His son Gerald, born in Cork in 1912, recalled that his father had been shown great kindness and hospitality by countrywomen in County Clare. On one occasion, Louis, who was a strict orthodox Jew, was invited into a cottage and offered a glass of milk by the woman of the house. He politely refused but offered instead to milk the cow. Befriended by the family, he was allowed to sleep in the house where – on other visits – he learned to sing lullabies in Irish which he later sang to his own children. It was, however, more usual for Louis to sleep in an outhouse while on the road. His was the common lot of the Jewish pedlar – a frequent sight in turn-of-the-century Ireland.

When prosperous enough in the mid-1880s, Louis rented a house in Mount Pleasant Avenue, off Colooney Street, in Limerick. He brought his mother over from Russia; Bubba (grandmother) Elka became a very strong force in his life, in that of his future family and in the life of the community. She became a much-loved member of the Limerick community and helped to maintain the Lithuanian Jewish family traditions. Louis, who used to travel to Cork as often as possible to buy stock for his business, frequently visited the home of the Sandlers at 13 Elizabeth Terrace, Cork. One day he saw a beautiful young woman scrubbing the wooden kitchen floor; it was Rachel, the girl he had first seen as an eight-year-old child when he had landed in Ireland in 1882. He was introduced to her by her mother. He was so impressed that he immediately visited an old friend from Akmijan, Zalman Clein, and told him that he wanted to marry the girl. He asked Clein to make the match. She was seventeen and he was twenty-four. Never allowed to 'walk out' together, the couple were married on 18 September 1891 at the *shul*, or synagogue, in 24 South Terrace, Cork. They went to live in Limerick at 50 Colooney Street, next door to Coll's public house; Louis ran a small grocery shop from the house and continued to travel as a pedlar.

Later in the decade, the family moved to 47 Henry Street, where Louis had a small drapery store. While the business did not provide the family with a luxurious standard of living, Bubba Elka was a strong woman known for her beautiful baking and her capacity to improvise. When, for example, kosher wine was not to be found in Limerick, she made it for special religious festivals. Rachel's mother also travelled from Cork, sometimes with her younger children, to help look after the household when her daughter had a child. By 1901, she had two daughters, Fanny and Molly (b. 1896) and one son, Henry (b. 1899). She had another boy in 1904. In all, Rachel had thirteen children who lived. Rachel's brother, Joseph Sandler, also lived with the family for a time, as did Louis's youngest brother, Solomon or Sol, later a significant figure in the Zionist movement. Thanks to Louis's financial help, his two other brothers, Bernard and Samuel, had also come to live in Limerick by the turn of the century. Samuel lived at 15 Emmet Place with his wife Rachel, and their two sons and two daughters; Bernard lived at 9 Colooney Street with his his wife Sima, and their three daughters and three sons. Their cousins, the Weinronks, lived nearby. According to the 1901 census, Bernard Weinronk lived at 27 Bowman Street with his wife Sarah and daughter Jennette. David Weinronk lived at 46 Colooney Street with his wife Sophia, daughter Hanna aged twenty and son Simon aged eighteen.

Fanny (Frances Rebecca) recalled from her childhood that for her 'there has never been anything so beautiful and so gracious as the Sabbaths we had in the kitchen in Colooney Street'. What follows is not a description of 'gracious living' but rather of the effort made by a family of committed Jews to observe the Sabbath with due solemnity:

> Bubba always did the cooking and serving, my mother looking after us children, and helping my father in the shop. The table was always beautifully laid with a white tablecloth, sometimes lace trimmed, with the candles lighting in the shining brass candlesticks. These candlesticks were brought over from Russia by Bubba. (When Molly got married, Uncle Sol who had kept them after Bubba died gave them to her.) The cutlery gleamed and a cruet stand was in the centre of the table with the various condiments in the cut glass bottles. The stand was old Sheffield plate polished to the gleam of silver. Wine was in a cut glass decanter, a very lovely one as I remember it.

On Friday evenings, the shop was closed and the older members of the Goldberg family changed into their best clothes and went to *shul*. Rachel remained at home with the children: 'When father came home there was the washing of hands, and Kiddush [prayer]. His exquisite baritone voice made every Kiddush a memory.' There followed the blessing of bread. A piece was given to each person seated at the table. The special bread was baked twice a week and it was 'beautiful in taste and looks. No bread has ever been so beautiful as that bread baked by my Buba Elka.'

Louis Goldberg and his brothers learned to read and speak English quite quickly. All had been well educated in Lithuania. Sol, for example, had studied to be a rabbi but had been expelled from the school very early in his career for reading late at night a work which had been placed on the banned list. In her memoirs Fanny records that they 'devoured newspapers and anything in print they could get hold of. How often I heard the names of Parnell, Kitty O'Shea, Michael Davitt and all the names of the famous Irish politicians of the day.' She recalls that her father was a staunch Parnellite all his life and blamed the British for his downfall. He felt that they had engineered the whole affair with Mrs O'Shea right from the beginning because he 'was a thorn in their side'.

The 1901 census provides details of the many other Jewish families who had settled in Limerick by this time. Solomon Arnovitch lived at 26 Bowman Street with his wife, son Isaac and daughter Edith. Solomon Shenkman and the Kramers lived at 25 Bowman Street. Samuel Racusen lived at 5 McNamara Place with his wife and four children. Marcus Jacob Blond resided at 40 Henry Street with his wife Esther, four daughters and a son. Jacob Barron lived at 48 Henry Street with his wife Rachel, four sons and two daughters. Julius Martinson, who had a son and a daughter, lived at 26 Richmond Street. David Cropman lived at No. 79 with his wife Ruth, two daughters and a son. Barnet Gould lived at No. 82 with his wife Eide, a son and a daughter. Barnet Graff lived at No. 23 with his wife Sarah and a daughter. Hyman Graff was in No. 77 with his wife Flory, two daughters and a nephew. Solomon Gerome lived at 19 Colooney Street; his wife's name was Hannah, and they had a son and a daughter, and a boarder Charles Berman. Benjamin Jaffe lived at No. 64 with his wife Rachel, son Sydney (who was a dentist educated at Queen's College Cork), and daughter Edith. Marcus L. Jaffe, a dental mechanic, lived at No. 31 with his wife Leah; they had one son and one daughter. Moses Keane, who was a shopkeeper, lived at 87 Colooney Street with his wife, Minnie. Rabbi Levin lived at No. 18 with his wife Annie, four sons and four daughters. A synagogue was situated at 63 Colooney Street, where Jacob Newman also lived. There was a second synagogue at No. 72, where Moses Velitzkein was the minister. Wolf Maissel occupied No. 24; he had a son and a daughter. Isaac Rosental, his wife Annie, their two daughters and a son lived at No. 81. Louis Sieve lived at 13 Colooney Street with his wife Johanna, their three sons, two daughters, a grandchild and a boarder, David Goldston. William Marcus Stein, who was a dental mechanic, occupied No. 27. Wolf Toohey lived at No. 74.

It is worth noting that, with the exception of the Jaffes where there was a dentist and a dental mechanic in the family and William Marcus Stein who was also a dental mechanic, the overwhelming majority of Jews in Limerick in 1901 were pedlars with a small minority describing themselves as drapery dealers and grocers. All the Jewish grocery shops were near to one another in Colooney Street, at the end near to the main street. Practically all the Jewish homes in Limerick listed in the 1901 census had a Roman Catholic servant. This did not reflect exalted status but it showed that many Jewish families were not to be ranked as being at the lowest end of the social register by 1901.

The first place of prayer the Limerick community had was a private house in Emmet Place. The congregation then moved to 18 Colooney Street. A more permanent place of worship was found at number No. 63. But schism over interpretations of observance of the law quickly divided the small community, and two rival houses of prayer emerged in the 1890s. Personal conflicts, which had sometimes ended in litigation, further complicated intra-community relations. The issue of moneylending was, according to the Limerick historian Des Ryan, also a source of conflict within the community and had been condemned by the chief rabbi of the United Kingdom, Dr Hermann Adler, on two visits to the city in 1892 and 1898. Louis Goldberg first opened a rival synagogue in his Henry Street home. The synagogue was moved to 72 Colooney Street in 1901. (Rabbi Levin's synagogue was at No. 63.) Letters from the rival groups appeared in the *Limerick Leader*. M. J. Blond wrote in January 1901 that the only authorised synagogue was at 63 Colooney Street. For the sake of 'our Christian neighbours and friends' the rival was a 'so-called Synagogue', he wrote. Goldberg replied that 'the principal reason for establishing the [new synagogue] is not to associate ourselves with moneylenders, and these are the full wishes of our Chief Rabbi, Rev. Dr Adler'. The Goldberg group had the support of about ten families, the oldest families in the city who, according to Louis, had 'built up the Jewish congregation, and this is not the first time in our Jewish history that our Tribe has had to make room for some upstarts. History repeats itself.'[38]

The purchase of land for a burial ground at Kilmurry, near Castleconnell, was a further occasion of public disagreement between the rival groups in the Jewish community. The site was bought from a local farmer, William Nunan of Ballyclough, for £150. The indenture was signed on 17 February 1902 by Rabbi Elias Levin and by Isaac Anonove, Marcus Jacob Blond, David Cropman, Hyman S. Cropman, Louis Clein, Barnet Graff, Hyman Graff, Philip Griff, Barnet Gould, Julius Greene, Moses Joseph Greenfield, Benjamin Jaffey, Sydney A. Jaffey, Marcus Lionel Jaffe, Solomon Jerome, Harry Levin, Maurice Maissell, Wolf Maissell, Barnett Shockett, Philip Toohy and Wolf Toohey.[39] On 24 May 1902, the president and vice-president of the Chevra Kaddisah, 63 Colooney Street, Wolf Maissell and Wolf Toohy respectively, appended a rule to the deed, which was passed unanimously, that there would be no charge for the ground for burial of a person belonging to the Jewish faith, 'whether a member of the Congregation or not' and that 'this rule shall exist for ever'.[40] That may have reflected an easing of the tensions within the Jewish community in Limerick. They were not, however, eradicated and the split continued to exist in 1904.

There were six Jews living in Cork, the largest city in Munster, according to the 1871 census. By 1881 there were ten but that figure had moved to 155 by 1891 and to 359 by 1901. The new arrivals settled in the Eastville area near the Hibernian Buildings on the south side of the River Lee. This area quickly became known, without any pejorative overtones, as 'Jewtown'.[41] It was 'a Lithuanian village inserted in the midst of a very parochial people'. Those who settled in Cork were almost exclusively from the districts of Vilna and Kovno.[42] Most had been neighbours in the village of Akmijan and sought to be so again – in Cork.[43] They were later joined by Louis Goldberg and his young family, who, like many others, moved to Cork to escape the Limerick boycott in 1904.[44]

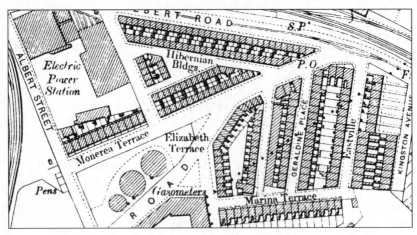

1. 'Jewtown', Cork, circa 1900

The majority of the Jews of Cork lived in Hibernian Buildings. According to the 1901 census, Solomon Cohen (aged 44), a pedlar, lived with his wife, Esther (36), and teenage daughter at No. 94. Louis Bookman (29), an illiterate pedlar, lived at No. 93 with his wife, Leah (28), their two daughters, Sarah and Anne, and two boarders, Moses and Abraham Bookman (both pedlars). William Goldberg (46), a house carpenter, lived with his wife Leah (45), three daughters and three sons at No. 92. Myer Lovity (45), an illiterate from Poland, lived alone at No. 88. Abraham Harwitz (43), an illiterate pedlar from Russia, lived at No. 87 with his wife Teresa (33) and their four children. Saran Hodis (74), a shopkeeper from Russia, lived at No. 84 with her sister, Jane, and two boarders, Michael and Joseph Spiro, both of whom were pedlars. Solomon Steinberg, a pedlar from Russia, lived at No. 82 with his wife, son and daughter, and a domestic servant. William Hershman (40), a pedlar from Germany, lived at No. 76 with his wife Clara (35), three daughters, one son and a boarder John Aranson. A pedlar from Russia, Joseph Spiro, lived at No. 74 with his wife Mary (36), three sons and four daughters. His neighbour in No. 73 was Mendel Cohen (35), a pedlar from Russia who could not read; he lived with his wife, Miriam, son and daughter, and a pedlar from Russia, Solomon Schorbig, who was a boarder. Rachel Lewis (34), from Poland, lived at No. 66 with her four sons, one daughter, and Alfred Fredman, a boarder. Maurice Goldwater (50), a pedlar from Poland, lived at No. 48 with his wife Fannie (36), four sons and two daughters. At No. 44 lived Bernard Smullen, a pedlar, his wife, Ethel (44), one daughter, two sons and a boarder, Jacob Phillips. Abraham Bizansky lived at No. 42; a rabbi from Russia, he had a son and three daughters. Esther Clein lived at No. 38; she had five sons, two of whom were pedlars, and two daughters. A pedlar from Russia, Samuel Brody lived with his wife, Hannah (30), and three daughters at No. 25. Solomon Hurwitch lived at No. 23; he had three sons and two daughters, and a servant, Mary Daly. Isaac Sandler, who has already been mentioned, lived at No. 16 with his wife Hannah, three sons and two daughters. Another daughter had married Louis Goldberg and lived in Limerick. Aaron Smullen, a pedlar from Russia, lived with his wife Minnie at No. 14. Marks Levin, also a pedlar from Russia, lived at No. 5 with his wife Hoda.

In neighbouring Elizabeth Terrrace, William Goldstein lived at No. 5 with his wife, Celia, and a boarder, Nathan Jackson. Both men were pedlars. Jacob Marcus (31), a picture frame maker, also lived in that street with his wife, Anna (29), four sons and three daughters. Israel Abrahamson, a pedlar who could read and write, lived at No. 7. He had five sons and one daughter. Isaac Berman (50), a pedlar from Russia, lived next door with his wife, Mira (50), daughter Fanny (20), son Abraham (19) and boarders, Bernard and Jamie Russo, both of whom were pedlars. At No. 9 lived David Medali (36), a pedlar, his wife Sarah (32), their two sons and a daughter. Moses Sayers lived at No. 13 with his wife, Maria, their daughter and son. Abraham Sandler (45), a pedlar, lived at No. 14 with his wife Mary (53), their three sons and one daughter.

Nathan Edelson, a pedlar from Russia, lived in Marina Terrace with his wife, daughter and two boarders, Joe Epstein and David Toohey. Lewis Herman, a pedlar, lived nearby with his wife, two daughters, two sons, a boarder, Arthur Sayers, and a servant. Harris Libesman (50), a pedlar, lived in Monerea Terrace with his wife Hannah (54), three daughters and two sons. Louis S. Clein, a draper and pedlar, lived at No. 4 with his wife Leah, four sons, three daughters and a servant. The Sayers family lived at No. 8; George (30) was a pedlar. He had a daughter and three sons. Next door lived Myer Elyan, a teacher of Hebrew, his wife, son and daughter, and two boarders, Jason and Israel Sless, both of whom were pedlars. Solomon Birkham, a pedlar and later shopkeeper, lived at No. 10 with his wife, Sarah, two sons, three daughters and a lodger, Aaron Serling, who was a shoemaker.

According to Gerald Goldberg, there was 'no real co-ordination' among members in the early years of the Cork community.[45] A congregation had been founded in the city in 1881, Isaac Epstein becoming its first president.[46] The community leased a cemetery at Kemp Street in 1885 and bought it outright in 1887. A *shtibl*, or room for prayer, was set up in 1 Eastville in 1884. Eventually a large synagogue was built on South Terrace close to the cemetery; the synagogue is still being used for services at the end of the twentieth century.[47] Cork did not differ greatly from Limerick. A schism developed.[48] As Gerald Goldberg wrote in 1945: 'The usual differences which are found among communities small in number made their appearances some forty years ago when Cork found itself possessed of two Synagogues and rival ministers.'[49] Though some 400 Jews (about fifty-five families) lived in Cork in the first decade of the twentieth century, only eleven families remained living in 'Jewtown' by 1939. The community had dwindled to a handful by the latter part of the 1990s.

'New' and 'old' Jews in Dublin and Belfast

Dublin, the administrative capital of the island, remained home to the largest Jewish community in the country. The 'foreign Jews' lived around the South Circular Road district, on the south side of the River Liffey. The area became known to locals as 'Little Jerusalem'. The new influx was to present a challenge for the forty or fifty Jewish families who were longer term residents in the city.[50] These tended to live in the vicinity of Mary's Abbey Synagogue, which was on the north side of the river.[51] The arrival of the new Jews meant that the axis of the community's social, economic and religious life in the capital shifted to the South Circular Road area.

Cultural and linguistic differences meant that the arrivals from Akmijan and the area around Kovno were virtually as isolated from their co-religionists as they were from the rest of the population. Those differences made an impact as early as 1883 when the immigrants broke away from the Mary's Abbey congregation and established the first of several *hebroth,* or brotherhoods, of their own at St Kevin's Parade; others followed at Oakfield Place (1885), Camden Street (1885), Lennox Street (1887), Heytesbury Street (1891), and Lombard Street (1893). That made for, as Hyman commented, a 'divided community' which was 'almost a moral necessity'. The newcomers felt much more at home in the new conventicles than in the 'English' synagogue.[52] Hyman adds:

> The newcomer was neither intellectually nor spiritually prepared to enter at once into liturgical fellowship with his Irish-born brethren-in-faith. Differences of language, character, and temperament kept them apart. There had to be a stage of transition in which the immigrant was adjusted to the new environment and contacts. The *hebroth* provided that interlude.[53]

The contrast between 'new' and 'old' Jews was also marked in Belfast. The community had grown from 55 in 1871 to 708 by 1901. There were two synagogues, one at Great Victoria Street and a second in Regency Street. There was a move to open a third. Sir Otto Jaffe, life-president of the Belfast congregation, sought to bring greater unity to the divided community by sponsoring the building of a new synagogue at Annesley Street, Carlisle Circus in central Belfast. Lady Jaffe laid the foundation stone on 26 February 1904, and Sir Otto, in his lord mayoral robes, presided over the opening of the new synagogue on 31 August 1904. It was consecrated by the chief rabbi of the British Empire, Rev. Dr S. Hermann Adler.[54] The new synagogue did not resolve all the differences in the Belfast community, but it did provide a place of common worship.

Fourteen years earlier, during a pastoral visit in 1890, Adler had attempted and failed to reconcile the differences between the four Jewish congregations in Dublin.[55] Nevertheless, shortly afterwards the local Jewish leaders acquired a site for a new synagogue and the building was ready for services within two years. The last divine Sabbath service held in Mary's Abbey was on 3 December 1892. The following day, Adler consecrated the new headquarters of the

Dublin Hebrew Congregation at Adelaide Road.[56] Adler said on that occasion: 'You have come here, my foreign brethren, from a country like unto Egypt of old to a land which offers you hospitable shelter. It is said that Ireland is the only country in the world which cannot be charged with persecuting the Jews.'[57] Rabbi Adler was generous in his remarks. The Irish administration in the nineteenth century did not persecute Jews. The new government of the Irish Free State, after 1922, did not do so either. Neither did the government of Northern Ireland. But Jews in Ireland, and the 'new' Jews in particular, did have to confront incidents of anti-Semitism.

Anti-Semitism and defence of the Jews

How widespread was the belief that Jews were a disruptive and an undesirable influence in Irish society in the 1880s and 1890s? A disturbance was recorded in Limerick on Easter Sunday, April 1884 when a crowd surrounded the house of Lieb Siev. Stones were thrown, and Siev's wife and child were hurt.[58] Two ringleaders were sentenced to a month in prison with hard labour. The mayor of Limerick, Alderman Lenihan, stated at the trial that the treatment to which the Jewish family had been subjected could not be tolerated in a civilised country. The *Cork Examiner* came to the assistance of the Limerick Jewish community: 'This country has long been honourably distinguished by its tolerance towards the Jews. . . . *Haud Ignora mali* – not ignorant of persecution and its evils, our own race ought to be especially careful to avoid its infliction.'[59] Two Jews were beaten up in the city in 1892, and in another incident, the house of Moses Leone was stoned on 24 November 1896.[60]

In Cork in 1888, two foreigners known as Katz threatened to import both cheap labour and cheap produce from abroad. The two were popularly believed to be Jews, although this has not been verified. Threats were made against the Jewish community by a number of trade unionists. The mayor of Cork, John O'Brien, wrote a letter to the London *Times* dissociating the city's population from these threats.[61] There were also indiscriminate attacks on Jews in Cork in 1894. Three of those responsible were imprisoned.[62] The leader of the Irish Parliamentary Party, John Redmond, said on 9 May 1894 that he had 'no sympathy with the persecution to which the Jewish community have been subjected in other countries'. He felt sure that 'the great body of Catholics in Ireland, who have in the past known what persecution for religion's sake meant, will never have any sympathy with the attacks upon the members of any creed'.[63]

In Dublin in 1886, there was an anti-Semitic poster campaign, supported by letters to newspapers, against the newly arrived Jews. Rallying to their defence, the *Freeman's Journal* wrote: 'This sudden antipathy to the Jewish community in the city is either the work of some hare-brained, or, what is more likely, the project of a set of ruffians having some ulterior object in view.'[64] On 13 July 1893 – less than a year after Chief Rabbi Adler's sermon praising Irish tolerance at the opening of the Adelaide Road Synagogue – the Land League leader, Michael Davitt, responded to a speech made by

Con Crowley from Bandon, County Cork, in which he had said at a meeting of the Labour Federation that 'the Jews ought to be kept out of Ireland'.[65] Davitt, who was to speak and write in defence of Jews in Ireland and in Russia on many occasions, repudiated such sentiments in a letter to the *Freeman's Journal*:

> The Jews have never to my knowledge done any injury to Ireland. Like our own race, they have endured a persecution the records of which will for ever remain a reproach to the 'Christian' nations of Europe. Ireland has no share in this black record. Our country has this proud distinction – freely acknowledged by Jewish writers – of never having resorted to this un-Christian and barbarous treatment of an unfortunate people.[66]

He recalled that the Irish House of Commons had passed a resolution in 1787 for the naturalisation of all Jews who wished to become Irish citizens.[67] Referring to anti-Semitic campaigns in working-class London, where it was alleged by Tory protectionists that trade depression was traceable to the influx of 'foreign workmen, mainly Jews', he said that 'no Irishman worthy of the name will sympathise with a mean and unjust crusade of so unscrupulous a character'.[68] As Irish men and women were scattered the world over, Davitt proclaimed:

> . . . we are bound in justice and in reason to extend to all who seek the shelter of our island shores the same treatment and hospitality which the members of our own race have received at the hands of so many nations all over the globe, when driven by persecution and unjust government from their own country.[69]

The *Lyceum*, a magazine associated with University College, Dublin, responded with an editorial written by Fr Thomas Finlay and entitled 'The Jew in Ireland'.[70] The editorial spoke about the necessity for the native Irish to adopt measures of self-defence, though not of persecution, against immigrants whose settlement in the country would constitute an economic danger:

> Our first duty is to ourselves and to our own people, and no sympathy with the suffering and persecuted Jews can avail to free us from this obligation. If the influx of the Jews into Ireland constitutes an economic danger to the industry of the wealth-producing classes amongst us, then it would be a duty to resist – not out of hatred of the Jews, but out of concern for ourselves.[71]

The editorial writer described what was happening in Dublin:

> In Dublin, where they are settling in ever increasing numbers, they do not gravitate towards the Coombe or the Liberties. They possess themselves rather of the quarter traversed by the South Circular Road. In this thoroughfare itself and in the streets opening off they have established a flourishing colony – so flourishing that for their religious needs a spacious synagogue has lately been built close by. In some of the streets that open off the South Circular Road one may walk along the pavement from end

to end and hardly hear a word of English spoken by the children who are at play on the footpath. We are in as completely a Jewish quarter as if we were wandering through some city of Poland or Southern Russia. But tenants of the houses which line the street are not of the social standing of the inhabitants of the Polish ghetto, nor are they given to the occupations of the 'sweated' Jew of London. They are respectable in their way, well dressed and well fed, not at all likely to compete with our poor tradesmen for the 'jobs' on which they depend for a livelihood.[72]

The editorial referred to the election of a number of anti-Semitic candidates to the German parliament, and offered an explanation of their political success: 'We may answer this question in a word by stating that their dislike of the Jew arises from the fact that the Jew amongst them is a gombeen man' and that he contrives 'by tricks of trade and the devices of the moneylender' to get control of 'the wealth that the toiling Christian creates'. The editorial claimed that the Jew became 'a hawker and trader first, then a moneylender, and, finally a lord of the Money Market and Stock Exchange where he holds the destinies of nations in his hands'.[73] Therefore the 'danger' to Irish social and economic life came from the Jew's 'gombeening propensities'.

We may notice him traversing the lanes of our cities, or visiting our country farm-houses when the 'good man' is abroad and only the woman of the household has to be dealt with. He carries bundles of cheap wares, or he is laden with pious pictures, or statues of the Christian Redeemer whose name and whose following he abhors. ... The Jew will be content to take his payment in weekly instalments. ... The 'Jewman' of Dublin, like the 'tickman' of Belfast, is an acknowledged acquaintance of the households with which he traffics and from which he collects his weekly contributions; it becomes easy for him to determine who are the 'good men' in his sphere of business, that is to say, in the Shylock's sense of the words, who are 'sufficient'.[74]

The editorial pointed out that the arrival of the Jew in Ireland as a trader coincided with a change in the law which gave the Irish tenant farmer a saleable interest in his farm, but trusted that 'it was no more than coincidence'. Nevertheless, the writer speculated on what Jews were doing driving along country roads 'in smart vehicles, making calls at the houses of some of the farmers as they go', without the familiar pack and without Christian pictures and statues: 'Their visits are not undertaken out of friendship or philanthropy. What then?'[75] The implication was that the newly arrived Jews were intent on taking over Irish farms.

After laying out those arguments, the editorial asked whether the Jew should be made welcome in Ireland. The answer was a qualified 'yes'. There ought to be a welcome if the Jew was to become an honest producer. But if he came merely 'as a parasite, not to produce by labour in the field or the workshop' but to live upon the fruits of the labours of others, then 'let him not be more welcome here than he is among the peasants of Germany or among the labourers of France'.[76]

The fears generated by the new arrivals in Ireland were exacerbated by growing anti-Semitism on the continent. The case of Alfred Dreyfus, a captain in the French army who had been convicted of spying for Germany and sentenced on 22 December 1894 to imprisonment on Devil's Island,[77] divided Irish society. Furthermore, the clash between church and state in France also had an impact on opinion in Ireland.[78] There was no publication in Ireland to rival *La Croix*, a Catholic daily paper edited by Fr Bailly for the Assumptionist order which was proud to call itself 'the most anti-Semitic paper in France',[79] or the even more extreme anti-Semitism that could be found in the writings of Edouard Adolphe Drumont and his paper, *La Libre Parole*.[80] Nevertheless, the founder of the Sinn Féin movement, Arthur Griffith, while no Drumont, allowed anti-Semitic views to be published in his newspaper, the *United Irishman*.[81] In late 1899, Griffith wrote in the *United Irishman*: 'I have in former years often declared that the Three Evil Influences of the century were the Pirate, the Freemason, and the Jew.'[82] Griffith, who had lived in South Africa, wrote of the 'swarming Jews of Johannesburg', and of a 'sorry gathering' in Hyde Park:

> Some thirty thousand Jews and Jewesses, mostly of phenomenal ugliness and dirt, had come out of their East End dens at the summons of their Rabbis. If they hated France, it was also evident that they detested soap and water still more acutely. It was a scene to recall Thackeray's
>
> > All the fleas in Jewry
> > Jumped up and
> > bit like fury. [83]

The Dreyfus case was taken up again by *La Croix* in France[84] and by the *United Irishman*.[85] The latter paper showed no sympathy whatsoever for Dreyfus, and, following the quashing of his guilty verdict and the ordering of a retrial on 3 June 1899, the *United Irishman* argued on 5 August:

> While the Dublin Editors have fed the Irish public on the fables of the Jew Telegram Agencies, every diplomatist in Europe knows why [General Gaston] Galliffet [chosen to review the guilty verdict in the Dreyfus case] has been chosen to be the Tool of the Jews at the French War Office. He has been for many years their servile debtor, absolutely living on their loans, and only able to pay as interest his 'aristocratic service' in getting rich Jews into 'good society'.[86]

Dreyfus was retried and condemned on 9 September but 'with extenuating circumstances'.[87] An article in an unrepentant *United Irishman* stated on 16 September:

> A few days ago a Jew traitor, who had sold the most vital secrets of France to her military enemies, was condemned to the mild punishment of imprisonment, after his guilt had been for a second time in five years demonstrated to a court martial of his comrades. . . . The simple fact is that the whole European world, with the exception of the Anglo-Jew coalition and its Irish sycophants, is utterly indifferent to the traitor's fate.[88]

Dreyfus was pardoned by presidential decree on 19 September 1899 and completely exonerated by the French government on 12 July 1906. The radical socialist, Frederick Ryan, spoke for many of his contemporaries when he wrote in a letter to the *United Irishman* on 26 August 1899:

> What do you think [Wolfe] Tone would have thought could he have seen a paper, allied with his memory, filling its columns with 'anti-Semitic' ravings – Tone, who was above all bigotries, and whose conspicuous service was to work for the emancipation of those of a faith [different] to that in which he himself was reared?[89]

Rumours about the activities of Jewish immigrants in Ireland continued to circulate at the turn of century. The rhetorical question posed by the *Lyceum* – quoted earlier – concerning the acquisition of land by the 'new' Jews was reflected in the actions of Dublin Castle. On 2 February 1903 the Under Secretary, Sir Anthony Patrick MacDonnell, requested the chief commissioner of the Dublin Metropolitan Police, Sir John Ross, and the inspector general of the Royal Irish Constabulary, Colonel Neville F. F. Chamberlain, to enquire into the causes for the sudden increase in the number of Jews in the country and whether Jews were 'endeavouring to get farmers into their hands with a view to the acquisition of land'.[90] They were further asked to ascertain whether there was any foundation in fact for the following suggestion:

> It has been stated that Jews are in the habit of collecting from hotels, and other large establishments of the sort, used tea leaves, drying them, mixing with them deleterious drugs, and selling the compound to the poorer classes as tea; and it had been suggested that this product must be injurious to health, even producing nervous disease and insanity.[91]

Inspector General Chamberlain circulated all the county inspectors for their response to the questions posed by MacDonnell.[92]

The county inspectors' reports provide a very full account of the life and occupations of many Jews in Ireland at the beginning of the twentieth century.[93] Sergeant J. Cusack reported from Belfast on 13 February 1903 that there were about eight hundred Jews living in the city:

> Belfast is considered by them a suitable place to live and carry on the several trades in which they engage i.e. such as making picture frames, cheap furniture, dealing in old clothes etc. etc.
>
> The better class of Jews keep house furnishing shops and supply their customers with goods given out on the hire-system. There are some Jews here who act as moneylenders but so far as I can learn none of them care to take land.
>
> The Jew moneylenders in Belfast do advance small sums of money to farmers and charge a high rate of interest for such loans but the money is not lent with a view to getting the farmers into difficulty.
>
> As regards the tea question. I have been round all the Hotels and principal restaurants in the city and none of them have ever supplied the Jews or any other people with the used tea leaves: nor have inquiries for such been made except in a few instances where the tea leaves were wanted for use in lifting the dust off carpets in some of the large shops here.[94]

The county inspector for the County Cork East Riding also reported on 13 February that Jews did not acquire land and that there was no reason to believe they were getting the tenant farmers into debt for the purpose of getting mortgages on their land.[95]

> With regard to the number of Jews in Cork City there is no increase since 1901. Some Jews work as tailors, others as pedlars – dealing in soft goods, pictures, furniture, musical instruments and cheap jewellery. They visit occasionally the Ballincollig, Mallow, Midleton, Youghal, Newmarket and Queenstown districts. They trade principally on the credit system . . . but as far as can be ascertained they are not getting the people into debt. Their operations are of a limited character, few people caring to deal with them. They don't take land.[96]

A report from the County Cork West Riding stated that there were no Jews resident in the area. However, the county inspector pointed out that:

> The principal towns and some of the villages near Cork are visited by Jew Pedlars who deal in soft goods, pictures and oddments, and also solicit orders for goods to be afterwards delivered. These are merely Pedlars, nor have they any dealing with land.[97]

He reported that there was no reason to believe that these Jews were getting tenant farmers into their debt: 'The payments made to them for their goods are made in cash as a rule, but they allow amounts up to one pound or one pound ten shillings to be paid by monthly instalments: they appear not to give credit unless that they are likely to be paid.'[98] He also reported that there were no itinerant or resident Jew tea-dealers in his area.[99]

Limerick, which was to be the focus of international attention in early 1904 for its treatment of Jews, presented a similar picture. A report from the county inspector on 12 February 1903 stated:

> The Jew pedlars have not got the peasants in the rural portions of this district into their debt to any great extent.
> They do not sell tea here; nor do they buy used tea leaves at hotels or other places. Enquiries have been made at the large drapery houses, hotels, etc. and used tea leaves are not sold.[100]

Another report from Limerick, also dated 12 February, stated that there had been a slight decrease in the number of Jews in the city since 1901.

> They are chiefly pedlars and small shopkeepers. A few of them control a Loan Fund Society. None of them have land.
> They do not lend money to a very great extent to tenant farmers, but a good many small farmers and labourers in the rural part of this district are in debt to them for goods sold and delivered and, in a few cases, for money lent. I do not think that this object is to obtain mortgages on the land. As a rule they do not allow the debts to run to a large amount.[101]

A report on 17 February from County Kilkenny stated that the Jews who visited there were 'small dealers in pictures, cheap jewellery and clothes, generally selling for ready money'.[102]

Having received reports from county and district inspectors throughout the country, Inspector General Chamberlain wrote to Under Secretary MacDonnell summarising the outcome of the exercise. He concluded that there was 'no reason at present to believe that Jews are obtaining any hold on farms'.[103] He added:

> No doubt the Jew moneylenders, and pedlars, give credit to farmers and others, and charge high rates of interest; but it does not appear that up to the present, at all events, they have taken mortgages on farms as securities, or in any way show a desire to obtain a lien on landed property.
>
> It is quite possible that the explanation of this is to be found in the fact that the Jews recognise the difficulty in Ireland, in view of the agrarian feeling, of enforcing a legal right to land with pecuniary advantage.
>
> If circumstances change, and land once more becomes a free marketable commodity, Jews would in all probability accept it as security, and deal in it to their own profit.[104]

Chamberlain told MacDonnell that, without exception, the county inspectors' reports supported the conclusion that 'there is no reason to believe that Jew tea Pedlars are in the habit of selling deleterious tea'.[105] Despite being exonerated in the eyes of the police, fear and suspicion continued to surround the presence of the 'new' Jews in the country.[106]

2

The Limerick 'pogrom', 1904

In the first decade of the new century, the impulse grew in Ireland to replace a foreign *esprit de domination* with a nationalist alternative. That new-found assertiveness is well illustrated in Fr Michael O'Riordan's *Catholicity and Progress in Ireland,* which was published in 1906 in answer to Horace Plunkett's *Ireland in the New Century* of the previous year.[1] Irish political Catholicism was not characterised by a hostility towards Jews which might be found among co-religionists on the right and on the left in France and other continental countries. On the other hand, Irish Catholicism was not noted for its toleration of other religious minorities. While most antagonism was reserved for Protestants, the liturgical and theological antipathy towards Jews was rooted in an intellectual foundation out of which a strong anti-Semitism might emerge at any time.

Michael Davitt stood out among his generation as a defender of the Jews.[2] In 1903, he reported on the pogroms in Kishineff (Kishinev) in Bessarabia, Russia.[3] A book based on his experiences there, *Within the Pale,* deservedly attracted international attention and gained him added respect for his commitment to humanitarian causes.[4] The year following his return from Russia, he was called upon to speak out on behalf of the Jews of Limerick.

Various writers have described as a 'pogrom' the events in Limerick of early January 1904. Is the retention of the term justified, considering nobody was killed or seriously injured? I believe it is, for the following reason: based on their experiences in Lithuania, the word pogrom came immediately to the lips of Limerick's Jews when they found themselves under attack in January 1904.[5] Those fears must further be seen in the context of a country which was overwhelmingly Christian. The radical asymmetry between members of the Catholic Church and the Jewish congregation in Limerick in 1904 may be illustrated by focusing attention on the size and activities of the Archconfraternity of the Holy Family, from a meeting of which first emanated the incitement against the local Jews. Founded on 20 January 1868 by the

Redemptorists, an order of Italian origin, the arch-confraternity had about 6,000 members in 1904. The numbers were so large that it met in sections three nights a week. It recruited its support mainly, although not exclusively, from the poorer sectors of Limerick city and countryside.

Fr John Creagh and anti-Semitism

Fr John Creagh took over as director of the arch-confraternity in 1902 at the age of thirty-two; he was the first Limerick-born priest to hold the office.[6] A contemporary newspaper article described him as an 'athletic, clean-built "figure of a man", with the characteristic cheerfulness and frankness of a son of the soil'.[7] Creagh has been portrayed by the Redemptorist priest, Samuel Boland as follows:

> His preaching was irresistible, said Sister Ignatius, a St John of God sister who remembered him vividly up to her death. One dour North of Ireland Protestant used to come each Sunday to 'sit under Fr Creagh', ostenta-tiously leaving the church after the sermon. He spared no one, and the people just loved it, regularly overflowing the church into the street.[8]

This description well fitted the man who was warmly received at his first arch-confraternity meeting in 1902 with the 'customary [Roman] salute'.[9]

From the outset, Creagh's preaching style was demagogic and revivalist, as can be seen by the manner in which he addressed the question of alcohol abuse in the city:

> I need not, my dear men, tell you that the great evil of today is drink. . . . There are publicans who have no conscience – no scruples. . . . What appeals to their conscience? Money – blood money. Money, the price of souls – the money of Judas. Judas sold his Master for thirty pieces of silver, and these publicans will sell souls, that Jesus Christ died to redeem, for the sake even of a pint of stout or a half glass of whiskey. Appeal to their conscience! Nothing would appeal to their conscience but the prison cell – the lash of the convict.[10]

In early 1904 those same forensic skills were directed against the Jews in the city.[11] It would appear that the priest had been approached by shop-keepers in the city who were hostile to the Jewish pedlars because they provided unwelcome competition. Although the topic of his sermon was not publicised, members of the arch-confraternity had been warned in advance to attend the Monday meeting on 11 January in large numbers. Creagh began innocently enough by talking about Christian charity and the duty to look upon all men as brothers, even those who hate or persecute Christians:

> [but] it would be madness for a man to nourish in his own breast a viper that might at any moment slay a benefactor with its poisonous bite. So too is it madness for a people to allow an evil to grow in their midst that will eventually cause them ruin.[12]

He then broke silence on the topic which was troubling him so much:

> It was that they were allowing themselves to become the slaves of Jew
> usurers. They knew who they were. The Jews were once the chosen
> people of God. God's mercy and favours toward them were boundless.
> They were the people of whom was born the Messiah, Jesus Christ, Our
> Lord and Master. But they rejected Jesus, they crucified Him – they called
> down the curse of His precious blood upon their own heads – 'His blood
> be upon us and upon our children', they cried, and that curse came upon
> them.[13]

Creagh continued in an even more strident tone:

> Nowadays, they dare not kidnap and slay Christian children, but they will
> not hesitate to expose them to a longer and even more cruel martyrdom
> by taking the clothes off their back and the bit out of their mouths.
> Twenty years ago and less Jews were known only by name and evil repute
> in Limerick. They were sucking the blood of other nations, but those
> nations rose up and turned them out and they came to our land to fasten
> themselves on us like leeches, and to draw our blood when they had been
> forced away from other countries. They have, indeed, fastened them-
> selves upon us, and now the question is whether or not we will allow them
> to fasten themselves still more upon us, until we and our children are the
> helpless victims of their rapacity.

He proceeded to describe how the fortunes of the Jewish community in
Limerick were being transformed.

> The Jews came to Limerick apparently the most miserable tribe imagin-
> able, . . . but now they had enriched themselves, and could boast of very
> considerable house property in the city. Their rags have been exchanged
> for silk. They have wormed themselves into every form of business. They
> are in the furniture trade, the mineral water trade, the milk trade, the
> drapery trade, and in fact into business of every description, and traded
> even under Irish names.[14]

Creagh then dramatically produced a copy of the *Limerick Chronicle*
which had just been handed to him. He read to his congregation the account
of a recent Jewish wedding in the city. Creagh was referring to the wedding of
Fanny Toohey and Maurice B. Maissell on Thursday, 7 January without using
their names. This wedding may have indirectly contributed to the growing
tension between local residents and a section of the Jewish community.
Fanny Goldberg, who was eleven at the time, remembered it well; she
recorded in her unpublished memoirs how childish curiosity took her unin-
vited (the schism in the Jewish community meant that the Goldbergs had
not been on the guest list) to the synagogue to see the bride:

> It was the usual kind of wedding with the horse drawn carriages, and white
> satin clad bride, and satin clad bridesmaids. And all men in top hats and of
> course the guests in their best. I thought the bridesmaids were beautiful in
> their long dresses, and coloured satin capes trimmed with swans down.
> There was a crowd of onlookers outside the [synagogue], with women in

ragged shawls, and overawed barefoot children. It was said at the time that this display of 'silks and satins' put the light to the smouldering fire.

That may or may not have been the case. But Creagh made the most of it. Reading from the *Limerick Chronicle* report, he recounted how, outside the synagogue, were those who wore 'poverty's motley', while those inside 'were clad in fine broadcloth, and silks and satins goodly to look upon'.[15] Creagh asked how Jews managed to make this money:

> Some of you may know their methods better than I do, but still it is my duty to expose their methods. They go about as pedlars from door to door, pretending to offer articles at very cheap prices, but in reality charging several times the value more than they were bought in the shops. The Jew is most persevering and barefaced in his statements as to the value of his goods. He does not mind to whom he offers his wares. . . . They force themselves and their goods upon the people, and the people are blind as to their tricks.

Creagh then outlined the evil of the weekly payments system where the client was often unable to make the repayments:

> When the summons is for less than 1.16s.8d. it must go before the Mayor's Court of Conscience; if for a larger sum it goes before another court. Then a decree is given, and the Mayor's sergeants are forced to become collectors of money for the Jews and the bailiffs are put in, and the little property seized and sold by the rapacious Jews.[16]

Creagh alleged that housewives were mostly the victims:

> The Jew has got a sweet tongue when he wishes – he passes off his miserable goods upon her. She has to spare and stint to get the money to pay off the Jew without her husband knowing it, and then follow misery, sorrow and deceit. The wife is afraid lest her husband should find out that she has been dealing with the Jews. . . . The wife . . . will beg the Jew not to come to her house – she does not want him to be seen coming, and then stealthy visits must be paid at night, in the darkness, lest the dealings might be found out.

He invited members of the congregation to stand at a prominent Jew's house at night

> and you will be surprised to see the number and the class of people who are going in and out, under cover of shawls, to pay the Jew his usury. Nor does the Jew care what excuse he makes to carry on business in the dark, if necessary, but after that comes the court day. Visit the Mayor's Court on a Thursday – you may not see it now for some time, for the Jews may hold their hands – but if you visited it during the past two years you would think it was a special court for the whole benefit of the Jews.[17]

Creagh told the congregation that he had in his possession an authentic document containing a list of the summonses issued by Jews during the past two years. He read out the contents:

In 1902 some 337 summonses were issued for 303.1s.1d. In 1903 226 summonses for 172.11s.4d. Surely this reveals a terrible state of things. If so many people had to be sued for money week after week, and for sums under 1.16s.8d., how many people, must we conclude, are constantly dealing with them? And those figures do not deal with processes in the other courts.[18]

Creagh was also concerned about the Jewish influence in the countryside:

They have made Limerick their headquarters, from which they can spread their rapacious nets over the country all round. When they came here first they had to carry their packs upon their shoulders. Now they can afford to have horses and traps to carry their goods, and they can go long distances by train, and succeed in making the farmers their dupes as well as those living in the towns. To make their traffic easier they will barter in kind instead of in money. They will take a hen or a goose, or a turkey, eggs or butter, and people will only receive half the market value of their poultry and dairy produce.

He admitted that some benefit might return to the local community if Jews bought their goods from local traders. But, he claimed, they did so only to a limited extent:

they prefer to get their goods from other Jews across the Channel, and week by week tons of goods of every description are landed in Limerick from Jews outside the country, and thus the Jews cripple local trade and industry. For instance, the furniture made in London deprives the local tradesmen of their work and the weekly wage to support their family.

Finally, Creagh turned his attention to the question of religion:

I do not hesitate to say that there are no greater enemies of the Catholic Church than the Jews. If you want an example look to France. What is going on at present in that land? The little children are being deprived of their education. No Nun, Monk or Priest can teach in a school. The little ones are forced to go where God's name is never mentioned.—.to go to Godless schools. The Jews are in league with the Freemasons in France, and they succeeded in turning out of their country all the nuns and religious orders. The Redemptorist Fathers to the number of two hundred had been turned out of France, and that is what the Jews would do in our country if they were allowed into power.[19]

Creagh advised his congregation to have no commercial dealings with Jews. If they had any transactions with them they should get out of them as soon as possible, and then keep far away from them.[20] His message was interpreted as a call for a boycott. He soon got his wish.

Michael Davitt, John Redmond and the Jews

Colooney Street, where most Limerick Jews lived, was only a few minutes' walk from the Redemptorist church. The hundreds who left the church after

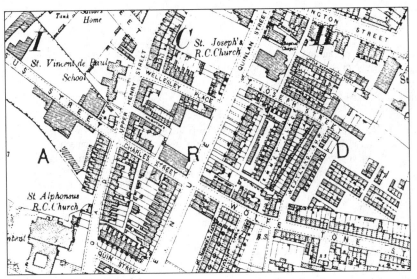

2. Jewish quarter, Limerick, near Colooney St

the meeting had to pass the top of Colooney Street on their way home. The Jewish community remained locked in their homes as the church militants passed by. Jewish shops, however, remained open and their owners felt menaced. One old Fenian – a member of the confraternity – single-handedly defended a shop from attack until the police arrived to mount a guard. Fearing an all-out attack on his community, Rabbi Elias Bere Levin wrote to Irish political leaders and to Jewish organisations in England asking for their public support. He told Michael Davitt in a letter on 12 January that the priest's allegations were 'devoid of any particle of truth'. He recalled that during the previous quarter of a century Jewish families in the city had lived 'in perfect peace and harmony with their Christian neighbours of all classes'. He added: 'The feeling of respect between them and their Christian neighbours seemed hitherto to be quite mutual, so that we are utterly at a loss to assign this very sudden event to any cause on our part.'[21] Levin asked Davitt to conclude for himself whether the anti-Semitic outburst had its roots in religious prejudices or had been 'promoted by local traders'. He sought Davitt's intervention to avert a general boycott of Jewish traders and prevent an anti-Semitic riot, as already 'several of us have been insulted, assaulted, and threatened with the most menacing language'.[22]

Davitt responded immediately. In a letter on 16 January to the *Freeman's Journal*, he said that it had been Ireland's unique glory that its original conquest to Christianity had been effected without bloodshed, and that the sons of St Patrick had truly upheld that reputation ever since:

> Irish Catholics have suffered every possible form of religious oppression known to the perverted ingenuity of the authors of the Penal Code, but it

is their proud boast that neither in Ireland nor in any land to which English rule has forced them to fly did they ever resort to a counter-religious persecution. . . . A few years ago, perhaps a dozen, the Chief Rabbi of London, on a visit to Dublin, declared that when he set foot on Irish soil he was in the only land of Europe in which his race had never suffered persecution.[23]

He protested as an Irishman and as a Catholic

against the spirit of barbarous malignity being introduced into Ireland, under the pretended form of a material regard for the welfare of our workers. The reverend gentleman complained of the rags and poverty of the children of Limerick as compared with the prosperity of the Jews, and on this ground deliberately incited the people of that city to hunt the Jew from their midst.[24]

Then, in a passage that was later to be challenged by Creagh, Davitt wrote against the charge of ritual killing: 'There is not an atom of truth in the horrible allegation of ritual murder, here insinuated, against this persecuted race . . . the dissemination of which has led to the slaughter of tens of thousands of innocent lives throughout Europe in past times.'[25] Davitt concluded by expressing his confidence in the city of Limerick, 'a stronghold of true Nationalist sentiment' which could not 'be induced to dishonour Ireland by any response to such unworthy and un-Catholic invitations'.[26] Praising the bishop of Limerick, Dr Edward Thomas O'Dwyer, Davitt encouraged the rabbi to seek a meeting with him.[27]

The leader of the Irish Parliamentary Party, John Redmond, also replied promptly in defence of the Limerick Jews: 'I have no sympathy whatever with the attacks upon the Hebrew Community in Limerick or elsewhere. I feel sure that the good sense and spirit of toleration of the Irish people will be sufficient to protect them from any wrong.'[28] Levin must have been comforted by the fact that no major public figure, no national politician or bishop, rushed to endorse Creagh's anti-Semitic attack.

The boycott begins

Besides seeking the support of major public figures, Rabbi Levin had also to ensure that the local police would protect the Jewish community from further intimidation. On 13 January, he sent a copy of Creagh's sermon to the Royal Irish Constabulary (RIC) county inspector, Thomas Hayes:

I beg to inform you that every member of my community regards his life at this moment in peril. As a matter of fact several of us have been already in this two foregone days *insulted, assaulted*, and abused with menacing language.[29]

Levin sought 'ample protection' and 'constables posted in every street in all parts of the City' as members of his community were 'obliged to go about everywhere to earn a living'.[30] District Inspector C. H. O'Hara was instructed on 14 January to make 'such arrangements with the local police as to *prevent their* [the Jews] *being molested'*. O'Hara reported on 16 January that he had personally visited two of the stations to give instructions to the sergeants. He had directed that special attention be paid to Jews by all the city stations, especially on the following Monday, 18 January, when they were due to collect the weekly instalments. O'Hara also visited Rabbi Levin at his home in Colooney Street. He asked Levin to let his people know that they would get every assistance from the police and to have them report any cases of assault or abuse. O'Hara also alerted RIC stations in the surrounding countryside to offer protection to Jewish pedlars.[31]

In view of the rising tension in the city, County Inspector Hayes called personally to see Rabbi Levin on the morning of 18 January. Levin was out, so Hayes left a message asking the rabbi to provide him with a written account of the position in which the Jews now found themselves. Upon his return, Levin wrote to thank the police: 'there is hardly any incident worth complaining of, except insults and abusive language given us to which we are no aliens'.[32] But a boycott was in operation against the Jews:

> Those of us who trade on the weekly pament [sic] system are literally ruined, I am informed that they hardly collect 10% of their usual collection, and as for selling goods that is out of the question, not one shilling's worth of goods having been sold by them for the last fortnight in the city of Limerick.[33]

The rabbi explained that economic sanctions against the Jews were on the increase:

> The people who have hitherto dealt with the members of my community say that they were ordered by Fr Creagh neither to pay their debts nor to purchase goods. There are six petty hucksters [sic] shops, whose owners until now managed to live, but whose ruin is already visible, having lost all their Christian custom since the first address on Jewish trade was delivered by Fr Creagh.[34]

Levin said that Jewish traders were being pressed for payment by wholesalers with whom they had done business for years 'and who had always placed the greatest confidence in them'. To give the county inspector some idea of what he meant, Rabbi Levin cited the example of two 'petty shopkeepers' who did business in the milk trade and were now being boycotted. One did business with a Mr James Gleeson of Kilpeacon Road.

> The latter used to supply him ten or twelve gallons of milk daily and since last fortnight, he refused to do so any more. The other petty shop-keeper who also deals a little in the milk trade has been given notice by the farmer who used hitherto to supply him with milk that he will not supply him any more. So much for the Jewish businesses in Limerick.[35]

Dublin Castle was advised by District Inspector O'Hara on 18 January that he had again issued 'instructions to the police to afford every protection to the Jews'. But the policing problem proved very difficult, as he told his superiors:

> To-day a number of them [Jews] – about 40 – went about collecting their instalments and *in most cases got nothing but abuse*. Crowds followed them hissing and, in some cases, throwing mud at them. It was difficult to keep an eye to them all *as they went in many cases to back streets without the knowledge of the police*. The names of several persons who followed them in a disorderly manner were taken and one boy, who had picked up a stone – thrown at them, was arrested and was, later on, discharged to be summoned to Petty Sessions.[36]

He felt, however, that 'things will probably settle down in a few days'.[37] O'Hara also reported on a meeting he had had that afternoon with the administrator of St Michael's parish, Fr J. Cregan, his curate Fr John Lee, and the priests of the neighbouring St John's parish. These parishes were located in the inner city and were the personal parishes of Bishop O'Dwyer. O'Hara was pleased to learn that Cregan and Lee were hostile to Fr Creagh's actions:

> Both these gentlemen exercise a very large influence here *and they disapprove of Fr Creagh's attack entirely* and I gathered from them that the latter – who is not one of the parochial clergy but belongs to the Redemptorist order, which has a church here – was not authorised by any one to speak as he did.[38]

O'Hara reported to Dublin Castle that Cregan and Lee would advise 'their people not to interfere with or molest the Jews and *I think after a while that the excitement will subside*'.[39]

The spiritual director of the women's confraternity in St John's Cathedral, Fr Murphy, denounced the violence against the Jews but otherwise offered little comfort:

> If the people owed money to the Jews they should pay it as they were bound to pay all their lawful debts. If it was their desire to get rid of the Israelites, this was the best way to accomplish it, and when this was done they need have no more dealings with them.[40]

An editorial in the *Limerick Leader*, which appeared on the evening of 18 January, was supportive of the boycott but sought to calm matters in the city in the interest of fair play:

> It has come to our knowledge that the Jews for the past few days have been subjected to ill-treatment and assault while passing through our public thoroughfares. We regret that such has been the case. We are living in critical times when every advantage is taken by unscrupulous opponents to misinterpret our acts and the cause of our religion. In such a crisis it is not wise to give a handle to vilification. If the people do not want the Jews, then leave them severely alone. Above all things have no recourse to violence. Such a policy only shows weakness, if not foolish vindictiveness, and will never succeed in accomplishing that which is, or may be desired.[41]

The Jews had not been left 'severely alone' throughout that day.

Rabbi Levin's mood had changed radically between the time he had written to County Inspector Hayes in the morning of 18 January and the late afternoon when he cabled the chief rabbi in London and Dr Ernest W. Harris: 'Anti-Semitic riots took place through the day. General boycott in force. Community in peril. Every member assaulted.'[42] A special correspondent for the *Jewish Chronicle*, reporting from the city on 18 January, wrote with Kishineff-like fear about what was likely to happen:

> My pen trembles as I sit down to write to you about the situation of the Jews in Limerick. I can hardly steady my nerves to give you a full and graphic account of the anxiety I feel lest, at any moment, some Jewish house should be attacked.[43]

Although only a week had passed since Creagh's sermon, the correspondent of the *Jewish Chronicle* felt that it was like an eternity. He thought he was back again in the Middle Ages, as he wrote that

> the miserable cry: 'Down with the Jews!' 'Death to the Jews!' 'We must hunt them out' is still ringing in my ears, and sends a cold shiver through my body. Today, Monday, the chief business day, Jews were attacked right and left. I myself witnessed one scene where a Jew was actually running for his life, and as he passed through one crowd he was actually hemmed in by another, till the police came on the scene. But that is only one case out of many! And this in a land of freedom, this in the twentieth century, this only two weeks after Christmas, when peace and goodwill to all mankind was preached throughout the land!

The correspondent concluded on a depressing note:

> When I witnessed the organised attacks today and heard the mob yell 'Down with the Jews: they kill our innocent children', all the horrors of Kishineff came back to me, and then, and only then, was I able to realise what Kishineff meant.[44]

The *Jewish Chronicle* wrote that 'the Jews of Limerick are living in a state of terror' and that Rabbi Levin feared 'a general boycott, and perhaps a regular anti-Semitic riot'.[45] The 'regular anti-Semitic riot' was not to happen.

Fr Creagh's second anti-Semitic sermon

Fr Creagh's sermon on Monday 18 January attracted international press attention.[46] Though members of the arch-confraternity were instructed to prevent journalists from being present at their meeting, the text of his sermon was published in the local papers the following day.[47] Creagh entered the pulpit to loud applause from the congregation. While seeking to be conciliatory in view of the disturbances in the city during the day, his sermon confirmed that he was an intransigent and unrepentant anti-Semite. He emphasised, at the outset, that he entirely and fully deprecated any violence towards Jews. Violence, he said, had never been his intention, and he felt that it would only ruin the people's cause. The Jewish religion – as a religion – had nothing to do with his statements, he said. He had only taken up the issue in order to save confraternity men from the 'ruinous trade of the Jews'.[48] And later on he concluded his sermon by admonishing members of the arch-confraternity:

> Remember, I warn you to do them no bodily harm. Such a thing I could never approve of. It would not be Christian like. But keep away from them, and let them go to whatever country they came from, and not add to the evils of our fates.[49]

However, in between these reproaches, Creagh's sermon was filled with an injudiciousness of language that only went to heighten and inflame emotions against Jews.

> Let the members of the Confraternity investigate Jewish dealings for themselves, and then if they find what I have said is true, and I am convinced that it is true, then I appeal to you not to prove false to Ireland, false to your country, and false to your religion, by continuing to deal with the Jews. If the Jews are allowed to go on as they have been doing in a short time we will be their absolute slaves, and slavery to them is worse than slavery to which Cromwell condemned the poor Irish who were shipped to the Barbadoes.[50]

Creagh claimed that, in view of the greatness of the evil, he would have considered himself a traitor to his religion and to his country if he had not raised his voice.[51] 'If Limerick is typical of other localities as regards Jewish methods', he added, 'then all I can say is God help our nation and our race, unless something is done, and done speedily also, to change such a deplorable state of things.'[52]

He then read out Davitt's letter in defence of the Jewish community which had been published in that day's issue of the *Freeman's Journal*. Creagh denied that he had ever insinuated ritual murder.[53]

> . . . but if Mr Davitt was in daily and hourly touch with the people here as I am – if he were to see the curse brought upon the poor by the Jewish trade, if he were to see the robbery that is going on by the weekly instalment system of the Jews, and the exorbitant prices demanded for wretched goods, if he were to see the misery and strife caused in the households by the dealings of the woman of the home with the Jews – if he were to see the result of their enormous usury and the efforts made by the poor to release themselves when they have become entangled in the Jewish nets, he might begin to think they were as bad an evil to Ireland as landlordism and over-taxation, and he might think that there was enough for me to mind without my trying to do what he and his colleagues failed to do on the floor of the British House of Commons.[54]

Creagh felt that it was fair to conclude that 'the Jews have proved themselves to be the enemies of every country in Europe, and every nation had to defend itself against them'. The priest told the congregation: 'Let us defend ourselves before their heels are too firmly planted upon our necks.'[55] Creagh's words were an incitement to violence.

Following the second sermon, the local RIC feared an outbreak of general disorder. But on 19 January, District Inspector O'Hara reported a general improvement in the situation. Although the endeavours of the Jewish traders that day to obtain the instalments due to them had failed, no attempt had been made to 'molest them or to follow them about by crowds as happened yesterday'. The police had taken measures to afford them 'all possible protection'.[56] Dublin Castle authorities, in the circumstances, did not see the need to send in extra police from outside. The RIC deputy inspector general, H. Considine, minuted on 19 January that the police were doing what they could to contain a problem which had been exacerbated by the fact that the Jews were 'moving about in the many lanes and back ways of the city'. The police had 'much difficulty' in preventing isolated attacks. But sending a 'large force of police in for such duty might only accentuate the feeling which has been so ill advisedly aroused'. He felt it was better to act as if 'nothing really serious has occurred', and to leave matters to the local police force and 'to the good sense of the people'. He concluded that 'after some little time no doubt with the assistance of the local Parish clergy . . . the matter will blow over'.[57]

Minuting his reaction to Creagh's second sermon on 21 January, Considine felt it probable that the worst of the matter had passed:

> The Rev Gentleman's second address makes it clear that he does not counsel nor desire overt acts directed against the Jewish Community – but he did and does advocate Boycotting; not so much because they are Jews as because their methods of dealing are in his judgment injurious to the poorer classes.[58]

But an unidentified superior did not entirely share that view:

> This may be the commencement of a very serious business: and calls for further inquiry. The Revd Mr Creagh's historical and religious references may be injudicious but this account of the methods and objects of these Jews is but a . . . repetition of methods which Jews have practised elsewhere to the great detriment of the — and thriftless mores.

The Under Secretary asked to review the file. O'Hara reported on 22 January that 'no further demonstrations against the Jews have taken place'. They had been 'transmitting their business without molestation for the last few days but in very many cases have been unable to recover instalments due to them'. He also reported that several people had been fined between 2s 6d and 10s 6d at petty session in Limerick that day for disorderly conduct and assaults on Jews the previous Monday.[59] The police had, without the need for outside reinforcements, contained a dangerous situation.

Bishop O'Dwyer and the Redemptorists

Limerick Jews – in anticipation of further attacks on the community following the second Creagh sermon – followed Davitt's advice and sought a meeting with the Catholic bishop of Limerick, Dr Edward Thomas O'Dwyer, in order to secure his intervention in the matter.[60] Rabbi Levin and another leader of the community, Sol Goldberg, went to the bishop's palace on

Tuesday, 19 January, where they were met by O'Dwyer's secretary. The bishop did not receive them himself, but asked the two men through his secretary to refrain from making any comment to the press.[61] No account of that meeting has been found in the archives of the Limerick diocese.[62] Nevertheless, the bishop's views may be inferred from the views of the priests in his personal parishes mentioned earlier: it is unlikely that Frs Cregan and Lee, who voiced opposition to Creagh, would have held views contrary to those of their bishop on the matter.

Rabbi Levin – influenced by Bishop O'Dwyer's request – made only a brief public statement on 21 January, stating that he was constrained from replying in full to Creagh by two considerations. First, Creagh's attack was against Jews as a whole and not against the Limerick Hebrew Congregation. Second, Levin had been informed by the Limerick Hebrew Congregation that it had been requested by a high authority of the Catholic Church to avoid public controversy in connection with 'this outrageous affair'.

How did Bishop O'Dwyer respond to Creagh's attack on the Jews?[63] Creagh was a member of a religious order and that made the question of disciplining him awkward for the local bishop. O'Dwyer's position was further complicated by the fact that, according to the provincial journal of the Redemptorists, a former consultor general of the order, Fr John Magnier, and the provincial, Fr Boylan, 'were with Fr Creagh on his attack on the Jews and consequently Fr Creagh continued his campaign against the Jews'.[64] (Creagh's immediate superior, the rector of Mt St Alphonsus house in Limerick, Fr Edward O'Laverty, was not mentioned.) The same source stated that 'Bishop O'Dwyer was certainly not defending the Jews, but he was offended because he was not asked beforehand about the sermons attacking the Jews'. It was further recorded that the bishop 'gave up coming to the house. He also declared that he would not come to the General Communion of the [Feast of the] Holy Family.'[65] That event took place in the autumn at the time of the annual retreat for the members of the arch-confraternity. Is it likely, therefore, that Bishop O'Dwyer refused to visit the Redemptorist house from January until the autumn? This episcopal 'boycott' might be mistakenly perceived as a weak and inadequate response: in the world of ecclesiastical diplomacy, it was a stiff and a stern rebuke to the Redemptorists.[66]

In the months that followed Creagh's sermons, the boycott of the Jews in Limerick received widespread attention in the international press. There was pressure on the leadership of the Irish hierarchy to intervene from prominent Catholic sources in England. The duke of Norfolk wrote to Cardinal Michael Logue to ask him to help put an end to the boycott.[67] The president of the London-based Jewish Board of Deputies, David Alexander, also wrote to the cardinal asking him to intervene: 'The fact that we Jews have always received active sympathy from the Church to which your Eminence belongs adds poignancy to the grief with which we regard this outbreak.'[68] Logue replied to Alexander's letter 'in sympathetic terms but stated that as Limerick was outside his Ecclesiastical province he had no jurisdiction to interfere except by way of friendly suggestion'. Logue said that he was expecting to meet O'Dwyer within a few days and that he would bring Alexander's communication to O'Dwyer's attention.[69] If the two men met – and that is probable – both would have wished to see an immediate end to the boycott.

The superior general of the Redemptorists, Fr Mathias Raus, visited Limerick on 22 July 1904. He was accompanied by his secretary, Fr J. Reuss. Raus, who was from Alsace where traditionally there was a fairly large Jewish community, was a mild-mannered man who did his best to avoid conflict.[70] He received a warm reception when he addressed the arch-confraternity, and Creagh was loudly cheered when he thanked the congregation for the welcome given to Raus.[71] The superior general 'called upon the Bishop upon his arrival and had a long talk with him at the Palace Corbally'. It is unlikely that the meeting passed without reference to Fr Creagh.[72] Bishop O'Dwyer did not return the visit.

Raus also received an address from Rabbi Levin respectfully requesting a meeting with the superior general and his intervention to stop the boycott.

> I regret I have to say to your Excellency, that at present it is useless for a Jew to keep open his shop for any trade, for the Catholic people who were their customers will no longer deal with them, under the mistaken idea that in so depriving us of our means of living they are complying with some religious requirement of which they would be breaking the requirements if they were to trade with us.[73]

Raus did not give Rabbi Levin an interview, but it could be argued that the superior general's visit to Bishop O'Dwyer and the Levin petition did have an impact. The *Limerick Leader* reported on 24 August 1904 that Fr Collier, formerly of Dundalk, had been appointed sub-director of the arch-confraternity. In the autumn, Bishop O'Dwyer signalled that he was prepared to visit the Redemptorist house for the General Communion of the Feast of the Holy Family but the reconciliation may not have been total.[74]

Local and international support for Creagh's anti-Semitism

Whether as a consequence of the displeasure of Bishop O'Dwyer or the action of a prudent superior, Creagh was sent in February 1904 on mission to Belfast for a few weeks. Before leaving, he found that he had much popular support in Limerick. A trade union group, meeting in the Mechanics' Institute on 20 January, passed a motion that 'we fully endorse the action of the Rev. Father Creagh regarding Jews as we consider their system of trading determential [sic] to the workers of our city. We also strongly condemn the action of Mr Michael Davitt for interfering in this matter.'[75] There was a special meeting on 22 January of prefects, subprefects and other officials of the Arch-confraternity of the Holy Family. Three resolutions were passed unanimously. The first stated that the meeting, representing 6,000 members, thanked Fr Creagh 'for his recent lectures on the ways and means of Jewish trading' and expressed the members' 'fullest confidence with their views'. The 'tone' of Michael Davitt's letter was condemned, and it was asserted that their spiritual director was 'actuated by no motives except the good of the Confraternity and the general benefit of the workers of this city, especially as regards its poorest members, and that he was in no way actuated by any feeling of malignity to the Jews'.[76] The final resolution stated that 'we condemn any violence towards the Jews in this city, and this Confraternity dissociates itself from any acts of violence towards them'.[77] Creagh later thanked the members of the arch-confraternity, saying that they all knew his action in the matter was 'actuated by only the deepest interest for the good of the people and to direct attention to what was a great evil and one likely to cause great danger to the common good if left to go unchallenged'.[78]

While in Belfast, Creagh commented in the local press that he had no animosity against the Jews as a race,

> and, as for the Jews in business, I am quite prepared to admit that there are many who are irreproachable. What people have been pleased to call my crusade has been directed only against a class of Jewish traders who grind and oppress those who are unfortunate enough to get into their power – who exact extortionate sums under the instalment system from those who can ill afford to pay them . . .[79]

Creagh stated that his sole object was to safeguard 'my people from ruinous trading'. He said that he had strongly deprecated any violence and had always used – and always would use – his influence to prevent it. He had simply asked the men of the arch-confraternity to 'have no dealings with them for their own sake'. However, he said that he was not 'the man to be frightened by threatening letters, and even if my life were really in peril through my action I should continue as I have been doing'.[80]

There is only one letter abusive of Creagh in the Redemptorist archives. A 'Galbally man and no Fenian' wrote:

> So you *low cur* had you nothing better to tell your people than to set them on the poor unfortunate Jews? You call yourself a minister of *God*. You are a minister of the Devil. You are a disgrace to the Catholic religion, you brute.[81]

Creagh, meanwhile, continued to receive many letters of support. For example, the secretary of the British Brothers' League sent the text of a reso-lution passed on 27 April. It thanked Creagh

> for the noble work he has undertaken to prevent a class of undesirable aliens who have received the hospitality of the Irish race from demoralis-ing the nation and bringing misery into the homes of our Irish Brothers and Sisters through their inborn instinct of greed, usury and arrogance.[82]

A letter from 'Milesian' in the London *Times* spoke about 'an invasion of low-class Polish and Russian Jews'. The feeling in the country had turned against the Jews 'but it is chiefly against their usury and extortion'.[83] An anti-Semitic illustration from France also found its way into the arch-confraternity's records; it was from the front page of an issue of Edouard Drumont's *La Libre Parole (Grand Journal Antijuif)*.

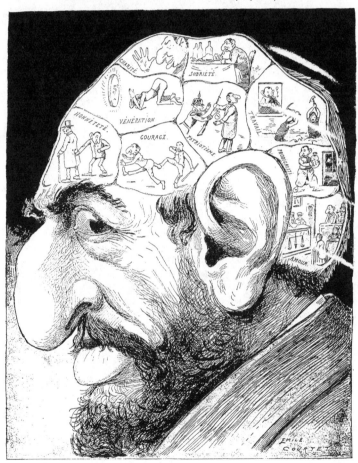

3. Anti-Semitic cartoon, *La Libre Parole* (*Grand Journal Antijuif*), circa 1900

Arthur Griffith's *United Irishman* commented that its sympathy went out to

> our countrymen the artisan whom the Jew deprives of the means of liveli-
> hood, to our countrymen the trader whom he ruins in business by
> unscrupulous methods, to our countrymen the farmer whom he draws
> into his usurer's toils and drives to the workhouse or across the water. In
> short, our sympathy is so much drained by that dreary weekly procession
> of our own flesh and blood out of Ireland that we have none left to bestow
> on the weekly procession of aliens coming in.[84]

Whereas twenty years before there were very few Jews in Ireland, the *United Irishman* argued that

> today there are Jewish magistrates to teach us respect for the glorious
> constitution under which we exist; Jewish lawyers to look after our
> affairs, and Jewish money lenders to accommodate us; Jewish tailors to
> clothe us; Jewish photographers to take our picture; Jewish brokers to
> furnish our homes, and Jewish auctioneers to sell us up in the end for the
> benefit of all our other Jewish benefactors. We are told the Jews are
> industrious people, and deserve to prosper. We do not object to their pros-
> pering by industry. We object to their prospering by usury and fraud. We
> object to their being given unfair advantages over the people whom they
> enter into competition with.[85]

The article ended:

> We are glad Father Creagh has given the advice he did. We trust he will
> continue to give it. We have no quarrel with the Jews' religion; but all the
> howling of journalistic hacks and the balderdash of uninformed senti-
> mentalists will not make us, nor should it make any honest man, cease to
> expose knavery, because the knavery is carried on by Jews.[86]

The front page of an earlier edition of the *United Irishman* stated: 'And what greater "persecution" could be inflicted upon the Jew than to prohibit him taking his pound of flesh – with interest, three pounds.'[87] Inside, the paper protested that it did not object to the Jew seeking an honest livelihood in Ireland but 'we object to his seeking a dishonest one, and howling out that he is being martyred for his faith when the people object to him putting his hand in their pockets'. The *United Irishman* then raised the emotional issue of emigration:

> No thoughtful Irishman or woman can view without apprehension the
> continuous influx of Jews into Ireland and the continuous efflux of the
> native population. The stalwart men and bright-eyed women of our race
> pass from our land in a never-ending stream, and in their place we are
> getting strange people, alien to us in thought, alien to us in sympathy,
> from Russia, Poland, Germany, and Austria – people who come to live
> amongst us, but who never become of us. When fifteen hundred of our
> strong men and good women sail on the liner from the Cove of Cork, we
> can count on receiving a couple of hundred Jews to fill their places by the
> next North Wall boat. But has Ireland gained or lost by the exchange?[88]

A letter from Jacob I. Jaffe, a member of the Jewish community, appeared in the *Jewish Chronicle*:

> I know that the utterances of Father Creagh do not voice the sentiments of Irishmen in general. But – and herein the danger lies – there exists in many parts of Ireland, especially in the South and West, a class of people who, brought up in the chains of Catholicism, and trained to unquestioning and unreasoning obedience to all the dicta of their priests, need but a slight stimulus to excite them, and to rouse them from their erstwhile friendly attitude to one of defiance and frenzied hostility.[89]

The sentiments of moderate 'Irishmen in general' were reflected in the nationalist *Freeman's Journal* and in the unionist *Irish Times*.[90] But while public opinion may have reduced the level of intimidation in the city, it did not stop the boycott.

Norah Keeffe, the Jewish pedlar and the parish priest

Throughout February and March the boycott of Jews continued. They could not sell their goods and, in some cases, they were not served in shops. Jewish children were being ostracised in the schools.[91] The RIC county inspector, Thomas Hayes, reported that he had visited some members of the Jewish community on 27 January. He 'encouraged them to hold out' and told them that 'the matter would blow over – probably'. He stated that '*the Police are affording all the protection they* [the Jews] *desire*. It is rather a difficult matter because if the Police are too prominent it will destroy their trade. They are quite satisfied that what is being done is ample.'[92] In the subdistrict of William Street, police acted upon a series of allegations made by members of the Jewish community. On 30 January they dealt with an alleged refusal to supply groceries to Mr Miessel by Messrs Egan. District Inspector O'Hara had investigated immediately and was assured by Mr Egan that he was quite willing to supply Jews and that his shop assistant told the Jew that the groceries could not be delivered. 'The Jew being told this was offended and went across the street to Quinn and Co. and was supplied there.'[93] The same day the police investigated an allegation that a member of the Jewish community, who had bought milk from James Gleeson of Kilpeacon, was no longer getting his supply: 'Gleeson assigned no reason to the Jew, but there was no scarcity of milk among the Jews as a farmer named Clancy supplied them.'[94] The police also investigated a complaint by Rabbi Levin that 'two of his community had been ill used at Newport' in County Tipperary. On 15 February, police investigated a complaint from Ephraim Goldman that he had been stoned while passing Bank Place. On 10 March a Mr Ginsberg complained that his house was being watched by two men. That proved groundless. On 25 March, Patrick Sheehan was fined £1 and costs for assaulting Mr Recusson on 18 March.[95]

There was also evidence of intimidation of Jews in rural areas. Isaac Sandler of 67 Henry Street was selling out of a car at Foynes, in the

Shanagolden area, in mid-March. He had just completed the sale of two blankets to Norah Keeffe, Kilbradran, when the parish priest of Kilcolman and Coolcappa, Fr James Gleeson, drove up. Sandler explained: 'When he saw my car he pulled up, and came off his car, and asked me what I had sold her. I said "a little not much".'[96] When Norah Harrington, who was with Norah Keeffe, saw Fr Gleeson coming, she ran into an outhouse and hid till the priest went away. In Norah Keeffe's own words, the priest told her:

> 'I will get you out of the parish for dealing with the Jews and be sure and be gone out of it before a week and to give out the blanket which you have bought from him at once.' I then took out the blankets the minute he told me. I don't remember him saying anything else to me. He then went as far as the door and told the Jew to clear off the road and that he would make him keep out of his parish. The Jew said he did not care about him nor his parish.[97]

According to Sandler's account, Fr Gleeson said 'something to the girl about buying goods from her equals'. Norah Keeffe returned the blankets, saying that the priest 'would not let me keep them'. The priest then said to Sandler: 'This is my parish and to clear out of it at once.'[98]

When Sergeant William McEvoy interviewed Norah Keeffe, he found that she was

> very frank in her version of the occurrence and appears also to resent Fr Gleeson's interference in such a manner. She is a poor herdsman's daughter and says only for the Jews that a good many of her class would often be in a bad way for clothing and bed covering.[99]

McEvoy reported to Dublin on 30 March 1904 that 'this priest's action is beyond anything I have yet had to encounter. Those Jews are examples of sobriety, industry and good conduct. They never break the law.'[100] McEvoy indicated that he was going out to the district but 'would take no action without direction'.[101] He did not interview the priest concerned.

When the matter was discussed in Dublin Castle, the RIC deputy inspector general, H. Considine, took a pragmatic view. He minuted on 8 April: 'This is a regrettable incident and I trust it will prove exceptional – but a prosecution even if sustainable (which is very doubtful) would unquestionably do infinitely more harm to the Jews than anything else.'[102] Another minute, dated 9 April, read: 'A police prosecution would be absurd.' No action was taken against the priest.[103]

Dublin Castle and pressure to prosecute Fr Creagh

Dublin Castle also withstood an appeal to prosecute Creagh. On 21 March the Jewish Board of Deputies in London wrote to Dublin Castle urging that Creagh be prosecuted, but the reply, drafted on behalf of the Lord Lieutenant, stated that there was not sufficient evidence to justify the institution of legal proceedings:

Even if it were otherwise, it would be undesirable to take any steps now that would tend to revive the excitement against the Jews in Limerick which is happily subsiding, or that might subject them to further injury or ill-treatment.[104]

The London committee sent another letter on 5 April, claiming that twenty of the thirty-five Jewish families in Limerick were stated to be now ruined and compelled to beg for a bare sustenance. It was further claimed that no member of the community was able to step out of doors without risk of bodily injury. The reply from Dublin Castle pointed out that the Lord Lieu-tenant had earlier directed the police force to 'afford every protection to the members of the Jewish faith' in Limerick and he was satisfied that those instructions had been fully carried out.[105]

Both the local police and Dublin Castle officials reacted negatively to corre-spondence in the press which painted – as they perceived it – a distorted and exaggerated view of the situation of the Jews in Limerick. The director of the Irish Mission to Jews, I. Julian Grande, had written to the *Irish Times* on 1 April 1904 claiming that 'no Jew or Jewess can walk along the streets of Limerick without being insulted or assaulted'. Justice, he wrote, had 'long since departed from lawless Limerick' where the police only gave the Jews 'passive protection'.[106] Grande also had a letter published in the *Daily Express* on 1 April.[107] An editorial in that paper on the same day spoke of the author-ities contenting themselves with the expression of 'pious opinions, and in the meantime the victims of religious hatred must go hungry':

> ... we think that it is a crying scandal that the educated bigots of Limer-ick should be allowed to make life intolerable for law-abiding and industrious members of the community, whose only offence is that they belong to a different creed.

The Jews were being denied their daily bread and were the 'victims of Limer-ick race-hatred'.[108]

Deputy Inspector General Considine, in Dublin Castle, minuted on 9 April 'That these people should suffer is earnestly a matter for regret to every one.' However, he insisted that the police 'have done, are doing, and will continue to do all they can to prevent any illegal interference with the members of the Jewish Community'.[109] District Inspector O'Hara also took issue with the allegations made by Grande and the *Daily Express*. In a report on 7 April, he stated that Jews were collecting their instalments but 'no new business is being done and no doubt the Jews have difficulty in obtaining sums due to them in many cases'. But he did not agree with the *Daily Express*'s claim that the 'only offence of the Jews is that they belong to a different creed', as he believed that 'the methods of doing business practised by the Jews are entirely responsible for the agitation'.[110] O'Hara repeated that point in a report on 13 April. He said that Creagh, who was 'a very excitable man', had advised his congregation to have no further dealings with the Jews 'by refer-ring in an inadmissible and injudicious manner to the past history of the Jews, *but there is no religious censure*'.[111] Neither did O'Hara believe that there was a 'general boycott of the Jews'. It was, he said, a rejection of the weekly payments system, and he added that, in time, their trade would return as 'the poorer classes cannot pay ready money in shops'.[112] In Dublin Castle, Considine minuted the Under Secretary saying that O'Hara might be correct in his view that Creagh wished to attack the Jewish system of trading and was actuated by no feeling of religious rancour. Considine himself had his reservations about the system but 'the Rev. Gentleman [had] selected both an unfortunate method and an unfortunate time'.[113]

The Chief Secretary for Ireland, George Wyndham, faced a question on Limerick in the House of Commons on 14 April. Asked by Thomas Sloan (Belfast South) whether he would order an inquiry into the whole matter in order to protect the rights of Jews, Wyndham replied that the police had received special instructions to protect the Jewish community from acts of molestation or violence. Eight cases had been prosecuted, and in two other cases proceedings were pending. Wyndham refused to give any response to a question from Michael Joyce of Limerick who asked: 'Is there any intention to introduce legislation to safeguard the people against extortional usurers who charge 200 or 300 per cent profit on shoddy articles?'[114]

The Raleigh case

The temperature in the city was again raised in the middle of April when a fifteen-year-old youth, John Rahilly or Raleigh (he was reported under both names), was sentenced to a month in prison at Mountjoy, Dublin. He was among a group of boys who threw stones on 4 April at Rabbi Levin and two other members of the Jewish community as they passed by Carey's Row. One of the group was struck on the ankle by a stone thrown by Raleigh. The *Limerick Leader* described how the youth cried bitterly as he was taken from the court.[115] In a long editorial, the paper said the sentence was 'extremely harsh' and regretted that there 'was not a single Catholic magistrate at the hearing of the case'.[116] A special meeting of Limerick Corporation was held on 20 April, during which angry speeches were made over the sentencing of the boy to a month in prison. A petition for clemency was sent to the Lord Lieutenant.[117]

Raleigh served his sentence and was released from Mountjoy on 12 May. District Inspector O'Hara reported that it had been the intention of the boy's friends to 'have a demonstration with a band and to march round the Jewish quarter'. He had warned the band and all concerned that such a demonstration would not be allowed, and in the end, according to O'Hara, 'only a few people took part in the affair which was confined to the locality in which Rahilly lives'. There were no disturbances, he told Dublin Castle.[118]

Readers of the *Limerick Leader* got a very different account of the homecoming. A report referred to Raleigh's imprisonment for 'alleged stone-throwing at the Jewish Rabbi' and said he was 'looking well after his experience'.[119] In contrast to what was reported by the district inspector, the local paper said that Raleigh was met at the station by a 'large crowd', who cheered him as he was carried shoulder-high to his home where he was presented with a silver watch and chain. Raleigh recounted how, in jail, one of the warders had said to him the morning after he arrived in Mountjoy, 'Come here you Limerick Jew slayer.' Calling over a number of other warders, he said: 'Here is our Limerick Jew slayer.'[120] After his fifteen minutes of fame, Raleigh walked out of Irish history.

Other instances of assault are recalled by Fanny Goldberg in her unpublished memoirs. David Weinronk and Louis Goldberg were taking their accustomed stroll through Colooney Street when, she explains,

> father was struck on the head and fell to the ground. His shout probably saved David a similar blow. He turned quickly and got a lesser blow in the face. A big burley man with a black shillelagh was flailing it about and shouting, 'I'll kill those bloody Jews.' Somebody picked father from the ground and he asked to be put in a side car and taken to Barrington's Hospital. This was quite a distance away. His head was bleeding profusely and I don't know how he could have got to the hospital on his own. I don't know how David Weinronk got home, but he was put to bed where he remained for some days suffering from shock. He gave mother and Bubba [grandmother] the news about father, and they were terror stricken. Father got home sometime later with stitches in his head and was in bed for a while. The shock upset him very much.

Weinronk, according to Gerald Goldberg, suffered a broken leg and was unable to appear in court when the attacker was brought to justice. The accused was declared insane and was sent to the local asylum. There the authorities declared that he was sane and he was released the following day. Another casualty was David Weinronk's wife, Sophia. She was, according to Fanny Goldberg, 'such a small little creature'. Venturing out one day to get some food during the troubles, she was attacked by a few young men in Bowman Street, off Colooney Street. One youth 'beat her head against the wall'. It was not clear how she managed to get away, 'but she too was in bed after that for a few weeks'. Violence was ever close during those early months of the boycott.

Bishop Bunbury and the boycott

At its meeting on 20 April Limerick Corporation heard strong criticism of the local Church of Ireland bishop, Dr Thomas Bunbury, who at the general synod of the Church of Ireland in Dublin on 15 April had vigorously defended the Jews of Limerick. He explained the 'persecution' of the Jews in his city to the general synod, stating that he was relying on information received from Rabbi Levin. The bishop was applauded when he related that the Jews did not charge one sixpence more on their goods than the respectable shopkeepers of Limerick.[121] He was also applauded when he said that the Jews in his city bought from wholesalers and that they made merely the legitimate profits allowed by those wholesale houses. Another accusation brought against them, he said, was that they went into country districts and, finding the parents absent, persuaded children or servants to accept goods, saying that they would call again for the money. Tea in particular was mentioned in that connection; it had been alleged that Jews left a 1 lb parcel of tea at a house and then overcharged for it. Bunbury said that he had asked Rabbi Levin about this, and Levin had replied that the Jews never did anything of the sort as they did not deal in tea. The people who went about the country were a different body known as teamen. That was a complete answer to the charge, the bishop told the synod to loud applause.[122]

Bunbury then spoke of the 'persecution' of Jews in Limerick, which was 'very severe'.[123] He did not think that there had been a more severe case of boycotting. Money had been collected in London and other places for the support of the local community. He explained that the Jews were not allowed to practise their trade and that money due to them could not be recovered. They did not bring actions in the courts for the recovery of this money. They were most forbearing in their dealing, the bishop said, and they were willing to accept small instalments spread over a considerable period of time. But despite all that, they were hooted at and assaulted in the streets. When summonses were issued and the offenders appeared in court, the magistrates did not deal properly with them.[124] The bishop said he felt fully entitled to say that the 'respectable Roman Catholic laymen in Limerick were entirely opposed to this persecution'.[125]

The general synod passed a motion drawing 'the attention of His Majesty's government and all Protestant members of parliament to the persecution of Protestants and Jews in Ireland'.[126] While the ugly situation in which the Jews of Limerick found themselves might be described as 'persecution', there was no evidence that Protestants shared the same fate. Not surprisingly, Bunbury's speech and the synod resolution were received very negatively in Limerick. District Inspector O'Hara explained to his superiors that the bishop had 'given offence locally as it is considered that he interfered gratuitously in a matter not concerning him and that he relied on statements made to him by the Rabbi without investigating their accuracy'.[127]

Members of Limerick Corporation and the local press were outraged. One Mr Donnellan told the corporation meeting on 20 April that he regretted the use of 'intemperate language' by the 'learned ecclesiastic' outside the city of Limerick; the bishop had taken his information 'from a contaminated source – from those immediately concerned, the Jews themselves'.[128] As far as the question of the Jews in Limerick went, Donnellan 'was one of those who believed that their presence in the city was not needed' as 'these people' charged 100 per cent profit on their goods.[129] The *Munster News*, in an editorial on 20 April, gave full vent to the charged emotion which underpinned some local reaction to the bishop's intervention:

> Let Bishop Bunbury then behave himself, as becomes one of his social position, and he may count on the courtesy which the Catholics of Limerick have always shown him. But to bear his Synodal slander in silence would not be courtesy but cowardice; and the days are gone when a Papist, ridden over by a Protestant fox-hunter, should crawl, hat in hand, to beg his honour's pardon for having been in the horse's way.

The irate editorial writer continued the history lesson:

> We are now in the dawn of the 20th century, but Dr Bunbury does not
> seem to have yet taken the cobwebs from his eyes. So wake up, bishop,
> and realise that a new light has come over Ireland, that the 'old order
> changes giving place to new, and God fulfils himself in many ways'. We
> don't object to your trying to convert us, but we protest against your plan;
> we take to truths but we take no notice of nonsense.[130]

William J. Moloney, writing in the nationalist weekly, the *Leader*, felt that
the entire episode had been exaggerated by Rabbi Levin and his supporters:

> You would naturally conclude from the reading of all the rancorous flum-
> mery that has appeared in bigoted Protestant journals, that Jews in
> Limerick are being roasted at stakes and crucified at corners, and that
> those who are happy enough to escape Catholic ferocity, are hid away in
> their wretched hovels, starving and singing the lamentations of Jeremiah.[131]

Moloney wrote that it was 'the opinion of shrewd people in Limerick that the
whole outcry is a money-making scheme on the part of the Jews'.[132] Bunbury,
he contended, had been contradicted in every single assertion he made:

> His speech has certainly been a disgrace to his position as a high Prot-
> estant dignitary, and would have been a disgrace also to his intelligence
> and good taste, if he were the happy possessor of either. . . . It is a high
> tribute to the extreme moderation of the people of Limerick that they
> have borne almost good-humouredly, the impertinent censure of a Prot-
> estant bishop.[133]

Moloney asked whether 'we in Limerick' had to 'close our eyes to the evil
influence on morality of the low-type Jews' who had come to the city during
the previous twenty years: 'Ireland is, at present, being drained of its Gaelic
population by emigration, and Jewish colonists are trooping in to fill up the
places of the emigrants, and to turn Ireland into a filthy Ghetto.'[134]

The legacy of anti-Semitism

However, Moloney's interpretation of what was happening in Limerick did
not accord with the reality of Jewish life. M. J. Blond, who was forced to sell
out his trading stock, had written to the *Times* on 10 April:

> It took me all these years, with the greatest pain and trouble and working
> unceasingly until I established myself comfortably and enjoyed a nice
> trade, until, all of a sudden, like a thunderstorm, spoke hatred and animos-
> ity against the Jews, how they crucified Lord Jesus, how they martyred St
> Simon, and gradually in one month's time, I have none of my previous
> customers coming into my shop. In fact, my business is nil at present.
> Would you call my trade a national evil? I defy anyone in this city to say
> whom I have wronged, what did I overcharge . . . since the beginning of
> the crusade of Father Creagh against the Jews we never got a fair chance to
> defend ourselves or to put our case rightly before the Public.[135]

Members of the Jewish community in the city, facing as they were financial ruin, offered to show their accounts in order to prove they were honest traders.[136]

Fanny Goldberg, in her memoirs, recalled that Jewish men and travellers were at a complete standstill as a consequence of the boycott. She remembered a visit to Limerick by the Jewish Board of Deputies to hold an inquiry and to raise funds for the relief of those suffering discrimination:

> I remember huge sheets of rolled foolscap came to father by post. I suppose from London. Everyone who had suffered losses (and who hadn't) came to our house and made a solemn declaration to father and to Mr [Solomon] Ginsberg who were in charge of the matter for our community. Every declaration was written out by Alec Ginsberg, the eldest son of the Ginsberg family. I do not know how much each person got in compensation, but after that came the exodus. Everybody had been ruined.

As the boycott continued into the autumn, there was a further attempt by an anonymous apologist for Creagh to fan the flames of anti-Semitism. A letter, signed by 'Lugaid', was published in the *Limerick Echo* on 1 October 1904:

> The simple facts are that the chosen people still issue from the ghetto with clockwork regularity on Mondays to pursue their beneficent avocations throughout the week in peace, their country customers are still faithful to them . . . and the wretched creatures in the purlieus of Limerick who flouted the Jewish creditors six months ago under the pressure of public opinion, have returned like the dog to its vomit, and are again robbing their families, damning their souls and forfeiting for ever their self respect by dealing with the garbage of Europe.[137]

'Lugaid' attacked the 'ignominious silence' of the local Catholic clergy and their failure to support Creagh. Left to stand alone, the Catholic press lived up, in his view, to its 'reptile traditions by sitting on the fence'. He felt that 'the humbler classes in this city are doomed for ages to come to be as Fr Creagh expressed it, "the slaves of Jewish usurers"' unless the 'manhood of Limerick, such as it is, arise and resolve, not in word but in deed', to organise a crusade against the 'evil'. He was convinced that if a determined effort was made, the Jewish colony in Limerick could be reduced to one-tenth 'and would no longer be a menace to the community'. He called for the holding of a public meeting to initiate and co-ordinate a campaign.[138] The local RIC and Dublin Castle viewed the letter as an attempt to 'kindle agitation against the Jews which had almost died out'.[139] 'Lugaid' did not get his way.

What impact did the boycott have on Jewish families in the city? This was a source of disagreement between the police authorities and the Jewish community. The county inspector, Thomas Hayes, reported on 12 March 1905 that 'the trade of the Jews has unquestionably fallen off in the city but the Jews who trade the country districts' were doing 'fairly well'.[140] Another report, dated 13 March 1905, stated: 'Their trade in the city is ruined: in the country except close to Limerick City, it has fallen off.' It was also stated that 'As a general rule they are left severely alone though there are one or two exceptions.'[141]

The official estimate in March 1905 of the effect of the boycott on the population of Limerick Jews was as follows:

> The police now report that, within the past year, 8 Jewish families (49 persons) have left Limerick. Of these, 5 families left directly owing to the agitation, as the breadwinners could no longer obtain employment as 'travellers'. The other 3 families left the town for private reasons – two having arranged before 1st January, 1904, to go to South Africa, and the third because its head (a Rabbi) was no longer needed as Minister. The 5 families which left owing to the agitation number 32 persons. 26 families remain, of whom 8 only are in good circumstances.[142]

The new Chief Secretary for Ireland, Walter Long, answered a question on the Limerick boycott in the House of Commons on 4 July 1905, using these figures.[143] Having read the reports of the Commons debate in the press, Rabbi Levin wrote to Long on 11 July stating that, according to their community records, 'the members of the Jewish Congregation who [have] been compelled to leave Limerick owing to the boycott, violence and constant abuse brought upon us by Fr Creagh [number] 75 individuals instead of 32'.[144] It is difficult to resolve the contradiction between the conflicting figures. Whatever the number, the Jewish community in Limerick had been dealt a severe blow which threatened its viability. The Ginsbergs left. The Jaffes left. The Weinronks followed the Greenfields to South Africa. The Goldbergs left for Leeds, before Louis brought his family back to Cork. Virtually the entire Jewish community in the city joined the exodus. The Limerick boycott was, as Louis Hyman described it, a 'sad but uncharacteristic and atypical episode' in Irish history.[145]

Life was never the same again for Rabbi Levin and the Limerick Jews.[146] Remaining in the city until 1911, the rabbi then went to Leeds, where he ministered until his death in 1936.

The departure of Fr Creagh

Fr John Creagh, meanwhile, opened a bank, a shop and the Workmen's Industrial Association in autumn 1904 in order to supply the 'poorer classes with clothing etc. on the instalment payment system'. The goods were supplied at ordinary retail prices provided security was given for the weekly payments.[147] During the following two years he directed his attacks towards the abuse of alcohol, evil literature and obscenity in the theatre. In November 1905, Creagh supported Bishop O'Dwyer's condemnation of the play *Sapho* by Mrs Bandmann-Palmer which was playing at the Theatre Royal. He was in excellent form when he addressed the arch-confraternity:

> And when such a play that was against morality was produced at the theatre he advised no one to look upon such foul representations because their eyes stimulated the mind and the imagination, and imagination easily worked upon the lower passions.[148]

Then, having served one term as director of the arch-confraternity, Creagh was assigned to the Redemptorist order's new missions in the Philippines in early 1906. That was in no sense a demotion. The local press paid homage to his achievements. The *Limerick Echo*, in an editorial on 24 April, spoke warmly of his successful battle

> with the usurers who grew fat on the people's want of thrift . . . The blows delivered were with no uncertain aim. Nor was the matter ended, as is only too often the case, when the talking was done.[149]

Another press report praised the man who had founded the Workmen's Industrial Association:

> To him is due the great movement dealing a great blow to the Jews, who had begun by their methods of usury to make life nearly intolerable for some of those poor struggling people who were so foolish as to buy their articles at most exorbitant instalment prices.[150]

The *Limerick Leader* added its voice to the chorus of appreciation on 27 April:

> To Fr Creagh is due practically the entire abolition of a system of credit trading with hawkers which had a demoralising effect on the poor families owing to the exaction in the shape of high interest levied for a deposit of the commonest class of good.[151]

An editorial in the *Munster News* on 9 May also recalled Creagh's 'success' of 1904:

> Later on Father Creagh discovered that much of the money earned by the poor people of the city was being handed over week by week to astute Hebrew harpies who, at that time, swarmed over the entire country and city. . . . Father Creagh . . . resolved to change all that; and change it he did beyond question, and that in a very short time . . . [by removing] the blighting influence of the Jewish pedlar from the homes of the people.[152]

The paper wondered whether his work would endure or whether he would watch from afar as the men for whom he had laboured so unselfishly 'handed themselves over to the tender mercies of the publican, the money-lender, the Jewman, the bagman, and the usurious purveyor of miscellaneous foreign shoddy'. There was no fear of that happening, the paper felt.[153]

At his final meeting of the arch-confraternity, Creagh was presented with an address which recorded his 'arduous and heroic service for the spiritual and temporal welfare' of the society. The address recalled:

> The indomitable effort you made to rescue the working classes of Limerick from the usurious grasp of foreigners planted in our midst and which resulted in a great victory, cannot easily be forgotten, and is a circumstance which will be proudly related to your credit in days yet to come by parents to their children. Let us hope that the lesson will not be forgotten when you are no longer amongst us.[154]

Fr Creagh, in his reply, stated that the establishment of the Workmen's Industrial Association had been the means of keeping the poor 'independent of the Jewish usurers'.[155] After benediction, a 'pathetic scene' took place in the church as large numbers of men crowded around the altar to shake Creagh's hand as he passed from the pulpit. At Fr Creagh's special request, the members sang the rallying song of the confraternity – 'Confraternity men to the fight'.[156]

On 12 May 1906, Creagh was seen off by a large crowd at Limerick railway station. He never returned to the city of his birth, dying in Wellington, New Zealand, in 1947.[157]

Nearly seventy years later, the Limerick county manager, Richard Haslam, discovered that the Jewish burial ground on the Dublin Road near Castleconnell had fallen into neglect. The cemetery had become overgrown and was in need of attention. Although strictly speaking the grounds were not under his jurisdiction, Richard Haslam undertook to have the grass cut at regular intervals and an identification sign erected. He corresponded with Gerald Goldberg in Cork about the long-term upkeep of the grounds. Eventually it was decided to place the cemetery under the trusteeship of two members of the local Jewish community, the late Louis Fine and Stuart Clein.[158] Under Richard Haslam's direction, a sum of £1,000 was voted by Limerick County Council to the Limerick Civic Trust to help restore the burial ground and pay for its upkeep.[159] The director of the trust, Denis Leonard, explained that his organisation has an indirect but ongoing role in the maintenance.[160]

An ecumenical service was held on 14 November 1990 to mark the completion of the restoration of the burial ground and prayer house.[161] The ceremony was presided over by Chief Rabbi Ephraim Mirvis, and the Catholic bishop of Limerick, Jeremiah Newman, and the Church of Ireland bishop of Limerick and Killaloe, Edward Darling, also took part. The two bishops were among those who planted six trees to mark the occasion,[162] which the *Limerick Leader* described in an editorial as 'possibly the most ecumenical occasion ever witnessed in Limerick'. It added that the monument inaugurated that day was 'an essential part of our shared heritage, Gentile and Jew. Let us treasure it.'[163] Chief Rabbi Mirvis referred in his address to the economic boycott and attacks on the Jews in 1904: 'This is a significant but sad occasion, for while we recall a period of bitterness and suffering endured by Jewish inhabitants of the city a few generations ago, we gather today in a wonderful spirit of fraternity, harmony and peace.'[164]

That small act of official generosity, initiated by Richard Haslam and executed by the Limerick Civic Trust, meant much to Gerald Goldberg and other members of the Irish Jewish community whose families had lived through the Limerick boycott of 1904. The ecumenical ceremony was a cross-community statement which explicitly acknowledged both the historical presence of Jews in the city and county, and that Jews were – and are – an integral part of that community, a fact that the late Jim Kemmy had repeatedly chronicled in the pages of the *Limerick Journal*.

3

Leopold Bloom, the Jewish
community and independent Ireland

During the first twenty years of the twentieth century the overwhelming majority of the new immigrant Jewish families continued to work as pedlars, tradesmen and small shopkeepers. They also continued to live with the consequences of economic anti-Semitism. The introduction of a highly restrictive Aliens Act in 1906 radically reduced the number of Jewish immigrants from Russia coming to Britain and Ireland. Nevertheless, there is evidence that the Jewish 'foreigners' were sufficient in number to continue to cause resentment in working-class areas of Dublin, Cork, Belfast and Limerick. The cartoon shown here, for example, appeared on 26 August 1911 in the *Irish Worker,* the egalitarian and strongly anti-sectarian paper of the labour leader James Larkin.

While anti-Semitism never became a feature of the trade union movement or of left-wing Irish politics,[1] the cartoon reflected the resentment, the discomfort and the sense of threat which the new communities of Jews posed to a closed society fixed in its ways and in its animosities. The tailoring trade in particular resented the presence of the new Jews. There were, according to the 1901 census, seventy-two Jewish tailors in Dublin at the turn of the century. The following advertisement from the Dublin Tailors Co-Partnership Ltd, 14 Bachelor's Walk, appeared in the *Leader* in 1904:

> Suits of Irish Material at Moderate Prices.
>
> All Garments made in our own Workshops under Trade Union conditions by Irish Tailors.
>
> (Irishmen, help us to stamp out Sweated, Jewish Labour, in the Tailoring Trade in Dublin.)[2]

That resentment did not fuel widespread anti-Semitism in Irish labour circles, but the economic basis for antagonism towards the new immigrants lingered.

4. Anti-Semitic cartoon, *Irish Worker*, 26 August 1911

Further evidence of antagonism towards Jews may be found in William Bulfin's popular and widely read *Rambles in Eirinn* which was published in 1907. He has left the following portrait of a Jewish pedlar he met on the Inny bridge near Ballymahon, Co. Longford:

> He smiled an oily, cross-eyed, subtle smile of self-apology and insinuating humility as he met my glance, and said in the best Hamburg English:
> 'That vos a warrm day, sar.'
> 'Do you find this country hotter than your part of Germany?', I asked.
> 'I vos from Dhublin, sar mineself, und not from Germany.'
> 'You are Irish, then.'
> 'Irish yes, from Dublin.'
> 'God help us! and were you born in Dublin?'
> 'With der help of Gott, sar.'
> 'Of Jewish parents, I suppose?
> 'No sar, Irish.'[3]

Bulfin wondered if he was the same Jew who had told the people around Forgny the week before that his name was O'Hara, and that it was 'patriotic to support Irish trade'. Or perhaps he was the Jewish pedlar who had visited Ballymahon, selling pens, rattles, egg-beaters and thimbles. He too had claimed to be Irish. One local said to Bulfin, 'He is descended from Solomon, if you ask me', to which another replied: 'I don't agree with you. . . . I don't think this man can trace his descent any farther back than the Impenitent Thief.' Bulfin then describes how the 'spiritless knave joined with well-feigned heartiness in the laughter against himself' and how, 'with the abject vileness of the renegade who is false to his blood, [he] tried to heap obloquy upon the Jews and the Jewish race, the stamp of which was indelibly set upon his every feature'.[4]

While in Longford, William Bulfin was given to understand that Jewish pedlars were to be met in many parts of Ireland. 'I was sorry to hear it', he wrote, and added that he had also been told 'that some of them, out of the profits of their trade, have already established themselves in Dublin and other cities as wholesale merchants and moneylenders'.[5] Bulfin's vignette illustrates the prejudice towards Jewish pedlars of both himself and his contacts in Longford and the midlands. He also records being told in Ballymahon that Moses and the duke of Norfolk were the two patron saints of the Jewish community – the latter because of his intervention in defence of 'some . . . money-lending Jews' who complained that an Irish priest was 'nefariously persuading his people' not to borrow from them. The duke of Norfolk, on reading of the case in the press, came to their defence, 'and since then the Sheenies in Ireland swear by him, and bless his name out of the depths of their profitable misery'.

Oliver St John Gogarty, medical doctor, man of letters and anti-Semite, shared Bulfin's prejudices; he contributed two racist articles to Arthur Griffith's new paper, *Sinn Féin*, in 1906 while in his final year at Trinity College Dublin. In the first, he wrote:

> . . . and this conviction of the Jew mastery of England at the same time grew stronger and more logical. England becoming Jewry . . . It explained how many things! that gross materialism; that shopkeeping, moneying instinct; that hatred of things generous or artistic – *make ye no graven images*; that filthy sensuality, unrelieved even by gaiety; that furtive and narrow timidity, and that panic-stricken cowardly way of taking revenge . . . the Jews are upon us? . . . This is the decline and now the fall.[6]

His second article was even more strident:

> Sludge in Ireland is Snudge. He has no money because he lives in a poor country: but he knows how to suck the best out of it. The blood in him is wormy and he fattens on decay. True son of his father, he extracts a thousand per cent. *He* can make a silk purse out of a sow's ear . . . I can smell a Jew, though, and in Ireland there's something rotten.[7]

Griffith, who tolerated the publication of that material, may have modified his views in later years. Michael Noyk, a Jewish solicitor in Dublin, was to become his close personal friend. In his memoir Noyk recalls spending many evenings in Griffith's home, 'where I got a very intimate knowledge of his character'; but at no time does he refer to Griffith as being anti-Semitic.[8]

Leopold Bloom and Dublin society

The 'pap of racial hatred'[9] in the *United Irishman* and in *Sinn Féin*, meanwhile, had produced a strong reaction in the young Irish writer James Joyce, who created in Leopold Bloom one of the strongest and most enduring refutations of anti-Semitism in western culture. Joyce had first gone to Paris in September 1902 at the age of twenty. As Richard Ellman points out, this was just after the Dreyfus case had reached another crisis and Anatole France had delivered a celebrated oration at the funeral of Emile Zola. Joyce made the connection between Zola, France and Dreyfus.[10] The culture of radical anti-clericalism was very much in evidence on his second visit to the French capital in 1903, a visit foreshortened by the terminal illness of his mother. Life in the Joyce household after her death was even less bearable for the young artist than when she was alive. His father, John, continued to drink heavily, coming home on one occasion and threatening to return to his native Cork: 'I'll leave you all where Jesus left the jews', he said,[11] in a typical example of the anti-Jewish prejudice which was prevalent in turn-of-the-century Dublin.

Joyce, who paradoxically enjoyed for a time the patronage of Oliver St John Gogarty, created from his imagination and his experience the celebrated character, Leopold Bloom.[12] Of Hungarian origin, Bloom may have been based on a Dublin Jew called Alfred Hunter.[13] The latter had rescued the writer, or so it is alleged, after he had been knocked down in the street by the escort of a young woman in January 1904.[14] Why did Joyce base the main character in *Ulysses* on an ethnic but non-practising Jew? He answered that question as follows:

> Bloom Jewish? Yes because only a foreigner would do. The Jews were foreigners at that time in Dublin. There was no hostility towards them, but contempt, yes the contempt people always show for the unknown.[15]

Contempt for the unknown is an arresting explantion for the widespread hostility to Jews in Joyce's Dublin.

In *Ulysses*, Joyce provides a vivid portrait of the Jew as 'foreigner' in Ireland. He evokes the atmosphere of the period through his sympathetic profile of Bloom, who, writes Ellman, is 'amiable and even noble in a humdrum sort of way, but [is] saved ... from sentimentality by making him also somewhat absurd as a convert, a drifter, a cuckold'.[16] This frequenter of the 'university of life'[17] had been baptised no less than three times, once by a Protestant clergyman, later by a Catholic priest, and the third time by James O'Connor, Philip Gilligan and James Fitzpatrick, together, under a pump in the village of Swords.[18] An advertising salesman, he converted to Catholicism before marrying an amateur singer, Marion Tweedy. He lives in comfortable circumstances in 7 Eccles Street, far from the Clanbrassil Street of his youth and far from his Jewish friends – Owen Goldberg, J. Citron, Philip Moisel, Julius Mastinsky and others.[19]

Born of a non-Jewish mother, Ellen Higgins, Bloom would not have been regarded as Jewish by the community in Dublin. (Jewishness in the orthodox tradition is traced through the mother.) Although never circumcised, Bloom is known to his acquaintances – to quote Joyce – as 'one of the bottlenosed fraternity',[20] an 'old lardyface' who would 'adorn a sweeping brush'.[21]

> Circumcised! says Joe – Ay, says I, A bit off the top. ... I had to laugh at the little jewy getting his shirt out. *He drink me my teas. He eat me my sugars. Because he no pay me my moneys.*[22]

Very average in many ways, Bloom displays courage and is capable of nobility when vigorously defending himself and his Jewish culture after being attacked in a pub by the 'citizen':

> – Those are nice things, says the citizen, coming over here to Ireland filling the country with bugs.

As Bloom pretends not to hear, the 'citizen' continues:

> – Swindling the peasants, says the citizen, and the poor of Ireland. We want no more strangers in our house.[23]

Echoing the sentiments in the articles of Oliver St John Gogarty, the citizen continues his tirade:

> It's on the march, says the citizen. To hell with the bloody brutal Sasse-nachs and their *patois*. . . .
> – Their syphilisation, you mean, says the citizen. To hell with them! The curse of a goodfornothing God light sideways on the bloody thick-lugged sons of whores' gets! No music and no art and no literature worthy of the name. Any civilisation they have they stole from us. Tonguetied sons of bastards' ghosts.[24]

Bloom, who had remained non-commital, finds himself being dragged into the conversation:

> But do you know what a nation means? says John Wyse.
> – Yes, says Bloom.
> – What is it? says John Wyse.
> – A nation? says Bloom. A nation is the same people living in the same place.
> – By God, then, says Ned laughing, if that's so I'm a nation for I'm living in the same place for the past five years. . . .
> – What is your nation if I may ask, says the citizen.
> – Ireland, says Bloom. I was born here. Ireland.
> The citizen said nothing only cleared the spit out of his gullet and, gob, he spat a Red bank oyster out of his right in the corner.[25]

Bloom feels obliged to respond:

> – And I belong to a race too, says Bloom, that is hated and persecuted. Also now. This very moment. This very instant.
> Gob, he near burnt his fingers with the butt of his old cigar.
> – Robbed, says he. Plundered. Insulted. Persecuted. Taking what belongs to us by right. At this very moment, says he, putting up his fist, sold by auction off in Morocco like slaves or cattle.
> – Are you talking about the new Jerusalem? says the citizen.
> – I'm talking about injustice, says Bloom.

As Bloom is insulted and called names, he continues:

> – but it's no use, says he. Force, hatred, history, all that. That's not life for men and women, insult and hatred. And everybody knows that it's the

very opposite of that that is really life.
— What? says Alf.
— Love, says Bloom. I mean the opposite of hatred.

At that point, Bloom makes his excuse and leaves as the citizen says:

— That chap? says the citizen. Beggar my neighbour is his motto. Love, Moya! he's a nice pattern of a Romeo and Juliet.[26]

The conversation turns to the question of 'dual loyalty' and the alleged inability of a Jew to love his or her country:

— And after all, says John Wyse, why can't a jew love his country like the next fellow?
— Why not? says J.J., when he's quite sure which country it is.
— Is he a jew or a gentile or a holy Roman or a swaddler or what the hell is he? says Ned. Or who is he?
No offence, Crofton.
— We don't want him, says Crofter the Orangeman or presbyterian.[27]

Bloom then runs foul of the drunken citizen who is leaving the pub shouting 'Three cheers for Israel'. Getting into the cab the citizen is still

on his high horse about the jews and the loafers calling for a speech and Jack Power trying to get him to sit down on the car and hold his bloody jaw and a loafer with a patch over his eye starts singing *If the man in the moon was a jew, jew, jew* and a slut shouts out of her
— Eh, mister! Your fly is open, mister!
And says he:
— Mendelssohn was a jew and Karl Marx and Mercadante and Spinoza. And the Saviour was a jew and his father was a jew. Your God.
— He had no father, says Martin. That'll do now.
Drive ahead.
— Whose God?, says the citizen.
— Well, his uncle was a jew, says he. Your God was a jew. Christ was a jew like me.
Gob, the citizen made a plunge back into the shop.
— By Jesus, says he, I'll brain that bloody jewman for using the holy name. By Jesus, I'll crucify him so I will. Give us that biscuitbox here.
— Stop! Stop! says Joe.[28]

In the same conversation, the French are described as a 'set of dancing masters' who were 'never worth a roasted fart to Ireland'. As for the 'Prooshians and the Hanoverians', the Irish had had enough of 'those sausageeating bastards on the throne'.[29] Bloom, of mid-European stock, has no sympathy with such provincialism and is the very opposite of Oliver St John Gogarty's vulgar caricature.[30]
Joyce again attacks racism in another scene:

— Mark my words, Mr Dedalus, he [Deasy] said. England is in the hands of the jews. In all the highest places: her finance, her press. And they are the signs of a nation's decay. Wherever they gather they eat up the nation's vital strength. I have seen it coming these years. As sure as we

are standing here the jew merchants are already at their work of destruction. Old England is dying.[31]

In reply to Stephen Dedalus's definition of a merchant as being 'one who
buys cheap and sells dear, jew or gentile', Deasy retorts:

> – They sinned against the light, Mr Deasy said gravely. And you can see
> the darkness in their eyes. And that is why they are wanderers on the
> earth to this day. . . .
> – Who has not? Stephen said.[32]

Running after Dedalus, Deasy continues:

> Ireland, they say, has the honour of being the only country which never
> persecuted the jews. Do you know that? No. And do you know why? . . .
> – Because she never let them in, Mr Deasy said solemnly. . . .
> – She never let them in, he cried again through his laughter as he
> stamped on gaitered feet over the gravel of the path. That's why.[33]

Ulysses, written between 1914 and 1922, is a work of fiction.[34] But is
Bloom Joyce's chosen method of refuting the thinking behind Gogarty's final
sentence in his second *Sinn Féin* article – 'I can smell a Jew, though, and in
Ireland there's something rotten'?[35]

'Old' Jewish families in Dublin

'New' and 'old' Jewish families alike lived in a country where Catholics were
the overwhelming majority. Living with the uncertainties which accompany
being a religious minority, they also had to accept that they were perceived
negatively as being 'foreigners'.

What was it like to grow up Jewish in early twentieth-century Ireland?
Much depended upon social background. For example, Maurice Solomons
was one of the most distinguished and well-known members of the Jewish
community in Dublin. He was born there in 1832 while his mother was on
holidays. Raised in London where he got a degree from London University,
he became an optician like his father and then moved to Dublin to expand
the family business. He maintained a consulting room at 19 Nassau Street,
where he tested eyesight and fitted glasses.[36] He gave up the optician business in later years and became a director of several commercial concerns.
He was also the Austro-Hungarian empire's honorary consul in the city.
According to his son, Bethel, 'He was a strong Imperialist, at a time when the
Imperialist cause was a declining force in the life of Southern Ireland. His
imperialism, however, did not prevent him from claiming Irish nationality
when he had no need to do so.'[37] Maurice died in 1922, having lived to the
age of eighty-nine, 'always in good health, loved by his children and grandchildren and respected by the whole of Dublin'.[38]

Rosa, his wife, was a Jacobs; she was born in Hull in 1842. A woman of
great beauty, she was a poet and a lover of music who played the piano very
well. Maurice and Rosa married on 21 March 1876. She died in 1926 at the

age of eighty-three. The couple were in the 'forefront of Jewish communal affairs' in the city. Rosa collected large amounts of money and, according to her son Bethel, was responsible 'more than anyone else for the new Dublin Synagogue' in Adelaide Road. Lovers of the theatre and of music, the Solomons enjoyed going to the Gaiety Theatre, where they had free seats every second week having subscribed for the debentures which were necessary to get it started.

Bethel Solomons, who was born in 1885 and died in 1965, was to become a distinguished gynaecologist and master of the Rotunda Hospital. He served as president of the Royal College of Physicians of Ireland in the 1940s. His elder brother, Edwin, born in 1879, became a stockbroker and a leading figure in Jewish circles in Dublin; he died in 1964. His sister, Estella, was born in 1882 and died in 1968. She was a leading artist of her time, painting landscapes and portraits and producing well-known etchings of old Dublin. Her portrait subjects included Jack Yeats and George Russell.[39] Interested in politics, she became a member of Cumann na mBan and was active during the time of the 1916 Rising. She married the Irish poet, Seumas O'Sullivan. The youngest sister, Sophie, trained to be an opera singer.

The Solomons children were raised in the privileged world of middle-class Dublin. After Bethel's birth in 1885, the family moved from 32 to 26 Waterloo Road:

> a spacious suburban house with a basement. Nowadays it would be considered impossibly inconvenient, but servants did not seem to mind then, when their wages were five shillings a week and all the outer doors were locked and bolted and they had to be in by ten o'clock on the one evening a week they were allowed out.[40]

While Bethel's parents went on a continental holiday every year, a house was taken in the summer for the children at Greystones in County Wicklow or, more usually, Howth in north County Dublin:

> Howth in those days was a marvellous place; there was neither tram nor bus there from Dublin or around the hill. The train was the only means of getting to and fro and those who lived on the hill used either the long car or the char-a-banc. . . . The place was delightfully secluded and we felt we owned Howth. Bathing, tennis and picnics were our chief amusements. Numerous cousins and friends used to come and stay with us, and we discovered caves under the cliffs; in fact we had variegated amusements of a simple kind. In the evening we played the piano, sang, danced and played games. Remember then there was no wireless, no cinemas nor motor cars![41]

The Solomons lived in a world of private dances and of outings to the Scalp in County Wicklow: 'How glorious it was to cycle home on a wonderful full-moon night with the precious Wicklow Hills around us and possibly with a girl one believed was the only girl in the world. They were indeed happy times.'[42]

Bethel Solomons was sent to St Andrew's School in Booterstown, Co. Dublin. There he developed a passion for sport, and rugby in particular, going on to play for Ireland ten times between 1908 and 1910 while a medical student at Trinity College.[43] Solomons recalled with good humour the probably apocryphal story of the spectator in a Dublin bar who commented after Ireland had beaten Scotland: 'That was a grand Irish team that won today.' His companion's 'devastating' reply was: 'Call that an Irish team with fourteen Protestants and one bloody Jew.'[44] Solomons's sense of injustice was aroused by the fact that 'women seemed to have an unfairly thin time'.[45] Such feelings may explain why later he became a founding member and first president of the Liberal Synagogue in Dublin.[46] Solomons married a classical musician, Gertrude Levy, in the Liberal Synagogue in London in 1916. His orthodox parents attended the service. 'I wish that some orthodox Jews of today', Bethel Solomons later commented in his memoirs, 'could be shaken up a bit and made a little more liberal in their outlook.'[47] He himself had helped encourage such a 'shake up' in his own lifetime.[48]

Growing up in 'Little Jerusalem'

While the Solomons enjoyed the security of growing up in middle-class Dublin, what was it like for children of the 'new' Jews? A. J. (Con) Leventhal

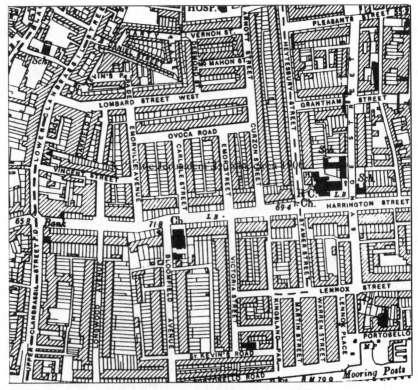

5. 'Little Jerusalem', Dublin, circa 1900

was born in Dublin in 1896. Described as a 'rather serious boy, passionately fond of books and culture in all forms', he went to Wesley College, Dublin, and entered Trinity College on a scholarship. He studied French and German and was later awarded a doctorate.[49] He became a lecturer in French at Trinity College, taking the position of his lifelong friend Samuel Beckett who had moved to Paris.[50]

Despite such later eminence, Leventhal was brought up in the working-class district of 'Little Jerusalem' in the Clanbrassil Street/South Circular Road area, and he has left an important description of his youth in an article which appeared in the *Bell* in 1945:

> It was at about the age of seven that I became aware of certain facts – not as one might imagine a precocious understanding of what were curiously called 'the facts of life', but of the boundary between certain Dublin streets. The cul-de-sac known as Oakfield Place, where I lived with my parents and co-religionists in the natural gregariousness of my people, was invisibly lined off from the lower end of Lombard Street West where non-Jews lived. Between them there might well have been a ghetto wall, so well drawn into their own loyalties were the young denizens of each locality.

Leventhal described the consequences of this segregation:

> Perhaps, at first, it was merely regional 'gang' rivalry, the battle of stones between neighbouring groups of ebullient boyhood ... Later, however, it became clear that we of Oakfield Place were regarded as strangers who, *as such,* ought to be liquidated.[51]

It seemed to Leventhal that 'we young Jewish boys must have appeared curious creatures to our young native neighbours'.[52] Though all the children in the neighbourhood attended the same primary schools and returned home to dinner at the same hour, there were definite differences:

> We looked foreign, to begin with. And in the afternoons when all school-boys left their homes to indulge in such street games as marbles, relievo, handball and the like, we were not available. Secular schooling for the day was over but we had still to spend a further two or three hours at Hebrew school. It was in the later afternoon, on our return from the severities of having Hebrew beaten into us by the *Rebbe* through the medium of Yiddish, that territorial tempers rose and first stones were cast with none to point the parable.[53]

Those 'Lombard Street Westerners', as Leventhal called them, had a battle-cry which was sung to the air of 'Villikens and his Dinah':

> 'Two shillies, two shillies', the Jewman did cry,
> 'For a fine pair of blankets from me you did buy;
> Do you think me von idjit or von bloomin' fool,
> If I don't get my shillie I must have my vool.'

The 'Oakfield Israelites', returning a rock for a rock, chanted in reply:

> 'Two pennies, two pennies', the Christian did shout,
> 'For a bottle of porter or Guinness's stout;
> My wife's got no shawl and my kids have no shoes,
> But I must have my money, I must have my booze.'[54]

Leventhal discovered that the term 'Jewman' was not always pejorative, as when he heard 'a mother teach a babe in arms his first lesson in racial differences by pointing me out as a Jewman'. But there were also times when 'it was no mere ethnic eureka but a contemptuous gibe' used by a corner-boy and often accompanied by a missile. Having learned the rudiments of boxing after Hebrew lessons from a co-religionist who later became a distinguished Irish patriot (probably Robert Briscoe), he defended himself and his territory: 'No varlet's cry from street to street would weave old Jewry's winding-sheet.'[55]

Leventhal felt that Jewish children in Dublin were 'too tied to our fathers' phylacteries', as they ascribed differences with their neighbours to a difference in creed despite the fact that the only Protestant boy who lived on the street fought by their side.

> It was Jew *versus* Christian not *versus* Irishman and the word 'Gentile', which we only knew in Hebrew form, *goy*, connoted 'Christian' to our minds. Thus, while the Sassenach might have referred to the drunken Irish, we merely saw tippling followers of Christ.[56]

Raised in the bosom of the Jewish community, Leventhal records how 'religion, even if not practised punctiliously, became part of my life, as it is part of every Jewish life'.

> I touched no milk or milk foods for six hours after eating meat. The Sabbath was observed with an asceticism that would have blanched a Presbyterian Scot. Pig, as food, was an abomination. And even before the age of thirteen, when such observances became obligatory, I joined the adult community in the abstention from all nourishment during the whole twenty-six hours of the Day of Atonement.

Apart from ritual, there was a sense of obligation to one's fellow Jews:

> He who would become an enemy of society knows that this involves the honour of all Jewry. Nowhere is the sense of communal sin and communal redemption through fasting, prayer and penitence more actual than on the Day of Atonement when hoarse, hungry voices are lifted in loud prayer, when breasts are beaten and a whole liturgical array of sins confessed – often impossible ones – which are designed to cover all eventualities. The Jew prays not only that all Israel may be forgiven but strangers too, for the whole world sins unwittingly.[57]

But of the teaching of Christ he knew nothing as a boy:

> A crucifix was a vaguely hostile symbol from which I averted my head. He who throws stones was to me a Christian; and I had yet to learn more thoroughly from life itself that the Jew is he who gets slapped.[58]

Leventhal's home life also made him aware of a rising Jewish national movement which aimed to found a home for Jews in Palestine: 'slowly and almost imperceptibly a national consciousness was added to my religious background'.[59] And added to this was a growing awareness of Irish nationalism. Leventhal found something more vital in national consciousness than he did in 'the automatic practice of religious rituals'. That was ever the young Jew's problem:

> he feels a dual loyalty. Patriotically he aligns himself with the country of his birth or adoption, whilst at the same time he is conscious of his own race and religion. That this could interfere with his duty as a citizen never enters his mind. The synagogue even provides a weekly prayer for the welfare of the State and its rulers. He loves peace; but patriotism is with him an equally passionate impulse. Generations of German Jews owed their first allegiance to the *Vaterland*; the desire to return to Zion was merely synagogal lip service. They died in the first great war, as British, French and American Jews died on the other side, in the complete conviction that they fought in a righteous cause fired by the proverbial Horatian *decorum*.[60]

Parallel Jewish lives in early twentieth-century Ireland

The Wigoder, Shillman, Zlotover, Berman, Nurock and Abrahamson families were among the 'new' Jews which came to prominence in the early twentieth century in business and in the professions. The newly arrived Jews placed great emphasis on the importance of learning and education. Within a generation, children from those families were counted among the most brilliant of their time in law, medicine and the academic world. It required great sacrifices on the part of their parents to ensure that their intellectual potential was realised.

Myer Joel Wigoder provides an interesting case study. Born in 1855 in Wegoda, close to Wexna in Kovno, Lithuania, he had no alternative but to emigrate in 1890 following the destruction of his house in a pogrom.[61] His journey to Ireland took him through Konigsberg, Halle, Leipzig, Magdeburg, Hanover, Telekapm, Amsterdam, Antwerp, Rotterdam, Hull, Leeds, Manchester and Liverpool.[62] Advised to go to Dublin where the Jewish community was small, his knowledge of Hebrew, Yiddish and Russian were not of much assistance in the Irish towns and countryside where he sold slippers door to door.[63]

He started a Hebrew school in the buildings of the Heytesbury Synagogue, near Kelly's Corner, Dublin. There he wrote his serious works in Hebrew while he conversed in Yiddish. He also conducted the services there, living in the basement under the synagogue. Selling slippers in the morning, he taught the children Hebrew in the evening for which he received a shilling a week per child.[64] About ten months after leaving Russia, Wigoder felt confident enough to send for his wife and five children in summer 1891. He changed his job to frame-maker in 1895, setting up a workshop in the basement of the synagogue where he was helped by his ten-year-old son, Saul Harris,

'Harry'.[65] The latter became quicker at making frames than his father, and, on leaving school at the age of twelve, he kept up the trade.

The family moved to a house lit by gas at 8 St Kevin's Parade.[66] They moved again to 33 New Street, near St Patrick's Cathedral, where they had a shop in which they sold pictures. Another shop was later opened at 11 Berkeley Road, on the north side of the city. Myer Joel continued to combine his business and religious activities, being president and secretary of the Chevra Gemara of the Camden Street Synagogue which he had founded. However, it was difficult for him to reconcile the clash of values between his 'old' world and Jewish life in Dublin. His son, Harry, explained:

> For in the communities of Lithuania there was one common characteristic never seen in the West. Scholarship had the highest value of all things in the community. A man might be wealthy but that mattered little. If a man were a scholar, the congregation would rise as he entered the Synagogue. The degrees of knowledge were the degrees of honour ... and he could never assimilate the standard of value which the West put upon money.[67]

In Ireland his father saw

> noble, respected persons standing near the entrance to the Synagogue because they cannot afford to pay for the higher seats whereas low and vulgar people are chairmen of Synagogues and public institutions and have the highest seats because they possess money.[68]

Harry was, for his family, the bridge between their Jewish world in Lithuania and the new world of Ireland. He prospered in business, where he was known to all as 'Barney'. He helped to further the fortunes of his family, which had since moved to 62 Charlemont Street. At the age of twenty, he opened a shop in Talbot Street under his own name. It sold picture frames, paint and wallpaper. Harry ensured that the younger members of his family were educated.[69] An accomplished sportsman, he was well known in later life in soccer circles in the city. He died on 15 August 1932.

Ada Shillman, who married a learned Talmudic scholar in the early 1880s in Lithuania, was another parent who strove to give a good education to her family. She and her husband came to Ireland and settled in Cork about 1888, where Ada studied for a diploma in midwifery at the Lying-in Hospital. They moved to Dublin in 1892, where she worked for the following forty years as one of the most popular and innovative midwives in the city. Among the thousands of babies she delivered were Robert Briscoe, who was to rise to prominence in Irish politics, and the Abbey Theatre/Hollywood actor, Arthur Shields.[70] Together with Bethel Solomons, who admired her pioneering professional work and described her as 'a magnificent woman',[71] she founded a free medical dispensary for Jewish women at 43 Bloomfield Avenue. She also helped found St Ultan's Infant Hospital in Charlemont Street. Ada was the mother of Bernard Shillman, the distinguished senior counsel and historian of the Jewish community in Ireland. When she died in 1933, Bethel Solomons wrote to Bernard:

I feel a definite personal loss. She was a friend of mine and she was one of the best midwives I have ever met. It is quite impossible to replace her. She stood above her fellows and I know she was as good a mother as a nurse.[72]

Unlike many members of the Jewish community who were educated in Church of Ireland schools, Bernard Shillman attended the Christian Brothers' School at Westland Row between 1906 and 1908:

I have the highest esteem and respect for the conscientious and zealous manner in which the Brothers themselves live their semi-claustral lives, discharge their teaching duties. The two and a half years that I spent in the class rooms of these Christian Brothers at Westland Row have left no bitter taste in my memory of tyrannous task-masters. On the contrary, I carried in my mind cherished memories of their kindliness as pedagogues.[73]

He singled out J. B. Whelehan as one of the brothers who befriended him and with whom he retained contact after Whelehan had left the order and become involved in Cumann na nGaedheal.[74] Shillman later married Molly Goldberg, sister of Gerald.

Joseph Zlotover and Lieb Berman were another two refugees from Lithuania who made their way to Ireland. Joseph and Deana Zlotover settled in Dublin where Joseph ran the Atlas furniture company at Mary Street. He became a prominent member of the Jewish community in the city, being the first president of the United Hebrew Congregation and the leading spirit in the building of a new synagogue in Dolphin's Barn in the mid-1920s. The Bermans first settled in Athlone where Lieb earned a living as a pedlar. They later moved to Dublin; their daughter, Hannah Berman, who was to become an author of international reputation, was educated at Donore School in Dolphin's Barn.[75]

William and Rachael Nurock were also from Lithuania. William was born on 31 May 1865 in Kurschany, Kovno, and Rachael (Zlotover) was from the village of Avesley, near Weksny, Kovno. They met in August 1884, were married in mid-1887, and came to Ireland in November 1887. Their first child, Amie, was born in Athlone on 26 January 1890. They had moved to St Kevin's Parade, Dublin, before their second daughter, Lib or Lizzie, was born on 5 June 1891. The next two children, Max (b. 28 April 1893) and Tillie (b. 21 November 1894) were born at 20 Oakfield Place – graphically described earlier in the writing of Con Leventhal – and the last two, Maurice (b. 14 March 1896) and Dinah (b. 12 October 1899) were born at 8 Emorville Avenue. The family later moved to 79 South Circular Road.

William Nurock, who was quickly to become one of the most respected members of the Dublin Jewish community, earned his living in business. Max, his oldest son, was a gifted scholar. He entered High School in 1904 where he became the editor of the school magazine, the *Erasmian*. One of his term reports for 1907 read: 'Very promising, except as to writing, and inattention in class'. His lowest mark on that occasion was 87 in classics. He went to Trinity College Dublin in 1911, where he had a distinguished academic career and was awarded many academic prizes.[76] He got a commission in the British army during the First World War and later spent most of his working life in Palestine where he was junior chief secretary to the high commissioner, Sir Herbert Samuel. He was awarded an OBE in 1933. Later he served in the Israeli diplomatic service.[77]

Leonard and Mervyn S. Abrahamson, sons of David Abrahamson of 10 New Street, Newry, Co. Down, had a different educational formation to the Nurocks. They – like Bernard Shillman – went to a Christian Brothers' School. Leonard received the highest marks in the country in Irish and Greek in the Intermediate Certificate in 1910. He wrote in Irish an appreciation of the contribution of the Christian Brothers to his education and to the education of the poor.[78] His educational achievements were all the more remarkable because he had been born in Russia. Winning further prizes in 1911 and 1912, he was awarded an Irish Sizarship to Trinity for four years. There he studied Irish and Hebrew, and was elected honorary librarian of the university Gaelic Society. A scholar of great brilliance, he also excelled in modern languages, taking French and German, before turning to medicine in 1915.[79] Befriended by Max Nurock, Abrahamson lodged with that family throughout his days in Trinity College. He married Tillie Nurock on 4 February 1920. His brother, M. S., qualified as a doctor in 1922.

Leonard Abrahamson, in common with many of his generation, was exercised by the prevalence of anti-Semitism. He supported the establishment of an Anti-Defamation League in 1914: 'The virus of anti-Semitic feeling, born of ignorance and fostered by unrelenting prejudice, still courses in the veins of numerous – if not the majority of – Britishers.'[80] The outbreak of the First World War placed further pressure on the Jewish community in Ireland. Abrahamson's own father was the victim of 'anti-German' insults and threats of assault in August 1914 by elements in Newry and Bessbrook who 'laboured under the impression that all Jews are German'. His father, who was born in Russia and a naturalised British citizen, appealed to a friend, William Moore, who wrote to the press in his defence: 'It is with great difficulty that Mr Abrahamson is able to conduct his daily business. I am confident that none of the respectable people of Newry and neighbourhood would give any countenance to such ignorant and intolerant conduct.' Moore added: 'Our Jewish fellow citizens are entitled to protection, with civil and religious liberty, under the British flag, equally with ourselves.' He said that the Jews were loyal to British interests 'and already in response to the call of our King, 600 Jews of London have volunteered for service in the war and at the present moment a large number of Jewish soldiers are on their way to the battle fields'.[81]

Leonard Abrahamson, prompted by the attack on his father, wrote in the national press:

> Since the outbreak of the war, the belief generally rampant that all Jews are Germans, has given rise to many unpleasant and reprehensible occurrences. Not only has this erroneous notion gained ground amongst the uneducated but it has been fostered by the repeated linking in several journals – amongst others, the 'Times' – of the term Jew and German. . . . The truth is that the Jews in Germany are but a very small

portion of the Jews in general. They are loyal subjects of the Crown, just
as the Russian, French and English Jews are loyal respectively to Russia,
France and England. . . .

He continued with a poignant defence of the loyalty of Jews to the country 'of
their birth or adoption':

Hardly a day passes but we learn of some new way in which the English
Jews – of all classes and descriptions – are showing their lasting devotion
and their heartfelt loyalty and gratitude to the kind country of their birth
or adoption. This war will bring desolation and sadness into many a
Jewish family bereft by love and sense of duty to England of those most
near and dear. To doubt Jewish loyalty at this juncture is the same as to
doubt the loyalty of those who may be at this moment sacrificing their
life's blood in the service of their country.[82]

But during the world war, Jews in Ireland continued to be viewed with
great suspicion. The Jaffes felt themselves under threat in Belfast. Sir Otto
Jaffe, who had lived in Northern Ireland for over sixty years, was a British
citizen. Although born in Germany, he was an Anglophile and a loyal
supporter of the crown. His eldest son, Arthur Daniel, was in the British
army, as was his nephew, Lieutenant W. S. Oppe. Twice lord mayor of Belfast,
Sir Otto resigned from the corporation in 1916 after twenty-five years of
service. The Jaffes took up residence in London, where Sir Otto died on 8
March 1929.[83]

If the Jaffes found suspicions about their loyalty intolerable, it may be
assumed that the Jews in Dublin's working-class 'Little Jerusalem', Cork's
working-class 'Jewtown' or the Jewish area of Belfast may have found those
early war years very uncomfortable if not, on occasions, menacing.[84] Such
anxieties may explain why, for example, the Dublin Jewish community used
the occasion of a visit to the city by Issy Smith VC, a Jew but not Irish, to
make a public profession of loyalty. Smith was honoured for his bravery at a
meeting in the Mansion House in late September 1915. Joseph Isaacs
presided. In making the presentation, Under Secretary Sir Matthew Nathan,
said that 'they of the Jewish faith lived in these islands in complete freedom,
in the enjoyment of equal advantages with their fellow-countrymen'. He
believed that 'a Jew born in Ireland was just as good an Irishman as any
Catholic and Irishman'. The Rev. Abraham Gudansky said he hoped that by
his bravery and self-sacrifice Corporal Smith had succeeded in removing the
cataracts from the eyes of some of their fellow citizens who would not see
the Jew in his proper light: 'If the Government thought it proper to enforce
conscription, there would be no opposition from the Jews', he said.[85]

The revolutionary years, 1916–23

Such compliance to the will of the British was not necessarily shared by
Leonard Abrahamson and other members of the younger generation of Irish
Jews. Abrahamson was disciplined by Trinity College Dublin authorities for

inviting the revolutionary nationalist, Patrick Pearse, to speak at the college Gaelic Society.[86] While no evidence has been found recording the reaction of the Jewish community to the execution of Pearse and his comrades in 1916, according to Melisande Zlotover, Dublin's Jews 'were most sympathetic [to the Rising] and many helped in the cause'.[87]

But such support did not prevent the publication of a virulent anti-Semitic attack shortly after the Rising in the *Catholic Bulletin*. Published since 1911 under the editorship of J. J. O'Kelly, the journal was an independent Catholic nationalist voice and never the official organ of the hierarchy. In its May–June issue of 1916, it published the first in a series of articles by a member of the diocese of Kildare and Leighlin, Fr T. H. Burbage, on 'Ritual murder among the Jews'.[88] The publication was accompanied by publicity posters which were hung up around the city, proclaiming: 'Murder by Jews'.[89] The article began:

> Does ritual murder exist among the Jews? This is one of those puzzling questions that is still awaiting a satisfactory answer. For centuries past and at frequent intervals Christians throughout the world have been shocked and alarmed by the discovery of murders that clearly belong to a special class. They show a startling similarity in their detail.[90]

The article brought bitter complaints; the honorary secretary to the Dublin Jewish community, J. Elyan, wrote on 10 June 1916 to the archbishop of Dublin, William Walsh, requesting a meeting concerning 'a very urgent matter'. Receiving no reply, Elyan wrote again to the archbishop on 23 June concerning 'a certain matter of pressing importance to our Community'.[91] On 12 June, Lorcan G. Sherlock, sub-sheriff of Dublin, wrote to Walsh on behalf of the Jewish community:

> Mr Joseph Isaacs T.C. brought under the notice of Alderman McWalter and myself an article in the *Catholic Bulletin* of this month relating to murder by the Jews, and made bitter complaints, not of the article alone but particularly of the poster which appears as follows 'Murder by Jews'. He pointed out that such publications were calculated to arouse public feeling in the city against the Jews as a class, and would tend further at this time of peculiar unrest to developments that might be very reprehensible.

He continued, outlining the preferred response of senior figures within the Jewish community which was remarkable for its moderation:

> The matter has been considered by the Jewish Board and suggestions were made to appeal to their London Authorities to try and prevent further publications of the sort, but Councillor Isaacs who is Vice-Chairman of the Public Health Committee succeeded in getting no action taken so that he might approach Your Grace in reference to the matter. Alderman McWalter agreed that I should bring the matter under your notice.[92]

Meanwhile, the police had intervened. The superintendent of the Dublin Metropolitan Police, Owen Brien, had sent on 5 June a copy of the article and the offending poster to the Chief Secretary's Office for his observations:

The article in question and the poster are of the most objectionable nature and calculated to stir up popular resentment against the Jewish Community. I have had an interview with two of the leading Jews in Dublin and they are very apprehensive of a campaign against people of their faith in the city.[93]

A letter of complaint was sent to the editor of the *Catholic Bulletin*. A reply was received from P. T. Keohane, the secretary of the journal's publishers, Gills, which stated that 'nothing could be farther from Fr Burbage's intention or ours than to excite public feeling against the Jewish community'. An assurance was given that no further reference to the subject would appear on the posters of the *Catholic Bulletin*.[94]

But the matter did not rest there. The editor J. J. O'Kelly remained unrepentant and he continued to publish articles by Burbage, with two more appearing in July and August. Dublin Castle declined to intervene,[95] and in September O'Kelly refused to distance the journal from the views of Burbage.[96] The latter, who had joined Sinn Féin, continued to write against the Jews and Freemasons in the *Catholic Bulletin*.[97]

The history of Jewish involvement in the Sinn Féin movement requires further research. Individual Jews may have opted for the cause of radical Irish nationalism to a greater extent than is realised; Fanny and Molly Goldberg, for instance, were both members of Cumann na mBan. Meanwhile, in the absence of documentary evidence, the novel *A Land not Theirs* by Fanny Goldberg's son, David Marcus, provides a realistic portrayal of the experience of Cork's Jewish community in the War of Independence.[98] The kidnapped Joshua Cohen, asked by his young Irish Republican Army (IRA) captor and would-be assassin, 'Wouldn't you fight for your home?', replies:

'For my home, yes, if I had to. But what is my home? My home is my self, my body. I live in my body, in my family. That's my home.'[99]

He is then asked whether or not he would fight for his country:

'What's that? A piece of land where I happened to be born. A piece of land ruled by tsars, kings, princes, politicians – people I have never met. People I don't know and cannot influence. People who don't care about me – or about you. Is that what I should fight for? Is that all my life is worth?'[100]

Even Joshua, sceptical of the political order, later plays an indirect role in the struggle for Irish independence by allowing an IRA friend to hide guns and explosives in his scrap yard.

His son Jacob, a medical student at University College Cork, is slow to commit himself to the country and to the city of his birth:

'I love its buildings, its rivers, its setting, its atmosphere. While I've grown up in it, it has grown up in me. I've lived my life in a ghetto – Jewish people, Jewish friends, Jewish history, Jewish affairs, Jewish concerns, that's been my world. And that world, that ghetto happens to be in the city of Cork. It's all I know and feel of Ireland, my physical surroundings. They appeal to me emotionally, aesthetically but not – not viscerally.'[101]

That world returns to haunt him at every turn:

> the one Jew among hundreds of Catholics and his Jewishness instead of
> making him vulnerable had in fact been his armour. It was as if the Jacob
> attending Presentation College was some 'doppleganger' sent to suffer the
> pinpricks of the outside world while the real Jacob remained cocooned in
> his Yiddish veldt. But now he saw that Jewish world for what it was – an
> anachronism not of time but of place – co-opted into the political
> struggle.[102]

Asked by a member of Cumann na mBan whether he felt he owed Ireland
something, Jacob's reply echoes Leopold Bloom:

> 'In the first place', he continued, 'what is Ireland? Is it "an island entirely
> surrounded by water" as I learned at school, or is it the Irish people? We
> can't be talking about Ireland, the physical land, because how can I owe
> its – how many? thirty-odd thousand square miles, is it? – how can I owe
> a piece of land anything? And if we're talking about the Irish people –
> well, it wasn't the Irish people who let the Jews into Ireland, it was the
> British government in Ireland. So, according to your reasoning, it's really
> the British I should support, not the Irish.'[103]

Jacob explains how his grandfather, a rabbi, and Jewish immigrants had been
made welcome in Cork. He is then asked the moral of that line of reasoning:

> Jacob shrugged: 'I suppose it would be surprising if the Cork Jews did not
> feel sympathetic to the Irish and their cause. If I had to take sides myself,
> I'd probably be in favour, too. But as to owing them anything . . . What, for
> instance? What am I supposed to do about it? I don't feel Irish – told you
> that – at least, not Irish enough to know the answer to that question.'[104]

Michael Noyk, a Jewish solicitor in Dublin who was active in the struggle
for Irish independence, is not a character from fiction. He worked closely
with Michael Collins, who was Minister for Finance in the Republican government under Dáil Éireann as well as being in charge of the IRA campaign
against the British. Noyk deeply admired Collins and once remarked that the
word 'cannot' did not figure in his vocabulary. There was a 'lot of the boy in
him',[105] Noyk recalled, adding that Collins had a command of bad language
'that even a British Tommy might have envied'.[106] Noyk remembered that
Collins, as Minister for Finance, was usually surrounded in his office by
about seven people to whom he was giving orders or dictation at the same
time.[107] Noyk has been described by Piaras Béaslaí – a biographer of Collins
– as 'the principal agent in the purchase of houses and offices for Dáil and
IRA work'.[108] He procured offices for Dáil Éireann at 22 Mary Street, which
remained a principal Department of Finance office until its discovery by the
Black and Tans shortly before the Truce in summer 1921.[109] Noyk also took
rooms for Dáil Éireann at 29 Mary Street, where a secret room was set up in
which books and papers were dumped whenever a raid was feared.[110] He
rented other rooms at 3 St Andrew's Street where a store of gold was kept.

Noyk practised in the Dáil Éireann courts held at North Great George's
Street. He was heavily involved in the defence of Sinn Féin prisoners

between 1919 and 1921; his offices were raided by the Black and Tans and papers in connection with the defence of prisoners were taken. He defended the famous commandant of the Longford Brigade, Seán Mac Eoin, who had been arrested in Longford on his return from a visit to Dublin in spring 1921. Collins, having mounted unsuccessful escape attempts, devised a plan to smuggle a couple of revolvers into Mac Eoin in order to allow him escape from the courtroom in City Hall, Dublin. Noyk agreed to do so, but the plan was abandoned.[111] Noyk remained one of Collins's closest advisers throughout this period.[112] Béaslaí also describes Noyk as 'an intimate friend of Arthur Griffith and as 'the most devoted and trustworthy of men'.[113] When he died in 1966, he was given full military honours by the Dublin Brigade of the IRA.[114]

Robert Briscoe, the first Jew to be elected to Dáil Éireann, also played an important role in the first wave of the Sinn Féin revolution between 1919 and 1921. He was born on 25 September 1894 in Lower Beechwood Avenue, Ranelagh, Dublin, but when he was five months old, his family went to live over their business, Lawlor Briscoe, on Lower Ormond Quay. A hand-made furniture workshop, Lawlor Briscoe also acted as a store for personal goods. His father, Abraham William Briscoe, had been born in the village of Zagar, in Kovno, Lithuania. He was sent to Dublin at the age of fourteen, where he earned a living as a brush salesman. Abraham's business took him to Leipzig where he stayed with a Jewish family; there he met Ida, one of the family's four daughters, whom he later married. Robert, their son, went to Kildare Street National School and then to the Presbyterian preparatory school, St Andrew's. He also attended the 'stylish Jewish school' at Townely Castle in Ramsgate, London, for two years. In 1912, Robert Briscoe went to Berlin with his brother to serve their apprenticeship in Hecht Pfeiffer. Following the outbreak of war, they returned to Ireland. In December 1914, Briscoe went to work in the United States where he remained until 1917. He married Lily Isaacs, the daughter of a close friend of his father, upon his return, and then became immersed in revolutionary politics.[115]

In the winter of 1919–20 Briscoe joined the staff of Michael Collins. Michael Noyk, acting on instructions from Collins, sent Briscoe to Germany on an arms procurement mission in 1922. There the paths of two Irish nationalists crossed for the first time – one a Jew and the other a strong anti-Semite. Charles Bewley, Quaker convert to Catholicism, senior counsel and diplomat, was a personality whose rising fortunes in the new Ireland caused anguish to the Jewish community. Appointed Irish consul to Berlin on 12 October 1921, he took up his post in December. He was to play an important role, in one guise or another, in the history of the Irish state and, in particular, in the relationship between the Jewish community and that state. Born in 1888, he was the eldest son of Dr Henry Bewley, a member of a distinguished Dublin Quaker family, and Elizabeth Eveleen Pim. He was the brother of Dr Geoffrey Bewley of the Adelaide Hospital, Dublin. Educated at Winchester and New College, Oxford, he won the Newdigate Prize for English verse – the first Irishman to do so since Oscar Wilde.[116] During his time at Oxford, Bewley converted to Catholicism. After graduating, he entered the legal profession and was called to the Bar in 1914.

During the early part of the War of Independence, he showed his nationalist credentials by defending IRA men.[117]

Bewley spoke Latin, Italian and German, linguistic skills which were utilised by the revolutionaries when he was posted to Berlin. However, he soon found himself engaged in an unseemly row with another Sinn Féin envoy, John Chartres, and Robert Briscoe.[118] On 21 January 1922 Briscoe complained to Chartres about Bewley's behaviour at a cafe in Berlin owned by a Jew:

> It seems Mr Bewley arrived there in the evening in a rather advanced state of intoxication, and on my name being mentioned burst forth into a string of most abusive and filthy language. His chief point of argument as an excuse for this attitude was my faith.[119]

In his memoirs, Briscoe records that Bewley was 'forcibly ejected' from the premises because he made 'extremely derogatory remarks about Jews in general, and himself [the Jewish proprietor] in particular. He repeated some of these insults to our race. They were the usual sort of thing.'[120] Bewley apologised when Briscoe and his companion, an IRA man named Charlie McGuinness, confronted him in his office. But the matter did not end there. Briscoe wrote to the Minister for External Affairs in Dublin demanding Bewley's removal: 'Such behaviour on the part of a man holding an official position is not conducive to attaining the results intended, nor will it help to bring credit to the people of Ireland.' Chartres recommended to Dublin that Bewley be immediately transferred elsewhere 'in the interest of decorum, national dignity and commercial prudence'.[121] He added: 'Moreover, an anti-Semitic outburst by an Irish official in a country where Jews are very numerous and very influential was an extraordinary indiscretion from the point of view of Irish material interest.'[122] Bewley sent a handwritten letter to Chartres on 28 January, outlining his version of events. Bewley claimed that one of the staff at the cafe had asked him if Briscoe was an Irish consul.

> I said that he was not, and added that it was not likely that a Jew of this type would be appointed. (The conversation was in German.) I regret having made the latter remark and have already expressed my regret to Mr Briscoe. At that moment, a German Jew who was sitting near said that I had insulted his race and after a further short conversation I left the cafe.[123]

It might have been possible to dismiss the anti-Semitic remark made by Bewley in a cafe as being the result of excess alcohol. However, Bewley, not content to make a graceless apology, sought to further blacken Briscoe's name. The latter had purchased the steamer *City of Dortmund* in 1921 to ply between Hamburg, Bremen, Belfast and Dublin. With an all-IRA crew, its purpose was to smuggle wanted men out of Ireland and to bring in arms and explosives when possible. Bewley, without any evidence, twisted the situation in order to imply that Briscoe was motivated by personal gain.[124] Then, when attempting to find a permanent residence for the Irish 'legation' in Germany some months later, Bewley commented, upon receiving an offer of rooms from two men by the names of Loewi and Jacobowitz: 'I am not suggesting that the offer of Messrs Loewi and Jacobowitz is one that should be accepted, as I think it likely that in any bargain with gentlemen of their ancestry we would not get the best of it.'[125]

However, Bewley had his supporters back in Dublin. His political superior, Minister for Trade and Commerce Ernest Blythe, took Bewley's side against Briscoe in the row discussed earlier. Perhaps Blythe's opinion of Briscoe was coloured by the fact that Briscoe had sided with Eamon de Valera against the Treaty settlement. Blythe wrote to the Minister for External Affairs, George Gavan Duffy, on 16 February 1922, saying that his enquiries had led him to conclude that Briscoe was 'a decidedly . . . shady character'. Another source had told him that Briscoe was 'out on the make'.[126] Blythe wrote to Gavan Duffy again on 11 March:

> There is no proof that this incident occurred further than the statement made by Mr Briscoe. You are aware of the character which this gentleman bears and I need scarcely point out to you that little weight should be attached to any statement made by him.[127]

Gavan Duffy had written consolingly to Bewley on 13 February: 'You cannot take too great trouble to cause the matter to be forgotten.' Writing to Chartres on 29 March, Gavan Duffy said of Bewley: 'I know that he is mad on the Jewish question and the incident you reported in your No. 1 was inexcusable; (the other gentleman referred to in No. 1 [Briscoe] is an undesirable person).'[128]

However, Chartres opposed giving Bewley the Berlin mission in his absence. On 28 March Gavan Duffy wrote to Blythe, stating that while Bewley might be a suitable envoy for Munich or Vienna, 'there is a great objection to appointing him to such a post in Germany, because his Semitic convictions are so pronounced that it would be very difficult for him to deal properly with all the persons and questions within the scope of an envoy to Berlin, where the Jewish element is very strong'. In the end, it went to Nancy Wyse-Power. Remaining in Germany for a while, Bewley returned to Dublin to practise law towards the end of 1922. Chartres had written that Bewley was 'unfamiliar with the canons of conduct to be observed by public men entrusted with the representation of Irish national interests abroad'.[129] We will see later how prescient that observation proved to be.

In that generation, it was not unfashionable to allow stereotypes of the Jew to influence popular discussion. Hilaire Belloc's controversial book *The Jews*, which was published in 1922, is evidence of a model of anti-Jewish thinking. The book was widely read and went into several reprints.[130] Professor Arthur Clery, a strong supporter of Sinn Féin, demonstrated that Belloc's views were not automatically accepted by Irish Catholics. In a review of the book in the Jesuit-published *Studies,* Clery wrote:

> Mr Belloc's *The Jews* is the wickedest book that has been written against Jews for a long time; all the more so as it is written in a strain of impartiality, really felt and yet in reality wholly absent. It is throughout the friendly criticism of an enemy, or (as a Jewish gentleman put it to me) the moral is: 'Don't nail his ears to the pump.'[131]

Clery outlined the Belloc thesis in the most unsympathetic manner:

> Belloc starts from the proposition that the Jew is of necessity an alien,
> incapable of absorption into any nation; he argues then that kind treat-
> ment, as in modern Britain, results in giving the Jew power without
> patriotism, that as this alien power increases, national feeling must rise
> against it, till it ends inevitably in persecution and expulsion.[132]

Belloc's remedy, Clery wrote, was 'that Jews should be openly treated as
and should admit to themselves to be foreigners', and that they should
develop separate institutions for Jews in each community as they had
already developed separate schools.

> The point which he stresses most is the controlling influence of Jews in
> finance, in the press, in the theatrical world, and in the ownership of
> certain essential metals, e.g., lead, nickel and mercury. The strongest
> point he makes against them is a tendency to combination under condi-
> tions of secrecy. As an argument that clinches all of his former ones he
> cites the prominent position taken by Jews in the recent Russian revolu-
> tion, and says in effect that this is the last straw in the matter of their
> toleration by Christians.

Clery wrote that the 'connection of a few excommunicated Jews with the
Russian revolution' was little more than an accident. Clery felt, however, that
the real explanation of the 'tendency to combination under conditions of
secrecy' lay elsewhere:

> If you look at the position of the Irish in America a generation ago – things
> are different now – you would find them engaged in secret combinations
> and connected with the least reputable institutions in the country – ward
> politics and the saloons. So in Ulster Catholic money was chiefly to be
> found in the retail liquor trade. No other lucrative occupation was allowed
> to them.[133]

Clery's arguments are worth recording for the clarity of his thought and
his exposure of the weakness of the anti-Semitic ideas so frequently repeated
in the pages of Catholic journals during the 1920s.

Rabbi Herzog and the Jewish community in the 1920s

Gerald Goldberg argues that partition had a very serious impact on the
unity of the Jewish community in Ireland. Both the Catholic Church and
the Church of Ireland, he points out, continued to be organised on an all-
Ireland basis: that was not the case with the Jewish community.[134] While
Jews in Northern Ireland remained affiliated to Jewish structures in Britain,
those south of the border which divided the Irish Free State from the North
were fortunate to enjoy the prudent leadership of the chief rabbi of Saorstát
Éireann, Dr Isaac Herzog.[135] The latter had served as a rabbi in Belfast since
1916. A year later, he married Sarah, the daughter of Rabbi Samuel Isaac
Hillman, who was originally from Kovno, in Lithuania.[136] The Herzogs' first

son, Chaim, was born on 17 November 1918 at 2 Norman Villas, Belfast; he was to become President of Israel in 1983. Scholarly but absent-minded, Isaac Herzog was very popular in Belfast. He visited Dublin on a number of occasions 'where he created a great impression on the entire community' and 'they all wanted him as their spiritual leader'.[137] He moved to Dublin in 1919 at the age of thirty.[138] The family first lived on the South Circular Road before moving to Bloomfield Avenue. A second son, Jacob (Yaakov), was born in 1921. He later became a distinguished Israeli diplomat. Admired by Ben Gurion, he was a senior adviser to Prime Minister Levi Eshkol, who 'treated him like a son'.[139] Jacob also became a close friend and admirer of Eamon de Valera.

Chaim Herzog recalls in his memoirs that his father was 'an open partisan of the Irish cause' and that 'the Jewish community as a whole gave a lot of help to the Irish'.[140] The rabbi, who shared with de Valera a love of mathematics, came to know the Irish leader as a friend. During those disturbed times, Herzog was of practical help. One source states that de Valera was hidden in the rabbi's home on occasions during the War of Independence.[141] The fighting during the Civil War in 1922–23 was among Chaim Herzog's first memories of Dublin. He recalls straying into the front garden of their home on the South Circular Road and witnessing the driver of a horse and cart being shot dead in crossfire only yards away on the road outside. Chaim Herzog also remembers that his father intervened to try to get prisoners to give up their hunger strikes at the end of the Civil War. De Valera continued to visit the Herzog household while he was in opposition during the 1920s 'and unburden his heart to my father'.[142] During one particular visit, de Valera humorously commented that a man of Herzog's linguistic capabilities ought to be able to speak Irish. Herzog agreed to study the language over the next three months, but as a quid pro quo the rabbi asked de Valera to learn to speak some Hebrew in the same period. When de Valera returned to Herzog's house, the chief rabbi spoke to him in Irish. But while Herzog had mastered some Irish, de Valera had to confess that he had not had time to learn any Hebrew.[143]

Herzog was also very friendly with the President of the Executive Council, William T. Cosgrave, and members of the Cumann na nGaedheal cabinet. In a divided society, it must have been difficult for the leader of the Jewish community to retain contact with both sides in the recently concluded Civil War. That was a transitory difficulty; the manner in which a religious minority might influence the policies of the new state in the direction of tolerance and inclusiveness was more problematical. The Free State's new constitution was very acceptable to all religious minorities. Article 3 granted citizenship to those 'who had been ordinarily resident in the area of the jurisdiction of the Irish Free State (Saorstát Éireann) for not less than seven years'. Article 8 stated: 'Freedom of conscience and the free profession and practice of religion are, subject to public order and morality, guaranteed to every citizen, and no law may be made either directly or indirectly to endow any religion . . .'

Unlike most of the other religious denominations in Ireland, the Jewish community depended for its viability upon its ability to bring in teachers and cantors from abroad. Consequently the country's immigration laws were of crucial importance. A brief evaluation of the policy of the Free State towards 'aliens' – the official term at the time for non-nationals – does not reveal any official antagonism to the admission of Jews in the 1920s. But it does show that Herzog was obliged to become involved from time to time in the admission process. The Free State continued the cautious British Home Office policy towards aliens. The existing Aliens Act was taken over by Dáil Éireann in 1922. At the time of the handing over of power, the British and the Irish authorities co-operated closely on drawing up mutually satisfactory guidelines for the admission of aliens. They had a shared interest in ensuring that both governments thought alike on this sensitive matter. Agreement between the two jurisdictions began to crystallise as early as May 1922.[144] Then in October a British Home Office official, W. Haldane Porter, who had been a central figure in the discussions about aliens, wrote to his counterparts in Dublin about the danger of unauthorised refugees coming to Ireland through Cobh:

> I feel sure from observations of the passenger traffic coming to Kobh [*sic*], even during the recent difficulties of transport, that there will be streams, possibly big streams, of aliens which will require very careful sifting if you are to protect yourselves, as incidentally Great Britain, against considerable additions to your population of undesirable aliens. I have no doubt that you have this matter in mind.[145]

Haldane Porter wrote on 8 November 1922:

> I am very glad to hear that your government intend to take steps to prevent any influx of undesirable aliens and I shall naturally be interested to hear further from you at your convenience as to the steps to be taken, especially as this would enable me to form some idea of when you can dispense with the services of my officers at your ports.[146]

He need not have been so concerned: the country was not flooded with applications from immigrants wishing to come to Ireland.

Applicants had to state their case to Irish representatives abroad and supply a character reference from the local police together with names of sponsors in Ireland.[147] Customs barriers between the Irish Free State and Britain became effective at midnight on 31 March 1923. Rabbi Herzog's name appears not infrequently in Department of Justice files as a result of representations he made on behalf of a small number of Jews who wished to take up employment in Ireland.[148] He wrote, for example, to the Department of Home Affairs on 10 December 1923 on behalf of an Austrian Jew:

> owing to the hieroglyphic character of my writing you have wrongly made out the name of the Reverend Gentleman in question . . . as consular officials are sometimes great pedants, I will give you his name in all its fullness as it was given to him on the day of his initiation into the Abrahamic covenant.[149]

Herzog wrote again on 27 December 1923 stating that the British consul at Munich had been willing to grant the necessary visa to allow the Austrian Jew in question to enter the Free State but had hesitated to issue passports for his family on the grounds that instructions from Dublin made no mention of them. Herzog continued: 'May I ask you kindly to send directions at your earliest convenience to the British consulate in Munich requesting them to include the family of the Rev. — in the visa, as it is his intention to bring them along with himself.' [150] They were allowed to come to Ireland.[151]

Rabbi Herzog had earlier made representations on behalf of the Limerick Hebrew Congregation, which had written to him saying that 'we are without a Minister to perform our Religious Ceremonies, and we have not been able to secure one during the last eighteen months'. Herzog recommended a Lithuanian minister, who was living in Moscow at the time, to the Limerick community, which unanimously agreed to engage him. Herzog then wrote to the authorities on 29 October 1923 requesting them to 'kindly give us the necessary permit to enable him and his wife to come here to Limerick'. He received a reply on 2 November stating that 'this Department is not aware of any objection to his admission to this country'.[152] Herzog's close friends, Moysha and Dwira Vilensky, were among those who came to live in Dublin in the 1920s. Moysha was a leading Hebrew scholar. Accepting the post of head of the Hebrew School, he proved to be a very successful teacher.[153] Among his students were the chief rabbi's sons, Chaim and Jacob Herzog. Overall, then, the state did not appear to pursue an active policy of discrimination against the admission of Jews in the first decade of its history.[154]

But while equality before the law – even for aliens – was not at issue in the 1920s, discrimination – often insidious and sometimes the work of a single individual – persisted. According to an oral source, Rabbi Herzog sought to have his two sons attend the Christian Brothers' School at Synge Street. When the superior discussed the matter with his confrères, all but one agreed to take the two children. A single brother voiced vehement objection. An embarrassed superior was obliged to refuse the Herzogs' entry.[155] Chaim and Jacob were educated in Alexandra College and later in Wesley College, and generally enjoyed a typically middle-class upbringing. They played cricket in the Jewish club in summer and cycled out each day to Blackrock or Dún Laoghaire to swim; in winter, they played rugby.[156] Yet they were always conscious of being 'different', Chaim Herzog explains:

> Ireland had no history of anti-Semitism, and while I did not feel outcast, I did feel different. I was always aware that somewhere in the background I was being judged by different standards. When a Jew was arrested for a crime, the entire Jewish community shuddered, because it was expected that all Jews would be thought guilty of the crime.[157]

Bethel Solomons wrote in his memoirs that he had never experienced anti-Semitism in his youth. He did not know 'such a thing existed'.[158] Yet, later in life he observed the anti-Semitism of affluent Dublin society:

Now, while there is no suggestion of pogroms in Ireland, and I do not believe there ever will be, there is an unpleasant and insidious movement. Social and sporting clubs are contaminated and in many there is an unwritten law that Jews will not be admitted. I am told that if one Jew is admitted he will bring a crowd. The answer to this absurd idea is that a man should be judged on his merits and a decent Jewish member of a club would be the first to try to prevent an undesirable person from being elected. If a Jew is seeking a position in a business or a hospital, he may not get it, because he is a Jew.[159]

In middle-class Cork and Belfast the situation was much the same.[160] Certain social, tennis and golf clubs simply kept Jews out.

That brand of silent anti-Semitism was reinforced by a view in contemporary pious Catholic literature that Jews were responsible for the eroding of moral values in Irish society. The bishop of Limerick, Denis Hallinan, wrote in 1919:

I have seen it stated on what I conceive to be reliable authority, that the principal designers of these modern fashions in women's dress are women, not men, and furthermore, that they are generally Parisian Jews and freemasons who are bitterly opposed to Christianity, and seek amongst other means, to uproot it by the introduction into Christian Society of those dangerous and indecent dresses.[161]

The Jesuit Richard S. Devane of Limerick was one of the priests who made the crusade against 'evil literature' a central focus of his life's apostolate. He, too, tended to hold Jews responsible for the corruption of society.[162] The founder of the Irish Vigilance Association in 1911, he had urged legal action against the proliferation of British publications when he met the Minister for Justice, Kevin O'Higgins, in 1926 as part of a delegation from the Priests Social Guild.[163] He complained to O'Higgins about a situation in the west of Ireland which he later explained before the Committee on Evil Literature:

I was on a mission in Ballina last year. There arrived in the town a Jew with a lorry . . . and he started selling contraceptives made up as pencil holders at 2/- each. Someone told the parish priest about the traffic and he found it was a fact. He notified the police who could do nothing. He then set up a court of his own and tried him and fined him £100. The jew paid £10 and cleared out.[164]

John Horgan has commented that Devane's advocacy of censorship and hostility to birth control 'had more than a tinge of anti-Semitism about it'.[165] The Censorship of Publications Act 1929 resulted from the hearings of this committee.[166]

Chief Rabbi Herzog's facility for diplomacy in dealing with leaders of both church and state helped his community greatly in that context. He became very friendly with the bishop of Down and Connor, Joseph MacRory, who later became cardinal archbishop of Armagh. Their good relations were in evidence at a state banquet in Dublin Castle when Cardinal MacRory chided Herzog jocosely for eating only fruit and not the excellent ham on offer: 'Let us discuss this at your wedding', the rabbi replied mischievously.[167] Friendship of that kind helped the rabbi make his views known to the cardinal or to the archbishop of Dublin, Edward Byrne, when necessity demanded. Catholicism, as the rabbi well understood, had its zealots. Yet the anti-Semitic undertow never became a driving force in the teaching of the Irish Catholic Church. Perhaps too much emphasis has been placed on the clerical extremists who wrote in the 1920s. It would be much more rewarding to speak of mentalities. There were other more tolerant Catholic nationalist intellectual currents than the one represented by Devane and his likes during the Cosgrave era. The Jewish community and other minority religious groupings had a secure place in that society, where many were leaders in the creative world of literature, music, cinema and painting.

One such person was Con Leventhal, who was among the first academics to publish a favourable review of Joyce's *Ulysses* which was published in 1922. When, however, the printers on the *Dublin Review* refused to set his text, Leventhal wrote the now famous line: 'a censoring God came out of the machine to allay the hell-fire fears of the compositors' sodality'.[168] Leventhal, not to be bested by such interference with academic freedom, published a single issue of a magazine which he called *Klaxon*. Writing under the name Laurence K. Emery, Leventhal stoutly defended *Ulysses* against attacks of being 'degenerate' and 'pornographic'.[169] He declared: 'One might as well label the Venus de Milo indecent, and just as that piece of sculpture has been the urge to centuries of artists, so *Ulysses*, with its strange modernity, will carry away young writers on its irrepressible tide.'[170] Leventhal found that there was 'no parallel to Mr Joyce in literature':

> He has that touch of individuality that puts genius on a peak. Rabelaisian, he hasn't the *joie de vivre* of the French priest; Sternesque, he is devoid of the personal touch of the Irish clergyman. Trained by the Jesuits, he can't guffaw like Balzac when he tells a good story.[171]

Joyce, he wrote, was scientific in his detachedness and had written 'a human book'. *Ulysses* was 'filled with pity as with the sexual instinct, and the latter in no greater proportion and of no greater importance in the book than any of the other fundamental human attributes'.[172]

Leventhal, a discerning Joycean scholar, went on to become both a friend of Samuel Beckett and a leading authority on his work.[173] In the 1920s, Leventhal was associated with the radical journal, *Tomorrow*.[174] A strong supporter of Zionism, he saw parallels between it and Irish nationalism. He was one of a new generation of Jews who helped win greater acceptance for his community in an Ireland experiencing its first decade of independence.

While members of the Jewish community contributed to the world of literary criticism in the capital, Dr Isaac Eppel was one of the country's pioneering film-makers. The owner of the Palace cinema in Dublin, he wrote and produced *Irish Destiny*, a love story set at the time of the War of Independence which received its premiere on 3 April 1926.[175] This was an important film and one of the earliest attempts to confront the destructiveness of the years 1919–21. It included a reconstruction of the burning of the Custom

House, and was a realistic depiction of the human entanglements and compet-
ing loyalties prevalent at a time of national struggle.[176]

The work of three Jewish artists, Estella Solomons, Stella Steyn and Harry
Kernoff, contributed greatly to the cultural life of the new state in the 1920s
and early 1930s. Solomons, a portrait painter and a fine water colourist, was
mentioned earlier as a member of the prominent Jewish family.[177] Kernoff,
originally from London, developed a strong interest in the 1920s in the
avant-garde and the Modern Movement. But he turned to realism in the
1930s and became one of the first artistic chroniclers of social life in urban
and rural Ireland. Left-wing in his political thinking,[178] Kernoff's woodcuts
were often used in republican and labour papers during the 1930s and 1940s.
Stella Steyn was born in Dublin to William Steyn and his wife Bertha Jaffe.
Like Solomons and Kernoff, she studied on the continent and was a friend of
James Joyce.[179] The 1920s proved to be a high point for the Jewish contribution to culture in Ireland.

The health of the Jewish community under the leadership of the chief
rabbi, Isaac Herzog, was reflected in the opening of a new synagogue,
Greenville Hall, by the United Hebrew Congregation as well as a major exten-
sion to the Dublin Hebrew Congregation's existing synagogue at Adelaide
Road. The United Hebrew Congregation project had been initiated in 1909.[180]
Land was acquired at Dolphin's Barn, Dublin, and the foundation stone for
the synagogue was eventually laid on 27 April 1924. It was consecrated by
Isaac Herzog. The service was conducted by the synagogue's new minister,
Rev. M. L. Rosenfield. The music was conducted by Leo Bryll, the new choir
master.[181] Then, on 13 September 1925, Morris Ellis presided at the opening
of Greenville Hall Synagogue. Rev. Abraham Gittleson was minister for most
of its existence. The synagogue, which closed due to dwindling numbers in
1981, came to play a very important part in the life of the Jewish community
in Dublin.

By the early 1920s the Adelaide Road congregation had become too large
for the synagogue, especially at High Festivals, and a decision was taken on
30 September 1923 to extend it. Arthur Newman, president of the congregation in the years 1920–23, was the driving force behind the expansion. The
reconsecration of the extended synagogue took place on 21 June 1925.[182]
Newman led the procession of scroll bearers, which was headed by the chief
rabbi.[183] Edwin Solomons was president of the Dublin Hebrew Congregation
by then, and remained so until 1964, when he was succeeded by Mr Justice
Herman Good.[184] Solomons's mother, Rosa, who had been centrally involved
in the original development of the Adelaide Road Synagogue in the early
1890s, was also present, and indeed wrote a poem for the occasion. She died
the following year at the age of eighty-three.[185]

Afterwards, Ernest Wormser Harris proposed a toast to the Irish Free
State, and Mr Justice Creed Meredith of the Supreme Court replied on behalf
of the government. He recalled that his father, Sir Creed Meredith, had been
present at the original consecration of the synagogue in 1892. He said that
although the members of the Dublin Jewish community who were in the
service of the government were only few in number, they were capable

officials and occupied prominent positions. He was glad to note in particular that a fellow lawyer, Lionel H. Rosenthal (president of the Dublin Hebrew Congregation in 1924), had been appointed deputy circuit judge for Cork City and County.[186]

Here was evidence that the Jewish community had achieved a position of respectability and a safe home in the Free State. But being a religious minority encouraged the community to display caution and shun the social and political limelight, no matter how protective the government was. This prudence and restraint is reflected in Maurice Abrahamson's story of the two Jews facing the firing squad. One said, 'I think I'll ask for a blindfold', to which came the immediate reply: 'You don't want to make any trouble.' Facing the turbulent 1930s, the Jewish community in Ireland had even greater reason to shun publicity: the you-don't-want-to-make-any-trouble mentality was prevalent in a Europe dominated by Hitler and Mussolini. Even in a relatively tranquil Ireland, the Jewish community sought to be left alone to live in peace and safety.

6. Wedding of John Aronson and Rebecca Hirshman (16),
Cork, 27 June 1902

7. Solomons family, early 1900s. Standing (left to right) Maurice (1832–1922),
Edwin (1879–1964) and Rosa (1842–1926); Seated (left to right) Bethel (1885–1965),
Sophie (1887–1972) and Estella (1882–1968)

8. Freedman's grocery store, Limerick, early 19(0s

9. Cohen's shop, Dublin, 1950s

10. Nurock family, Dublin

11. Moisel family, Dublin, early 1900s

12. Chief Rabbi of the Irish Free State, Dr Isaac Herzog

13. Robert Briscoe and Eamon de Valera

4

Irish society and the
culture of fear, 1932–37

In early 1932 Chief Rabbi Isaac Herzog's friend, Eamon de Valera, defeated
Cumann na nGaedheal in a general election and formed a minority Fianna
Fáil government. Robert Briscoe remained the only Jewish member of Dáil
Éireann. A founder member of Fianna Fáil, he had first been returned to the
Dáil in September 1927 for the Dublin constituency of South City; it was his
third attempt at the polls.[1]

Being a Jew in public life in an overwhelmingly Catholic country could
sometimes have its awkward if perhaps humorous moments. Briscoe recalls
in his memoirs a visit to Ballyseedy, County Kerry, in the late 1920s where
he was brought along to the local Catholic church for an after-Mass election
meeting. When the local organiser for Fianna Fáil, Willie O'Leary, saw that
Briscoe had not gone in to Mass he asked him to do so. Explaining why he did
not attend Mass, Briscoe received the unsympathetic reply: 'Everybody goes
to Mass here, you'll have to do likewise.' When Briscoe remained uncon-
vinced, he was told firmly: 'Haven't we enough bloody trouble explaining
Fianna Fáil without having to explain you as well?' Briscoe agreed with
O'Leary's suggestion to go to the door and *pretend* he was going to Mass.
After the meeting, the speakers returned to O'Leary's farmhouse where
Briscoe was confronted by a plate of cabbage and bacon. His host, with a
twinkle in his eye, told him immediately that he had a special meal for him.[2]
Thanks to O'Leary's 'courteous recognition' of his faith, Briscoe enjoyed a
'sumptuous breakfast of eggs and great glasses of foamy milk with home-
made bread and farmer's butter'.[3] It was not the last time Briscoe would
encounter such understanding in public life.

Yet, despite being a veteran of the War of Independence and a politician of
vast experience and long service, Briscoe was never given a ministerial post
or even made a parliamentary secretary (junior minister) in a public career
that lasted until the mid-1960s. De Valera, it seems, wanted to promote him
but did not do so because he felt that the appointment would provoke

opposition. This pointed to an undercurrent of hostility towards Jews in the country which even de Valera disappointingly adjudged better left unprovoked. Briscoe, however, readily understood and accepted de Valera's reasons for not promoting him.[4] The Jewish community in the 1930s were well aware of the need to display a capacity for common sense and a willingness to be accommodating towards the beliefs of the majority Catholic community.

There was a further illustration of this pragmatism in 1932 when a priest donated a crucifix to the Oireachtas which he had asked to be hung in the Dáil chamber. The Committee on Procedure and Privileges met to discuss whether the gift should be accepted. Briscoe, who was a member of the committee, later wrote that the exchanges, for once, were not along strictly party lines. There were arguments in favour of acceptance on the grounds that Ireland 'was, in fact, a Catholic country' while others opposed because it might provide confirmation for those who accused Irish people of religious prejudice:

> Because I was the only deputy of the Jewish Faith, I carefully abstained from expressing an opinion. Pro and con were so evenly divided in the committee that they finally came to me and directly asked my view. 'Gentlemen', I said, 'if having the Crucifix in the Dáil will make you any better Christians, I certainly have no objection.'[5]

The crucifix was hung in the chamber.

If Briscoe exhibited a willingness to compromise, he had also been very much aware of the need to take action to remove the stigma of moneylending which had continued unfairly to blight the good name of many members of the Jewish community. While in opposition in 1929 Briscoe sought to introduce a private member's bill to regulate a trade which had inflicted so much misery on Irish society.[6] Supported by his Fianna Fáil colleague, Patrick Little, Briscoe explained on 20 February 1929 that the measure was directed against those he would describe as

> nothing else but money hawkers. They go from house to house offering and inducing the wives of working men to borrow money, for the purpose of getting them into their power, and keeping them paying perpetually certain sums weekly, without any regard to the original amount lent, or any morality with regard to reasonable rates of interest.[7]

On 27 March 1930 the Bill was referred by the Minister for Justice, James Fitzgerald-Kenney, to a select committee of Dáil Éireann.[8] The committee was nominated on 11 April 1930 with the power to send for persons, papers and records. The Minister for Justice was a member, as were Briscoe and nine other TDs (members of the Dáil). The Garda commissioner, Eoin O'Duffy, told the committee that 80 per cent of the country's registered moneylenders (147 out of 180) were in Dublin. There were, he said, about fifty unregistered moneylenders in Dublin, seven registered and thirty-six unregistered in Cork, three registered and none unregistered in Limerick, three registered and three others suspected of being moneylenders in

Waterford, and in Galway there were neither registered nor unregistered moneylenders.[9]

In the course of the committee's hearings on 20 November 1930, C. A. Jackson Jellie, who had acted as an auditor to various moneylenders in Dublin, revealed that the rate of interest could be as high as 166 per cent per annum, but that would be rare.[10] O'Duffy linked crime to moneylending where people were driven to desperation because of the pressure exerted on them: 'Our returns also show that moneylending has been responsible for many cases of suicide, for indulgence in gambling and drink, and for domestic quarrels', he said.[11] O'Duffy, in supporting the Bill, said that the gardaí found it difficult to secure evidence for convictions – there had been only six prosecutions since 1925.[12]

The change of government in 1932 temporarily delayed the Bill becoming law. In response to Briscoe's representations, Fianna Fáil quickly reintroduced the measure. One deputy, at least, made a coded anti-Semitic comment during the debate in the Dáil. The former Minister for Justice, Fitzgerald-Kenney, asked the House about letting Belfast moneylenders work in Dublin:

> Does the Deputy think that any moneylenders who may come down here from Belfast would be of the Celtic race? Well, at least, any moneylender who came here from Belfast would have acquired a Celtic veneer. He would have 'wrapped the green flag around him' and that, at least, would have recommended him to us and we would have claimed him as our own.[13]

The Moneylenders Act, originally sponsored by the only Jewish TD in Dáil Éireann, was eventually put on the statute-books in 1933. This did something to undermine, but not to eradicate, a popular prejudice that the 'Jew' was the 'culprit' yet again.

The state, meanwhile, had granted financial support to Rabbi Herzog to provide for the growing educational needs of his community. During the latter years of the Cosgrave administration, the Jewish community had set up a committee, led by the minister of the Adelaide Road congregation, Rev. Abraham Gudansky, and the indefatigable Arthur Newman, to address the matter. They first approached the Minister for Education, John Marcus O'Sullivan. The interviews were arranged by the Jewish civil servant, Robert Kahan. The Cumann na nGaedheal government approved a grant to cover one-third of the cost of £10,000 for a school. A site was found in Bloomfield Avenue in Dublin in 1931, where it was also decided to build an assembly hall. The total cost would be £12,000, of which the government would pay £4,000. Arthur Newman acted as chairman of the building committee and Bernard Shillman was honorary secretary. On 19 December 1932, Newman laid the foundation stone. Four cornerstones were laid by Dr George Wigoder, David Cohen, Joseph Zlotover and Isaac Tomkin. Chief Rabbi Herzog and Rev. Gudansky led the prayers which preceded the ceremony. A reception was held later that day at the Rathmines town hall at which Herzog thanked the Jewish community for their generosity. Zion Schools were officially opened on 25 March 1934. A portrait by David Hillman of Arthur Newman, who had been the main driving force behind the project, hung in the assembly hall.[14]

Dublin Corporation recognised *Shehitah* – the traditional Jewish method of slaughtering livestock for human consumption – in 1934, following an intervention by Herzog who argued the case convincingly before the authorities. Kosher butchers were permitted, under the new bye-law, to cut the throat of the animal. An abattoir was built for the use of the Jewish community.[15] But despite the passage of the bye-law, ritual slaughter remained in the 1930s a target for anti-Semitic jibes.

The Jewish community were fortunate to enjoy such a high quality of leadership in the early 1930s, something that was recognised internationally. The president of the World Zionist Organisation, Nahum Sokolow, visited Dublin in May 1933.[16] He was received at Dún Laoghaire by the local treasurer of the Jewish Agency, William Nurock, and by the president of the women's section, Mrs Leventhal.[17] Sokolow had visited Dublin seven years before. On that occasion he expressed pleasure that the Jewish community stood in high repute with their fellow citizens and that men and women of eminence in the arts and in commerce in the city were Irish-born Jews. He also singled out for praise the work in Palestine of William Nurock's son, Max. Sokolow was received on that occasion by the Governor General and by the President of the Executive Council, William T. Cosgrave.[18]

Herzog, Newman and Briscoe were among those who accompanied Sokolow to a meeting with Eamon de Valera at Government Buildings in 1933. They had an hour-long interview, during which de Valera promised that the Irish Free State would use its good offices to have the issue of Jewish settlers in Palestine raised at the League of Nations.[19] A public reception was held in Sokolow's honour at the Oak Room of the Mansion House, and before departing he also addressed a meeting of the Zionist Youth in the Shelbourne Hotel.[20] He left Dublin with a very favourable impression of de Valera and the vigour of the local Jewish community. Briscoe, who sided with Zionist revisionists, kept the leader of the Irish government informed about the Palestinian question.[21] He accompanied de Valera on a visit to Israel in 1950 where they met Prime Minister Ben Gurion.

By the early 1930s, Herzog's leadership had helped give greater confidence and cohesion to the Jewish community in a new state. He had seen the Adelaide Road Synagogue undergo renovation and extension. He had successfully encouraged the opening of the Greenville Hall Synagogue. State funding had been received for a Jewish school. The Jewish community was strongly represented in business, in the professions, in the academic world and in the arts. However, Herzog found it reassuring to have his close friend Eamon de Valera in government at a time when minority elements in Irish society, too, manifested aspects of the intolerance of the anti-Semitic movement in Europe. Herzog remained confident that in de Valera's Ireland anti-Jewish prejudice would not become part of official government policy any more than it had been in the Cosgrave decade. Compared with the growing climate of intolerance in continental Europe, the two states on the island provided a reassuring and relatively tranquil environment in the early

1930s. But still, life for religious minorities – and the Jews in particular – was not without its difficulties and, on occasions, a sense of menace.

Catholicism and sources of anti-Semitism in Ireland

From whatever source anti-Semitism might emanate, Herzog and the leaders of the Jewish community confronted that menace by private representations to the relevant church or state authorities. That was the preferred course of action. Public statements were made by the leaders of the community only when absolutely necessary. The constraints imposed by such an approach did not recommend themselves to some of the younger generation of Jews.[22]

In the 1930s some 62 per cent (9.5 million) of the world's Jewish population of 15.3 million lived in Europe where the forces of fascism and Nazism took a firm hold. The largest Jewish communities were in the east; Poland had a population of 3 million Jews, the European part of the Soviet Union had 2.5 million, Romania had 980,000, and there were about 255,000 in the three Baltic states. There were 565,000 Jews in Germany, 445,000 in Hungary, 357,000 in Czechoslovakia, 250,000 in Austria, 300,000 in Great Britain, 225,000 in France, and 160,000 in the Netherlands.[23] In contrast, there were less than 4,000 Jews in Ireland. But even if the Jewish community in Ireland in the 1930s was very small, that did not prevent an undertow of hostility and – in some cases – naked anti-Semitism from emerging.

The first source of concern were the popular Catholic journals and newspapers which carried radical anti-Jewish articles. The *Irish Catholic,* the *Catholic Bulletin*, the *Irish Mind,* the *Irish Rosary* and the *Cross* wrote often about the subversive influence of Moscow, linking Jews to the spread of communism in many articles and editorials. Two writers in particular, the Holy Ghost priest Denis Fahey and the Jesuit Edward Cahill, gave Herzog cause for concern. Both depicted the Jew as being responsible for the moral corruption of western society and for the fomenting of world revolution.

Professor of theology in the Holy Ghost Fathers' seminary at Kimmage, Dublin, Fahey's theories were part of a broader right-wing continental Catholic tradition which had so profoundly influenced the Limerick Redemptorist, Fr John Creagh, during his priestly formation at the end of the nineteenth century. Fahey was ever-conscious of the influence of freemasons, Jews and communists in the plotting of world conspiracy. He was also ever-mindful of the alleged hidden hand of Jews in the economic, political and moral subversion of Irish society.[24] He was a prodigious writer, and may have written even more but for the fact that he eventually ran into difficulties with the ecclesiastical censor.[25] While his writings had some popular influence in Ireland, they were not viewed with sympathy by de Valera's government.[26]

Fahey argued that the 'real forces behind Bolshevism in Russia are Jewish forces' and that communism was 'the most recent development in the age-long struggle waged by the Jewish Nation against the Supernatural Messias, our Lord Jesus Christ'. Despite questioning the authenticity of the Protocols of the Elders of Zion, he continued to cite that spurious document in his work.[27] In his book *The Mystical Body of Christ in the Modern World*, Fahey laid out the contrasting programmes of Catholicism and international Jewry:

PROGRAMME OF CHRIST THE KING THROUGH HIS MYSTICAL BODY, THE CATHOLIC CHURCH	PROGRAMME OF THE JEWISH NATION SINCE THE REJECTION OF CHRIST BEFORE PILATE AND ON CALVARY
FIRSTLY	FIRSTLY
I) *The Catholic Church, Supernatural and Supranational*, is the *One Way* established by God for the ordered return of human beings to Him. All States and Nations are bound to acknowledge it as such, and all men of nations are called upon to enter it as Members of Christ.	(I) *The Jewish Nation* under the *Natural Messias* will establish union among the nations. That necessarily involves aiming at the elimination of every vestige of the Supernatural Life that comes from Christ.
SECONDLY	SECONDLY
II) *The Catholic Church* is the *solely divinely-appointed Guardian* of the whole moral law, natural and revealed.	(II) *The Jewish Nation* under the *Natural Messias* will decide what is moral and what is immoral.
THIRDLY	THIRDLY
(III) *Christian Marriage*, the foundation of the Christian Family, as the Symbol of the union of Christ and His Mystical Body, is *One and Indissoluble*.	(III) *Divorce and Polygamy* will take the place of Christian Marriage.
FOURTHLY	FOURTHLY
(IV) *Children* must be educated as *Members of Christ's Mystical Body*, so that they may be able to look at everything, nationality included, from that standpoint.	(IV) As the doctrine of membership of Christ is a corruption of the true Jewish message to the world, *all trace of membership of Christ and of the Supernatural Life of Grace must be eliminated from education*. Non-Jews must be trained to accept submission to the Jewish Nation, and non-Jewish nationality must not conflict with Jewish world-wide supremacy.
FIFTHLY	FIFTHLY
(V) *Ownership of property* should be *widely diffused*, in order to facilitate families in procuring a sufficiency of material goods for their members. Unions of owners and workers in Guilds will reflect the solidarity of the Mystical Body of Christ.	(V) Complete *Socialization of property*, either in the form of ownership of everything by the State or by the relatively few financiers who control the State, must be aimed at. *Ownership of property*, especially in land, makes for independence, *so it must be eliminated*.

SIXTHLY

(VI) *The Monetary System* of a country is meant to be *at the service of production* in view of the virtuous life of Members of Christ in happy families.

SIXTHLY

(VI) Money is the instrument by which State-control or State-socialization is brought about. Instead of the correct order of finance for production and production for Members of Christ, *men must be subservient to production and production to finance*. State-control can be maintained by means of financial control.[28]

His central historical thesis is summarised thus in his own words:

> The spread of the spirit of the French Revolution has caused the Rights of God to be obscured. They must be unequivocally proclaimed, and the Divine Plan for order through membership of Christ made known. We have to undo the triumphs of Judaeo-Masonic Naturalism and guide aright the national reactions that have come or are coming everywhere against the domination of the two naturalistic Internationalisms of Jewry and Freemasonry.[29]

Fahey also wrote about the alleged 'dual citizenship' of the Jew, a charge that had been made in earlier anti-Semitic literature published in Ireland. Intent on domination, according to Fahey, Jews 'entertain considerable contempt for the national patriotism of non-Jews, though in public pronouncements they may pander to it for the sake of their own interests'. The situation was much more straightforward for an Irishman, according to Fahey:

> The primary allegiance of an Irishman, who has become a citizen of the United States, is to the United States. He may retain his sympathies with Irish national aspirations, but to put it mildly, he is not imbued from birth with the idea that the Irish nation is destined to rule over the Americans and all other nations.[30]

Fahey argued that the

> naturalistic adventure upon which Europe embarked on the French Revolution has been disastrous for the nations of Western Europe, for it has simply meant, as we have seen, that they have allowed the Jewish Nation to impose its national form upon them and thus bring about their downfall and decay.[31]

The Jesuit Edward Cahill was a strong proponent of views similar to those held by Fahey. The founder of Catholic Action (An Rioghacht) in 1927, he sought unsuccessfully to establish it throughout the country.[32] Supporters used the pages of the *Irish Mind* as a vehicle to popularise their thoughts. The organisation founded *Outlook* in 1932 but it failed within a year. Other short-lived Catholic Action publications followed: *Up and Doing* in 1934, *Prosperity* in 1935 and *Hibernia,* which was taken over by the Knights of Columbanus, in 1936.[33] Cahill was a prolific writer. His major work, *The*

Framework of a Christian State, was published in 1932.[34] Cahill, like Fahey, was concerned about the legacy of the French Revolution and the spread of liberalism in Europe.[35] In his sermons and writings, he sought to provide an alternative model to liberal capitalism, and he identified freemasons in particular as an obstacle to the achievement of that objective.[36] Independence, he believed, had presented the Irish people with an opportunity:

> The people of the Irish nation have now in large part regained the owner-ship of the land; and over the greater portion of the country have also secured a very large measure of political independence. Their religious faith and fervour being what they are, what was impossible during the last four centuries is feasible under the new political conditions, namely, to in-augurate a social reconstruction on a definitely Irish and Catholic basis.[37]

But it was necessary to be vigilant against the advance of socialism and against the 'predominance of capitalist interests among the Judaeo-Masonic leaders'.[38] He blamed Jews for the contamination of western society through their 'control' of the international press and cinema:

> The great capitalist Press of the United States, England, Germany and France, is now almost entirely controlled by the great Jewish Inter-national financiers. Of the papers not directly owned by Jews, Jewish influence usually predominates in the management. In such cases the editor or art critics or principal foreign correspondents, or all of these, usually are Jewish.

Cahill continued:

> Not only what is called the Capitalistic Press, but even the Socialistic Press of the world, is in large part owned and controlled by Jewish financiers. . . . What is said here of the Press applies with equal or greater force to the Cinema; practically all of which over the two continents of Europe and America is in the hands of the Jews.[39]

Cahill was a friend of Eamon de Valera.[40] Despite this, however, the Fianna Fáil government did not heed any of his anti-Semitic ideas. Fahey's writings had even less political impact. While de Valera and his cabinet colleagues were no admirers of aspects of their British political inheritance, they were supportive of the liberal democratic philosophy on which the Irish Free State was founded.

The Blueshirts movement, founded by General Eoin O'Duffy who had been sacked as commissioner of the Garda Síochána in 1933, was a second area of potential concern to the Jewish community. Its failure to become a mass movement was as welcome to Herzog as it was a disappointment to those in Berlin and Rome who viewed Ireland as fertile ground for the sowing of fascist and authoritarian ideas. O'Duffy – who was never elected to Dáil Éireann – was the 'duce'. Dressed in paramilitary-style beret, blue shirt and dark trousers or skirt, the Blueshirts chose the cross of St Patrick as their insignia.[41] Blueshirtism attempted to build a coalition among the anti-Fianna Fáil parties by seeking to combine the ideologies of nationalism, Catholic corporatism and fascism.[42] Pius XI's *Quadragesimo Anno* and Benito Mussolini's corporatism were both viewed as models. Cumann na nGaedheal changed its name to Fine Gael and became the party of the Blueshirts. That new departure in Irish politics did not enjoy the support of William T. Cosgrave, who remained throughout the leader of the parliamentary party.

The organisation's newspaper, the *Blueshirt,* displayed tinges of xenophobia. On 8 June 1935, a contributor expressed the hope that 'when a Blueshirt Government is elected its first act will be to send all the foreign exploiters who have come in here during the past 12 or 13 years back to the land or lands of their birth'.[43] But the writer rejected charges that the organisation was anti-Semitic:

> I suppose there are not many who are silly enough to believe that the National Guard [one of a number of names adopted by the Blueshirts] is Nazi or anti-Semite. It is true that the new Constitution confines membership to Irishmen who profess the Christian Faith. . . . It is definitely a Christian organisation to those who are Christians, but it is not out to persecute, injure or attack those who are not Christian.[44]

Although the Blueshirts attracted individuals who were anti-Semitic, the leadership continued to claim that the organisaton did not subscribe to such views. However, the leadership of the Irish Jewish community was sufficiently worried for Arthur Newman to write to the former Minister for Finance, Ernest Blythe – a Presbyterian and a most enthusiastic supporter of the fascistoid organisation – seeking clarification about the nature of the Blueshirts. Blythe completely disavowed any association of the Fine Gael party with anti-Semitism. Writing on 29 October 1934, he assured Newman that 'your apprehensions concerning the attitude of the United Ireland Party [Fine Gael] towards the Jewish community in the Irish Free State are quite unfounded'.[45] Blythe stated that his party stood 'for toleration and full liberty for all law-abiding citizens of every denomination'. Fine Gael had never discriminated between persons of different religious beliefs in their treatment as citizens and never intended to do so.[46] Blythe said his party believed that every person who conformed to the law of the state was entitled to the full enjoyment of the privilege of citizenship without any discrimination. He said the rumour that Fine Gael intended to propagate a 'campaign of victimisation against the members of any community is absurd and malicious'.[47] A month earlier – on 21 September 1934 – O'Duffy had resigned as president of Fine Gael.[48] The National Corporate Party was founded in June 1935 by a remnant loyal to O'Duffy. That, too, ended in farce. The Jewish community did not weep over its early demise.

Unlike some other European countries during the 1930s, anti-Semitism was never permitted to become a defining feature of Irish Catholic culture. Frank Duff, the founder in the 1920s of the popular Catholic lay organisation the Legion of Mary, was an able defender of the Jewish community, as was his civil servant friend, León Ó Broin. Both men were very sensitive to the ignorance, the ambivalence and the prejudice towards Jews to be found in much Irish popular Catholic literature. They represented a tolerant strand in

Irish society, a strand of thought shared by a Dr Moody, the writer of a 1938 Catholic Truth Society pamphlet entitled *Why are the Jews Persecuted?*[49] The text systematically disposed of many of the arguments which had received such widespread attention in the popular Catholic press:

> The attitude of many towards the people of Israel may be summed up thus: 'Let them cease to be as they are, and we will like them.' We might as well say to the man: 'Stop being six feet tall, and I will care for you.' Just as a man's height is conditioned by the law of growth, so a people's character is moulded by their history, and traits can be broken down only by that same slow process by which they were introduced.[50]

The writer further emphasised:

> To deny the actuality of the forces which determined the formation of the Jewish soul is to deny the obvious testimony of history. To pass strict moral judgement upon a people who have been bred in the bitter cauldron of hate and oppression is to neglect the basic laws of justice and charity. It is far more reasonable to try to understand the modern Jew in the light of the conditions which have shaped him. Nor is it beside the point to insist that, not only is this the rational view, but it is the only one consistent with the high principles of our Christian faith.[51]

The idea that Jews were predisposed to radicalism was challenged:

> Can you imagine our indignation if someone attacked us for the activities of an Azaña [Spanish republican] or a Cárdenas [Mexican republican], both of whom are baptized Catholics? What would be our response were we to be accused, because the radicals there happen to have come from Catholic parents, of trying to overthrow civilisation in Spain? Yet the Jews who support communism have rejected both the Jewish religion and every other distinguishing mark of their people.[52]

Dr Moody argued that nationalism had replaced religious and economic factors as the root cause of anti-Semitism:

> It is not hard to see that the same complaints formulated by the ardent nationalists against the Jews apply equally to ourselves. Whatever a Catholic may think of the Jews, he cannot escape the fact that he and the Jews have a common enemy in extreme nationalism. . . . Nationalism has reached a point in its evolution in which it is equally dangerous to the Jewish and the Christian concept of life . . . [53]

Chief rabbi defends his community

The *Cross*, published by the Passionist Fathers in Dublin, carried a letter in May 1934 from Liam Ua Cheannfhaolaidh which laid down a challenge to Herzog. The chief rabbi had repeatedly said that the attempt to link Jews and communism was one of the most outrageous libels ever invented; the letter writer did not agree: 'Notwithstanding the protests of the Chief Rabbi in

Dublin, volumes could be written to show that the Jews lead the Communist and Masonic bodies.'[54] This charge was added to by the managing editor of the *Cross*, Fr Edmund Burke, who spread fear about the increase in the Jewish population:

> The anti-Jewish movement on the Continent has brought a large influx of Jews to Ireland. They have been received with kindliness and hospitality. Has the policy of peaceful penetration begun? Everybody speaks of it in private, but few dare mention it in public. Why? Is our country already enmeshed in the net of the International Judaeo-Masonic alliance?[55]

Herzog drafted a detailed response to the magazine in which he rebutted the accusation that the socialist movement was almost entirely controlled by Jews.

> The fundamental principles of Socialism were originally propounded and advocated by the Englishman Robert Owen, the Frenchmen Baboeuf, St Simon, and Fourier, and the Germans von Thuenen and Weitling – all non-Jews. Karl Marx was simply the systematiser, and although he was born a Jew he was baptised at the age of six, brought up as a Christian, and never had any associations with the Jewish community or came under Jewish influence. Engels was not even born a Jew: he was born and died a Christian.[56]

The chief rabbi also rejected the linking of Jews to international finance: 'The remark about "Jewish International Finance" controlling and guiding "Communist and Revolutionary propaganda" is the sheerest nonsense that cannot deceive any intelligent person.'[57] He then issued a word of caution:

> You conclude by referring to the persecution of the Jews now raging on the Continent. May I remind you that the same power that is scourging the Jews in Germany is also persecuting the adherents of the Catholic Church ... Is it not time that you discarded belief in the bogey of an 'international Judaeo-Masonic alliance' and all the hocus-pocus engendered by fanatical imaginations reminiscent of the worst passions of the Middle Ages? Happily, not all Catholics are minded as you are.[58]

Herzog deemed the matter serious enough to write to Archbishop Edward Byrne of Dublin.[59] Pointing out that an article in the *Cross* was putting forward sentiments that were liable to 'sow the seeds of hatred', Herzog said he believed it was contrary to the principles of the Catholic Church to foster anti-Semitism, which, as the example of Germany was showing, logically turned first against the Old Testament and in sheer consistency would end up by turning against Christianity.[60] He wanted the archbishop 'to put an end to nascent anti-Semitism sheltering itself under the *Cross*'.[61]

Whether the archbishop wrote a restraining letter to the *Cross* is not known, but the magazine printed the chief rabbi's letter with an unrepentant rejoinder: 'Whilst it is true that many of the principles of Socialism are to be found in the writings of the men mentioned by Dr Herzog, the real founders of Socialism as well as its most ardent apostles have been Jews.'[62]

One of the sections most offensive to Herzog in the reply referred to the Jews in Germany:

> The Chief Rabbi's reference to the 'pretexts' given for the ill-treatment of the Jews in Germany is particularly unfortunate. A writer in the *Catholic Bulletin* (June, 1934, p. 476) gives a useful summary of the situation. The Jews in Germany 'had used the power which they attained under the Weimar Constitution in a ruthless drive to repeat their Muscovite success, to create in Germany a second commanding Marxist State in which, as in Russia, they would be *uber alles*. Their activities make sinister history. . . . It is not suggested that all German Jews were either Socialists or Communists, but the leaders of both movements have been Jews.' A volume of evidence is available to substantiate the above indictment.[63]

Much of Herzog's time in the 1930s was spent having to track and refute such sentiments.

There were other isolated examples of anti-Semitism. An envelope was opened in early 1935 in the offices of the Commission of Inquiry into Banking, Currency and Credit which was addressed in Irish to 'Guggenheim and Jacobson's people'. The undated contents, signed by Conor MacNessa, read in translation: 'If you do not leave Ireland soon you will be shot. Death to Judah.' The letter included a printed excerpt from a speech by Hitler.[64] This remark has to be seen in the context of attempts by some people associated with Irish fascist organisations to foment anti-Semitic feelings in the country aided and supported by elements in the German and Italian legations.[65]

Charles Bewley and the Berlin legation

The Herzog debate with the *Cross* prompts the question: how well informed was the Irish government in the 1930s about the growth of anti-Semitism in continental Europe? Apart from published sources, the government depended for information upon the Irish diplomatic service which was very small in number. In 1935, there were missions in Paris, Geneva (League of Nations), Berlin, Madrid, the Vatican, London and Washington. There was no Irish envoy accredited to the Italian government until 1938. The Irish envoy in Berlin, Charles Bewley – whose anti-Semitism in the early 1920s was discussed in chapter 3 – occupied a central position in that chain of communication. Unfortunately many of his despatches on the treatment of the Jews were more in the nature of an uncritical recitation of National Socialist doctrine than informed, analytical reportage.[66]

Before he had had an opportunity to present his credentials in August 1933, Bewley, in an interview with a Berlin paper, contrasted Nazi Germany with the Weimar Republic and added that 'one can perceive a new hope in the people' under Hitler.[67] He immediately sought to distance himself from the anti-Nazi views of his predecessor, Daniel Binchy, who had – following his retirement from the Irish diplomatic service – publicly criticised Hitler and National Socialism in print.[68] Presenting his credentials to

President Hindenburg on 31 August, Bewley spoke of the 'national rebirth' of Germany.[69]

Many envoys representing democracies in Hitler's Berlin did not attend the annual Nazi Party rally at Nuremberg. Bewley pointedly did so until he was replaced in 1939. On 4 September 1933, after attending two major National Socialist rallies, Bewley reported that Hitler was 'incomparably the finest orator that I have heard'.[70] He was impressed by the devotion of the masses to one man: 'It is a personal devotion hard to realise by those who have not come into personal contact with it', he wrote.[71] While such initial enthusiasm might have reflected lack of experience on his part, he had had time to adjust his thinking when he wrote his memoirs in the 1950s:

> For myself I needed no argument to convince me that National Socialism whatever might be its defects, should be upheld by the Western Powers as the strongest, perhaps the only, force which could prevent the spread of the Communist Empire over half Europe – and sufficient events have more than sufficiently confirmed my view.[72]

Did Bewley count the Holocaust merely as one of the 'defects' of National Socialism?

Bewley's anti-Semitism pervaded his reports to Dublin. He reported on 19 February 1934, for example, on a speech by the Minister of the Interior, Dr Wilhelm Frick, on the 'race' question:

> It was noticeable that Dr Frick, again no doubt in view of his audience,[73] did not say a word about the 'demoralising' influence of the Jews in the press, literature, the stage, etc., which forms the bulk of anti-Jewish propaganda. This thesis is best summed up in a book by Rosenberg entitled 'Der Sumpf' (The Morass) in which quotations of indecent, unpatriotic, or blasphemous character are given from the works of prominent Jews.[74]

Bewley then made comments upon two other questions not dealt with by Frick – 'the large Jewish emporiums and marriage between Jews and Germans'.[75] He reported that the SA had been instructed in many districts not to deal with Jewish businesses, though no action had as yet been taken against them because to do so would disturb the economic situation and throw a large number of Christians out of employment: 'It is anticipated that in time they will probably be compelled to go out of their business in its present form.'[76] Bewley also predicted that marriage between Jews and Aryans would be forbidden, 'and it undoubtedly would be in harmony with the opinions of the vast majority of Germans today'.[77] Whether that would apply to baptised Jews would depend upon the circumstances, he said.[78] It is worth noting that Bewley's observations were based upon a conversation with 'an influential member of the Berlin police' who informed him that

> in the inspections which his force makes of the various cabarets and places of entertainment in Berlin, special attention is paid to German women seen in the company of Jews, and that in many cases they are kept in the police-station for the night, as a reminder of their duty to the race.[79]

His informant had also referred to 'the project of insisting that all Jews, particularly the baptised ones, should bear distinctively Jewish names, so that Christians should not marry or deal with them under any misapprehension'.[80] Bewley's informant may have been none other than Hermann Göring, about whom he later wrote a partisan biography.[81]

Reporting at length on the internal situation on 11 May 1934, Bewley argued that 'it would be an absolute error' to suppose that anti-Semitism was 'imposed' by Hitler on the German people:

> I have not the slightest doubt that it was one of the most popular planks in the programme of the National Socialist party and brought it more recruits and votes than perhaps any other item. But the Government, on coming to power, found it necessary on economic grounds to leave untouched the vast majority of Jews in Germany, who are living exactly as they did before, though excluded from some public positions.[82]

It was simply not accurate to report that Jews were 'living exactly as they did before' in Germany in May 1934.

Bewley argued that Jews were left untouched in order to conciliate foreign opinion, and said that Nazi Party members had, for the same reason, been disciplined for attacks on Jews. Such a modification in the original programme of eradicating the Jews from the life of the country was undoubtedly the cause of considerable dissatisfaction, Bewley reported, but there were indications that the policy against the Jews might be carried further: 'whatever opposition it might meet within the "upper classes", it would certainly be extremely popular with the workingman', he told Dublin.[83]

Bewley explained on 6 June 1934 the background to German policies against the Jews, which, he added, represented the 'belief of a very large number (I think personally a great majority) of the German people'. The three beliefs, according to Bewley, were:

1. the Jews 'regard themselves as a special "chosen" race, or, as it is expressed in the Talmud, they regard themselves as men, and non-Jews as only equivalent to animals. . . . No Jew is bound by any duty towards a non-Jew (i.e., he may injure him in body or goods or misuse non-Jewish women without any sin).'[84]
2. the Jew, being 'in no way bound by the ordinary moral law (whether Christian or Germanic) in his relations with non-Jews, is a pernicious influence if permitted to associate on equal terms' as he 'will live by usury, embezzlement, etc., or by catering for the vices of his non-Jewish neighbours (white slave traffic, immoral literature and theatre, etc.)'.[85]
3. the Jew 'is hostile to non-Jewish patriotism and to non-Jewish religion and morals. He therefore strives to destroy both when allowed into positions of power or influence. Cf. the last fifteen years in Germany.'[86]

Based on these beliefs, the German authorities had concluded that the Jew

> must therefore be removed from all positions enabling him to exercise this demoralising influence, e.g., judge, professor, lawyer, doctor, etc. His

economic power must also be limited, so as to prevent his virtual enslave-
ment of the peasantry by usurious mortgages, etc.[87]

Bewley told Dublin that all the measures taken by the German government
to date had been based on 'this theory', adding that, if the premises were
admitted, it was 'only logical for the government to take steps to eliminate an
influence ex hypothesi so fatal to the race'.[88]

He reported that while the question of ritual murder was not essential to
the theory, 'it is often adduced in support of it, and is fairly generally believed
in, not only Germany, but in Poland, Hungary, Russia and other Eastern
countries'.[89] He continued: 'This belief is held, to my own knowledge, by
many well educated and intelligent people.'[90] He sent literature to Dublin
dealing with the matter:

> In the circumstances, on the assumption that ritual murders do not in
> fact take place, it seems regrettable that the Jewish authorities do not deal
> more circumstantially with the very detailed charges made. A general
> denial or denunciation of 'medieval superstition' is an unsatisfactory
> method of meeting accusations which give dates and names, nor does it
> explain why at all periods and in all countries this particular charge
> should have been fastened to the Jewish race alone.[91]

Bewley did not report what was happening to Jews in Germany. He had
personally absorbed the arguments of the National Socialists and made them
his own. A professional diplomat would have felt obliged to report that the
Nazis had set up concentration camps immediately after coming to power in
1933 at Dachau in the south, Esterwegen in the north-west, Sachsenhausen
in the north-east and Sachsenburg in the west.[92]

In the summer of 1935, Bewley reported on the growing hostility to the
Jewish community.[93] On 26 July, he wrote about statistics which purported
to show that the percentage of crime committed by Jews in Germany was
proportionately much higher than their 1 per cent of the population.[94] The
codification of anti-Semitism in the Nuremberg laws of 1935 did not come as
a surprise to Bewley. Neither was he very sympathetic to the Jews' plight: 'As
the Chancellor has pointed out, it amounts to the making of the Jews into a
national minority; and as they themselves claim to be a separate race, they
should have nothing to complain of.'[95] Bewley, reporting on the prohibition of
marriage between German Aryans and Christian Jews, said the measure was
justified 'by the frequent practice of Jews of becoming nominal Christians for
material reasons: the example of the Jews in Spain in the Middle Ages is very
frequently quoted'.[96] Reporting on the law prohibiting the employment of
non-Jewish females under the age of forty-five in Jewish homes, he said it
was justified by the very grave moral danger to the employees in question:
'certainly a perusal of the criminal reports in the German press would make
it appear that the danger was not in any way exaggerated', he commented.[97]

The *Irish Press* and the *Irish Times*, using agency copy, reported on the
Nuremberg laws more objectively than did Bewley.[98] The *Irish Times*, for
example, stated in an editorial entitled 'A Jewish free land' on 12 September
1935:

> The resolve of the Hitlerites to bring about the complete elimination of Jewry from German life makes it essential that some refuge shall be provided for the victims of Nazi fury; and civilised people in every country would welcome an arrangement that would provide a means of escape for them.[99]

Generally speaking, the prevailing opinion throughout the 1930s in the Irish government was not unsympathetic to the plight of Jews on the continent. But, while Bewley's reports did not influence de Valera's policies, as Irish envoy in Berlin he could exercise considerable personal authority – without reference to his superiors in Dublin – over the reception of, and advice given to, prospective Jewish refugees.

The case of Julius Pokorny

Reading Bewley's sanitised reports, it is difficult to sense the immediacy of the menace and the institutionalised violence which characterised the Nazi regime. Although travel to the continent from Ireland was not as frequent as it later became, the professional classes in Dublin were kept very well informed about the growing anti-Semitic climate in Europe. Academic contact with the continent was particularly strong in subjects such as folklore, Celtic studies and languages. The case of Julius Pokorny, a distinguished Celtic scholar from Prague, provides an example of the nightmare which befell so many academics affected by Germany's anti-Semitic laws. In his case, the outcome did not have a tragic ending. Good fortune allowed him to escape from Germany to Switzerland in 1943 and survive the war.[100] Pokorny's case illustrates both the extent to which his predicament was known to his academic colleagues in Dublin and also the willingness of de Valera's government to help scholars who found themselves the victims of Hitler's racial laws.

Pokorny had succeeded to Professor Kuno Meyer's chair of Celtic in Berlin in 1920. But after speaking out in defence of a colleague, Ernst Lewy, he became the target of police investigations in 1933 and finally lost his chair in the wake of the Nuremberg laws in 1935. He wrote to the director of the National Library in Dublin, Richard Irvine Best, on 5 May 1933 explaining the background to his problems:

> This Easter I got a form from the Government, asked to give particulars about my grandparents. To my astonishment my father informed me, that my mother's father had not been 'Aryan'. He had died before I was born and I had never known it. According to a new law, everybody, *one* grandparent of whom is a Jew, is looked upon as Jew and to be dismissed from his office, except if he has fought in the war or been in office before August 1914. Though a lecturer since April 1914, *I have been suspended from office.*[101]

Pokorny said that he had been in contact with the Irish chargé in Berlin, Leo T. McCauley, who had sent his full particulars to Dublin. He sought to have the Irish government intervene on his behalf and he had given Best's name as a reference. The case being made was that 'my person was an important link between Ireland and Germany'.[102] He warned Best to 'please remember that any anti-German propaganda may ruin me'.[103] He admonished in a covering note on 4 May not to write to him directly.[104]

If the Irish government intervened – and it is probable that they did so – Pokorny still had not been reinstated by October 1933. Writing in the middle of that month, he told Best that he had gone through 'terrible weeks'. He had not had any disagreeable personal experiences

> but to be suddenly an outcast is no pleasant experience. You know, that according to German law everybody with even *one* non-Aryan grandparent is treated exactly like a Jew! I am still suspended from office, but I get my salary as usual, a definite settlement is probably being put off until the end of the winter term.[105]

Charles Bewley, who had arrived in Berlin between the sending of the letters, was described by Pokorny as being '*very much* in favour of the Nazis as you probably know. When writing to me, please don't ever mention German politics!'[106]

Pokorny wrote to Best again on 27 December 1933 stating that he had been restored to his office: 'I am sure I owe a lot to the interventions from Banba, and I wish to thank you, too, for all the business shown to me in those days.'[107] Two years later he told Best that his position had been saved 'by the intervention of the Irish government'.[108] In an undated letter (perhaps early 1934) to Best from Bologna, Italy – which he ordered him to burn after he had read it – he wrote:

> In the meantime I have been worried and at present on my honeymoon in Italy. To be alone is not nice in these uncertain times. So far I have never been molested. I got reinstated 'owing to the service done to German science', but after all I count as a Non-Aryan and nobody knows what will happen after Hindenburg's death. There is general talk still of stricter revolutionary and 'Aryan' measures.[109]

Pokorny's academic post survived for two more years. His marriage, however, did not. He was divorced in October 1934 having, as he explained to Best, 'fallen in love with a most beautiful and charming woman and married her too fast'.[110]

But the Nuremberg laws had changed his situation for the worst. Pokorny wrote to Best in October 1935 outlining his fears:

> As regards my chair, I am afraid, scientific considerations have nothing to do with it. It is merely a question of 'blood and race'. By the way, the paper by Krogmann is rubbish, but I had to take it, since he is an important member of the Party. So is Muhlhausen, Professor of Celtic in Hamburg, older than I am, though he is no good at all, has published nothing but a worthless vocabulary to the Mabinogion. . . . I am afraid everything will have been in vain. Yesterday I got orders to give strict account of my great-grandparents. They just may spare me, for diplomatic reasons, but I have no great hopes.[111]

He warned Best:

> Now, in replying, please be very careful not to say anything that may hint
> at the suspicion, that I had complained about Germany. Also, for heaven's
> sake, be careful in talking to friends – a little slip, and they have spies
> everywhere. Nobody ought to guess that I am not completely happy. It is
> too dangerous![112]

Pokorny was suspended in the middle of November and pensioned off
towards the end of December.

He wrote to Best on 1 May 1936 warning him to be careful about discussing the content of the letter with anyone 'as it may land me in prison'.
He wrote that about sixty to seventy scholars had lately been deprived of
their chairs 'but not a line appeared about it in any of the newspapers'.
Pokorny explained how, when he had been approached by a journalist from
Reuters bureau, he had phoned the dean in his university who replied: 'I
forbid you to talk about your deposition, it is an internal affair (!!)'.[113] The
journalist then went to the ministry and was told that Pokorny had been
'deposed with all the others, but they hoped "to keep me"'. However, a few
weeks before he wrote this letter to Best in May 1936, Pokorny heard that
the ministry had asked the dean to convoke a commission about his chair:

> They all agreed, there was nobody to fill it, only our new Dean a Sanskrit
> professor from Bonn rose up and said Muhlhausen was an 'excellent
> man'!! Since both are storm-troopers and since he could not know
> anything about him, it is clear, that he had been asked to look after the
> interests of the Party.[114]

And he did. Pokorny continued to live a precarious existence in Germany.
Further efforts by the Irish government to get him out of Germany before
and during the war failed. Fortunately, he survived.

Two general conclusions may be drawn from Pokorny's case. Firstly, the
academic world in Dublin had been alerted very early in the 1930s to the
general plight of non-Aryan professors in the German university system, particularly in the areas of folklore, Irish and Celtic studies. Secondly, it may be
inferred from the palpable fear in Pokorny's letters to his close friend Best that
there were those in Irish academic circles who were not to be trusted. That may
have been because they were simply blabber-mouths or because they sympa-
thised with the new political ethos in Germany. Pokorny may have suspected,
in particular, the bona fides of the director of the National Museum, Dr Adolf
Mahr, with whom Best, as director of the nearby National Library, was obliged
to have a close working relationship. Pokorny would have had good reason to
do so. Mahr was the head of the Dublin branch of the National Socialist Party.

Nazi and fascist influence in Dublin

An Austrian, Mahr had been appointed keeper of the Irish antiquities division of the National Museum in September 1927. He was promoted to

director on 16 July 1934. The assistant secretary of the Department of External Affairs, Frederick Boland, described him in 1945 as 'the most active and
fanatical National Socialist in the German colony here'.[115] The head of Irish
military intelligence (G2), Colonel Dan Bryan, minuted in the late 1930s:
'Mahr makes no secret of his activities.'[116] Boland recalled that Mahr had
'organised the German colony's steamboat excursion outside the three-mile
limit in 1936 or 1937 to vote in the National-Socialist plebiscite in that year',
and that he had received from Hitler the title 'Herr Professor' for his zeal.[117]

Mahr richly deserved such a reward. He was, until December 1938, *Gruppenleiter* (group leader) of the Dublin branch of the Nazi Party's
Auslandsorganisation (organisation abroad). The Dublin 'club' was formed
in 1934, and Mahr and his associates sought to make the German director of
the Irish Army School of Music, Colonel Wilhelm Fritz Brase, its first chairman.[118] Brase wrote seeking permission from his superior officer. In a letter
on 14 May 1935, he gave his word that nothing would happen 'which might
be disloyal or detrimental to the interests of the Irish Free State, my adopted
country'. He further assured his military superiors that it was 'a strict and
rigid rule issued by the Reichskanzler Adolf Hitler not to interfere with political and other matters ... [and] not to have any connection whatsoever
with political parties and fascist movements'. He was refused permission.[119]
Brase, like Mahr, was given the title 'Herr Professor' by Hitler.[120]

Mahr instead became leader of the Dublin Nazi group. According to an
Irish military intelligence profile of him, Mahr was 'closely in touch with
German Legation and with Nazi H.Q. in London and German Press Agency
(Deutsches Nachrichtenbüro) in Dublin'.[121] According to Boland, Edouard
Hempel, the German envoy in Dublin since 1937, always had 'a strong dislike
and distrust' of Mahr.[122] That may not have been the case between 1937 and
1939; throughout the 1930s Mahr enjoyed an intimate relationship with the
German legation in Dublin. Mahr was helped in his efforts by his second in
command in the Nazi group, Heinz Mecking, who took over from him at the
end of 1938. Mecking was manager of the Turf Development Board. Others
associated with the Nazi Party in Dublin were Karl Kunstler, Karl Krause,
Otto August Reinhardt (employed in the forestry section of the Department
of Lands) and Robert Stumpf. Throughout the 1930s, Mahr conducted party
meetings in a German social club behind the Court Laundry in Dublin.[123] A
Friends of Germany group met in the Red Bank restaurant in Dublin.

It is difficult to make a direct connection between the activities of Mahr's
group and the spread of anti-Semitism in Dublin. But it is more than probable that the spread of Nazi propaganda had a direct bearing on the
anti-Semitism of radical nationalist groups in Ireland in the 1930s. Mahr was
closely watched by G2, whose head, Colonel Bryan, wrote in December 1945
that Mahr 'was an open and blatant Nazi and made every effort to convert
Irish graduates and other persons with whom he had association, to Nazi
doctrines and beliefs'.[124] As director of the National Museum, he was in a
position to observe as an insider Irish politics and society.

A branch of the Italian Fascist Party, another source of antagonism
towards the Jews, met regularly in Dublin during the 1930s in the premises

of an Italian cafe owner. Although relatively small, the 'Fascio di Dublino Michele D'Angelo', which was part of the Fasci Italiani all'Estero (Italian Fascists Abroad), had a loyal membership. It was led by Count Eduardo Tomacelli from Naples, who came to Dublin in 1935 and took a position at Trinity College as a teacher of Italian.[125] G2 had two intelligence sources in the universities, code-named 'Rome' and 'Paris', and they both supplied information on the activities of both Mahr and Tomacelli to Colonel Bryan.[126] Tomacelli, described in 1938 as the secretary of the Fascist Party in Ireland, was reported by Bryan to be 'hand in glove with the [Italian] Legation'.[127] The assertively pro-fascist activities of Tomacelli and his cronies were a cause of distress to members of the Italian community in the capital who were exiles from the Mussolini regime.

Together Mahr and Tomacelli helped spread the secular gospels of fascism and Nazism in Ireland. As anti-Semitism was an integral part of National Socialist beliefs – and was officially grafted on to Italian fascism after the adoption of the Manifesto of Fascist Racism in July 1938 – Mahr and Tomacelli were duty-bound to proselytise in Dublin. Their most likely targets were radical nationalist cultural groups as well as revolutionary organisations like the IRA, which was weakened significantly after the departure of many left-wing activists to fight in the Spanish Civil War.

Paddy Belton and the Irish Christian Front

The spontaneous reaction of many people in Ireland following the outbreak of the Spanish Civil War in summer 1936 was to support the side led by the insurgent, General Francisco Franco.[128] That war gave rise to strong expressions of confessional fervour which sometimes manifested themselves in anti-Semitic form. Paddy Belton, a former Blueshirt, was to the fore in founding on 21 August 1936 a pro-Franco solidarity group, the Irish Christian Front.[129] This organisation claimed to stand against the 'crimes of Godless capitalism' which were no more attractive 'to the Church of Christ than the crimes of communism'.[130] Besides being a corporatist, Belton was anti-Semitic – evidence of which he had first displayed in Dáil Éireann during the Ethiopian crisis in 1935:

Mr Mac Dermot:	Does the Deputy think the Italians will go and live in Abyssinia?
Mr Belton:	I know the British did not go to live in South Africa, and I remember that war.
Mr Davin:	They got the gold.
Mr Belton:	No, the Jews got it, and I daresay there are Jews there or thereabouts in Abyssinia, too.[131]

The Jews were also 'there or thereabouts' in Spain, according to Belton.

At the end of 1936, Belton gave further evidence of his anti-Semitism, using the issue of the ritual killing of animals for human consumption (*Shehitah*) as his excuse to attack the Jewish community. At a meeting of

Dublin Corporation's board of health in December, he attempted to have the bye-law which permitted this practice rescinded. In moving the motion, Belton produced a letter allegedly received from 'a good Jew' which addressed Belton as 'you pig, you swine, you should be bumped off, your attack on the chosen people will not do you any good'.[132] He attacked Jews in his speech and suggested that communism and Judaism were interchangeable. He also blamed Jews for the Spanish Civil War: 'I can't forget Spain because I don't want to see the Spanish situation brought here. I don't want to see special facilities given to these people who created the situation in Spain, and are doing their damnedest to do the same in Ireland.'[133] A. W. Rollins, supporting the motion, said he believed in 'Ireland for the Irish' and not for anyone else: 'Why should privileges be given to foreigners in this country? It might be said that this was a religious matter, but if cannibals come to this country should they be allowed to eat the people because it was their religion?'[134]

Herzog responded to the attack. He enclosed newspaper cuttings of the board of health debate when he wrote to Archbishop Edward Byrne of Dublin:

> From the enclosed cutting Your Grace will note the rise of an anti-Semitic campaign by Mr Belton, the leader of the Christian Front. The press has not fully reported all the venom which Mr Belton poured out about the unfortunate Jewish people who, after all, are only represented by a negligible number in the country, at most, 6,000 souls in a population of several millions.

Herzog continued, emphasising Belton's use of religion as a cover for his anti-Semitism:

> The whole campaign is simply a disgrace to Catholicism and to Ireland. The trouble really is that Mr Belton is preaching his Jew-hatred and his insulting attitudes towards the Jewish religion under the colours of Christianity. Therein lies the danger, lest, God Forbid, popular passions become inflamed and serious disturbances result as a consequence.[135]

The chief rabbi said that all the talk about Jews and communism was 'a tissue of lies'. There were, of course, people born of the Jewish race who were communists, but so 'there are communists of the Anglo-Saxon, of the Irish race etc.' The overwhelming majority of the Jewish race were not communists, and he thought that, perhaps 'with the exception of one or two', there were no communists among the Jewish community in Ireland.[136] (For the record, one Irish-born Jew, Maurice Levitas, fought on the side of the Spanish Republic.[137]) Herzog appealed to the archbishop to make a pronouncement on the matter since 'Belton is simply re-echoing Nazism and Hitlerism'.

Meanwhile, the former member of the IRA, Frank Ryan, had gone to Spain in 1936 together with other volunteers to fight on the side of the Republican government. Eoin O'Duffy had taken a 'brigade' to fight for Franco.[138] Belton had also travelled to Spain to visit pro-Franco church authorities and the forces of the insurgents. Writing in February 1937 to Cardinal Joseph MacRory, Belton identified as a growing problem in Ireland the 'fact' that the major political parties 'remain passive in the face of Jewish immigration and the export of food to the Reds in Spain'.[139] In a further letter to MacRory on 29 December 1937 he claimed that the situation in Ireland was critical:

> The problem here is bigger and more urgent than many people imagine. The Jews have a stranglehold here and present arrivals mainly consist of those expelled from European countries for their communist activities. They have an international organisation and they control money. They did their job well in Spain and could do it here if not checkmated.[140]

Ironically, MacRory was a close friend and admirer of Chief Rabbi Herzog. He is most unlikely to have been favourably influenced by Belton and the Irish Christian Front, which self-destructed in the early months of 1937. But the undercurrent of anti-Semitism which that organisation represented did not disappear.

Contrary to the anti-Semitic stereotypes held by Belton of the parasitic 'Jew', Herzog and many members of his community had taken a special interest in the question of poverty in the city of Dublin. Following a major exposé in the *Irish Press* in summer 1936, the chief rabbi strongly advocated the establishment of a fund to help do away with the slums. He had been so shocked and mortified with the slum conditions that he had observed in the city that he broke his rule never to issue statements to the press on feast days. In a letter to the *Irish Press* he stated:

> I have been hoping and praying for some time now that some such movement as your newspaper has started, would be launched for the purpose of eradicating the awful slum evil from the city. Dublin, from what I have seen, has the worst slum conditions anywhere in Europe. In my boyhood days in Lomza, Poland, I thought I had seen some horrid slum conditions. Yet now that I compare them with what I daily see in Dublin's tenement sections, they diminish in misery, because there was some air around them for the people to breathe owing to the spacing of that city.[141]

He felt that the Dublin slums were also far worse than what he had seen in Leeds in England, where he had lived for a while as a boy. He was particularly struck by the manner in which the conditions affected the physical, moral and spiritual well-being of children. In a passage that revealed his own deep humanity, he wrote:

> The sight of some of those poor children of the slums is really horrifying. I have no doubt that both the physical growth and the moral and mental development of the children are seriously hampered by these miserable conditions. Who can gauge the tremendous loss this means to the Irish nation and to humanity in general? ... If we are to ensure that our Dublin childhood is to be spiritually healthy we must guarantee clean, decent homes, for a healthy body and a healthy morale can only exist in a clean home.[142]

He encouraged all citizens, irrespective of creed, to unite in seeking a remedy for such an evil.[143] Herzog was a social reformer, and his commitment to Ireland was manifest in the manner in which he had led his community to play the role of exemplary citizens in the new state – completely contrary to the theory on which Bewley had claimed German anti-Semitic doctrine was based.

Herzog leaves Ireland

The measure of Dr Isaac Herzog's achievement in Ireland[144] was reflected in the genuine warmth of the international reception which greeted the news that he had been selected on 1 December 1936 as the next chief rabbi of Palestine, a position which required him to represent that community 'not only to Jews everywhere but also to Moslems, Christians, and the British Mandatory authorities'.[145] He left the following April. But news of Herzog's selection was also tinged with sadness. While the local Jewish community felt justifiably proud of the honour which had been bestowed upon their rabbi, they knew he would be a great loss to them and very difficult to replace.

During Herzog's last few months in Ireland it would seem that his close personal relations with de Valera were reflected in his being taken into de Valera's confidence when the new Irish constitution – Bunreacht na hÉireann – was being finalised during early 1937.[146] The Irish leader undertook a round of consultations between 3 April and 27 April 1937 with all major church leaders in order to draft the final wording of the religious article in the constitution; Herzog's name is surprisingly absent from a comprehensive list of those consulted in the de Valera papers.[147] However, according to an oral source, Herzog was consulted on that important matter by de Valera on more than one occasion.[148] Herzog had a great legal mind, and that alone would have made him an obvious person for de Valera to consult. The relevant section of the final text of Article 44 read:

> The State also recognises the Church of Ireland, the Presbyterian Church in Ireland, the Methodist Church in Ireland, the Religious Society of Friends in Ireland, as well as the Jewish Congregations and the other religious denominations existing in Ireland at the date of the coming into operation of this Constitution.[149]

The new constitution was adopted after Herzog left for Palestine.[150]

Two episodes shortly before his departure must have caused the chief rabbi considerable distress.[151] Herzog will no doubt have read a report in the *Irish Times* on 6 April 1937 giving the contents of an interview by envoy Charles Bewley to the Berlin evening paper, *Uhr Blatt*:

> My government will always do everything to promote the old friendship between Ireland and Germany. Undoubtedly our growing patriotism helps us to find recognition especially in countries in which people are willing to stake their lives for liberty and honour. That your Reich and its leaders have many admirers among our youth is a well-known fact.[152]

This was another of Bewley's gaffes. He was making a purely personal observation – without any supporting evidence – and was not following a policy instruction from headquarters. This was a source of professional embarrassment to de Valera who was Minister for External Affairs. The *Irish Times*, no supporter of the Fianna Fáil government, questioned in an editorial how

> a democratic state administered by a democratic government, which has made no secret of its abhorrence of dictatorship . . . could approve the German system, which, for all its admirable elements is based upon dictatorship and the negation of liberty.[153]

The *Irish Times* thought that Bewley's 'expressions of kindness' were indiscreet at the very least.[154] No stranger to indiscretion, the Irish envoy in Berlin had done it again.

Herzog must also have been aware before his departure of the ugly libel case pending which further underlined the existence of anti-Semitism in middle-class Dublin. Oliver St John Gogarty, the surgeon and novelist who wrote anti-Semitic articles in *Sinn Féin* in 1906, published a volume of memoirs in 1937 entitled *As I Was Going Down Sackville Street*. This became the subject of a libel action taken against him by a member of the Jewish community in Dublin, Henry Morris (Harry) Sinclair. His twin William, who had married Cissie Beckett, an aunt of the writer Samuel Beckett, was nicknamed the Boss, the Beard or Sink. A lover of the company of artists and poets, he had enjoyed the friendship of Gogarty for a number of years.[155] In *Ulysses*, Leopold Bloom remarked in the Lestrygonians episode: 'Or I will drop into old Harris's and have a chat with young Sinclair? Well-mannered fellow. Probably at his lunch.'[156] The twins had inherited the Nassau Street antique business from their grandfather, Morris Harris, to whom Gogarty referred in his memoirs as 'the ancient chicken butcher', an 'old usurer' who had 'eyes like a pair of periwinkles on which somebody had been experimenting'. Gogarty also alleged that the older Morris Harris grew 'the more he pursued the immature, and enticed little girls into his office', adding: 'That was bad enough; but he had grandsons, and these directed the steps of their youth to follow in grandfather's footsteps with more zeal than discrimination.'[157]

Three weeks before William died in destitution on 4 May 1937 in the county home at Rathdrum, County Wicklow, he read these remarks in Gogarty's memoirs. He also read a description of himself:

> But Willie spent the sesterces
> and brought on strange disasters
> Because he sought new mistresses
> More keenly than old masters.[158]

These comments had greatly disturbed the dying man and Samuel Beckett, a nephew, promised William that he would testify on behalf of the twins. He duly signed an affidavit on 12 May 1937 which read in part:

> I was aware that their grandfather Mr Morris Harris deceased carried on
> the business of Art Dealer and Jeweller at Nassau Street, Dublin and that
> on his death his said two Grandsons succeeded to the said business and
> have since carried on the same and that they were twins and profess of
> the Jewish Faith.[159]

Samuel Beckett stated that the lines commencing 'Two Jews in Sackville
Street' referred to the Sinclair twins and that the words 'old usurer' referred
to Morris Harris and his grandsons.[160] He said the words constituted a very
grave charge against the twins. Henry Sinclair in his affidavit described the
book as a 'reservoir of filth and the grosser form of vulgarity'.[161]

The case was tried in November 1937 and proved to be an ugly affair,
Samuel Beckett being subjected to a very severe cross-questioning.[162] When
asked whether he would describe himself as a Christian, a Jew or an atheist,
Beckett replied to defence counsel that he was 'none of the three'.[163] Gogarty
lost and was fined £900. His biographer, J. B. Lyons, argues that the charge of
anti-Semitism 'in the real sense of the term' cannot be sustained against
Gogarty whose 'brand of "anti-Semitism" is the parallel of today's Kerryman
jokes'.[164] That view was not shared by Henry and William Sinclair: neither
was it the view of the judge. Gogarty, fulminating against de Valera's Ireland,
left that year for New York where he died in 1957.

In contrast, Chief Rabbi Herzog had left Dublin much more reluctantly. A
farewell reception was held for him in the Mansion House on 8 April 1937.
Representatives of Fianna Fáil, Fine Gael and Labour were present, together
with leading members of the Jewish community.[165] Eamon de Valera, who
sent a message regretting that he was unable to attend, was represented by
his parliamentary secretary, Patrick Little. De Valera had it conveyed to the
meeting that he felt sure that Herzog would bring the same spirit of peace to
the task which he was approaching as he had brought to his people in
Ireland. He regretted that they were losing Herzog, but the Jewish community in Ireland would be consoled with the thought that while he was not
with them physically he was still their spiritual leader.[166]

Letters of apology for absence were also read from the two primates, Dr
Charles Frederick d'Arcy and Cardinal Joseph MacRory. The latter wrote
that he would be with the gathering in spirit:

> I have known the chief rabbi for nearly twenty years, and have always
> admired his ability, sincerity and untiring zeal for the welfare of his
> people. My best wishes go with him, and I hope he will be happy in the
> exalted and very onerous position of chief rabbi of Palestine.[167]

Leonard Abrahamson, who presided, said that he had known Herzog for
nearly twenty years, and in all that time – in times of joy or sorrow, in suffering or in health – the community had found the rabbi and the man were
'inextricably mixed'. He was a great divine, and Abrahamson also felt that he
was 'one of those rare examples of real greatness'.[168]

Herzog had made history when he became the first chief rabbi of the Irish
Free State. He had also made history in other ways and his new appointment
would allow him to continue to make it in a much wider sphere. Tributes

were also paid by the chief minister of the Dublin Hebrew Congregation, Rev. Abraham Gudansky, and by the president of the Zion Schools, Arthur Newman. The latter recalled the work done for Jewish emancipation by Daniel O'Connell in the nineteenth century; Newman suggested that if O'Connell were present with them in such a historic setting

> to see representative members of the leading parties of the State, and representative members of [the Jewish] Community gathered together on the one platform in order to do honour to a great Rabbi and a great scholar, and all animated with feelings of loyalty to Ireland and hopes for her future advancement, I am sure he would feel well compensated for his noble efforts on behalf of our persecuted people, which he did out of the greatness of his heart and when he was at the height of his political career.[169]

Replying, Herzog said that the call of Zion was irresistible. He was being asked to go to Palestine 'at a great moment, at a turning point in the history of Israel'. He then went on to pay tribute to Ireland:

> Long before he set foot on Irish soil he felt a kind of romantic interest in this country, where Jews had never even in the Middle Ages, suffered any persecution. Its attitude towards the Jewish citizens was the truest criterion of a country's level of civilisation, and it was precisely in times of great trouble that the true character of a nation was decided. Measured by that standard, Ireland emerged with a record which they might well regard with a just and noble pride. A few isolated unfriendly utterances in recent times could not in the slightest degree mar so noble a record. He was convinced that those uncharitable utterances were not native products – they were imported from abroad.[170]

According to an *Irish Times* editorial, Herzog was 'not only a scholar of high distinction' but he also possessed 'the great gift of leadership, and in all probability nobody better suited for the high office could have been found anywhere'. His appointment reflected 'high honour upon our nation', the paper said, and added:

> We claim no special credit for Ireland because she never has persecuted the Jews – for therein she has behaved merely as any civilised country ought to behave. On the other hand, it is difficult to read the speeches which were delivered at Thursday's [farewell] function without, at least, a faint glow of pride. . . . Here in Ireland the Jews are not a separate people; they are part of the nation to whose welfare they have contributed in large measure. They have done fine service to our industry, our commerce and our art, and, if we have tolerated them – to use an objectionable phrase – we have been more than repaid by their presence in our midst.[171]

The editorial also commented upon the remarks of Leonard Abrahamson, the chairman of the farewell ceremony, concerning the 'few isolated unfriendly utterances' which had been directed in recent times against the Jews in the country.[172] The *Irish Times* concluded:

> Every nation has its complement of boors, and we do not think that these
> occasional and uncharacteristic outbursts will affect in the slightest
> degree the attitude of the mass of the Irish people towards their Jewish
> fellow-citizens. The choice of Dr Herzog will bring the name of Ireland,
> and Ireland's reputation for kindliness, before the notice of many millions
> of Jews throughout the world. Our hope is that the reputation will be
> maintained unimpaired in the years to come.[173]

Herzog was the guest of honour at a banquet in the assembly hall of Zion
Schools on Bloomfield Avenue on 11 April, where he performed his last official act in Ireland; blessing about three hundred Jewish children, he urged
them to strive to grow up exemplary citizens of the Irish Free State, and to
pray daily for the rebuilding of Jerusalem and for the redemption of the
Jewish people from lands where they were being oppressed. An *Irish Press*
reporter commented that there were tears in the eyes of many of the parents
present: 'I will always remember you and pray for you. I wish you to pray for
me, also', he said.[174]

The Herzogs departed Ireland and were joined by their eldest son, Chaim,
in Alexandria; he had made the journey to Egypt on the trans-Sinai train
which was loaded with Bedouin chieftains and their harems.[175] Chaim
boarded his parents' ship, and together they sailed to Haifa where Herzog
received a 'royal reception'.[176] They travelled by train along the coast,
stopping in the towns and settlements to be greeted by the crowds who had
come out to meet the new chief rabbi. In Jerusalem, thousands lined the
streets and he acknowledged the crowds from the balcony of Amdursky's
Hotel. Herzog, already noted for his learning, was a wise choice for the
changing times.[177]

While he may have left Dublin, the new chief rabbi of Palestine and his
two teenage sons, Chaim and Jacob, maintained very close contact with the
Jewish community in Ireland. And though Herzog did not visit Ireland again
until after the Second World War, he worked closely and successfully with
'his personal friend' Eamon de Valera on the refugee problem during and
after the war.[178]

5

Irish refugee policy,
anti-Semitism and the approach
of the Second World War

Chief Rabbi Isaac Herzog's departure for Palestine in 1937 deprived the Irish Jewish community of the services of a universally respected leader. It was not easy to fill a position held by a person of Herzog's moral authority, erudition and plain common sense. The Jewish community in Dublin temporised and disagreed over the appointment of a successor. Herzog was not replaced until the appointment of Immanuel Jakobovits in 1949.[1] That inability to find a consensus meant that the community was without a chief rabbi during the years of unprecedented international turmoil leading to the Holocaust and its aftermath.[2]

Then in 1938, the Dublin Jewish community lost two of its leading members. Joseph Zlotover died at the age of seventy-nine on 1 February. His name, wrote Chief Rabbi Herzog, 'deserves to be recorded in golden letters in the annals of Dublin'.[3] William Nurock, one of the 'best beloved of the pioneers' according to his lifelong friend Arthur Newman, died in May, also aged seventy-nine.[4] Nurock, who had celebrated his golden wedding anniversary the previous year, was a great loss to the community.[5] The obituary in the *Jewish Chronicle* described him as being 'an orthodox Jew of considerable Hebraic knowledge' who 'combined orthodoxy with a luminous and intelligent tolerance'.[6] His wife, Rachael or Rocha, died in 1952. The leadership of the Jewish community had passed to a younger generation.

In his later years in Dublin Herzog had built a small advisory group around himself, and in 1938 this was institutionalised as the Jewish Representative Council (JRC). It was mandated to deal with all matters internal and external affecting the Jewish community of Ireland and to act as an advisory body to the chief rabbi. Bernard Shillman states that the creation of the JRC was largely due to the efforts of Professor Leonard Abrahamson and the solicitor, Herman Good.[7] The community was also fortunate to have articulate spokespersons in Bethel Solomons and his brother, Edwin. While the JRC's style was cautious, discreet and non-confrontational, it remained an effective defender of Jewish interests with easy access to Eamon de Valera and to his government ministers – an access the JRC did not choose to exercise except in situations of necessity.[8] The JRC had a difficult assignment since the two years which followed Herzog's departure saw a growing clamour for refuge as anti-Semitic laws in many continental European countries intensified. Ireland did not prove to be a safe haven of hope for many fleeing persecution on the continent.

The developing refugee crisis

The Irish Nationality and Citizenship Bill became law on 10 April 1935.[9] A national was defined as a person born in Saorstát Éireann (Irish Free State); a person born outside Saorstát Éireann whose mother at the time of the person's birth was ordinarily resident in Saorstát Éireann; or a person who at the relevant time is and for not less than five consecutive years immediately preceding that time has been ordinarily resident in Saorstát Éireann.[10] The Act also provided for the granting of citizenship to children born of one Irish parent.[11] The Act therefore granted citizenship to the children of immigrants.[12]

The Aliens Act 1935, a second piece of legislation relevant to this study, was administered by the Minister for Justice who possessed wide-ranging powers.[13] Other departments might also be involved in any decision regarding the fate of an alien, such as the Department of External Affairs and the Department of Industry and Commerce; the Garda Síochána might also be called in to investigate a case. However, the final decision in routine cases usually rested with the Minister for Justice. The legislation provided that any alien, other than an alien coming from the United Kingdom, might not land in Ireland except with the permission of an immigration officer. An alien wishing to take up employment in the state was required, before he or she was given leave to land in the country, to produce a copy of the permit issued to the employer by the Minister for Industry and Commerce.[14] Aliens who did not possess an employment permit had to satisfy the immigration officer that they were in a position to support themselves and their dependants. They also had to have proper identity papers duly visaed where necessary.[15]

There was a large increase in the workload of the aliens section in the Department of Justice from the mid-1930s onwards, yet this continued to be administered by virtually the same small staff until after the war. P. J. Ruttledge was Minister for Justice in the late 1930s until he was replaced by Gerald Boland in 1939. The secretary of the department, S. A. Roche, held that position from 1934 until he was replaced in 1949 by the assistant secretary in the department, J. E. Duff. The latter took direct responsibility for the aliens section during the period under review. A future secretary of the department, Peter Berry, was private secretary to Roche. There were less than twenty professional administrative staff in the department at the outbreak of war and its budget was £82,912.[16]

The aliens policy administered by the Department of Justice was 'not liberal', according to Tom Woulfe, a former civil servant in the department.[17] The evidence presented in this chapter will demonstrate that that was practised understatement. As the political and religious persecutions in continental Europe intensified during the late 1930s, the Irish government had already the necessary legislation in place to control, and prevent where desirable, an influx of aliens who were likely to wish to become permanent residents. The Irish envoy accredited to the League of Nations, Frank T. Cremins, was regularly instructed to defend an 'illiberal' policy.[18] The League of Nations, under the high commissioner for German refugees, Sir Neil Malcolm, was seeking to establish international agreement for the adoption of a protocol on the legal status of refugees coming from Germany. An intergovernmental conference was called for 2 July 1936, and the Department of Justice prepared a memorandum on the subject. The memorandum stated that the Minister for Justice was opposed to putting 'such refugees in a more favourable position than other aliens'. He did not agree that the powers under the Aliens Act to refuse admittance to an alien should be in any way limited. Each case had to be dealt with on its merits.[19] Cremins was sent a copy of the memorandum and urged to study it carefully.[20] He was instructed that he should 'resist any efforts to impose additional obligations on the Saorstát in relation to such refugees'.[21]

In the end, Cremins was unable to attend the conference, which was chaired by Malcolm. Fifteen countries took part while Finland and the United States sent observers.[22] The conference, according to Michael Marrus, secured agreement on a provisional arrangement providing a certificate of identity and certain legal guarantees to German fugitives abroad. But, Marrus points out, the agreement merely referred to existing refugees: it said nothing about new arrivals and remained silent about German policy.[23] As the situation worsened in Europe, Malcolm continued his work on the drafting of a refugee convention in Geneva.

In Dublin, there was little support within the Departments of Justice and Industry and Commerce for any relaxation in the laws covering entry into the country. The fact that visitors to Ireland from the United Kingdom did not require leave to land continued to worry officials in Dublin. Furthermore, the 270-mile land border with Northern Ireland made checks on entry through that route very difficult. That situation gave rise to a general concern about Ireland being vulnerable to illegal entry by aliens.

When the preliminary draft convention concerning the status of refugees coming from Germany was circulated in May 1937, the secretary of the Department of Industry and Commerce, John Leydon, wrote to the Department of External Affairs on behalf of his minister, Seán Lemass:

> Owing to the number of persons unemployed in this country it is desired
> that there should be no relaxation of the existing arrangements for the
> control of aliens entering Saorstát Éireann for employment and that
> aliens entering Saorstát Éireann from Great Britain or Northern Ireland
> should be subject to similar restrictions in the matter of entering employ
> ment in Saorstát Éireann.[24]

The Department of Industry and Commerce did not propose to promote legislation for the purposes of altering the existing arrangements and was not disposed to recommend that Saorstát Éireann should be a contracting party to the preliminary draft convention.[25] The Department of External Affairs conveyed that information to Cremins in Geneva, together with the news that the Department of Justice had no comment to make on the draft.[26] Cremins was told to inform the secretary general of the League of Nations that Ireland was not prepared to accept the draft convention.[27] Despite opposition from a number of countries, Malcolm had succeeded by February 1938 in getting agreement for the Geneva Convention on Refugees Coming from Germany. According to Michael Marrus:

> This agreement repeated previous measures of protection, improved conditions for refugees in countries of asylum, and limited the recourse to expulsion. Once again, the document mainly protected refugees who had already escaped Germany. Ignored by the major West European countries, it probably emerged at the last possible moment – just before a new flood of refugees occasioned by Anschluss. Henceforth . . . governments resisted any move that might possibly suggest new obligations to refugees.[28]

Hitler's troops crossed into Austria on 12 March 1938 and triumphantly entered Vienna – the home of 165,000 of the country's 180,000 Jews.[29] An editorial in de Valera's *Irish Press* stated that Hitler 'has wiped from the map a Nation with a history going back for more than a thousand years, and he is convinced that he can do so with perfect impunity'.[30] The result, according to the editorial, was that there 'is not one of the smaller States which do not feel that their security, if not their very existence, is threatened'.[31] Although the editorial writer did not dwell upon the question of anti-Semitism and the refugee problem, Hitler's Anschluss – the forced union of Austria with Nazi Germany by which an independent Austria ceased to exist – had the most serious consequences for neighbouring states. Vienna had been, up to that point, a refuge for Jews from Germany, Romania, Hungary and Poland.[32] But not any more. The newspapers of Austrian Jews were closed down on 12 March. Within a few months, all Austrian Jews lost their means of livelihood. In many cases, they also lost their property and their homes.[33] Adolf Eichmann, a name which was to grow in infamy as the war progressed, was entrusted with the task of directing Jewish emigration. Some 50,000 Jews fled Austria between April and November 1938, and that figure rose to 126,500 by November 1939.[34] By the end of the war, 65,000 Austrian Jews had lost their lives.[35]

The Polish government had authorised on 31 March 1938 the cancellation of citizenship for anyone living outside the country for more than five years – automatically blocking the return of the 20,000 Polish Jews then living in Austria. When Hitler expelled all Polish Jews from the Reich, the Polish authorities responded by blocking their entry to Poland. Thousands of Jews were forced to camp on the border between Poland and Germany until finally they were admitted to Poland in July 1938.[36] In Romania, King Carol supported a law which denationalised 225,000 Jews, representing 36 per cent of the country's Jewish population. Hungary, with a population of 445,000 Jews, passed a law in May 1938 which cut down the number of Jews in business; further anti-Semitic laws were introduced later in the year. A great dispersion of Jews and other victims of Nazism followed this wave of repression across central and eastern Europe, a relatively small number of whom sought to come to Ireland.

Ireland and the Evian refugee conference

President F. D. Roosevelt, responding to the mounting pressure from pro-refugee groups in the United States, called an international conference at Evian-les-Bains in the south of France in July 1938.[37] Roosevelt's representative at the conference, the multi-millionaire former head of US Steel, Myron C. Taylor, presided over the first session and was later elected permanent president.[38] In all, thirty-two countries were represented. The British Dominions Office encouraged the dominions to be represented, and the reluctance of both Canada and Australia was eventually overcome.[39] The Irish envoy in Geneva, Frank T. Cremins, led the small Irish delegation, which was in attendance throughout the proceedings.

The Taoiseach and Minister for External Affairs, Eamon de Valera, had told the Irish delegation that 'no commitment of a financial nature should be entered into at the Conference without his antecedent approval'.[40] Cremins stuck rigidly to that brief when he told the plenary session that his country was effectively closed to refugees. Remarking that Ireland was not 'in a position to make any substantial contribution to the solution', he outlined the position thus:

> Ireland is a small country with jurisdiction over a population of something less than three million people. Notwithstanding the steady progress which has been made in recent years in regard to the creation of new industries, by far the greater part of our people still derive, and will continue to derive, their living from the land. I need not attempt to explain the land problems which have arisen in Ireland; it is sufficient to say that there is not enough land available to satisfy the needs of our own people.[41]

Cremins explained that the new industries were 'not yet capable of absorbing the regular increase in our population' and consequently thousands of people emigrated each year. That being so, he said, 'it is obvious that we can make no real contribution to the settlement of refugees'.[42] Cremins was instructed to state that due to overcrowding Ireland was also closed to members of the liberal professions. So while the Irish government felt obliged to express its hope that the 'mass of human suffering involved in the refugee problem' might 'by some means, be substantially alleviated', there was little that Dublin felt it could do to contribute towards the resolution of the situation. Cremins argued that the only alternative was the opening up of new or underdeveloped territory and 'the Irish government have no such territory under their control'.[43] Cremins stated later in the conference that the Irish government could not

> make any promises or give any undertaking. Apart from the disappoint-
> ment to which unfulfilled promises would give rise, the government feel
> that there is grave danger that ill-considered promises or promises hedged
> round with conditions the full implication of which may be realised only
> too late, may actually result in an increase in the hardships inflicted on
> what we may call 'prospective refugees'. The greater the hopes held out by
> potential countries of refuge, the greater may be the pressure brought to
> bear on these unfortunate creatures.[44]

Hubert Butler, the distinguished essayist, recorded how he met two of the Irish diplomats (one from Berne and the other from Paris) who had attended the Evian conference. One remarked to Butler: 'Didn't we suffer like this in the Penal Days and nobody came to help us.'[45]

What was the verdict on this international gathering? Tony Kushner concludes as follows:

> It would be wrong to dismiss totally the Evian conference as a cruel
> facade, even if the progress made in liberalizing immigration restrictions
> was limited. Apart from some mainly empty promises from Latin Ameri-
> can countries, it was clear from the conference that no major power was
> willing to state publicly that it would open its doors more widely to Jewish
> refugees.[46]

However disappointing the outcome, the Evian conference had recom-mended the establishment of an intergovernmental committee in London. The committee was entrusted with the task of negotiating with Germany in order to try to stop the chaos caused by mass expulsions. The committee also held out the possibility of negotiating more liberal refugee policies with other countries. But the outcome proved to Jewish refugee organisations that many European countries, despite the turmoil of 1938, were not prepared to receive refugees in general and Jewish refugees in particular.[47] Ireland's painfully frank statement of its position raised no false expectations.[48]

Monitoring Ireland's alien population

Before discussing the evolution of Irish refugee policy in relation to Jews, is it possible to estimate how many aliens were resident in the country by 1939? The files of the Department of Justice and Irish military intelligence (G2) provide the most meticulous information on the place of residence, occupa-tion and activities of every individual in that category. Aliens under suspicion had their mail intercepted, translated when necessary, and a photographed copy of the original kept on file. This was the practice, in many cases, long before the outbreak of war. After September 1939, surveillance became even more intense. Therefore, a survey of these files makes it possible to provide a comprehensive picture of Ireland's alien population.

The number of aliens in 1939 was given as 2,354.[49] This number was broken down by nationality, the largest group being US citizens at 1,143; there were 194 Germans, 188 Italians, 142 Belgians, 133 Russians, 113 French, 93 Dutch, 86 Czechs, 52 Austrians and 41 Swiss. The heaviest concentration of aliens was in the Dublin Metropolitan Division of the Garda Síochána, which had 864 aliens in 1939. Again US citizens were the most numerous at 162, followed by 141 Italians, 123 Germans, 117 Russians, 57 French, 36 Austrians, 33 Belgians and 28 Czechs. In the Dublin–Wicklow Garda Division, which included Bray, Dundrum, Baltinglass and Wicklow, the 120 aliens listed were more thinly spread.

Number of aliens in Ireland by nationality, 1939

	Country	Dublin Metropolitan Division	Dublin–Wicklow Division
American	1,143	162	55
Argentinian	10	4	0
Austrian	52	36	0
Austro-German	1	0	0
Bavarian	1	0	1
Belgian	142	33	2
Chinese	1	1	0
Czech	86	28	0
Danish	24	5	2
Danziger	1	1	0
Dominican	1	1	0
Dutch	93	37	13
Ecuadorian	1	1	0
Egyptian	9	9	0
Estonian	1	1	0
Finnish	1	1	0
French	113	57	7
German	194	123	24
Greek	3	1	1
Hungarian	15	4	1
Iraqi	5	1	0
Italian	188	141	4
Japanese	1	1	0
Latvian	12	10	0
Lithuanian	12	11	0
Luxemburger	2	0	0
Norwegian	2	2	0
Ottoman	2	0	0
Palestinian	1	0	0
Polish	39	36	0
Portuguese	1	1	0
Romanian	6	6	0
Russian	133	117	4
Siamese	3	2	1
Spanish	10	3	4
Swedish	3	3	0
Swiss	41	24	1
Stateless	1	1	0
Total	2,354	864	120

Besides keeping a personal file on every alien in the country, the Department of Justice also kept a general file on their places of employment. There are, for example, individual files on the Irish Steel Mills,[50] the Electricity Supply Board,[51] the Irish Glass Bottle Company,[52] and the Drogheda-based Irish Oil and Cake Mills.[53] The department also held comprehensive files on theatrical and circus performers,[54] air crews at Shannon, merchant sailors, foreign religious, and musicians in the Radio Éireann orchestra. The Department of Justice's system was as efficient as it was comprehensive. When deemed necessary, surveillance, be it of an individual or of a group, was carried out with great expertise by both the gardaí and military intelligence. The exigencies of national security were interpreted by the Irish authorities in a very liberal fashion in the years leading up to the war.

It is difficult, therefore, to separate the question of national security from policy towards aliens in this period. That linkage was made by the officials in the Department of Justice and G2. There was, moreover, solid ground for the grave concern felt in both agencies about the subversive activities of certain prominent aliens in the country. Therefore, the security factor must be added to the Evian guidelines when attempting to evaluate Irish policy towards aliens and refugees prior to the outbreak of the Second World War.

Given those constraints, what was the *modus operandi* for an alien to make an application for residence in the country? The initiative might come from within the country by friends, relatives or a potential employer. Alternatively, an alien might make a request directly through one of the Irish legations on the continent at Paris, Rome, Berlin or Madrid. The legations generally referred each case to the Department of External Affairs, which in turn referred it to the Department of Justice and, where necessary, the Department of Industry and Commerce.[55] But what was the policy of the Irish government towards Jewish aliens and Jewish refugees?

The Department of Justice and Jewish refugees

The growth of anti-Semitism in continental Europe during 1938 – and the spread of the German sphere of influence with the absorption of Austria – increased the demand for refuge in Ireland. In August 1938 – shortly after the ending of the conference at Evian – the governing body of University College Dublin sought permission to allow twelve Austrian students to study at the college. The request had come from Catholic sources in Austria. After some reflection, the Department of Justice drafted a letter to the president of the college, Denis J. Coffey, which effectively refused permission unless there was a guarantee that the students would return to Austria after completing the course. How could that be guaranteed in the context of Anschluss as Austria had ceased to exist? The draft letter to Coffey was sent on 22 August by the Department of Justice to the Department of the Taoiseach. A covering note from the secretary of the Department of Justice, S. A. Roche, who was anxious that the matter should receive no publicity, suggested that Coffey be called in and have the matter explained to him. However, the recommended refusal was reversed in the first week in September, and the students were given permission to study in the country.[56] That was due to the direct intervention of the Department of the Taoiseach, where the secretary, Maurice Moynihan, was very much opposed to the inflexibility of the Department of Justice.[57]

This pattern was to be repeated up to and throughout the war years. The Department of Justice interpreted Irish policy towards aliens in a very restrictive and conservative light. The Department of the Taoiseach, and de Valera when informed of a particular case, tended to act more liberally. A number of cases in early 1938 will help illustrate this pattern.

Bernard Hollander, an Austrian who became a naturalised German in the 1920s, was appointed in December 1937 'First Reader and Cantor' in the Lennox Street Synagogue. He had arrived in England in 1937 to study music and was allowed to land there on condition that he would not take up employment. He had told immigration officers that he was a concert singer.[58] A Department of Justice minute recorded that the department had been advised about Hollander's appointment by letter from the solicitor, Herman Good, and that the chief rabbi had approved the decision. As there was no chief rabbi in Ireland at the time the reference in the minute is mistaken. It undoubtedly referred to Rev. Abraham Gudansky, the chief minister of the Dublin Hebrew Congregation.[59]

The department, as was the practice, requested a report from the Garda Síochána. The report indicated that the Lennox Street congregation consisted of thirty-eight people who met in a single room over a shop at No. 32, and that a Dublin-born Jew named Gittleson was acting as reader, cantor and secretary of the congregation at a wage of 12s 6d per week. The gardaí were convinced that the congregation would not be able to pay Hollander a living wage and that he would have to seek further employment.[60] The Department of Justice minute concluded that it 'looks as if the Jews are trying to use the Readership of the Lennox St. Synagogue as an excuse for introducing aliens who would take up some other employment when established here'.[61] Rev. Gudansky had called to the department on 23 March 1938 to petition on behalf of Hollander. He was asked how Lennox Street had operated without a cantor since 1933. Gudansky explained that Gittleson had carried out part of the work, but not being a clergyman he could not perform all the services. The president of the congregation, Eli Isaacson, had performed the remainder but he was getting too old to carry on. Therefore, it was essential that a qualified reader and cantor should be appointed. There were, he said, no facilities in Ireland or in Britain to train cantors. It was, therefore, necessary to bring them in from abroad.[62] But the outcome was not favourable. A handwritten minute reads:

> Herman Good was informed [in December 1937] that Hollander would not be allowed in, but despite this the alien came to Dublin. Mr Briscoe made representations on his behalf, which were rejected, but Hollander refused to leave until a deportation order was made against him.[63]

There was, however, a successful outcome to two other cases in which

Robert Briscoe was involved. The success, however, was achieved despite the objections of the Department of Justice. One case concerned Rabbi Israel Frankel and the other an orphaned Latvian girl whom an Irish Jewish family wished to adopt. Both help to shed further light on the working of the 'official mind' in the Department of Justice.

Rabbi Frankel was a Polish national who had come to Ireland on 2 March 1937. At the request of Chief Rabbi Herzog, he was granted a three-month extension in order to undertake religious and philosophical research in Dublin in university libraries. Frankel was given a further extension for two months and he left the country on 5 August 1937 for Belgium. An application had been sent before his departure to the Department of Justice requesting residency for him. Under great strain, he wrote in very poor English to Briscoe on 19 August 1937 from Antwerp:

> I know that I should not bother you again, but my situation is very bad here and this upsets me therble, I cant even sleep tru the nights thinking what is going to happen with me, as in no place they would let me stay, except Dublin is the only chance for me, and all my thoughts are only consinstrating that you would be the only person who can help me, and thats why I have to write you again, so I beg forgiveness once again for troubling you.[64]

A few weeks later Briscoe received a letter pointing out the vulnerability of Frankel's position.[65] The TD took up the case on the grounds that the Lower Ormond Quay Synagogue wanted the rabbi to take charge of a particular service. Briscoe sent a telegram to Frankel which the rabbi produced to immigration officers. It read: 'Your presence required, conduct service here on Tuesday night; will personally take responsibility for you vis a vis authorities.'[66] Frankel, entering the country on 14 September, wrote a note of thanks to Briscoe.[67] By March 1938, however, he was in difficulty again. His extension to remain in the country expired on 7 March and he was in danger of being deported.[68]

In the case of the Latvian girl, the assistant secretary of the Department of Justice, J. E. Duff, reluctantly recommended a refusal. He wrote to Roche on 31 March 1938:

> It may sound harsh to refuse sanctuary in cases of this sort, but in the long run it may be best for all concerned (excluding perhaps the girl herself). . . . It is difficult to explain to him [Briscoe] that there is a feeling in this country that there are an undue number of Jews resident here, and that any increase in the present number might easily lead to a definite anti-Semitic agitation arising. In my opinion the best thing for the Jewish community in this country would be to prevent any more Jews taking up residence here.[69]

The secretary of the department, S. A. Roche, sent a minute to the minister, Patrick Ruttledge, on 1 April 1938 saying that he agreed with Duff.[70] Ruttledge agreed with the negative advice received in both cases.

However, when the matter of Briscoe's involvement in the case was brought to the attention of the Department of Justice – in particular the text of his telegram to Frankel – the reaction was far from friendly. Ruttledge wrote to Briscoe on 11 April and told him of his decision, which, he said, had been dictated by policy considerations.[71] He explained more fully:

> In general, I think that the Jewish community in this country should not be increased by way of immigration, except in cases where the immigrant is a definite acquisition to the State. So long as we have (in common with so many other countries) the problem of unemployment, I feel that it is wrong to admit aliens about whom we cannot be certain that they will not compete with our own citizens in the labour market.

Ruttledge continued, pointing out that such certainty would be very difficult to establish:

> the immigrant may be, at entry, as in the case now before me, merely a child or a person invited over temporarily for religious duties but there is no certainty, and no promises or guarantees can give any certainty, that in a few years' time they will not be found competing in the labour market and it may then be found impossible to secure their departure.[72]

The minister outlined what he saw as the dangers of Jewish immigration:

> There has never been in this country any feeling against Jews on the scale which has shown itself in some other countries but there *are* anti-Jewish groups in the country which would be only too glad to get an excuse to start an anti-Jewish campaign and those groups could get no better slogan than that the native Irish worker was being ousted by cheap imported labour.[73]

Ruttledge drew the following policy inference:

> The conclusion I am inclined to draw, is that the existing Jewish community in this country would be well advised in its own interests not to encourage Jewish immigration, and that is a point of view which I would like you to bear in mind when efforts are made to secure your support in facilitating such immigration.[74]

He said he would like to see 'a greater effort made towards self-reliance' in the particular matter of religious ministers as, in too many cases, it had been represented that a particular synagogue could not carry on unless 'an alien is allowed to come in as Rabbi'.[75]

However unwelcome the minister's letter may have been, Briscoe had received a most comprehensive statement of government policy regarding the admission of Jews into the country. The Fianna Fáil TD was very angry when he replied to Ruttledge on 22 April, saying that he was still anxious to secure a permit for a leading member of the Jewish community in Dublin to bring an orphan girl into the country. He also wished to see Rabbi Frankel remain in Ireland:

> Nobody is more conscious of the difficulties that the Government would have to face in the event of being generous in the granting of permits to aliens of my persuasion. I have, as a result of my knowledge of all the

implications in such matters been most careful in associating myself with applications for permits for aliens. Further, I have been more than careful in associating myself with applications by aliens resident in this country for naturalisation requests, and in view of the fact that I am the only member of my persuasion elected to An Dáil I do not think I could be charged with attempting to seek over-indulgence in matters of this kind.[76]

Briscoe stated further: 'I am the bludgeon with which any Minister can be beaten and, consequently, I am quite wide awake to what is correct for me to apply for.'[77] He was dismissive of the idea that the Jewish community in Ireland was capable of producing its own rabbis, and replied by making an 'equally ridiculous suggestion':

Has the time not now been reached when China can produce its own Priests and Bishops to the exclusion of those who are sent out after graduation from Maynooth; or perhaps it might interest your Department to know that the National College of Art in Dublin has selected and appointed as its Professor of Design (Gaelic) a Dutchman; as its Professor of Sculpture an Austrian; as its Assistant Professor of Sculpture an Englishman. Surely I could equally say that Ireland should be able to produce masters, from the national point of view, from its own nationals.[78]

Briscoe then became even more pointed in his criticism:

Might I respectfully point out that our Instructor of Music in the Army [Colonel Brase] is a German who has not seen fit to become an Irish national; that our Director of the Museum [Adolf Mahr] is an Austrian whose allegiance is firstly to Mr Hitler who recently honoured him in his Birthday Honours for his services – not to Ireland but Germany. I could give you a whole lot more instances but I do not wish to be too unreasonable and, consequently, I now await the permits in both these cases referred to in this letter.[79]

Ruttledge chose not to reply personally. Instead, Roche responded in a long letter which cast further light on Department of Justice thinking.[80] On behalf of the minister, he agreed that Briscoe was correct to state that 'a number of non-Jewish foreigners have been appointed to official posts in this country'.[81] But the minister was 'unable to see its relevancy to the present discussion':

When it is found necessary or desirable to appoint a foreigner to a public post in this country after public competition or by special Government sanction, this office, when dealing with the immigration aspect of the matter, is indifferent as to whether the person appointed is or is not a Jew: the same facilities are given in either case. The view is taken that any such person has, in effect, been declared by competent authority to be 'a definite acquisition to the State' so that his or her case falls in the privileged category, open equally to all races and religions, to which the Minister referred in . . . his letter to you. The Minister is unable to see in what way this procedure is unfair to the Jewish community or how it can be related to the question of the admission of people like the girl X or Rabbi Frankel.[82]

Roche then raised the issue of Briscoe's comparison between bringing a rabbi into Ireland and sending Maynooth missionaries to China:

> The Minister is quite unable to admit that the suggested comparison is well-founded or that the conclusion sought to be drawn from it has any validity. He considers the argument to be not only fallacious but even mischievous, in the sense that any attempt to rely upon it, in public, as a reason for granting facilities for Jewish immigration into this State would tend to prejudice the position of the existing Jewish community here.[83]

Since rabbis could not be trained in Ireland, the minister wondered why it was not possible 'for members of that community to get the necessary training, elsewhere, as was commonly done by Catholics in this country at a time when the law did not permit them to be educated for the priesthood in their own country'.[84] Roche added that the minister could not consider as satisfactory

> a state of affairs in which the Jewish congregations in Dublin are pressing him (as they are at present) to admit three aliens, simultaneously, on the ground that all three are necessary for the spiritual and religious welfare of these congregations, and he is the more concerned about the situation because he has no assurance that these requests, if conceded, will not be followed by other requests.[85]

Despite the outright opposition of the Minister for Justice, Frankel remained in Ireland during the war years. Moreover, the Department of Justice was obliged to change its mind over the admission of the Latvian girl – almost certainly due to an appeal over the head of Ruttledge to Eamon de Valera. A Department of Justice minute on 23 May 1938 stated: 'Minister has decided that this alien is to be admitted. Please authorise visa.'[86]

De Valera also intervened personally in at least two other cases. Professor Ernst Lewy was studying Irish in Galway in 1938 with the assistance of funding from the Society for the Protection of Science and Learning in London. De Valera sought his help in the establishment of an Institute of Celtic Studies in Dublin. On de Valera's intervention, a visa was granted to Lewy's daughter.[87] In another case, the Department of Justice temporised over the granting of a visa to Dr Bacher, an analytical chemist from Vienna. Bacher was a Jew whose family's wealth had been confiscated after Anschluss, but they still had sufficient means outside Austria to ensure that he would be self-sufficient. The Department of Justice was unsure about issuing a visa because Bacher was in a concentration camp. De Valera directed the secretary of the Department of External Affairs, Joseph Walshe, to inform Roche:

> the fact of this man's internment in a concentration camp is not, in itself, a reason for withholding the grant of a visa and accordingly, if the applicant were, in the opinion of your Department, otherwise qualified to receive a visa, this Department would raise no objections.[88]

It is not known whether Dr Bacher succeeded in getting to Ireland.

Given the severity of the restrictions on entry, is there any evidence that

members of the Jewish community sought to bring in refugees illegally from
Britain and from the continent? There is evidence to suggest that one
member of the Jewish community was suspected of such a practice. A Garda
report in May 1938 gave a negative recommendation on an application by a
member of the Jewish community to bring in his brother and sister-in-law.
The Department of Justice was informed that 'X is actively associated with
the Jewish Board of Guardians and is suspected of assisting aliens of undesirable character who enter the country by surreptitious means'.[89] This was,
undoubtedly, an isolated case and an extensive search of Department of
Justice files did not reveal any other cases of this kind. Why? Briscoe, in his
letter to Ruttledge quoted above, indicated that he was 'the bludgeon' with
which the minister could be beaten. That concern influenced him to be very
careful and selective in the cases he took up. The Jewish community in
general was equally cautious in its activities, for three main reasons. Firstly,
the Jewish community was emphatically opposed to breaking Irish law even
for a cause as worthy as the bringing to safety of refugees trapped on the
continent. Secondly, representations to the authorities sometimes yielded
positive results. Thirdly, the smuggling of refugees would be immediately
tracked down by the authorities and would ultimately undermine the collective credibility of the Jewish community leadership. In fine, a combination of
good citizenship and respect for the law were the defining characteristics of
the Irish Jewish community.

It was not the practice, or so it was stated by the Department of Justice, to
record the religion of aliens entering the country. But, in reality, the Irish
authorities knew when an alien was Jewish. It made a difference too. As 1938
advanced, the numbers wishing to come to Ireland increased dramatically.
The deteriorating situation in Europe meant that aliens, once admitted, would
not be allowed to return to their country of origin. The secretary of the
Department of External Affairs, Joseph Walshe, wrote to his counterpart in
the Department of Industry and Commerce, John Leydon, on 16 August 1938
with regard to the granting of visas to German nationals of Jewish origin:

> the Minister for External Affairs is satisfied that it is more than probable
> that all such persons, once out of Germany, will be deprived of their
> German nationality and consequently permanently debarred from return-
> ing to Germany. They cannot be allowed to return as deportees or in any
> other way, as the German authorities will refuse to allow them to land in
> any circumstances. The country granting the visa is accordingly bound to
> keep them, despite the fact that the validity of the visa or of the permit to
> reside may have been restricted to a very short period. This has already
> been the experience of a number of countries.[90]

Walshe further told Leydon that de Valera felt that 'every possible precau-
tion should be taken to prevent an influx of persons who could subsequently
not be removed from this country'. Walshe proposed, therefore, that in the
case of all German and formerly Austrian nationals to whom it was proposed
to give an employment permit, the permit be sent to the Department of
External Affairs for transmission to the Berlin legation:

If and when the Minister Plenipotentiary were satisfied that the person named in the permit would not be debarred from entering Germany on his return, then he would deliver the permit. If, on the other hand, he were not so satisfied, then he would hold the permit, and report immediately to this Department his reasons for so doing.[91]

That was, in the opinion of de Valera, the only effective method of controlling the entry into the country of people who might be left there for the rest of their lives.[92]

The assistant secretary at the Department of Justice, J. E. Duff, agreed also with de Valera's line of argument.[93] In a letter on 23 August to John Leydon, he wrote:

The only person in a position to obtain this information [concerning aliens being debarred] is the Irish Minister at Berlin, and, in cases where employment in this country is not contemplated, the practice of this Department has been to leave the granting or withholding of the necessary visa to the discretion of the Minister Plenipotentiary.[94]

It was a matter of expediency and policy, therefore, to allow the anti-Semitic Charles Bewley, Ireland's envoy in Berlin, wide discretionary powers in the granting or withholding of visas.

Charles Bewley and Irish refugee policy after Munich

In September 1938, Mussolini ordered all foreign Jews, about 20,000, to leave Italy. Anti-Semitic laws had been introduced in July.[95] The 'Munich bother', as the Irish poet Patrick Kavanagh termed appeasement's crowning achievement,[96] culminated with the agreement signed on 30 September by which the Sudetenland in Czechoslovakia was ceded to Hitler. An editorial in the *Irish Press* said:

There can be few people in neutral countries who have watched the development of the crisis in recent months but will sympathise with the gallant Czech people in the partial dismemberment of their Republic. ... Their self-sacrifice in the interests of peace will not, let us hope, go unrewarded.[97]

The paper endorsed de Valera's statement that 'a comprehensive examination should be made of the remaining problems that might again threaten European peace'.[98]

Following the ceding of the Sudetenland, the Czech capital Prague had over 130,000 refugees – many of them Jews trying to flee the country before Hitler completed his absorption of what remained of Czechoslovakia. That was to occur in March 1939 with the seizure of Bohemia and Moravia where 117,000 Jews lived.[99] Between the Munich crisis in September 1938 and Hitler's march into Prague on 15 March 1939, Dublin was obliged to take further measures to deal with the growing number of applications from people seeking refuge in Ireland.

Charles Bewley responded to instructions from the Department of External Affairs in a report on 6 October 1938 concerning 'those persons of Jewish or German origin who have left or will leave the parts of Czechoslovakia occupied by Germany, Poland and Hungary'. Still in possession of validly issued Czech passports, they would not be allowed back into their own country. Bewley had visited the Czech minister in Berlin on 5 October, and was told that

> many Jews had already left Czechoslovakia, having first taken care to export as much of their capital as they could transfer. I gathered that the feeling among the Czechs is now strongly anti-Jewish, as they feel that their present situation is at least in part due to a policy pursued more in Jewish and anti-German interests than in those of the Czech people.[100]

Bewley's following paragraphs may have caused alarm in the Department of Justice: 'The net result will in all probability be that a large number of Jews and German Communists will be at large in Europe, with Czech passports, but without the possibility of returning either to Czechoslovakia or Germany.'[101] He pointed out that if people with Czech passports entered Britain freely, it would be almost impossible to prevent them from landing in Dún Laoghaire. He added:

> In any event, I consider that it would be very unsafe to assume that Jews or German Communists who may come to Ireland from the part of Czechoslovakia now ceded to other countries can be returned to Czechoslovakia. . . . I am satisfied that in many cases it would be impossible to repatriate.[102]

The Department of Justice took note and drew up guidelines for Irish immigration officers on 12 October 1938: 'Leave to land should be refused also to persons from Czecho-Slovakia proper who in the opinion of the immigration officer are likely to become refugees.'[103] Then on 19 October the secretary of the department, S. A. Roche, wrote to John Leydon at the Department of Industry and Commerce about the need to take measures to stop the issuing of work permits to 'any person who seems to belong to that class unless the need for the services of such person is so great as to justify his acceptance as a *permanent* resident in the State'. The people of 'that class' were those from 'Czecho-Slovakia who are of Jewish origin and/or political refugees'. Roche urged that the Minister for Industry and Commerce, Seán Lemass, might 'bear in mind the tendency of certain classes of aliens who have already gained admittance to this State to press for the admission of their relatives and friends who are still in Central Europe'.[104]

On 27 October, Bewley reported on a further conversation with the Czech minister in Berlin. The Irish envoy had asked him whether he anticipated a great efflux of Jews from Czechoslovakia. In reply, Bewley was told that Czéchoslovakia 'would under no circumstances permit the Jews who had become naturalised since the [First World War] to remain'. (Many German emigrants since 1933 had been allowed to become naturalised Czechs by the Beneš government, he reported.) He was also told that many

Jews had been expelled and were now camping between the Czech and the German borders.[105]

As the refugee situation worsened, J. E. Duff wrote to Boland at the Department of External Affairs on 26 November stating that the minister for Justice believed there was 'a danger that Jews and other persons who are personae non-gratae to the authorities' of Czechoslovakia, Italy, Poland and Hungary might gain admission to Ireland to take up employment and become refugees. Aware that the Department of Industry and Commerce could not ascertain in every case whether a person was likely to become a refugee, the Minister for Justice believed that, if 'an arrangement similar to the arrangement by which permits for German nationals are issued through the legation in Berlin could be made for the issue of permits to Czecho-Slovak, Italian, Polish and Hungarian nationals, the danger of refugees being admitted would be lessened'.[106] The Minister for Justice proposed that the Irish legation in Rome be used for permits being issued to Italian nationals while Irish permits for Poles and Hungarians – Ireland not having legations in their countries – could be sent to the British passport control officers, who would only give them out when they were certain that the aliens would not be prevented from returning to their own countries.[107] That latter arrangement was accepted by the British.[108]

This still left the problem of aliens who at the time had valid work permits and who, if allowed to remain, would almost certainly become refugees. Duff wrote to John Leydon at the Department of Industry and Commerce stating that Minister Ruttledge suggested

> accordingly that when the employment permits for such persons expire, the possibility of their becoming refugees should be taken into consideration and that extensions of their permits should not be granted unless the Minister for Industry and Commerce is satisfied that the need for the services of the aliens is so great as to warrant their acceptance (and the acceptance of their wives and families) as permanent residents.[109]

Leydon wrote back to Roche at the Department of Justice agreeing with the proposals. He pointed out, however, that in connection with permits being issued for Hungarian, Polish or Czechoslovakian aliens, it would be difficult, from the information available in his department, 'to determine whether or not an alien is Jewish'. The Department of Industry and Commerce therefore 'proposed to consult your Department before extensions of permits are granted in respect of the employment of aliens of these nationalities'.[110]

Czechoslovakia may have been a far away country for Neville Chamberlain. It was even further over the horizon for the Irish Minister for Justice and certain civil servants who may have had an opportunity to read only select passages from Bewley's reports circulated by the Department of External Affairs. The Irish envoy's reports in the latter months of 1938 were alarmist and anti-Semitic. Bewley reported in detail on 25 October on the anti-Jewish laws which had been implemented by the Czech government – measures which amounted to the de facto expulsion of Jews as they were dismissed from the universities and the professions. He referred to the banning of the Communist Party and the Masonic order, which were both 'in overwhelming proportions composed of Jews'.[111] He then gave his superiors in Dublin the benefit of his wisdom on the character of Jewish emigrants from Middle Europe:

> the Department will no doubt be aware from the Belgian press that there has been a great increase of criminality in Belgium owing to the influx of these undesirable types. The Belgian government has in fact interned some thousands, and those left at large are obliged to sign undertakings to refrain from association with the Belgian population. The latter step was, according to the *Handelsblad van antwerpen*, rendered necessary by the Jewish practice of entering into formal marriage with Belgians in the hope of thus being exempted from expulsion.[112]

Bewley was approached in late 1938 by a British Labour Party member, Mr Karran, seeking to have German medical students continue their training in Ireland. They would then, he assured Bewley, go to New Zealand. He was told by Bewley that visas would not be issued unless they produced evidence that they would be allowed to re-enter Germany. Bewley also wanted to know why 'the Jewish medical students' could not be educated in England or New Zealand. He wrote to Dublin on 2 November:

> The danger that if they had completed their medical studies they would not be admitted to practise in either of those countries [England and New Zealand] seems to be a considerable one. . . . Mr Karran is the type of Englishman who is fond of doing good at other people's expense . . .[113]

Bewley's swansong

In view of the growth of radical anti-Semitic laws in continental Europe, the Department of External Affairs requested Bewley in November 1938 to provide a review of the state of anti-Semitism in Germany and in other specified countries (Italy, Hungary, Poland and Czechoslovakia). Bewley warmed to his task, giving a report on 9 December which uncritically mirrored the central Nazi ideas on anti-Semitism.[114] He began:

> The Governments of the countries mentioned have been led by their experience to the conviction that Jews, even when settled in a particular country for centuries, do not become assimilated to the people of that country, but, when the interests of the country of their birth come into conflict with their own personal or racial interests, invariably sacrifice the interests of the country of their birth to Jewish interests.[115]

Bewley repeated the claim that German Jews acted against German interests during the First World War. He argued further that as soon as England had 'definitely espoused the cause of Zionism', the Jews worked for Germany's defeat in the war. The same conviction, he said, was held in Hungary. The Irish envoy continued:

> The Italian Government has stated that, when relations were strained between Italy and England in 1935, the whole body of Italian Jews (who

should have been assimilated if assimilation was possible, owing to the fact that their ancestors had in many cases been over a thousand years in Italy) openly declared themselves Zionists, or in secret conspired against Italian interests.[116]

Bewley then developed the thesis, citing Fr Denis Fahey's *The Rulers of Russia* as evidence, that Jews were invariably the 'chief supporters and organisers of Communism'. The Bolshevist movement in Russia, he claimed, 'was almost entirely led by Jews' ('a fact so well known as to need no emphasis') and had been 'financed by American-Jewish banking houses'. He also said that 'the majority of the leaders' of the 'Communist' governments in Hungary and Bavaria after the First World War were Jews. Bewley continued:

> In recent years the governments of all the mid-European states have formally prohibited the Communist Party, and have effected very numerous arrests for illegal Communist activities. The vast majority of the guilty persons in each country have been Jews ... [that] is proved by perusal of the reports of trials of Communists in any country in Central Europe.[117]

Bewley then spoke about the dominance of Jews in business, finance, academia and politics. He claimed that in Germany and in the other countries he had mentioned

> the Jews had acquired so dominating a position in the financial world that they were in a position to control public policy, and up to a certain point public opinion, that they monopolised the learned professions and held important positions in the universities out of all proportion to their numbers, and in fact had become a force in face of which the lawfully elected government was in many cases powerless.[118]

He claimed that in Germany before 1933 the 'whole press, theatre, cinema, stock-exchange, the banks were completely under Jewish control'. In Berlin and the other major towns, 'the medical and legal professions were composed of roughly 70 per cent Jews and 30 per cent Germans'. Even hospital nurses in many nominally non-Jewish hospitals were exclusively Jewish, he wrote. Jewish professors who held important positions in universities were, he claimed, 'frequently anti-Christian, anti-patriotic and communistic'. While that situation no longer existed in Germany, Bewley said it continued to be the case in Warsaw, Budapest and Prague, adding that 'at the present day ... measures are being adopted to alter it in those countries also'.

Bewley reported that another reason for the taking of special measures was that Jews did not work as manual workers, labourers, farmers or artisans. Financial scandals were, he said, attributable to Jews. But even at the lower levels of commerce it was felt that Jewish behaviour was marked 'by a want of scruple' which obliged governments 'to intervene in the interests of the native community against the usury and fraud of Jewish money-lenders, employers, and middlemen'.[119] The same difficulties arose, he claimed, even in countries to which Jews had been allowed to emigrate in the previous couple of years. Various diplomats in Berlin had confirmed to him that Jews refused to remain on the land 'but very soon deserted it for the purpose of exploiting the inhabitants of the country'.

Bewley felt that 'members of the Jewish race' tended to shirk national service. Recently published figures revealed, he claimed, that 'the proportion of Jews [killed in the course of duty] was minimal in comparison with that of Germans, Frenchmen or Italians, whether Protestant or Catholic'. The inference could therefore be drawn, according to Bewley, that 'the Jew endeavours with success to avoid doing his duty in defending the state in which he resides'. He added:

> Anyone who witnessed the immigration into Ireland of English Jews after the introduction of conscription in England will feel inclined to adopt the German view. When it was found in Germany, as in many other countries, that the Jew has not only succeeded in avoiding military service but also in enriching himself during the agony of the country, it is comprehensible that popular feeling has tended to become anti-Semitic.[120]

The envoy then advanced a further reason for discrimination against Jews – their 'demoralising' influence on the community among which they live.

> It is a notorious fact that the international white slave traffic is controlled by Jews. No one who has even a superficial knowledge of Germany can be ignorant that the appalling moral degradation before 1933 was, if not caused, at least exploited by Jews. The German stage was the most indecent in Europe; it was a Jewish monopoly. German papers appeared of a purely pornographic nature: the proprietor and editor were invariably Jews. Jewish members of the Reichstag were responsible for the introduction of a number of measures abolishing legal penalties for abortion and a number of other practices which are visited by the most severe punishments in every Christian country.[121]

Bewley claimed that 'Jewish emigrants in the countries which they have been permitted to enter have created and are creating grave moral scandals and are a source of corruption of the populations among which they live'. Referring to his time as a senior counsel on the western circuit in Ireland during the 1920s, he wrote:

> Anyone familiar with the criminal courts even in Ireland must be aware that every Jew convicted of a crime can count with confidence on the Chief Rabbi testifying on oath that he knows the man intimately and is convinced that he could not possibly be guilty of the crime of which he has been found guilty by an Irish jury.[122]

All the 'facts' cited by Bewley were, he claimed, 'well known to everyone who has lived in Central Europe, or who has taken the trouble to make enquiries from non-Jewish sources into the situation as it really is'.

In consequence of those 'facts', Bewley said that Germany, as well as the other countries in central Europe, had 'felt itself obliged to eliminate the Jews from the public life of the state' with the result that 'Jews are now for practical purposes completely isolated from Germany'.[123] He added: 'It is perhaps well to refer to the fact that very few, if any, of the measures introduced in Germany in relation to the Jewish problem cannot be paralleled in the measures introduced by the Popes in relation to the Jews of Rome.'[124] He defended Germany's record:

If every state which has experience of Jews, including those with Catholic clergymen at their head, finds it necessary to introduce similar special measures restricting their activities, it is impossible to take up with any degree of reason the attitude that they should be treated like ordinary citizens of the country. ... Naturally this would not apply to cases of deliberate cruelty on the part of the Government, but I am not aware of any such towards Jews on the part of the German Government. There has been no episode in connection with Jews in Germany which could even remotely be compared with the atrocities of the Communists in Spain or Russia or the English in Palestine.[125]

Bewley claimed that the German situation was being distorted because of Jewish control of the international press and the international wire services. This meant that, in the long run, Irish public opinion on foreign affairs and public policy on international relations were formed 'not by the Government of Ireland but by anonymous agencies acting on the dictation and in pursuance of the policy of persons who are neither Irish nor Catholic but bitterly opposed both to Irish Nationalism and to the Catholic Church'. Bewley then launched an attack on the Irish daily press where reports of 'persecutions' of Jews were invariably 'featured'. But crimes of anti-fascists were 'systematically suppressed'. He concluded:

It is ... clear that if the Irish press and public opinion indulge in parox-ysms of moral indignation at the treatment of Jews but remain blind and deaf to atrocities committed on Christians in other parts of the world, they lay themselves open to a charge of ignorance or hypocrisy, and scarcely contribute to an amelioration of the general international situation.[126]

That piece of propaganda, masquerading as diplomatic reportage, was Bewley's swansong.[127] He was living on borrowed time as the Irish represent-ative in Berlin. Dublin was very dissatisfied with his professional performance during late 1938. Walshe wrote to him on 26 January 1939 expressing de Valera's disappointment about the fact that the last comprehensive report on the international situation had been sent in July 1938, 'notwithstanding the gravity of the September crisis and the predominant part which is being taken by the German Government in a situation which might at any moment bring our Government face to face with issues of vital importance to the Irish People'.[128]

Bewley wrote six reports between February 1939 and his departure in August. His final valedictory despatch to Dublin on 2 August was insolent and offensive. It spoke of the 'failure' of the Department of External Affairs and of Irish foreign policy to distinguish itself from Britain:

Ireland, at the end of ten years' separate representation at Berlin, is regarded by the German Government, as by the other Governments where it has representation, as a British dependency, with autonomy but no real independence either political or spiritual.

This report was accompanied by a petulant note from Bewley to de Valera: 'I enclose copy of report on the general situation, which I trust you will do me the honour of reading.'[129] He left the diplomatic service days later in a welter of acrimony.[130]

But for as long as he had remained at his post, Bewley had only to refer to Dublin the visa applications of those seeking to work or set up industries in Ireland. He had, on the other hand, been granted exceptional powers to decide over who should or should not be recommended for refugee status. As he was the only Irish diplomat resident in Berlin, did he allow his prejudices to influence his unsupervised consular decisions?

George Clare and Kristallnacht

George Clare, a Viennese Jew, provides some evidence to show that Bewley's anti-Semitism influenced his treatment of those who came to the Berlin legation. Clare was in his late teens when Hitler entered Vienna. His father, Ernest, was a banker and a friend of Emil Hirsch; the latter owned a ribbon factory in Austria and managed to get some of his machinery out of the country. He set up Hirsch Ribbons Ltd at 24 Suffolk Street, Dublin, and the Castle Hat Company also at 24 Suffolk Street and in Castlebar, Co. Mayo.[131]

The Clare parents and their son, George, had applied for visas to live in Ireland in return for the provision of capital to help Robert Hirsch set up a ribbon factory in Longford.[132] In August 1938, the family received a cable in Vienna informing them that their immigration permits had been granted and that their visas were awaiting them at the Irish legation in Berlin. They closed down their flat, stored their furniture and took the train to Berlin, arriving on 2 September.[133] They then took a taxi to the Irish legation at Tiergartenstrasse 34A in Berlin's diplomatic quarter, where they found that a Frau Kamberg and Charles Bewley constituted the entire staff.[134]

Clare's father produced the telegram from Dublin. But after a search, Kamberg, who appeared to be sympathetic, said that the visas had not yet arrived. She managed to convey that she would try to help as much as she could but that, as George Clare later recounted, 'the Minister himself might be somewhat less keen'.[135] She advised the family to contact their agent in Dublin directly and to return to the legation a week later; she also agreed to call Dublin provided she was given permission by Bewley to do so.[136] Returning the following week, George Clare's mother was disappointed to find the visas had not arrived. Kamberg, who risked being sacked, courageously gave her the following explanation:

> A policy decision and not Irish distaste for speedy action was prolonging our stay in Berlin into one *mañana* after another. A letter from Dublin had arrived at the legation that morning explaining that the Irish authorities thought it too risky to allow a Jewish family to enter their country before they had confirmation that Hirsch's machines, which were what mattered to them, were on their way.[137]

The machinery was likely to take a further six weeks to get there.

George Clare and his mother waited in Berlin in a climate of intensifying persecution of the Jews. After six weeks, his father travelled to Paris to take up a post in a bank, but he could not get entry permits into France for his wife and son. Forced to wait another four weeks in Berlin, George Clare and his mother lived through the terror of Kristallnacht (the night of broken glass) on 9 and 10 November in the Jewish Pension Lurie on the Kurfurstendamm: 'With the other guests we sat in fearful silence in the lounge listening to the howls of the organised mob smashing the windows of Jewish shops. We all had but one thought. When would the SS come and take us away?'[138] The historian Karl Dietrich Bracher described Kristallnacht as a night of orchestrated pogrom in which, to the strains of Beethoven's *Eroica* symphony, about 100 Jews were murdered and almost all the synagogues in Germany were destroyed together with 7,000 Jewish-owned stores.[139] Michael Marrus has called Kristallnacht 'the culminating barbarity, the definitive expression of Nazi implacability towards the Jews'.[140]

The distinguished Celtic scholar, Julius Pokorny, narrowly escaped being rounded up on that occasion. He wrote to the director of the National Library in Ireland, Richard Best:

> You probably know, that . . . the order had been given, to arrest 40,000 Jews (and Non-Aryans as well), especially intellectuals. I had been warned in time and gone away for a few weeks. I still have not given up hope and shall try to remain in Germany as long as possible. But, I am afraid, the chances grow worse from day to day, and in the end I shall probably be obliged to leave the country as a *scoláire bocht*![141]

Meanwhile, nothing happened that night to either the Clares or the other guests in the Pension Lurie. All remained in their boarding house throughout the terror of the Kristallnacht riots.[142]

The following day, George Clare and his mother both went to the Irish legation. Writing later, George was suspicious that 'our visas had actually been granted by Dublin some days earlier, but that Mr Bewley, the Minister, for whatever reason, had sat on them'. He surmised that Kamberg had persuaded Bewley that morning to issue the visas without delay: 'It just seemed too pat somehow that authority from Dublin should have arrived on the very morning after the Kristallnacht.'[143] Clare and his mother arrived in Ireland on 12 November 1938 and went to Galway. On 27 February 1939, George Clare went to Longford with Robert Hirsch, Ernst Sonnenschein and Alois Gobl to set up a ribbon factory. They returned to Galway on 4 March. Both George and his mother travelled to London on 27 March to meet his father who had arrived from Paris. George returned alone to Longford, where another alien, Kende Ludwig, joined the group.[144] Separated from his parents who were now in Paris, George Clare sought to join the British army and rejoin his fiancée, Lisl Beck, who was living in England. Prevented from joining the army because of his age, he remained in Ireland for a further two years. Writing to his parents on 18 January 1941, he sought to disabuse them of the notion that Ireland offered the future they sought together as a family: it 'does not exist, never did exist and never will exist. Put Ireland out of your head.'[145] Eventually, Clare joined the British army and survived the war. His parents were less fortunate. Rounded up in Paris, they died in a concentration camp. The terrible tragedy was that they both had visas to live in Ireland.

Religious bodies and refugees, 1938–39

The need to help refugees fleeing political and religious persecution on the continent was a source of growing pastoral concern for the Irish churches and religious groups. Prominent among those organisations was the German Emergency Committee of the Society of Friends (later the Society of Friends' Committee for Refugees and Aliens) which had been established in 1933.[146] Lucy O. Kingston's family looked after a German Quaker girl, Annelies Becker, who came from the Rhineland in 1934. The family joke was that she came for three weeks and remained for nineteen years.[147] Other Irish people who helped in the reception of refugees were the labour activists, Louie Bennett and Helen Chenevix.[148] The Jewish Refugee Aid Committee of Éire, established in 1938 with an address at 43 Bloomfield Avenue, South Circular Road, Dublin, was also very active.[149] The honorary president was Rev. Abraham Gudansky and the chairman was Leonard Abrahamson. The vice-chairmen were Arthur Newman, Max Newman (Cork), Edwin Solomons and H. Tomkin.[150] The Church of Ireland and the Catholic Church also had comparable organisations.[151] But what the various bodies lacked was unified co-ordination in the face of a most restrictive national refugee policy. That was to come about in late autumn 1938.

Many members of the Jewish community in Ireland were particularly outraged when not even the overtures of the chief rabbi of Palestine, Isaac Herzog, could persuade the medical profession to allow Christian Jewish doctor refugees to practise in Ireland. On 9 October 1938, Herzog wrote to de Valera appealing to him, 'In view of the noble stand which you have made on behalf of those unfortunate victims of blind hatred', to admit a quota of Jewish refugee doctors and dentists to practise in Ireland on the same conditions as in the United Kingdom. 'Perhaps Éire might feel particularly interested in Jewish doctors and dentists of a particular area or locality within the zone of anti-Semitic persecution', he suggested.[152] The appeal did not meet with success.

This ungenerous and small-minded example of the restrictiveness of government policy contributed to the growing appeal of prominent academics and churchmen to co-ordinate the individual endeavours of the various humanitarian bodies. Thanks to the diplomatic skills of the professor of medicine at University College Dublin, T. W. T. Dillon, administrative obstacles were removed expeditiously. Recognising the unsatisfactory nature of existing arrangements, de Valera responded positively to overtures. The Departments of Justice and Industry and Commerce may not have been quite so co-operative. However, on 10 November 1938, Dillon acknowledged progress to the Taoiseach: 'I think I may say that, thanks to the good offices of Mr [Frank] Fahy [the ceann comhairle or speaker in the Dáil] and the generous support you gave us, we have now established friendly working relations with the Departments concerned.'[153] De Valera met Dillon soon afterwards with a delegation of the ad hoc Irish Co-ordinating Committee for Refugees, and a working group had been set up by 14 November; it outlined its position in a memorandum of that date:

> These proposals relate only to Christians with Jewish blood. The Co-ordinating Committee are of opinion that this country should confine itself to such persons as there are adequate funds subscribed by the Jewish Communities in other countries to deal with the cases of professing Jews.[154]

The memorandum stated that a large number of applications had already been received from doctors, dentists and other professional men who wanted to settle in Ireland: 'The Minister for Industry and Commerce has expressed the opinion that it would be highly undesirable to permit foreign Doctors to practise in this country and in the absence of very special circumstances the Minister for Justice agrees.'[155]

It was also proposed in the memorandum that applications from refugees who wished to establish themselves in the country would be entertained by the government only when received through the committee:

> Up to the present numerous applications have been received from genuine and well-meaning people in this country for permission for refugees to settle here. It was clear, however, that in many cases the applicants knew little or nothing about the persons for whom they were seeking asylum and it would be almost an impossible task for any Government Department to distinguish between different applications from private individuals.

Prepared to undertake the task of sifting applications for permission to settle in Ireland, the committee expressed itself willing to put forward names 'only of persons whom they are satisfied will be suitable in every way'.[156] The memorandum argued that, if the government recognised the committee, it would be possible to fix the number of refugees in specified categories and allow the committee to select the persons for admission. The committee's proposals related to three different classes.

Firstly, the committee proposed that fifty people who had already some training in agricultural work in the Kagran group near Vienna should be admitted for further training. They would then go to either Australia or South America. Adequate funds had already been provided. Two private houses had been put at their disposal and the Minister for Agriculture had promised to co-operate fully. Three visas had been authorised already by the Minister for Justice, and the first party was expected shortly. Secondly, the committee had received offers from well-to-do people who were prepared to maintain indefinitely if necessary certain adult refugees. (The term 'adult' was understood to mean over sixteen years.) Many of these were refugees who were waiting to emigrate to the United States. The committee guaranteed that none of these people would become a public charge or enter into competition with nationals for jobs. The figure of twenty in that category had been put forward, and the Minister for Justice was disposed to agree. Thirdly, numerous applications had been received for permission to educate children in Ireland. While it was usual for such children to go to another country afterwards, the committee could not give a 'binding undertaking' that that would happen. But in many such cases, the committee felt, there were strong 'claims to sympathetic consideration' and some children had already been admitted on guarantees that funds for their maintenance and education would be available. The committee wanted the discretion to select about twenty such children, and again the minister was disposed to agree.[157]

The Irish Co-ordinating Committee for the Relief of Christian Refugees from Central Europe was launched at a meeting in the Mansion House, Dublin, on 4 December 1938.[158] The meeting established an executive committee and issued an appeal for financial support. The ceann comhairle, Frank Fahy, was elected chairman and T. W. T. Dillon vice-chairman.[159] The following organisations were represented on the Co-ordinating Committee: the Church of Ireland Jews Society (for Hebrew Christians); the Society of Friends' German Emergency Committee; the Jewish Refugee Aid Committee; and the (Catholic) Irish Committee for Austrian Relief.[160] The committee, it was stated, had been recognised as the channel through which applications for visas for refugees 'must be presented', and the government had agreed to facilitate the committee in every way.[161] However, it was acknowledged that the position of refugees was the same as that of other aliens in regard to permanent residence: that could only be considered in exceptional cases where there was reason to believe that the presence of the alien would be of definite value to the country.[162]

The public appeal emphasised that 'Ireland has so far taken a very small number and should now do her share'.[163] The objective was to provide hospitality and training for refugees who were expected to emigrate to other countries later:

> In former days when the great Famine and other disasters lay heavy on this land, many of our people sought and received the hospitality of other countries. Let us now show that we, too, can be generous and prove to the world that the Irish people believe that Christians of whatever race or blood are sons of the same Father Whose brotherhood is shown, above all, in this, that 'they love one another'.[164]

Cardinal Joseph MacRory was the first to sign the appeal. The following day's *Irish Press* carried the lead headline: CARDINAL LEADS APPEAL FOR REFUGEES. The initiative was supported by Catholic and Church of Ireland archbishops, leading clergy, members of the professions and leaders of public life generally.[165]

While the appeal met with a mixed financial response, the committee achieved much. Professor Mary Macken rescued a number of refugee children, placed them in Irish schools, and arranged for annual holidays. The committee had, as stated, received lists of names of applicants from various sources. The Society of Friends was responsible for a major success. Through its international centre in Vienna, it assisted the Irish committee in the task of selecting the most suitable cases. The essayist Hubert Butler went to work with the society in Vienna, and there he was put in charge of the Kagran group, which was one of the specific categories mentioned in the Irish committee's November memorandum. Named after a suburb in Vienna, the group was made up mainly of Jewish converts to Christianity who intended forming an agricultural community abroad.[166] Erwin Strunz, a left-leaning journalist, was one of the group. Strunz had converted to Judaism when he married his Jewish wife, Lisl. As he was in danger of being arrested at any time by the Gestapo, Hubert Butler and Emma Cadbury of the Society of Friends had him invited to a conference in London. They succeeded in getting himself, his wife and two children out of Vienna. The family then made its way to Ireland, where the Butlers offered the four a temporary home.[167] That story had a happy ending. Strunz and his family settled in Dublin, where they later ran the Unicorn restaurant with the help of their Austrian friend, Fritz Lederer.

Butler, together with Emma Cadbury and the London Society of Friends' German Emergency Committee, helped get out all the members of the Kagran group. Many settled in England. Meanwhile, prominent members of the Irish Society of Friends opened up their homes to Jewish refugees. The Irish Co-ordinating Committee for Refugees and the German Emergency Committee contributed towards maintenance. The solicitor, Stella M. B. Webb, ran a home for refugees at 'The Haven', Clonliffe Road, Dublin. It remained open until it was sold in the 1950s.[168] The Butler holiday home in Dunmore East, County Waterford, was also used for the same purpose, as was Philip Somerville-Large's house 'Vallombrosa' in Bray, County Wicklow. Sir John Keane's house in Ardmore, County Waterford, was a refuge where the artist, Mary Odell, acted as warden.[169] One family that stayed there were the Schlessingers; Odell provided initial rest and shelter for a few weeks and then they moved on to 'Vallombrosa'. Many of the children of the refugee families – including the Strunz, Schlessinger and Kamerau families – attended the Society of Friends' school in Newtown Park, Waterford.[170] While these refugees were few in number, it was a tribute to the Society of Friends in Vienna, London and Dublin that the trickle reached Ireland.

Reviewing progress on the refugee situation within the context of the categories agreed in November 1938, the vice-chairman of the Irish Co-ordinating Committee for Refugees, T. W. T. Dillon, sought to

> pay a warm tribute to the patient courtesy and kindness of our officials who have to administer these regulations. They have gone to the extreme limit to facilitate the refugee committees in their task, and the work has been carried out in an atmosphere of mutual trust which has done much to lighten the labour.[171]

Nevertheless, after months of trying to meet the criteria laid down for bringing refugees into the country, Dillon was forced to admit that it was 'extremely difficult' in practice to meet those requirements in most cases:

> Where a refugee has friends or relations in this country, or where he has managed by fair means or foul to smuggle out some money the thing is possible. For the ordinary refugee who knows nobody, who has nothing to recommend him except his Christianity, who is in fact a complete liability, it is desperately hard to find the guarantee required. And yet these people are just as deserving of help as the others, and they need it much more urgently.[172]

Dillon cited the case of a girl who had arrived in Ireland a few days before he wrote the article quoted here:

> She is 13 years of age. She told us that her parents were reduced to buying dog biscuits before she left. They had nothing left to sell. There is no hope for these people. Slow starvation or emigration – that is the ugly choice. The Catholics are in the worst position.[173]

He stated that the sum collected from the public 'was only sufficient to provide for about 70 refugees, of whom 25 are being maintained by the Society of St Vincent de Paul'. He said that the only Catholic committee working in Ireland was the University College Catholic Committee for German and Austrian refugees, which dealt with students and scholars.[174] He also referred to an effort being made to reorganise Catholic refugee agencies.[175]

The puny response of the Irish government ought to be measured against the efforts of other countries. Between 1933 and 1939, an estimated 439,000 Jews were forced to emigrate from countries in Europe with strong anti-Semitic laws. About 42,000 went to Britain, 12,000 to Switzerland, 15,000 to Belgium, 27,000 to the Netherlands and 30,000 to France. Some 85,000 went to the United States, another 85,000 to Latin America, 18,000 to Shanghai and 7,000 to Australia and Africa. Some 80,000 went to Palestine, 65,000 of whom arrived in 1935, and many more would have made their way there if a restrictive British policy had not prevented entry. However, even after such a mass exodus, in 1939 there were still 290,000 Jews (including 65,000 non-Aryans) in Germany, 125,000 Jews (including 70,000 non-Aryans) in Austria, and 90,000 Jews in Bohemia and Moravia, together with 20,000 Jewish refugees and 15,000 non-Aryans.

The parsimony of refugee policy must be viewed in the context of official Irish fears that the country might have to cope with thousands of refugees seeking permanent residence. Official concerns of that kind led to feelings of great frustration and even desperation within the Jewish community in Ireland, particularly amongst those members who had relatives and friends living in grave danger on the continent. For example, Muriel Bennington Cooper, an Irish woman living in Brussels, wrote to de Valera on 10 - December 1938:

> Through my travels as an artist, I made several friends of Jewish faith in Germany, all people of 1st class standing, who would like to find a new home. I beg you to tell me if such people with means could not emigrate to Ireland. They are willing to pay in your hands Pounds Sterling ONE HUNDRED each, to be used by you for any charity requiring help. Besides

they will bring into the country: Capital and New Industries and give work to a certain number of unemployed. The export of Ireland will certainly increase tremendously.[176]

She wanted to know whether those people could become citizens, as they needed assurances before establishing factories and investing money.[177] On 16 December, Frederick Boland at the Department of External Affairs sent her letter to S. A. Roche at the Department of Justice.[178] A similar letter, written on 7 December 1938, was received from Julius Jakobovits, Amsterdam. He, too, wanted to know if there was 'a possibility in principle that Jewish people [might] emigrate into the Irish Free State'.[179] Bennington Cooper wrote to the Department of External Affairs again on 15 February 1939 and yet again on 9 May; she was finally informed that 'the only refugees who are admitted to this country are persons whose cases are recommended to the Minister by the Irish Co-ordinating Committee for Refugees, 4 Eustace St., Dublin'.[180] Other enquirers had been given the same advice throughout late 1938 and early 1939.[181]

Robert Briscoe's wife, Lily, received a similar answer when she wrote to her friend, the Minister for Justice, Patrick Ruttledge, on 5 April 1939:

> My brother-in-law, Bob's brother in Paris, wishes to get permits for his wife's brother and sister-in-law who are anxious to go to America but cannot leave Czechoslovakia without a visa. Would it be possible for the Irish government to grant them visitors' visas for those months, in all probability they would not remain for the full duration of this period and as they are very comfortable people would in no way cause any difficulty. I would feel most grateful to you for using your influence on their behalf.[182]

Peter Berry, writing on behalf of the minister, told her that Ruttledge was not prepared 'to consider any application for the admission of refugees into this country except applications made by the Irish Co-ordinating Committee for Refugees'.[183]

Gerald Goldberg recalled an episode in Cork during 1939 in which he was involved.[184] It concerned a German Jew who jumped ship at Cobh, some ten miles away, and was allowed by a friendly customs official to come ashore. A blind eye was turned to the man's lack of documentation, and the Jewish community in Cork agreed to set him up in business.[185] This unnamed individual was a deserving case. His family had been forced to split up because of the Nazi persecution of the Jews. He was in danger of being arrested and deported to a concentration camp if he were returned to Germany. All efforts failed, including a direct appeal to de Valera. The man was sent back and was arrested on landing. He spent the war years in a concentration camp but was lucky to survive.[186] Subsequent attempts by the Goldberg family failed to bring Jewish refugees to Cork during the war.[187]

The Department of Justice was involved in another case which ultimately had a happier outcome. A Jewish man from Przemysl in Poland (formerly part of the Austro-Hungarian empire) first came to Ireland on 20 August 1938 as the holder of a Greek passport.[188] He was ordered out of the country in November when the department became aware of his presence. He left for

France but returned to Ireland in early January 1939. Told to leave again, he departed for England. His case was comprehensively reviewed in March 1939. The department, suspicious of the authenticity of his passport and the quality of his 'character', refused him permission to set up in business in Ireland despite his claim that he had £3,500 to invest in the project and had a near relative living in the country. The assistant secretary at the department, J. E. Duff, minuted on the file: 'Professor Michael Hayes told me that X admits that X is not a Greek subject and that he had no right to hold a Greek passport.'[189] He was refused permission to return. Taking up residence in Belfast, he remained there until May 1941 when the deportation order against him was withdrawn on compassionate grounds. In declining health, he was allowed to return to the country and live with his near relative.[190]

'We possess our soul in patience'

Occasionally, even miracles happened. The German Jewish banker, Hugo Wortsmann, and his wife, Erna, had no doubt but that they owed their lives to Frank Gallagher (director of the Government Information Bureau), his wife, Cecilia and a friendship which had begun decades before. While this chapter has amply demonstrated the negative impact of a restrictive refugee policy, the Wortsmanns' story reveals the generosity which was evident in Irish church circles and from private citizens when given the opportunity to show it.

A letter written in broken English arrived in Cork (written Pork), dated 25 December 1938, and addressed to the chief burgomaster.

> Dear Sir,
>
> Allow me to lay before you the following matter: During the year 1912 there was a young lady: Miss C. Saunders 14 Jriars Walk, Pork, Jreland, in the boarding school at Wiesbaden in Germany together with my wife. Now we want her adress for a special matter (humanity).
>
> Be so kind as let me know fuller particulars, where she and her family is living now, is she married, with whom and where. Does she live in easy circumstances. Are the parents still alive and where are they living. Which is the profession from each of them.[191]

The woman in question was Frank Gallagher's wife. She had taught English in a Jewish school in Germany before the First World War. Somehow the letter was sent on to them in Dublin, and Gallagher, using one of his pseudonyms, David Hogan of Talbot Press, replied to Wortsmann seeking more information.[192]

Wortsmann wrote back on 13 January 1939. His wife's name was Erna, born Walter, from Windsheim (Bavaria); she was at Wiesbaden during 1911–12 and became acquainted with 'Miss C. Saunders'. Wortsmann wrote: 'In remembrance of that happy youthful time Lady Saunders wrote in blank-book of my wife a few lines out of Othello.'[193] The lines in question were from *Othello*, Act 3, Scene 3, which he enclosed together with a copy of the page from his wife's book:

> Who steals my purse steals trash;
> 'tis something, nothing,
> 'twas mine, 'tis his and has
> been slave to thousands,
> But he that filches from me
> My good name,
> robs me of that which not
> enriches him
> and makes me poor indeed.

Wortsmann explained:

> My wife is married with me since 1926. My father and myself, we both
> were the proprietor of the old Banking-firm Emil Wortsmann at Nurem-
> berg. But through the events, well known to you, we both, must, like the
> other Jews, leave Germany. We would like to go to America.[194]

He said they would like to move to England while waiting on their US visas,
and asked Gallagher and his wife to use their influence: 'We appeal upon
your heart. . . . I am sure that you have heard enough about our fate and I
believe further you will participate in it.'[195]

Wortsmann wrote again on 18 February, giving Gallagher details of the
German Jewish Aid Committee in London that was handling their case.[196]
'As we have no relations in Great Britain, allow me to appeal to you to do
something for us. The committee will communicate on our behalf with you
direct, as I read in the letter from the German Jewish Aid Committee.'[197]
Gallagher was in the United States when this letter arrived. Upon his return,
he wrote to Wortsmann pointing out that he had heard nothing from the
London aid committee. In the meantime, Gallagher had got in touch with a
number of his influential friends to take up the case. Wortsmann wrote again
on 15 June thanking him for his efforts: 'Next time my wife, Erna, will write
to you, but for today you must excuse her, then her mother goes next week
to Holland and you can imagine what it means for mother and daughter.'[198]
He was concerned that Jews could not transfer money out of Germany.

> I must apply again renewed to you to help us, to support us in furnishing
> the necessary funds for our stay in England. I think and I am sure you will
> do the same for us, what we have done during many years, we kept it for
> our duty to be humanely and mercifully against everybody who knocked
> on our door. But we never thought and kept it for possible that the fate is
> so terrible with us.[199]

Gallagher continued to work for the Wortsmanns. He got news that they
hoped to get to England by August.[200] Gallagher got confirmation on 27 June
that the Wortsmanns' application for a visa had been made to the British
Home Office, and he informed Wortsmann of this by letter. Wortsmann
replied that he did not know when they would get to England as they had yet
to settle with the German authorities: 'It is all not so easy as the people
believe. We possess our soul in patience.' He thanked the Gallaghers for their
efforts: 'We are very lucky that you was and are prepared, especially in the

last months, do all what is in your power and what could be done to alleviate our lot.'[201] He then enquired: 'My wife has learned last year to stuff carpets and clothes. Is this a profession in Great Britain to earn the living? Are shops of this branch in your country or would England welcome such a branch, because I think there will be many carpets which need to be stuffed.'[202] Word was sent on 28 July to Gallagher from the German Jewish Aid Committee that the British passport control officer in Frankfurt had been authorised to issue a visa to Mr and Mrs Hugo I. Wortsmann.[203]

In the meantime, Gallagher had collected funds from his friends for the support of the couple when they arrived in England. These included Robert Barton, Erskine Childers, John Moynihan, Francis MacManus and Sinéad de Valera.[204] Gallagher got a letter from Wortsmann upon his arrival in London on 12 September 1939: 'I can't enough English to express our feelings in words. You will understand, believe me, as great is your sympathy, your feeling about our persecution, as great is our love, our heart to you.'[205] Another letter on 14 September read:

> It is wonderful to know human beings, who have sence (?) for a human fate. It is once more wonderful when one can reckon on people who are prepared to help with hand and heart. We are only thankful for your aid, but we esteem especially your very nice lovely good meaning words which we always found in every of your letters. You may have much luck in all your enterprises for all your good doings on us.[206]

Gallagher continued to find resources to support the Wortsmanns. Cecilia Gallagher's sister, Hilda Saunders, who lived in London, met them while they were there. The Wortsmanns went to relatives in the United States in 1940 where they settled in Savannah, Georgia. The two families never met, but every Christmas during the war years when rationing was severe the Wortsmanns sent a wonderful parcel to the Gallaghers as a gesture of appreciation to those who helped with 'hand and heart'.[207]

Anti-Semitism in Ireland on the eve of war

How did Irish refugee policy on Jews appear to the German minister in Dublin, Edouard Hempel? Reporting to Berlin on 7 December 1938, he stated that Irish people were 'beginning to be more lucid than before about the dangers of an increase in the Jewish population in Ireland and of the necessity of a fundamental solution of the Jewish question'. The German envoy had the view put to him in various milieux that the immigration of 'Jewish elements' into Ireland, the initial sign of which was an increased number of Jewish businessmen, was being viewed 'with overt unease'. He added:

> The Irishman as such is generally not well disposed to Jews, in so far as he knows any. A particularly bad impression was created here by the fact that during the September [Munich] crisis many English Jews, some of them of German birth, fled to Ireland to find security here and at the end of the crisis returned to England.

Hempel further reported that there might be some reservations in government about allowing in a large number of Jewish refugees; he believed that the government feared further disturbances.[208]

Anti-Semitic disturbances in Dublin had not been very frequent throughout the 1930s. But in the latter part of the decade a number of radical nationalist groups gave expression to anti-foreigner and anti-Semitic ideas. On 20 November 1938, the 1916 Veterans' Association passed the following motion: 'That we hereby register our emphatic protest against the growing menace of alien immigration, and urge on the Government the necessity of more drastic restrictions in this connection.'[209] The *Irish Times* carried the text of a manifesto from the Irish–Ireland Research Society on 23 February 1939. Addressing 'Irishmen and Irishwomen', the society declared that it refused to 'stand by and allow the Jewish hold on our economic life to develop'. The statement continued:

> Unhappily the whole question of racial aliens, their special moral code and values, is never widely appreciated until it is too late. When at last a remedy is applied to the evils engendered by leading Jewish propaganda the public is given no opportunity to judge for itself.[210]

It concluded:

> Is this, in spite of Father Fahey's warnings against those with dual citizenship, to be the reality behind the green, white and gold? Are Hamar Greenwood, Jewish Commander-in-Chief of the Black and Tans, and Copeland of the Partition Boundary Commission, to be our secret, pitiless dictators? Our society is ranged against world money.[211]

In an editorial, the *Irish Times* described the statement as the 'crudest form of anti-Semitic propaganda' and continued: 'We would treat this effusion with the contempt which it deserves but for the fact that attempts have been made of late to stir up anti-Jewish feeling in this country, which is famed justly for its tolerance.'[212] The editorial went on to state that 'the Jewish citizens of Éire are good citizens' and if some of them were successful it was due to their own hard work. Many of them had made valuable contributions towards the national well-being. The paper was convinced that the great majority of the Irish people shared the view of the editorial. The *Irish Times* concluded: 'Anti-Semitism in any country is foolish; in Ireland it is almost criminal.'[213]

The manifesto was printed in the Nazi Party paper *Völkischer Beobachter* on 26 February, probably having been sent to Berlin by the German legation in Dublin. In an article signed by 'CNP' and filed from Dublin, the writer attempted to put the statement in context. He wrote that recently there had been 'increasing signs in Ireland of a widespread enmity to Jews', which was caused 'not least of all by the "refugee" policy of the Government'.[214] He explained that

> Irish anti-Semitism is still fairly young. Until about 50 years ago scarcely any Jews were to be seen in Ireland. After the war, however, the Jews streamed in here, too, and in the meantime they have been able to gain a

strong position in business and politics. At present emigrants from
Germany are granted permission to remain temporarily in Ireland. The
Government has made a fund available for the support of these mainly
Jewish immigrants. It is an open secret that the prohibition against the
taking up of employment by emigrants is not everywhere strictly
observed.[215]

'CNP' said that anti-Semitism had been previously demonstrated in Ireland
'merely by occasional attempts to establish a boycott of Jewish shops and
firms'. But the manifesto, he claimed, showed that Irish anti-Semitism
'appears to have taken a more definite form'. The article recorded that the
manifesto was sent in the post to 'the most prominent citizens of Dublin'
with an invitation to join. The manifesto, 'CNP' concluded, 'takes for the first
time an anti-Semitic aspect' and 'quietly takes its place in the All-Irish Front,
whose unofficial slogan is "Ireland for the Irish"'.[216]

A leader of growing importance in the Dublin Jewish community, the
lawyer and later distinguished member of the judiciary, Herman Good, gave
an indirect rejoinder to the writers of the anti-Semitic manifesto.[217] On 28
February 1939 he lectured in St George's parochial hall, Temple Street,
Dublin on 'The Jewish Question'. Declaring that Irish people were fortunate
to live in a country where democracy held sway and where justice still meant
something, he pointed out that 'recently, however, there had been examples
here, too, of that anti-Semitism which was coming back into the world'.[218]
He referred to the work of a well-known cleric, probably Fr Denis Fahey, who
had accused the Jews of being a revolutionary people, anxious to undermine
the whole Christian world, and ready to commit acts of violence, even
murder, to gain their ends. Good, dealing with what he called the 'fallacy of
Jewish wealth and power', observed: 'So powerful are we that we cannot get
back even our own small country for our own.'[219]

Gardaí made enquiries and concluded that the Irish–Ireland Research
Society did not exist. Their investigations revealed that 'this Society never
existed in fact but efforts to organise it were made by Mrs Clarke, Journalist
. . . and that she sent out the circulars in the fictitious name of A. J.
Browne'. The circulars had been stencilled at Mrs Clarke's address by herself
and two employees of the *Irish Press*. They had printed over two hundred
and sent about eighty by post to people in the city and country. The gardaí
also understood that a sum of money, 'source unknown and amount not
ascertained', had been placed at Mrs Clarke's disposal for anti-Jewish activities. While the gardaí did not speculate on the source, it is probable that it
came from propagandists within either the German or the Italian legation.
Mrs Clarke had attempted to interest the IRA in an anti-Semitic campaign
but to no avail.

A plasterer named Thomas Curran had also taken an active interest in
spreading anti-Semitic literature in Dublin. He had secured subscriptions
from business people for the campaign, and had been particularly active in
1937. But the gardaí concluded that he was in it for personal gain. When
questioned by the gardaí, he said he had given up that activity, and that it
was 'in better hands now'. He mentioned names and told the gardaí that now

'a few more "bigshots" were running the anti-Jewish campaign' from the premises of a loan society.

During the first week in February 1939 the words BOYCOTT JEWS were written in cream-coloured paint on walls around Dublin. The gardaí were convinced that one person had done all the painting. About the same time, notes were received by a number of Jews in the city warning them to 'clear out of the country or they would meet the same fate here as the Jews in Germany'. The gardaí believed that George Griffin, who ran the Irish Christ-ian Rights Protection Association, was responsible for both activities. He was helped in his anti-Semitic campaign by his wife, a typist, who had worked in the Hospital Sweeps Trust. Griffin, who was about thirty-eight years of age, was known to be in receipt of a substantial disability pension obtained under the 1934 Pensions Act. The gardaí felt that Griffin was 'not a very intelligent person and in fact is inclined to be slightly abnormal'; he was 'easily led' and 'suffering from anti-Jewish mania', but was 'not addicted to violence'.

The gardaí believed that the Irish Christian Rights Protection Association also had no membership, 'but the Griffins have a certain following consisting of people who have received loans from Jewish moneylenders and who were advised by Griffin to discontinue payments. These people, on his advice, handed him their account books and he in turn communicated with the moneylender concerned telling him to call to [Griffin's home] . . . to collect his accounts.' The gardaí were convinced that Griffin was responsible for the slogan painting and the threatening letter campaign, and that there 'is reason to believe that he is being used for this type of work by an organisation known as "the International Fascist Movement" emanating from the Italian legation and sponsored by Captain Liam D. Walsh, who is employed there'.

Walsh was merely one of a number of prominent fascists and Nazis in Dublin who had grown arrogant with the political success of the radical right in Europe. Prominent among these was Dr Adolf Mahr, leader of the small but vigorous Dublin branch of the Nazi Party. He had done his job well by the time he allegedly resigned from the National Socialist Party by letter to Berlin in 1938. In a letter to his superior, the secretary of the Department of Education, Seosamh Ó Néill, he pointed out that his resignation did not indi-cate a loss of faith in the gospel of Hitler.[220] Mahr did not believe that membership of the Nazi Party was an impediment to being a good employee: 'On the contrary, the National Socialistic outlook on life implies that a German citizen living abroad, who submits to party discipline, is a more desirable guest of the country of his sojourn than a German who shuns such voluntary discipline.'[221] Mahr felt that he was in a position to be a good employee: 'Hence I have a perfectly clear conscience as to the time during which I was the "Dublin Nazi No. 1" or, as some people may now prefer to call it, "Public Enemy No. 1".'[222] Mahr was resigning merely to avoid govern-ment embarrassment: 'This is not a council [sic] of fear. I am perfectly aware of the fact that nothing I may or may not do at the present moment can obscure or undo my openly-professed adherence to the Party.'[223] Rooted in his unflagging loyalty to Hitler and to the triumph of National Socialism, he had no doubt about who was to become the future master of Europe.

Mahr, in fact, did not resign from the party. He simply stepped down as *Gruppenleiter* in December 1938 in favour of Heinz Mecking.[224] There was an unfounded rumour in May 1939 that the director of the Irish Army School of Music, Colonel Wilhelm Fritz Brase – who, as was seen earlier, was the preferred choice for the position in 1934–35 – had taken over.[225] Mahr continues to be described as 'party comrade' in correspondence in June 1939 (which G2 intercepted) by senior *Auslandsorganisation* official, Admiral H. E. Menche, who had visited Dublin that February: 'Please tell P[arty] C[omrade] Mahr to be prepared to receive an official invitation to Nuremberg in the role of a worthy scientist serving abroad.'[226]

Ironically, as director of the National Museum, Party Comrade Mahr was privy to Ireland's top secret plans to hide treasures from the National Museum, the National Library and the National Gallery. At a meeting of relevant senior officials and an army officer on 23 March 1939 in the Department of Education, Mahr 'proved troublesome'; he told the meeting that an invasion was unlikely or remote, and that if one did come to pass 'it would be by a highly cultured nation who would value articles of art, culture etc., as much as we did'. Mahr wanted tunnels dug under Kildare Street, the site of the national repositories, to store the treasures. At the meeting he displayed a 'surprising and detailed knowledge of the geography of the country' which was attributed to his knowledge of archaeology. It was noted that he was 'fully familiar with ARP [air-raid protection] proposal'.[227]

Mahr left Ireland on 9 August 1939, presumably for his Nazi rendezvous in Nuremberg. Ostensibly, he was to represent Ireland at the Sixth International Congress of Archaeology in Berlin. Caught in Germany with his family by the outbreak of war, he was unable to get a 'safe conduct' back to Ireland.[228] According to G2, Mahr stayed for a while in Bad Ischl, Austria, when he also visited Bolzano. He moved to Berlin where he was without a job and very badly off.[229] His fortunes changed when he wrote a long report and approached one of the German intelligence sections which was dealing with the possibility of a landing in Ireland. He was given employment there. Boland stated in 1945 that, though Mahr was ostensibly concerned with cultural matters, there was some 'slight evidence' to show that he knew of, and was connected with, some of the attempts at German secret service activity in Ireland.[230] Mahr survived the war but never returned to Ireland.[231]

His party comrade, Otto August Reinhardt, left Ireland on 18 August 1939 on annual leave from his job as director of forestry in the Department of Lands, a post he had held since coming to the country from Germany on 16 November 1935. Described by G2 in a report dated February 1945 as a typical military man in appearance, he was 'very charming and is something of a "gay dog"'. He was believed to have known the country very well and to have had a particularly thorough knowledge of the eastern seaboard. A friend and associate of Karl Petersen of the German legation, 'he was on intimate terms with the Budina brothers [Karl and Kurt] of Kilmacurra Park Hotel [Kilbride, Co. Wicklow] and was a frequenter of that hotel, where Nazi meetings are known to have been held'. In 1939 the hotel was used for at least one Hitler Youth rally, attended by children of German nationals living in the country. Nothing was known of his activities during the war, but it was believed that he worked for German intelligence on Irish matters.

Helmut Clissmann was another party member who left Ireland at this time. Departing on 26 August 1939, he was seen off by Hempel and Henning Thomsen of the German legation. Clissman had first come to Ireland as an exchange student in Trinity College Dublin and then as a German lecturer sent by Deutscher Akademischer Austauschdienst. He ran classes in German and, according to G2, seemed to have exercised supervision and control over German exchange students in Ireland. By 1936 he was being regarded with suspicion. When his permit came up for renewal in the Department of Industry and Commerce in October of that year, the Department of Justice pointed out that he was 'frequenting extreme elements', and on 19 November the permit was refused. But following the intervention of the German legation and the Department of External Affairs, his permit was extended to 4 June 1937. It was extended again to 4 December 1938 at the request of the Austauschdienst. Suspecting that he was under suspicion, he took to using different letterboxes when posting letters. He married an Irish woman known to G2 to have strong republican views. Both were followed on one occasion to a rendezvous with a person allegedly known to G2 to be senior in the Irish Republican Army hierarchy. G2 also intercepted a letter to him from Adolf Mahr which began 'Dear Party Comrade Clissman' and ended 'Heil Hitler, Dr Mahr, Party Group Leader'. G2 also had a report that Clissman sought to negotiate an exchange programme between Clann na h-Éireann groups and the Hitler Youth. That plan was never realised.

Clissman, who died in Dublin in November 1997, spent the war in Copenhagen, Berlin, Rome and elsewhere. G2 suspected that he worked in intelligence and quoted from an intercepted letter of his wife to her sister dated 23 March 1943: 'Helmut is away doing his bit in the south but should be back soon.' He was also believed to have written the text of some English-language broadcasts to Ireland. He frequently met Francis Stuart in Berlin, according to G2 sources. Colonel Dan Bryan, head of G2, wrote upon Clissman's return to Ireland in October 1948 that 'it is well to remember that he was, during the Emergency, connected with activities directed not merely against this country but also against Great Britain'.

Hitler would have been proud of the thorough manner in which German agents had undertaken their intelligence gathering during the 1930s. The fruits of that work are partially contained in a book of maps, photographs and detailed drawings of landing points on the southern Irish coast. Dated 31 May 1941 and published in Berlin, it was found by an Irish-American officer in Luftwaffe headquarters in Bavaria in 1945 and returned to Dublin via the Irish Consul General in New York. This was a German manual for invasion known as Case Green (Fall Gruen). The quality of the photographs, many of which had been taken in Ireland in the 1930s, was most striking. Although some were taken from published sources, such as the *Cork Examiner* and international magazines like *National Geographic*, many were the result of careful photography – probably by more than one person – over a number of years. Nazi agents in Ireland had indeed been busy during those pre-war years.

The plans for the invasion envisaged a sea landing between Cork and Cobh which was itself a 'gateway or entrance' offering 'a peaceful or complete surprise landing in which the considerable natural obstacle of the hinterland can be overcome before the development of any strong enemy counter-operation'. The book provided elevated maps of Crookhaven, Mizen Head, Baltimore Harbour, Glandore Bay, Kinsale Harbour and the Port of Cork, Youghal and other points along the south and west coasts as far north as Donegal. The German plans also provided aerial views of all strategic installations in the south, east and north, including the most detailed aerial photographs of Dublin, Belfast, Bangor and Larne. Berlin had left nothing to chance. Abwehr did not have to rely upon the intelligence-gathering skills of the Irish Republican Army in order to bomb Belfast or any other Irish city. Much of that work had already been undertaken by German agents living in the country working on behalf of the 'fatherland'.[232]

On the eve of war, the Jewish community in Dublin – together with many others on the island – were fearful of a German invasion. In all likelihood, details of the names and addresses of members of the Irish Jewish community were already lodged in Berlin. But few people in Ireland could have believed that the war would result in the Holocaust. Yet, Robert Briscoe appears to have anticipated those terrible events when he wrote on 22 September 1939:

> How often did I tell American Jews when speaking to them in America that if they did not make up their minds quickly the problem would be solved by extermination. You probably remember my phrase so often used that the only solution was Palestine and the only alternative was extermination.[233]

The truth of the statement was grasped only very slowly by an uncomprehending international community in the latter months of 1942 and early 1943.

6

Ireland, the Second World War and the Holocaust

Sometime towards the end of the Second World War Leonard Abrahamson's young son, David, did a drawing of Churchill beside a Union Jack on a home-made card. Underneath he wrote the words of the British prime minister: 'Hitler must and will be defeated.'[1] There was never any doubt about where the wartime allegiances of the Irish Jewish community lay – they hoped for an Allied victory. So, too, did Eamon de Valera and his government, but the primary objective of Irish foreign policy from the outbreak of the war was to keep the country out of all hostilities for as long as possible. De Valera's task was made all the harder because Northern Ireland, as part of the United Kingdom, was at war. The Northern capital, Belfast, was about 100 miles from Dublin, and the two states shared a 270-mile land border. Despite Ireland's military weakness and dependence upon Britain's goodwill, de Valera refused to allow the British either to repossess or to use the Treaty ports which had only been returned to the country in 1938.[2]

The wartime relationship between Dublin and London, often tense and sometimes overtly hostile, did not, however, prevent the emergence of a strong measure of co-operation in support of Allied war goals. De Valera and his closest advisers, as the leaders of a neutral state, worked for the defeat of the Axis powers. There was no room for romanticism in the Irish govern-ment about the ultimate intentions of Germany. While the German minister in Dublin, Edouard Hempel, a Nazi Party member, conducted diplomatic relations with his hosts in a professional fashion, his legation worked closely with German intelligence, Abwehr, and with its secret agents in the country who were in contact with the collaborationist Irish Republican Army (IRA).[3]

'Michael', a friend of the prominent republican Connie Neenan, provided evidence on 2 September 1939 of the pro-German attitude of that organisa-tion. Writing to 'Catherine' in New York, he said:

153

I still think I am right about what I called the 'Yanks'. Roosevelt is trying to drag USA into the war which has just begun. Are the Americans fools? What have they to gain by going to war? Nothing, but they have everything to loose. Men, money and maybe her Independence, who got the spoils from the last war, did America? Did she ever get the twenty billion dollars owed to her by England and France? No. Cannot one white nation keep out of war and save the world from the yellow race? Yes. . . . All Europe will be destroyed and the yellow race will rule then. If America stays at home from the war there is a chance that she will be able to lick the yellow man when the time comes. . . . This is why I say that I am right about the Yanks. Is it the Jewish people who are backing Roosevelt to go to war or is it to avenge the death of his son who was killed in France in 1918? It is up to the non Jewish people in America to unite and keep America from war. De Válera would throw us back into the fight but for the IRA. They have the people of Ireland behind them so he is afraid to stir.

The letter writer, who was an IRA activist, went on to outline the plans of that organisation:

All the fellows are waiting for England to declare war on Germany then we will march North and take the Six Counties from the Orangemen. They are already leaving for the Border in twos and threes just to look things over. Of course I don't know what will happen. Headquarters may send a demand to London to hand them over and if she don't the fun will start. England may hand them over because she knows we are in earnest about it and that we will blow London and all the other big cities over to Berlin and all the Public Works and Services as well. We will have no mercy for them, also we will cause unrest among the British troops. . . . I have just heard that the HQ have made it known to De Valera their intention to take the North and if he tries to stop us it will mean civil war which above all the Lord grant won't happen.

Neither de Valera nor close administrative and military advisers shared such views. Colonel Dan Bryan, who was to take over as head of military intelligence (G2) in 1940, strongly favoured an Allied victory. More than any other individual in the administration, he was aware of the skulduggery of the Nazis in the country. His unwavering hostility to the Axis powers was shared by the chief of staff of the Irish army, Lieutenant General Daniel McKenna. The secretary of the Department of the Taoiseach, Maurice Moynihan, was equally keen to see Hitler defeated. De Valera was in a strong position to silence all dissent and maintain party unity. The opposition parties – and the Fine Gael leadership under William T. Cosgrave in particular – were also strongly pro-Allies.[4] De Valera and Cosgrave shared a common desire for an Allied victory; that perspective drove Irish wartime policy.

The Jewish community and the outbreak of war

Uncertainty about the future was the dominant reality for members of the Jewish community in Ireland during the early war years. Family ties kept many close to the brutality of Axis-controlled continental Europe as they confronted the possibility, or probability, of a German victory. That sense of vulnerability was felt by Irish Jews long before a meeting of leading Nazis in the Berlin suburb of Wannsee, on 20 January 1942, sought to intensify the 'final solution' – the mass annihilation of Jews and other non-Aryans.[5] That meeting considered a table showing the number of Jews in each country, including those in neutral and non-belligerent states: Finland 2,300, Portugal 3,000, Spain 6,000, Sweden 8,000, Switzerland 18,000, Turkey-in-Europe 55,000, and finally Ireland 4,000.[6] The magnitude of what was being planned defied the comprehension of even those who understood the depth of Nazi anti-Semitism. Irish political leaders did not know about the Holocaust until late 1942.

In posing the counterfactual historical question of what might have happened to the Jews had Ireland been occupied, the experience of continental countries that were occupied may offer signposts.[7] Would the Irish have behaved like the Danes, who helped Jews escape to Sweden?[8] Or would they have actively collaborated in the destruction of the Jews like many members of the political elites in, for example, France, Belgium and Holland?[9] Robert Briscoe's son, Joe, reflecting in the 1990s on the nightmare of what might have been if the Nazis had seized control of the country, stated that nothing would have happened at first. But:

> After a couple of months, an announcement would be made that food rations could only be collected at the local town hall. I would have gone to Blackrock Town Hall and there would have been a big sign saying: All Jews must state the fact that they are Jews. I had never hidden the fact that I was Jewish. There would have been an Irish Garda standing behind the Nazi officer. I would say my name is Briscoe and they would take a big red stamp and put a J on my card. This would have happened all over Dublin, all over Ireland.[10]

Then what?

> Some time later, an announcement would be made on the radio that all Jews were required to go to South Circular Road within forty-eight hours, bringing only those belongings they could carry. So with my handcart, my wife and my little son, we would go there. The houses would be empty and waiting for us. We would be curfewed. Then a wall would have been put up one night at Kelly's Corner and they had you. It's as simple as that.[11]

The Jews would then, he feels, have been taken out of Ireland by boat to the continent and 'that would have been the end of it'.[12] Dr Conor Cruise O'Brien is of a similar point of view:

> The Gestapo had listed the names of the Jews of Ireland, and if our Department of External Affairs had been right about the outcome of the war, the Germans would have demanded and obtained – in one way or another – the handing over of the Jews of Ireland for destruction.[13]

Anyone who protested against the handing over of the Jews, argued Cruise O'Brien, would have shared the fate of the Jews.

Counterfactual speculation apart, Gerald Goldberg in Cork harboured these same fears in late 1939. In the event of a Nazi occupation, he arranged for his son to be hidden by Christian neighbours who would raise him as their own son but in the Jewish faith. He would, at the earliest opportunity, be sent to his relatives in the United States. Goldberg had an alternative emergency plan which involved sending his son to the family of Mary Lynch, a West Cork woman who worked in their home.[14] Happily, the need never arose. The Solomons family in Dublin bought a house in Kildare where they planned to take refuge if the Nazis occupied the country.[15] Many other Jewish families throughout the country equally must have felt a need in late 1939 and 1940 to make contingency plans for their children. Others chose to enlist. Bethel Solomons's sons, Michael and Bethel jun., both doctors, were among the many thousands of Irish people who joined the Allied forces. Michael served in the British air force while Bethel jun. joined the British navy. Both survived the war.

While a significant number of the Jewish community in Southern Ireland joined the British armed forces and served courageously in the war, many others served in the Local Defence Force (LDF), the Local Security Force (LSF) or in Air Raid Protection (ARP). One Garda report, written on 7 May 1940, viewed that development with apprehension:

> It has come to the notice of this Branch that the Jewish section of the population is making a concerted movement towards enrolment in the Local Security Corps. It is reported that Robert Briscoe, TD, now returned from his recruiting campaign in South Africa on behalf of the British forces, has called a meeting of the men of his community and instructed them to enrol, not in the Army, but in the local security volunteers.

The writer of the report advanced the view that the presence of a large number of Jews had discouraged recruits from other religious backgrounds. He further reported that 'certain responsible citizens, on finding a large number of young Jews in the Local Security Body – one said he thought he had wandered by accident into a synagogue rather than into a Garda Station – immediately abandoned their intention of serving in that Body'. While the writer did not wish to question the quality of the services of the Jewish community or the sincerity of their intentions, it was 'earnestly pointed out that a concerted movement on the part of any section of the population is bound to have a deleterious effect on the recruitment of other circles, apart entirely from 'the present widespread objection in the civil population to the Jewish community, recently much swollen in numbers'. The writer further argued that 'the same objection as to the Jews applies also to the Ailesbury Road or Killiney type of look' – presumably a reference to members of the Church of Ireland.

It was suggested that 'this grave danger to recruitment' could be averted by the drafting of a 'period of residence clause in the conditions of service for the Local Security Corps, a clause which . . . could be waived in the case of persons unorganised and with a genuine desire to help protect the country from the threat of invasion, from whatsoever quarter it may come'. No such clause was ever invoked. But further hostility towards Jews was shown when Robert Briscoe sought an independent unit for his co-religionists – a request that was turned down by the Minister for Defence on advice from the armed forces. A G2 profile of Briscoe, dated 3 November 1942, showed the hostility of the anonymous writer towards the Jewish TD. He was described as a frequent visitor to London who 'interests himself in visas for Jews on the Continent and is, as is to be expected of one of his race, an internationalist indulging in any and every line of business that will bring financial benefit'. Army intelligence stated, in another report, that it had definite information which showed that 'Briscoe holds a high place in the councils of international Jewry and was in 1941 a member of the nessiut or supreme body of the new Zionist Organisation which has its headquarters in New York'.

Do these Garda and G2 documents in part reflect a suspicion about Jews playing a role in the Irish armed forces during the war? Gerald Goldberg holds the view that there was discrimination against Jews who joined the local defence forces. He claimed that those who deserved it were never given promotion to officer rank. Only further research will reveal whether he is correct. But a historical fragment from military intelligence files is quite revealing of one view. The unsigned report was written in late 1941 in response to a request by Robert Briscoe to the Minister for Defence to have a parade of Jewish members in the LDF on the first Friday after 4 December – the Feast of Dedication: 'It is presumed that the . . . request is based on the precedent that has already been established in the granting of permission to both Catholic and Non-Catholic members of the LDF and other branches of the Forces, ARP Service etc. to hold church parades.' The report writer felt that a request for a

> Jewish church parade is not in exactly the same category as that of Christian persuasions, primarily for the reason that the Jewish religion cannot be divorced from the super-national character of the Jewish race.
>   In the light of this information it behoves us to tread warily in a direction which may tend to give the Jewish element in our Forces anything approaching the character of a separate entity, and while it is thought that there are no very strong immediate grounds for refusing the request for a church parade, any tendency on the part of the Jews to get themselves into a distinctly Jewish unity should be firmly countered.

There was further a feeling that

> the ostensible object of stimulating the recruitment of Jews into the LDF or LSF is, in the light of the foregoing, of doubtful advantage, while the relevant provisions of the Constitution in relation to the Jews are not lost sight of, it would be foolish to ignore the fundamental characteristics of the Jewish people in that they have not national allegiance and are described by those who have studied the Jewish problem as being super-national or international in character.

How widely shared were such opinions in the Department of Defence and in G2? Did those views, as claimed by Gerald Goldberg, lead to a policy of discrimination against Jews in the Irish forces?

Many Jews joined the Irish local defence forces and served with distinction during the war and afterwards. Among them was Herman Good, who was one of the few Jews to be promoted to the rank of officer. Robert Briscoe's son, Joe, became the longest serving officer in the local defence forces in the late 1980s. He retired with the rank of commandant. In all his years of service, he recalled only one remark which might be described as anti-Semitic. To the horror and embarrassment of his fellow officers, he was asked in the mess by one officer, 'When are you going home?' But it was an isolated incident. Dr Rudi Neuman, a German Jew who came to Ireland in the 1930s and served in the same local defence unit in Dublin as Joe Briscoe, was once asked why he bothered to turn out every weekend for training over the years. He replied that he was honoured to put on the uniform of his country, a country which allowed him to wear it without discrimination. During the war, all Irish Jews wore the uniform of the armed forces of their country for the same patriotic reasons as did members of the Catholic Church, the Church of Ireland, and other religious communities. Writing in 1945, Con Leventhal put this well: 'Patriotically [a Jew] aligns himself with the country of his birth or adoption . . . He loves peace; but patriotism is with him an equally passionate impulse'.[16] During the war, Irish Jews did their duty.

Northern Ireland was in the war. There were, according to the 1937 census, 1,472 Jews living there, 1,284 of them in Belfast. Many joined the armed forces. Among those was Billie Goldstone.[17] Others like Louis Friedlander would like to have done so: 'I would have joined up, like my brother, but I was too young.'[18] Rada Hyman's father, who was in the furniture business, joined the Home Guard and had responsibility for the strategic Dock Yard area.[19] The Northern Irish Jewish community was well represented in the British forces during the war. However, all interviewed denied that any Jewish family in Belfast had contingency plans at the beginning of the war to evacuate or to hide their children in the non-Jewish community. They expected to share, for good or ill, the common fate of the wider community. The war years offered Irish Jews, north or south of the border, no space to harbour illusions about what was likely to happen if Hitler's forces landed anywhere on the island.

The Department of Justice and Irish policy towards aliens and refugees, 1939–42

The immediacy of the German threat ought to have been particularly well understood in the Department of Justice, which on a daily basis handled the applications of those wishing to flee persecution on the continent. It would, however, be an error to project backwards to 1939 a knowledge of the realities of the Holocaust. It would be equally wrong to attribute to those departmental officials a concept of the closeness of the continent which has developed since Ireland joined the European Economic Community in 1973. Moreover, the idea of 'happenings elsewhere' is not confined to the 1930s and

1940s. It continues into the 1990s. The Polish Nobel prize winner, Czeslaw Milosz, wrote in his poem 'Sarajevo':

> While a country murdered and raped calls for help from the
> Europe which it had trusted, they yawn.
>
> While statesmen choose villainy and no voice is raised to call it by
> name. . . .
>
> Listening with indifference to the cries of those who perish
> because they are after all just barbarians killing each other[20]

Austria, Czechoslovakia and the 'Munich bother' may have appeared remote to senior officials in the Department of Justice who went about their increased workload conscientiously and efficiently as they faced the unprecedented demands for refuge. The civil servants' concern was how to hold closed the 'flood-gates'.

In the weeks leading up to the outbreak of war, many 'visitors' had arrived from Britain, since there were no restrictions on British citizens entering the country. Confronted by this new situation, senior officials in the Department of Justice on several occasions discussed the imposition of restrictions on entry from Britain. The outcome was 'the fairly unanimous feeling that things should be left as they are'.[21] According to S. A. Roche, the secretary at the department, this view was based on a number of pragmatic considerations. First, the north-east land frontier (i.e. the border with Northern Ireland) 'cannot or should not be controlled, and so long as that is so it seems futile to try to control traffic direct from English ports'.[22] Second, it was believed that most of those coming to Ireland were people to whom the authorities could not or would not refuse admission – 'our own nationals and British people with money'.[23] Third, those aliens who got into the country illegally could be deported.[24] Roche, however, was in no sense complacent. Outlining these views to the Minister for Justice on 5 September, he said that 'the present position is open in theory, and possibly to some extent in practice, to the objection that this country is offering itself as a refuge to every useless mouth in Great Britain, of whatever nationality'.[25]

It was decided to send a memorandum to government on the matter.[26] Circulated in late September, the document argued for the retention of the status quo: 'Traffic at the ports could be controlled, at the cost of great delay and inconvenience to travellers, but the cost of controlling traffic on the Border would be prohibitive.'[27] During the drafting of the memorandum, one official wrote to the Department of Justice on 13 September:

> Continental refugees, temporarily resident in Great Britain, may also seek to come to Ireland and the British would be glad to get rid of them.
>   These various people (Jews, for example) may cause Irish people loss of employment. In any case, all are additional mouths to fill. It will obviously be to the advantage of Britain to get rid of surplus, useless population. . . . I believe, for example, that practically every Jewish house on the S[outh] C[ircular] Road has additional tenants, and these (and others) should be accounted for.[28]

It is important to stress that the memorandum flatly contradicted this assertion: 'The rumours which are circulating regarding an influx of British Jews
may be discounted'; it added, however, that 'numbers of women and children
and elderly people have come also, and it is probable that a high proportion
of Jews have arrived'.[29]

The cabinet was further informed that the Department of Justice had
arranged for traffic from Britain to be kept under observation by the Irish
authorities. The memorandum explained that the Minister for Justice, Gerald
Boland (who had replaced Patrick Ruttledge on 8 September 1939), considered it necessary to have the power to deport from the country any person,
other than an Irish citizen, whenever 'he deems it to be conducive to the
public good so to do'.[30] The minister also wanted the power to oblige all
recently arrived aliens, and all aliens over sixteen years of age, to register
with the gardaí immediately.[31] The gardaí had traced about seventy aliens:

> Practically all of them are persons without means and without any special
> qualifications. Their presence here would not be any advantage to the
> country, and they are being warned to leave. If they do not leave, the
> Minister for Justice proposes to deport them to Great Britain under the
> Aliens Order. An exception is being made, however, in the case of
> Germans who have fled here from Britain. These people are not being told
> to leave, but the German Legation are being asked whether they can
> arrange for their repatriation through Holland. Only 18 Germans who fled
> from Britain have been traced by the police so far.[32]

Sweeping emergency powers were granted to the minister under the
Emergency Powers (No. 11) Order 1939.[33] Roche explained on 5 December:

> The main purpose of this Order is to deal with the Jews and other unde-
> sirables who came here in August and September. If we find, after six
> months or so, that there is no longer much need for the Order, and that it
> is in any way interfering with the visits of wealthy English people, we will
> be quite ready to consider revoking it altogether.[34]

Roche's reference to 'the Jews and other undesirables' ought to be read in
context. It was not so much an anti-Semitic comment as a reflection of the
pressing difficulties which departmental officials faced in dealing with the
growing numbers of aliens seeking refuge. However, the order was not
revoked for the duration of the war, and thus began a system of surveillence
on aliens, subversives and Irish people who corresponded with anyone who
might be held in suspicion by the authorities. Military intelligence, the gardaí
and the Department of Justice combined to create the infrastructure of a de
facto national security state. The following list of 'undesirable aliens
(German, Austrian etc.)' illustrates the detailed knowledge held by the
administration on each person. Without using names, the date of arrival and
the description on the file of a selection of aliens are given:

| 18 October 1938 | Active Nazi and propagandist. Associate of German agent Clissmann. |
| 4 October 1932 | Nazi. Application for citizenship refused. Extensive export |

	business without permit.
4 September 1939	Immoral.
4 February 1939	Refugee. Attempted smuggling, employed in Turf Development Board as draughtsman and translator.
25 August 1939	Refused permission to land in 1933. On British passport black list. Both said to be Nazis and in touch with extreme elements here.
3 June 1939	Immoral (Homosexual suspect).
27 August 1939	Nazi. Came here in 1939 to avoid arrest by British. Married to Frenchwoman, now in France. Loose morals.
1923	Inner circle Nazi. Major suspect association with Hoven, Rehmann, known German agents who were here before the war.
1 July 1932	Nazi official. Contact with known German agents, Clissmann, Rehmann and Schmidt who were here before the war.

Files were kept on every single alien. All aspects of their life, relationships and activities were known to the authorities and kept on file in G2 headquarters. When the Irish Co-ordinating Committee for Refugees could not guarantee that 'all the refugees under the care of the Committee were reliable', the Department of Justice was supplied with a list of all relevant names.[35] The Minister for Justice, Gerald Boland, signed blank deportation forms in bulk: senior officials had only to fill in the names. Many aliens, some seventy in the first five months of the war, received a terse order to quit the country.

Were Jews the target of especially illiberal treatment by the Department of Justice during the course of the war? It is difficult to interpret certain references in official correspondence in any other way. Roche outlined the position very clearly in a letter to Maurice Moynihan in 1946:

> Our practice has been to discourage any substantial increase in the Jewish population. They do not assimilate with our own people but remain a sort of colony of a world-wide Jewish community. This makes them a potential irritant in the body politic and has led to disastrous results from time to time in other countries.[36]

The Department of Justice's interpretation of policy remained consistent throughout the war: the admission of Jews was to be generally discouraged. It is possible to detect a number of recurring concerns underlying this rigid attitude within the department: first, the admission of a Jew meant that he or she was likely to become a permanent resident; second, Jews did not 'assimilate', to use Roche's language; and third, any significant increase in the size of the Jewish community was likely to exacerbate the anti-Semitism that already existed in the country to a worrying degree. It is important at this point to make a distinction between the cases which were handled exclusively by the Departments of Justice and Industry and Commerce and those applications which were brought to the attention of the Departments of the Taoiseach and External Affairs. In the former category, the policy tended to be applied in an illiberal and ungenerous fashion. In the case of the latter, however, the wider the process of consultation the more likely there was to be a favourable outcome. Nevertheless, the recommendation of Colonel Bryan in G2 usually had a decisive influence on any case.

There were instances where visas, provided by the Irish authorities, were not taken up; the case of the Clare family, reviewed in the previous chapter, falls into this category. The case of the manager of Les Modes Modernes factory in Galway, Serge Philipson, had some similarity. He failed to gain admission into the country in 1939 for his father and mother, Abraham and Hanna S. Philipson, his sister Sola Siemion, and his six-year-old niece Myrian Siemion. They perished in the Holocaust.[37] However, Philipson's G2 file reveals that permission was granted to his wife and immediate family to come to Ireland. Remaining in France too long, they were caught when 'the Axis made a round up of Jews'. According to a G2 minute, a daughter aged seventeen was left and the rest were taken.[38]

Philipson's superior, Marcus Witztum, was described by the head of G2, Colonel Liam Archer, as being widely used by 'alien Jews to secure entry' into Ireland.[39] Witztum was only modestly successful in that regard. But Archer wrote on 23 July 1940 in connection with an application for the admission of Witztum's father-in-law:

> On the question generally of admitting aliens to this country my point of view is that no others of the fraternity [Jews] should be allowed to enter under any circumstances as we have more than enough to do to control and supervise the numbers of aliens already here.[40]

Again, Archer's attitude is that of a beleaguered administrator determined to keep down the number of aliens in the country – particularly the number of Jews.

The complexities and inconsistency of the official Irish mind regarding the admission of Jews into wartime Ireland are illustrated by the contrasting manner in which the Department of Justice dealt with applications for admission by two rabbis – Gittel Bisko and Hillel Medalie. Bisko, a Lithuanian, was, according to the secretary of the Association of Orthodox Jews of Dublin (Lombard Street Synagogue), Albert Siev, 'a profound scholar in the Talmud and is well known, respected, and liked by all our people here'.[41] Accompanied by his wife, Bisko had been allowed to come to Dublin in September 1939 to give a lecture. The local Jewish community wanted him to stay on in Dublin and minister to them. Bernard Shillman urged the Minister for Justice, Gerald Boland, to allow him to remain as the community was thinking of opening a seminary and putting Bisko in charge. However, Boland wrote to the Biskos on 26 September saying that he was 'not prepared to permit them to reside in the country'.[42] Siev explained to Boland in a letter on 14 October that the Association of Orthodox Jews of Dublin had agreed to appoint Bisko as its rabbi for a period of one year, subject to him being allowed by the minister to stay:

> Since Rabbi Dr Herzog left Eire to take up his position in Palestine, the Jews in Dublin have not been able, unfortunately, to agree on the appointment of a Rabbi for the whole Community, with the result that though *we*

are well served with Ministers or Readers, there is not one man in
Dublin with sufficient authority to advise us on matters of every day
need.[43]

Siev explained that Rev. Gudansky, who had 'served the Jewish Community
in Dublin well and faithfully for a considerable number of years', was about to
retire. Rabbi Elkan Eliezer Gavron, he said, was not able, 'through old age
and ill-health', to continue his work, and 'we have now no one else'.[44] The
correspondence continued with the department but to no avail. Despite
widespread support for the rabbi within the Jewish community, on 19
January 1940 Boland signed a deportation order for Bisko. He had no alternative but to leave for Belfast; his wife, who was in hospital in Dublin, joined
him some months later as she, too, was threatened with being deported.[45]

Following the harsh treatment meted out to the Biskos, the Jewish Representative Council requested a meeting with Boland. Although the JRC
delegation, led by Leonard Abrahamson, knew that it could not change the
fate of the Biskos, it volunteered to advise the minister in connection with
future applications for the admission of rabbis.[46] Roche, on behalf of Boland,
asked for the advice of the JRC on 12 July 1940, following the receipt of an
application from the Rathmines Hebrew Congregation for the appointment
as rabbi of a Palestinian living in Manchester, Hillel Medalie.[47] The JRC
received a delegation from the Rathmines congregation on 5 September, and
then wrote to the minister in support of the appointment, declaring that the
rabbi's qualifications 'are of a very high order and there is no Irish citizen of
comparable ability or standard available. There is a qualified Rabbi of Irish
citizenship in Dublin at the moment, but he is not acceptable to the Congregation.'[48] The JRC explained that the Rathmines community wished to
change their existing arrangements; until then they had had to rely upon the
help of a lay minister who had not been consecrated a rabbi and had no
rabbinical qualifications. The hundred-strong congregation had bought a
premises and now wanted to appoint a fully qualified rabbi.[49] Reviewing the
case for the minister on 9 September, Roche recommended that permission
should be granted for the entry of Rabbi Medalie:

> The Jews have always imported their Rabbis into this country, and they
> say that this is necessary as there are no schools in this country in which
> Rabbis can be trained. Although there is an Irish citizen available to fill
> this post, I doubt if anything would be gained by our trying to compel the
> Congregation to appoint him instead of Medalie.[50]

Boland endorsed the recommendation the following day.

The case of Paul Léon, James Joyce's friend, had quite a different outcome. It also shows the relative powerlessness of the Irish authorities to save
the life of anyone who had been arrested by the Germans. Léon, a Russian
Jewish refugee, had been brought up in St Petersburg where he studied law.
He came to Paris in 1921 after living in London for three years. He met Joyce
in 1928, and he has been variously described as Joyce's agent, unpaid secretary, collaborator and closest friend.[51] This relationship lasted until 1939
when a disagreement led to a temporary rupture. Both men were reconciled

in Saint-Gérand-le-Puy, in Vichy France, following the German occupation of Paris. After spending the summer of 1940 together correcting misprints in *Finnegans Wake*, Léon returned in September to Paris where he continued to live at great personal risk.[52] He helped rescue a section of Joyce's library from the family flat on the rue des Vignes; the remainder he bought back at an auction which was held illegally by the landlord.[53] The books and archives were handed over to the Irish chargé in Paris, Count Gerald O'Kelly, to be sent back to the National Library in Dublin. Léon, who had done the Irish state some service, refused to leave Paris. Samuel Beckett met him in the street on 20 August 1941 and was told that he was going to leave the following day as his son was finishing his school examinations.[54] He was arrested the next day and imprisoned at Drancy and Compiegne. Through his wife Lucie Léon Noel, Beckett sent him his bread ration and also some cigarettes. (Beckett had joined the resistance movement on 1 September 1940.)[55]

On 31 October 1941, the Society of Swiss Writers sent an appeal to Dublin requesting the Irish government to intervene on behalf of Léon. The government on 5 November duly notified the Irish envoy in Berlin, William Warnock: 'In case there is danger that Léon be shot please intervene with Foreign Office on his behalf.' Warnock replied on 8 November, observing that certain South American countries had made similar representations and that 'their actions had been received very badly'. He added:

> In my opinion there is danger that intervention on behalf of L. might be regarded as interfering in internal German matters where no Irish citizen is involved and might even have some effect on our good relations. I beg to suggest that if Department feels we should intervene case might be mentioned to German Minister in Dublin.[56]

Dublin wrote back on 21 November agreeing that no action should be taken. Joseph Walshe, the secretary of the Department of External Affairs, minuted: 'No action possible at present.'[57] Léon, who was beaten and tortured in prison, was shot at a camp in Silesia on 4 April 1942, dying a year after his great friend, James Joyce.

Esther, or Ettie, Steinberg was the only Irish-born Jew to die in the Holocaust. She was one of a family of seven children who were reared in Raymond Terrace, South Circular Road, Dublin. Originally from Czechoslovakia, her family had come to Ireland from London in 1926. 'She was a beautiful girl, tall and slim with wonderful hands. She was a fantastic dressmaker and embroider', recalled her sister-in-law, also Ettie. In 1937, at the age of twenty-two, Ettie Steinberg married a twenty-four-year-old goldsmith from Antwerp, Vogtjeck Gluck. The couple moved to Belgium, where their son Leon was born. When the Germans invaded the Low Countries, Ettie and her family went into hiding. By a strange irony, the Steinbergs in Dublin had secured visas for Ettie and her family through the British Home Office in Belfast. The visas were sent immediately to Toulouse but they arrived too late. Ettie and her family had been rounded up the day before and sent to the camp at Drancy, outside Paris. They were transported to Auschwitz and to their immediate death.[58] But would the arrival of the visas in time have made any difference? That same question may be asked in so many other cases during the latter years of the war.

But there was one outstanding success on the island during the early war years regarding Jewish refugees. Before the outbreak of war, a committee in Belfast decided to rent a farm of seventy acres at Millisle, Co. Down, to 'assist in the work of giving refugees from the continent a fresh start in life'.[59] Official clearance was given to receive a number of families. The Hyman family used their business in Belfast to collect and supply furniture for the huts on the farm. A number of Jewish children who had arrived in England after Kristallnacht in November 1938 had been sent to Belfast for schooling. These children arrived at the farm in July 1939, two months after about thirty German Jewish boys accompanied by some adults had taken up residence. By the beginning of the war, there were eighty in the Millisle community, including about twenty adults from all over central Europe.[60] The boys learned how to farm, and when they reached the age to enlist they immediately joined the armed forces. There were about thirty left at Millisle in 1944. The farm closed in 1948.[61]

Relations between the Millisle group and the local Jewish community were good but not without tensions. Rabbi J. Shacter from Belfast visited the community frequently. The children were sometimes taken to Belfast, and during the summer many of them were invited to Dublin for two weeks' holidays in local Jewish homes – usually two to each family.[62] While conditions at Millisle were somewhat basic, the community provided education for the children and an opportunity to develop a fluency in English. They survived.

The Jewish community and anti-Semitism in wartime Ireland

The first two years of the war had passed without a German invasion. But the ungenerous nature of the country's alien and refugee policies had left many members of the Jewish community dejected, knowing that the provision of Irish visas for their relatives and friends on the continent would certainly have saved some lives. But if relations between the Department of Justice and individual families were strained, the Jewish Representative Council sought to maintain a good working relationship with the government. They found right of audience with de Valera and other cabinet members easy to secure. The Fianna Fáil TD Robert Briscoe, meanwhile, continued to act as an unofficial emissary for the community.

The JRC had to attend to very practical matters, such as providing for the evacuation of Jewish children in the event of heavy bombing raids or invasion. (Dublin, the capital of a neutral power, had in fact escaped very lightly during the early war years.) An emergency committee was established by the JRC; Arthur Newman, Edwin Solomons, Herman Good and Leonard Abrahamson were again to the fore in organising the community's affairs. A delegation had an interview in early 1941 with Seán Moylan, Parliamentary Secretary to the Minister for Defence. During the meeting an undertaking was given that the government would, in the event of occupation, provide certain buildings for Jewish evacuees.[63] However, it is not clear how much progress was ever made on this issue. On 7 May 1941, Arthur Newman, a member of the JRC, met a Mr Egan, the Department of Defence official in charge of the evacuation of the capital in the event of invasion. Newman felt that the situation had worsened since the meeting with Moylan, as Egan claimed that he had not yet sufficient buildings allocated for the general public. He suggested that the JRC should insert advertisements in the press to locate suitable premises. In the meantime, he promised to send a list of houses in the country which the JRC could inspect.[64] On 14 May Egan wrote to the JRC under the direction of Moylan to state that enquiries were being made about the provision of houses for Jewish children in the event of evacuation. A list would be sent to the council within a fortnight.[65] Newman wrote to Rev. Abraham Gudansky the following day enclosing the Department of Defence letter, but it is not known if anything became of these exchanges.[66]

Members of the JRC were also vigilant in combating the growing incidence of anti-Semitism in wartime Dublin. A letter from the archbishop of Dublin, John Charles McQuaid, who was appointed to that position in December 1940, provides evidence of that fact. Writing on 26 May 1949 to the new chief rabbi, Immanuel Jakobovits, he said: 'During the war, it was happily possible for me, with the very alert sagacity of Mr Edwin Solomons, to help to forestall incidents which could have provoked retaliation or aroused unjust antipathy.'[67] While details of the incidents are not outlined, it is probable that the archbishop was indirectly involved in having the support of Catholics withdrawn from the shadowy People's National Party which was led by George Griffin – whose pre-war anti-Semitic activities under the guise of the Irish Christian Rights Protection Association were discussed in chapter 5 – and included among its small coterie of members the former leader of the Blueshirts, Eoin O'Duffy.[68]

This party broke away from Cumann Náisiúnta, or the Irish Friends of Germany, which had been set up by Liam D. Walsh in early 1940 with an address at the Red Bank restaurant, D'Olier Street, Dublin. The Friends of Germany met in the home of Walsh, who worked at the Italian Legation and was a close friend of General O'Duffy. They also held meetings in Wynn's hotel, where the inaugural meeting was held. Between forty and fifty people attended a meeting at the Red Bank on 31 May 1940, where Griffin, an ex-Blueshirt, lectured on the 'Jewish stranglehold on Ireland'. A detailed account of what he said was sent to G2:

> He gave details of a harrowing nature of various unfortunate people who had fallen into the clutches of the Jews, especially in matters of money-lending and the Hire Purchase of Furniture. Then he said that he belonged to another small society which had 'blacklisted' some of the worst of the Jews, the first of whom was buried on Whitmonday and the rest of whom would follow in due course.

Griffin mentioned many Dublin Jews by name and said that 'we should never pass a Jew on the streets without openly insulting him'. He said that 75 per cent of the rateable property in Dublin was owned by Jews and that the other 25 per cent was mortgaged to Jews. Ireland, he said, was Jew-ridden. He then spoke about the Jewish presence in Dáil Éireann:

> An Taoiseach's father was *Portuguese Jew*. Erskine Childers' grand-mother was a Jewess. Mr Ruttledge has Jewish connections by marriage – and 'Jew' was written all over the face of Mr Seán Lemass! Practically all the Fianna Fáil TDs are in the clutches of the Jews! ... The Fianna Fáil selection committee dropped Briscoe, but Mr Lemass threatened to resign, whereupon the committee was compelled to adopt Mr Briscoe rather than face the sensation that would be caused by the resignation of a Minister. Mr de Valera's Jewish masters had forced him to protect them by name in the constitution.

Griffin then went on to commend Hitler's treatment of the Jews.

Another speaker, Alex McCabe – also an ex-Blueshirt – said that they were not a 'fifth column'. The only fifth column in Ireland was the British secret service, which must be smashed. They wanted to see the very life-blood squeezed out of England and therefore they wished Germany well, he declared. The authorities recorded: 'It is reasonable to conclude that McCabe's sympathies are predominantly pro-German and that he would be disposed to facilitate the German espionage system insofar as it may exist in this country.'

Another front organisation in which a number of these people were also engaged, the Irish Neutrality League, attacked the national press on 28 May 1940 for being 'very definitely biased against Germany and in favour of the British Empire'. G2 and Garda reports stated that in May and June 1940, the Friends of Germany 'manifested an intense interest' in German successes. They anticipated a German victory and the probability of strong German influence on the government of Ireland. The Irish authorities swooped on the ringleaders in June, and McCabe and Walsh were imprisoned in Cork. Not intimidated by that move, another meeting of the Friends of Germany was held in Swiss Chalet in Merrion Row, Dublin on 26 June. Griffin told his dwindling band of followers that he had been checking on all firms in the city which were run by Jews or freemasons. He mentioned that there was talk of McBirneys taking over Clerys premises, and that the Jews were behind this move.

In the absence of McCabe and Walsh, Maurice O'Connor took over the leadership of the Friends of Germany. According to G2, O'Connor had a long chat with General O'Duffy on 28 July 1940. While O'Duffy felt that there was not time to organise anything in the nature of a pro-German political party, he told O'Connor to get as many people as possible together as the military situation might change overnight. O'Connor mentioned an upcoming meeting, but O'Duffy said that he would prefer not to attend in case his presence would bring them to the attention of the authorities. He stated, however, that he would give all the help he could, and that he would send two trusted men to the meeting, one of whom would be Colum Kenny of Kenny's Advertising Agency.

The meeting took place in Broadway Soda Fountain and Café, 8 O'Connell

Street, on 29 July. O'Connor told those present that the IRA had signed a
document asking for German aid in their activities. There was discussion on
contact with the Germans. O'Connor said that he intended to compile a
register of sympathisers and to link up with the IRA and German nationals
living in the country. He would get in touch with the IRA leader Seán Russell,
who had been in Berlin but was believed to have landed by parachute in the
country recently.

Superintendent Gantly was convinced of McCabe's importance to the
organisation. On 5 May 1941 Gantly reported on McCabe's release from
prison: 'I have no knowledge of the conditions under which he was released,
but whether he continues personal activities or not the object of his release
has been achieved, because on this date I have received reliable information
that Maurice O'Connor, in referring to the release, has stated "I have now got
the names of the German and IRA contacts in this country".' McCabe continued to be active and in close contact with O'Duffy. But the group had lost its
momentum. O'Connor was arrested in October 1940 and released on an
undertaking that he would not break the law. By mid-1941, the group
appeared to be defunct.

Griffin, meanwhile, frustrated by the limitations of the Friends of
Germany, sought in summer 1940 to found a political party based on the
ideology of National Socialism. There were references in police reports on 24
July 1940 to Griffin having founded a new organisation with an associate,
Patrick Moylett – the People's National Party. Brendan Kennedy was the trea-
surer: 'He has anti-Jewish sympathies and holds pro-German views.' George
Sinclair was vice president.

According to Garda reports, Griffin and Moylett spent most of August
collecting subscriptions from business people in Dublin. They handed out
leaflets, the opening sentence of which read: 'For eighteen years we have
seen our country decay and become a prey to British and Jewish Financial
Economic Penetration.' The gardaí reported that at least one leaflet was
placed in the letterbox of a Jew, 'but whether this was done deliberately or
not is not known'. They also distributed a leaflet headed: 'The Jewish Question must be faced'. It urged more people to study the 'Jewish problem':

> It is the power of the Kabal which has prevented the Government from
> taking adequate measures to stem the tide of immigration of east Euro-
> pean Jews into this country. It is Judaism which is responsible for the
> alliance between High Finance and Bolshevism.
>
> The existence of a Jewish problem at all was hotly denied in 'Eire' about
> five years ago. The problem is now being discussed throughout the land
> but is ignored completely by every political party. This conspiracy of
> silence must be broken. Every Club, Society, and Church should have its
> library of books on the Jewish question, so that the Jews can be discussed
> intelligently and fearlessly.

The gardaí reported that Griffin was believed to have received subscriptions from many shopkeepers in the city, and both Griffin and Moylett
appeared 'to be in very affluent circumstances'. (Moylett split with Griffin in
the autumn.) Mrs Griffin was quoted as having said that the new party was

'purely Nazi in outlook' and that 'they are out to overthrow the Government'. She claimed that her husband was not receiving funds from the Germans. But on 11 October 1940, after receiving a letter from Griffin, the German envoy Hempel asked the Irish authorities: 'What [is] this party? It seems to be anti-Jewish.'

The People's National Party remained on the periphery of the periphery of Irish politics. It may have received encouragement, if not financial support, from the propaganda wings of the German and Italian legations.[69] *Penapa*, its short-lived paper, appeared for the first time in December 1940. The first issue carried a cartoon on the front page of a Jew sitting on bags of money. The government press censor immediately ordered its editor to submit all copy for the next issue to his office for vetting. The second and final issue of *Penapa* reported on the first 'monster' meeting of the People's National Party in Borris, Co. Carlow, where Griffin alleged that certain non-Christian elements were attempting to get control of the world – even Ireland. (A voice: 'We won't let them.') He said that he would not tolerate the conduct of certain non-Christian elements in Ireland.[70] It also carried a poem on the 'Origins of the National Flag of Ireland'.

> A little bit of Heaven fell from out
> the clear blue sky,
> Two Jewmen, when they saw it, at
> each other winked the eye.
> Said Moses unto Aaron, 'don't it
> look so sweet and grand,
> What is there to prevent us making
> this our promised land; . . .
> We'll fleece them of their birthright
> with laws both new and old,
> Give them the banner Green and White
> but collar all their Gold.'[71]

In another article, the author took a futuristic look at 'The Red Cross Chase of 1960 – or Sooner?' At the racecourse in Leopardstown, Dublin in 1960, the writer

> asked a big fat fellow with a parrot nose what won. He said he should not have vonit the favourite he Vould Vall at de last fence. I asked him what was favourite, he said, my horse 'Easy Terms'. . . . They talked so fast you could hardly understand them but one fat fellow behind me was telling another of these Olive Oil Nationals, that Mark Goldman's horse 'The Moneylender' Vould Valk the Race. . . .[72]

The gardaí understood that some members of the Jewish community intended to make representation to the government because of the frontis-piece of the paper 'which they regard as being particularly offensive and likely to leave them open to contempt and ridicule'. On 15 January 1941, members of the aliens supervision section of detective branch seized 1,974 copies of *Penapa* following the issue of a direction by the censor. Griffin was reported by the gardaí to have been in communication with both Archbishop

MacRory of Armagh and Archbishop McQuaid of Dublin concerning the Jewish problem; it seems probable that both would have condemned his anti-Semitism out of hand and advised the priests of their respective archdioceses to do likewise. That may have been one of the occasions, to which McQuaid referred in his 1949 letter to Jakobovits, when he helped forestall an anti-Semitic outbreak during the war years. The second issue was confiscated in its entirety by the authorities, and Griffin found himself in court in December 1941 being sued for failure to pay the printing costs of both issues. Griffin decided it was not worth his while bringing out the paper again.[73] It was not missed. The People's National Party also faded away.

But organised anti-Semitic groups continued to be active in Dublin. Griffin continued to be to the fore. A Fr Carey remained in contact with him, and together they organised a number of meetings to which they invited Axis ministers. Griffin, however, used another tactic to continue his attacks on Jews. He appeared in the Dublin District Court on 20 August 1940 to object to the renewal of the moneylending licences of a number of Jewish firms, and he repeated that action in September 1941, December 1942 and June 1943. The JRC was in contact with Superintendent McGloin on 10 December 1941 about 'inscriptions on walls in public places of an anti-Jewish and inflammatory nature on a number of occasions recently'.[74] McGloin promised that the matter was receiving 'special attention'; he said that 'any further inscriptions coming under notice' would be 'immediately obliterated' and that the necessary steps to have the offenders prosecuted would be taken.[75] There is evidence of another anti-Semitic incident a few months later. Bethel Solomons wrote on 29 June 1942 to Professor Jacob Weingreen of the JRC concerning the anti-Semitic actions of a particular group: 'I think there is a committee watching these people, and I would like to suggest that they should once or twice a year, send a full note of their activities to every member of each of the congregations in Dublin.'[76]

The *Weekly Review of the German News Agency* and *Radio Stefani – News from Italy* were among the most persistently anti-Semitic publications circulating in Dublin during the war years.[77] Those efforts were supported by propaganda radio broadcasts from Germany given by, amongst others, Lord Haw Haw (William Joyce, from Galway) and the novelist, Francis Stuart.[78] The Italian bulletin of 21 April 1941 referred to Jews as 'these rodents'.[79] The JRC complained immediately as did the Fianna Fáil TD, Erskine Childers. Vincenzo Berardis, the Italian envoy, was summoned to the Department of External Affairs by the secretary of the department, Joseph Walshe. 'When he had got through some of his usual incomprehensible world theories, I drew his attention to two recent editions of "Radio Stefani" sent out from his legation', minuted Walshe.[80] The Irish authorities, he informed Berardis, could not allow any legation enjoying Irish hospitality to circulate material which was an insult to the intelligence of Irish people and 'only fit for natives or aborigines'.[81] Berardis was summoned again on 7 May. Walshe told him that the recent bulletins were in the 'worst bad taste' and displayed an 'attitude towards the government of this friendly neutral country which can only be described as a gross breach of the privileges of hospitality which you enjoy'.[82]

But the agents and dupes of the Axis powers were not the only voices of anti-Semitism in wartime Ireland. The Holy Ghost priest Fr Denis Fahey wrote on 20 October 1941 to the leader of Fine Gael, William T. Cosgrave:

> When I learned that Jews had been given full citizenship by the new Constitution, I remarked to the present Archbishop [John Charles McQuaid]: 'That finishes our nation.' I made that remark because I am aware of what that has meant in the case of other nations such as France and Austria. The Jews, utilising other anti-Catholic forces, will strive to get control of supplies, so that people will be afraid to act; they will corrupt and debase our ideals by the cinema etc. and they will lead our subversives 'from behind'.[83]

Concluding his letter, Fahey stressed that he knew

> what the Jews are aiming at, and it is possible that they may have got very far already. . . . Quite a number of our people will be gripped by them and paralysing fear will keep them quiet in misery. I am afraid it is useless to appeal to ordinary Irishmen to wake up quickly to organise against the evil. The priests, however, are still independent and could organise.[84]

Cosgrave did not acknowledge the letter, and certainly did not share Fahey's views.

The occurrence of such anti-Semitic outbursts in wartime Dublin motivated a small but influential group of lay Catholics, led by Frank Duff (brother of J. E. Duff, assistant secretary at the Department of Justice) and León Ó Broin (a senior official in the Department of Finance), to establish the Pillar of Fire Society. The desire to foster Christian–Jewish dialogue came at a time when rumours had begun to reach the country about the mass killing of Jews on the continent.[85] Frank Duff had already established the Mercier Society to encourage discussion between Protestants and Catholics. Ó Broin was selected to present a paper at the first meeting, and on 25 September 1942 he wrote for help to a Jewish friend and fellow civil servant, Laurence Elyan:

> I feel, as the founders of this new Society do, that nothing but pain and hardship lie in store for the Jews in this country if the present lack of understanding between Jew and the majority of the people of Ireland continues.[86]

Ó Broin, who said his views on the subject were 'pretty well known in Catholic circles', felt very unhappy about certain negative developments:

> One hears too much wild talk around and sharp criticism, not always well informed, to be too happy about the way things are shaping, and I, for one, would like to do all that I could to get intelligent and influential Jews to meet intelligent and influential Catholics to talk things out in a convivial atmosphere. Only in that way can the seemingly intolerable experiences of Jews in almost every other country, at one time or another, be avoided. As an Irishman and a Catholic I don't want that crime ever to be laid at my country's door.[87]

Ó Broin asked Elyan to give him 'an honest-to-God statement' of his reactions.[88]

Elyan replied immediately, offering Ó Broin 'all assistance' in the project as he felt that they would be doing 'God's work' in promoting contact between 'our co-religionists'.[89] Plans were carefully laid, and a large group attended the first meeting of the Pillar of Fire Society. It was a resounding success, and a member of the Jewish community gave the next talk.[90] Joseph Walshe, secretary of the Department of External Affairs, read a paper at the third and what was to be the final meeting of the society. Why did it cease its activities? The following is a tentative explanation. Archbishop McQuaid had monitored the activities of the Pillar of Fire Society with interest and with some disquiet. A number of clergy had been asked by the archbishop to report to him fully and directly on the attendance and the content of the proceedings. His anxiety was aroused because laymen, as distinct from trained theologians, had articulated the official Catholic position at the meetings. He expressed those views in an exchange of letters with Ó Broin, who showed an independence of mind and an assertiveness which McQuaid would not normally have encountered among the laity at the time. The archbishop sought to replace the system of alternating Jewish and Catholic speakers with Catholic speakers – preferably clergy/theologians – at all meetings; he did not want any lectures to be given by Jews. Fr Michael O'Carroll, León Ó Broin and the other Catholic founder members were angered by the unreasonableness of the restrictions.[91] In view of the insult which such a change in structure would have caused Jewish members of the society, Duff and Ó Broin decided not to hold any further meetings.[92]

The demise of the Pillar of Fire Society removed the only inter-faith group in Dublin capable of fighting a recrudescence of anti-Semitism. One example of the anti-Semitism Ó Broin had spoken about was provided by Oliver J. Flanagan, the Monetary Reform candidate for the Laois–Offaly constituency, when he wrote to Fr Denis Fahey during the general election campaign in May 1943:

> Just a line letting you know we are going ahead with the Election Campaign in Laoighis-Offaly against the Jew-Masonic System which is imposed upon us. The people are coming to us – but it's hard to get the people to understand how they are held down by the Jews and Masons who control their very lives. I did as you told me to – placed my trust in our Blessed Lady and I am sure I will get a good vote here. The cause is a great one – for God and Ireland, and I hope we will win.[93]

Flanagan polled 4,379 first preferences, the third highest in the constituency.[94] He took his seat in Dáil Éireann and spoke in the chamber on 9 July:

> How is it that we do not see any of these Acts [emergency orders] directed against the Jews who crucified Our Saviour 1,900 years ago and who are crucifying us every day of this week? ... There is one thing that Germany did and that was to rout the Jews out of their country. Until we rout the Jews out of this country it does not matter a hair's breadth what orders you make. Where the bees are there is the honey, and where the Jews are there is the money.[95]

Flanagan apologised for those comments many years later.[96]

Further evidence of anti-Jewish prejudice was provided by a campaign in local councils to highlight the number of Jews who were allegedly making their names more Irish. In August 1943, for example, Longford County Council passed this resolution: 'That the attention of the Government be directed to the fact that several foreigners, mainly Jews, have succeeded in having their names changed to names of Irish origin.'[97] Tipperary South Riding County Council unanimously passed the same resolution in October. This issue also concerned a letter writer who wrote to Eamon de Valera on 18 June 1943 under the name of 'Brian Boru (late Abraham Goldstein)'.[98] Attaching notices of name changes from the *Official Gazette*, the anonymous writer claimed such notices were growing in frequency:

> Already I know of O'Brien, O'Sullivan (late Solomon), Sheridan, Byrne, etc. and now we have Collins. At this rate the Irish people will very soon be known by their characteristic noses and live complexions, not to mention their thieving propensities. Do you not think the time has come to give up [the] study of Irish and replace it in the schools [with] Yiddish, as undoubtedly the latter is going to become the language that matters in Ireland.

That was representative of the undercurrent of anti-Semitism which persisted in Ireland even after news of the Holocaust had become well known in the country.

Irish refugee policy and the Holocaust, 1942–45

The papal nuncio in Berne, Monsignor Armand Bernardini, received in March 1942 a memorandum which told of mass killings in Poland and in parts of Russia. The first news of the mass killings of Jews had reached Britain and the United States in 1941. There was definitive confirmation of mass exterminations about June 1942.[99] The representative of the World Jewish Congress in Geneva, Gerhart R. Riegner, sent a memorandum to Washington and London on 8 August 1942 giving details of the 'final solution'. The Vatican had evidence in August 1942 that the poisonous gas Zyklon-B was being used for mass extermination of Jews. Myron C. Taylor, Roosevelt's special representative to Pope Pius XII, gave a report on the exterminations to the Holy See in September 1942.[100]

When did news of the final solution and the Holocaust first reach Ireland? Fr Michael O'Carroll recalled that there were fragments of news about the mass extermination of Jews circulating in Dublin in the summer and early autumn of 1942; it may indeed have been a reason for the sense of urgency in setting up the Pillar of Fire Society. It may be assumed, therefore, that members of the Jewish community and of the political and administrative elites in Ireland knew about the final solution in late autumn 1942.

If leading members of the Jewish community had received news through the post of the Holocaust at an early stage, military intelligence would have known immediately. Colonel Dan Bryan and his associates were kept very well informed about the international contacts of the Jewish community through the interception of letters under wartime censorship regulations. A large collection of copies of letters remains on file from private individuals who were in many cases leaders of their community, such as Victor Waddington, Herman Good and his father Rev. Abraham Gudansky, Leonard Abrahamson, Ellis Sampson, Arthur Newman, A. Benson, M. Jacobson, Joshua Steinberg, Rev. W. Garbarz and Rabbi Alony. The mail of Jewish and Zionist organisations in Ireland and abroad was also intercepted and copied for the files by the censor, although the date of the beginning and the duration of that practice are not clear. The correspondence on the files relates to the activities of the Jewish Representative Council of Éire; Zion schools, Dublin; the Jewish Refugee Aid Committee, Dublin; the Dublin Daughters of Zion; the Zionist Society of Éire, Dublin; Harry Goodman, Aguda, London; the Zionist Federation of Great Britain; the Jewish National Fund, London; the new Zionist Organisation of America, New York; the Anglo-American Committee for a Jewish Army, New York; the Jewish Fellowship, St Albans, England; the Jewish Defence Committee, London; and the United Jewish Relief Appeal, London. Though scrutiny of them was quite systematic, a review of the intercepted and copied letters gives no indication that they provided the Irish government with an early warning of the Holocaust.

The government received news of the Holocaust from an unimpeachable source in early December 1942.[101] The chief rabbi of Palestine, Isaac Herzog, sent de Valera a telegram:

> REVERED FRIEND PRAY LEAVE NO STONE UNTURNED TO SAVE TORMENTED REMNANT OF ISRAEL DOOMED ALAS TO UTTER ANNIHILATION IN NAZI EUROPE GREETINGS ZIONS BLESSINGS.[102]

De Valera replied on 5 January 1943: 'I know you will believe that everything we can do as a neutral state to prevent or alleviate suffering anywhere we shall do to the utmost of our power.'[103] Herzog sent another telegram to de Valera on 30 January:

> AMERICAN STATE DEPARTMENT ANNOUNCED TWO MILLION EUROPEAN JEWS PERISHED, FIVE MILLION THREATENED WITH EXTERMINATION. DEPORTATIONS FROM GERMANY HOLLAND BELGIUM FRANCE NORWAY TO POLISH GHETTOES THENCE CENTRES MASS EXECUTIONS CONTINUE UNABATED. UNDERSTAND VARIOUS PROPOSALS MOOTED FOR REMOVING JEWS FROM GERMAN OCCUPIED TERRITORIES TO NEUTRAL COUNTRIES PRELIMINARY TO SUBSEQUENT TRANSFER OVERSEAS. EXECUTION THESE PLANS DEPEND ASSENT GERMAN AUTHORITIES. BEG YOU USE GOOD OFFICES STOP MASS DESTRUCTION EUROPEAN JEWRIES AND SECURE PERMISSION GRADUAL DEPARTURE. PLEASE APPROACH HIS HOLINESS FOR SUPPORT BOTH DIRECTIONS. MAY OUR HEAVENLY FATHER VOUCHSAFE YOU HIS COUNSEL AND GUIDANCE AND MAKE YOU PROVIDENTIAL AGENT FOR SALVATION MILLIONS INNOCENT MEN WOMEN CHILDREN FACING THREAT IMMINENT THREAT ANNIHILATION.[104]

De Valera, unable to do very much, sought to gain further information from the Irish high commissioner in London, John Dulanty. The director of the Agudas Israel World Organisation, Harry A. Goodman,[105] met Dulanty on 7 April and suggested a meeting with de Valera to discuss the following:

a) the granting of blocks of unnamed visas to your consuls in neutral European countries, especially Spain and Portugal, enabling cases of special hardship to be dealt with on the spot by the consul.

b) the granting of visas of a temporary nature to such persons as the British authorities have expressed their willingness to allow to come to this country once they have left enemy controlled territory. This would enable refugees now in such territory to obtain a transit visa then through neutral countries.

c) the possibility of the establishment of an internment camp for a limited number might be envisaged; the United Nations would supply food, clothing etc.

d) the use of neutral shipping to take refugees say from Bulgaria to Turkey en route for Palestine.[106]

On 10 April Dulanty suggested to Joseph Walshe at the Department of External Affairs that he should meet Goodman 'from the point of view of gathering first hand information'. The high commissioner reported that 'Goodman seemed to be a reasonably minded man and he stated his organisation is the most representative of the various Jewish bodies dealing with the problem of refugees'.[107] Rabbi Solomon Schonfeld, who was the executive director of the chief rabbi of Great Britain's Religious Emergency Council (and Chief Rabbi Joseph Hertz's son-in-law), confirmed that Goodman was authorised to negotiate with the Irish government on the question of rescuing victims of the Nazi massacres. Schonfeld guaranteed to maintain any Jews who were given temporary Irish visas. He also undertook to ensure that the Religious Emergency Council would 'use its utmost efforts for the subsequent re-emigration to Palestine or elsewhere of the persons for whom such visas have been given'.[108]

Walshe met Goodman in Dublin on 2 May 1943 where he repeated his proposals to the Irish government. He suggested that a limited number of visas, say 100, should be given to such people as were recommended by the Religious Emergency Council. The question was also raised of giving power to Irish envoys in Rome, Berlin and Vichy to grant at their discretion a limited number of visas to individuals whose emigration was of an urgent character. Such refugees, Goodman claimed, would not become a charge on the Irish state.[109] He also suggested that some visas be granted to refugees who intended to go to Palestine. There was a further proposal to allow a limited number of orphaned child refugees to settle with Jewish families in Ireland. That might be done through the Red Cross and the US representative in Lisbon. (Britain had taken more than 10,000 child refugees before the outbreak of hostilities.) Goodman also suggested that the Irish government might charter a boat to take Jewish child refugees from Bulgaria (where 5,000 had been granted release by the government) to Turkey or Palestine.[110] These proposals were redrafted on the advice of Walshe.[111]

Before leaving Dublin, Goodman expressed the hope that he would meet de Valera on his next visit. He also discussed with the secretary of the Irish Red Cross, Martin MacNamara, the possibility of sending food parcels to civilians in Poland.[112] Robert Briscoe was Goodman's main contact in Dublin.[113]

However, Walshe, who regarded Goodman as being somewhat self-important, discovered that he had deeply upset the leaders of the local Jewish community. That was not entirely due to his personality. Goodman was a member of Rabbi Solomon Schonfeld's Union of Orthodox Hebrew Congregations. The JRC leadership in Dublin seemed to share the view of many Jews in Britain that Schonfeld and Goodman were representative of 'a small ultra-Orthodox group of troublemakers'.[114]

Dublin had contacted John Dulanty about the possibility of chartering a boat. He met Goodman again, and the Irish were assured that the chartering costs would be borne by the Jewish organisations directly involved.[115] The International Red Cross would arrange 'security'. Goodman called to the British Foreign Office on 13 May where he saw A. W. G. Randall, the official in charge of the refugee department. (The latter had attended in April the unsuccessful Bermuda Conference which had failed to secure agreement on the rescue of Jews in Europe.[116]) Randall thought that the proposals were practicable and was prepared to assist in their realisation. In relation to the visas for 100 recommended individuals and for child refugees, he felt that there would be no difficulty in arranging for transit through Britain. Randall was, according to Goodman, particularly interested in the transit of women and children from Bulgaria.[117]

The Foreign Office took up the idea of the Irish government hiring a boat to ferry refugees in the Mediterranean. Randall discussed the matter on 21 May with the Irish high commission in London and said that 'it would be of considerable assistance to us in dealing with one very difficult area' – the removal of Jewish women and children from central and eastern Europe via Istanbul.[118] However, Dulanty reported on 7 June that the Bulgarian government had gone back on its word to release the women and children.[119] There the matter rested.

But 'local difficulties with the [Irish] Jewish community' now impeded the advancement of the refugee work. Goodman and Chief Rabbi Joseph Hertz discussed the situation with Dulanty at a meeting on 2 July.[120] Hertz undertook to write to the Jewish community in Dublin to try to resolve the 'local difficulties'. Meanwhile, in Dublin Edwin Solomons and Leonard Abrahamson of the JRC went to see Joseph Walshe about the matter. Solomons replied to Hertz on 13 July, saying that they were planning to meet de Valera: 'I well understand the tragic fate of our brethren on the European Continent, and you may rest assured that Dr Abrahamson and myself will endeavour to press the matter as much as possible next week.'[121] Goodman, writing to Walshe on 23 July, felt that 'it appears as if the difficulties are being overcome' and suggested that Dulanty might discuss the matter with the Jewish community while on a visit to Dublin. Goodman and the chief rabbi were prepared to travel to Ireland 'if that would assist in solving the problem'. He emphasised that in the three months since his visit to Dublin the position had deteriorated on the continent, 'and I feel sure that a number of cases which might have been saved, in regard to which we already had the papers, have since been lost'.[122] Goodman referred again on 9 August to the 'local difficulties' and stressed to Walshe that there were a number of 'grave cases awaiting your decision'. He pointed out that 'nothing tangible has yet resulted', and added:

> It may be that the German authorities would not allow these people to leave, but we can but try. . . . Amidst all the vital problems of State, the saving of a few individuals is really all we can do. I do hope that this matter will not be delayed and am prepared to come over if you thought that would be useful.[123]

In the weeks that followed, the chief rabbi of Great Britain personally, according to Goodman, 'put right' the 'difficulty with the Jewish community in Dublin'.[124]

Meanwhile, another telegram from Herzog arrived on 10 July 1943:

> HORRIFIED BY REPORT SOME 80000 JEWS IN ITALY NATIVE AND REFUGEES THREATENED WITH DEPORTATION TO POLAND WHICH MEANS CERTAIN DEATH. PRAY INTERCEDE IMMEDIATELY WHICHEVER WAY POSSIBLE ALSO PLEASE PETITION THEIR BEHALF HIS HOLINESS THE POPE. GREETINGS BLESS-INGS.[125]

Walshe immediately contacted Ireland's envoy at the Holy See, Thomas J. Kiernan: 'Can you say if there is any truth in report that 80,000 Jews in Italy are threatened with deportation to Poland?'[126] A telegram was sent to Robert Briscoe from London in late July requesting the Irish government to intervene through the Vatican to prevent the deportation of over 3,000 Jews who had been on their way to Palestine and were interned in Ferramonti Tarsia camp in the province of Cosenza.[127] Kiernan replied on 24 July giving the total number of Jews in Italy not as 80,000 but as 40,000, of whom 32,000 were Italians of mixed blood. The 8,000 of pure Jewish blood were interned and were being deported.[128] On 10 August 1943, Walshe wrote to Briscoe – on the basis of information he had received from Kiernan – giving him permission to tell Leonard Abrahamson that 'it is now confidentially hoped that all discriminatory racial laws [in Italy] will soon be repealed'.[129] That was not to happen.

The Irish envoy in Berlin, Con Cremin, sent a telegram on 3 September 1943 concerning the case of the noted Gaelic scholar Julius Pokorny who has been referred to in previous chapters.[130] Cremin reported that Pokorny was still in Berlin and that the 'visa did not help him. Police are averse to letting anybody out of Germany; they are afraid that information might leak out.'[131] The best efforts of the Irish authorities notwithstanding, Pokorny had a remarkable escape, as he explained to his friend Richard Best in a letter on 30 August 1945. Writing from Zurich, he said:

> My father reached 87 years in spite of the terrible moral persecutions of the Nazis. He was only spared deportation on account of his purely Aryan second wife, whose brother happened to be vice-president of the Vienna Police, who did his best to protect him. He saved my life in dying on the 10th of April 43, for on account of his death I was absent from Berlin the very day the Secret Police came to arrest me in my Berlin flat! My luck has been really enormous. Not only could I cross the Swiss frontier quite easily in plain daylight, but I was never interned in a camp but got

permission to live in a boarding house, and after 8 months I got a small lectureship both in Berne and Zurich. But the pay is very little.[132]

Pokorny died on 8 April 1970 after being struck by a car while crossing a road in Zurich. He was eighty-three.

The Department of External Affairs, meanwhile, continued to act on Goodman's initiative.[133] On 25 August 1943 Dublin informed the Irish envoy in Vichy, Seán Murphy, that the government had been approached to grant temporary visas so as to enable a number of prominent Jewish personalities to get out of German-occupied territory. It was the understanding of the government that there was no prospect of these people being able to get German exit permits in the present circumstances. Murphy was asked to make enquiries.[134]

Dulanty told Goodman on 7 September that Irish enquiries at Vichy and in Berlin had not been successful. He also mentioned the case of an Irish national, a relative of one of the government ministers, who had been refused an exit permit by the Germans.[135] Despite the lack of success, Goodman sent Dublin a list of Jews he thought were in imminent danger of being deported to the death camps. He encouraged Dulanty on 17 September to try again because the British Foreign Office remained of the view that while exit permits would not be granted by the Germans, the giving of visas to individuals by neutral countries might prevent the holders from being deported to the east.[136] A second list of names was added by Goodman on 24 September. A month later, he wrote to Dulanty claiming that the Irish government had been somewhat inactive:

> Many months have now elapsed since this matter was first raised with the Dublin Government and we were under the impression that instructions had been given for the visas to be granted. In the tragic position of the European Continent today and the planned destruction of millions of men, women and children of the Jewish faith nothing that could be done to save a few individuals should be delayed.[137]

Goodman repeated his view that while the German authorities would not grant exit visas, anyone receiving a visa from Ireland would not be deported to the east; and even if they were interned they would be put in separate internment camps.[138]

Dulanty was approached in London on 26 October 1943 by Baron Floris Pallandt, the minister plenipotentiary and acting head of the political division of the Netherlands Foreign Ministry, with a request to have the Irish government intervene with the German minister in Dublin on behalf of 'important members of the Dutch Jewish community'.[139] Between 300 and 450 Dutchmen of Jewish origin had been interned by the German authorities in a country house near Barneveld, Holland. The Dutch government in exile had learned that they had been transferred to 'the ill-famed concentration camp of Westerbork in Germany' and had reason to fear 'their imminent transportation to Poland, which, in most cases, will mean their extermination'.[140]

Walshe wired Cremin in Berlin on 1 November, to enquire whether it was true that Jews holding visas from neutral countries were exempt from deportation and bad treatment. Cremin was advised that Dublin had been asked to give visas to a number of named Jews in Holland and Belgium as a protection, whether they came to Ireland or not. 'Would such steps be good or bad for the Jews concerned?', Cremin was asked.[141] He replied on 18 November saying that the German authorities regarded the question of the Jews as an 'internal matter'. In his enquiries he had been refused any general information; each case, he was told, would be considered individually. 'I have asked Swedish Legation what their experience is and they have told me visa is rarely any use.' Cremin added that it might, however, be interesting to try a few test cases.[142]

The Irish envoy in Berne, Frank T. Cremins, was asked by Dublin on 4 November if the Swiss had intervened in the case of the Dutch Jews. He replied on 10 November that the Swiss Foreign Office had no information on the matter and said that the Swiss 'would find it extremely difficult to intervene even semi-officially in view of their many other interests in countries concerned. They are unaware visas would have results stated.'[143]

Seán Murphy in Vichy was again asked by Dublin about the usefulness of possessing an Irish visa. He replied on 16 December that the Vichy Foreign Office had told him unofficially that it did not afford protection. Murphy added, however, that the Vichy Foreign Office 'considered that it is possible that German authorities might agree to allow us to take a certain number of Jews of a defined nationality but were quite sure that in the absence of agreement nothing could prevent foreign Jews being deported'.[144]

The Irish government was involved in another round of diplomatic initiatives after 15 December 1943 following the receipt of another telegram from Herzog:

> TWO HUNDRED MOST RESPECTABLE JEWISH FAMILIES POLISH REFUGEES IN VITTEL FRANCE HOLDING SOUTH AMERICAN STATES PASSPORTS IN EXTREME DANGER THREATENED WITH DEPORTATION. PRAY GRANT THEM VISAS TO ENTER AND TEMPORARY PERMITS STAY EIRE. THEIR MAINTENANCE WILL BE FULLY GUARANTEED BY RESPONSIBLE JEWISH PUBLIC BODIES. JEWRY WILL BE EVER GRATEFUL TO EIRE FOR SAVING THESE FAMILIES IN GRAVEST DISTRESS. ANTICIPATORY THANKS HEARTFELT BLESSINGS.[145]

De Valera replied to Herzog on 17 December: 'Am having possibilities examined'. Walshe cabled Murphy in Vichy requesting him to find out whether the Germans would allow the Polish Jewish families in Vittel to come to Ireland, and to ask Vichy to intervene with the Germans.[146] Murphy replied on 29 December that the German authorities had informed the Vichy Foreign Office 'that they are not prepared to accept French intervention on behalf of foreign Jews in France'. Murphy had been advised that the Irish government should try to arrange matters directly with the German government. The Vichy authorities, he was told, would facilitate departure so far as possible.[147]

Dublin cabled Cremin in Berlin on 4 January 1944 asking him to find out whether the 200 Polish Jewish families living at Vittel would be allowed to come to Ireland temporarily if transport could be arranged; whether 500 French Christian children could be transferred to Ireland for the duration of

the war; and whether specifically named Jewish families could be transferred from occupied territories.[148] As might have been anticipated,
Cremin's enquiries yielded no results. He had seen the deputy director of
the political department of the German Foreign Office, who had promised to
make enquiries. But Cremin was not optimistic. He restated to Dublin the
difficulty in getting exit visas, even for Irish citizens. He cited the case of a
person named McConville, possibly the relative of the minister mentioned
earlier. Cremin was keeping the question of children 'separate from that of
Jews'. He concluded:

> It seems improbable therefore that these Jews would receive more
> favourable consideration. You will also appreciate that German authori-
> ties are inclined to regard action by other countries as indirect criticism
> of their Jewish policy.[149]

Walshe cabled Cremin again in mid-February, laying particular emphasis on
the case of the French Christian children. Cremin replied on 6 March; he
understood from German officials that it was unlikely the children would be
granted visas, and even more unlikely that Jewish families would. On 17
March Cremin informed Dublin that the visas for the children had been
refused.

> As regards Jews [I] have been asked by Internal Affairs section of Foreign
> Office why we want them to go to Ireland whether it is intended that they
> become citizens or only remain until end of war and whether any of them
> have relatives there. I gather no hope of visas except for such families as
> may have relatives and even then I think little chance. The official
> concerned seemed inclined to read political implications into our enquiry
> thinking that it had something to do with Anglo-American refugee
> scheme.[150]

The Polish refugees remained in Vittel.

Also on 17 March Harry Goodman wrote to Dulanty in London urging that
Dublin issue Irish visas to Jews on the continent.[151] Dulanty wrote to Walshe
some days later, enclosing this letter and offering the following explanation
for Goodman's persistence:

> As I have mentioned before, Mr Randall of the British Foreign Office,
> thinks there is good ground for believing that the granting of our visa
> would secure for its holder relatively humane treatment. In certain cases,
> he says, a South American visa has prevented Jews being sent to
> Poland.[152]

Meanwhile, the US envoy in Dublin, David Gray, had seen Walshe on 9
February to discuss President Roosevelt's setting up of the War Refugee
Board. Walshe told Gray that the Irish government was prepared in principle
to receive 500 Jewish refugee children. Gray sent news of the offer to Washington, and on 22 March he sent Walshe a copy of Washington's reply:

> Please inform the appropriate Irish official that this Government accepts
> with deep appreciation the generous and humanitarian offer which we

understand the Irish Government is prepared to make to receive and provide haven for 500 Jewish refugee children.

Gray also asked Walshe whether the Irish government would be willing to guarantee admission after the war to an additional 500 Jewish refugee children. Such a commitment, Gray said, might enable the War Refugee Board to induce the Swiss government to accept larger numbers of refugee children from Vichy for the duration of the war.[153] The secretary of the Irish Red Cross Society wrote to Walshe on 1 April to indicate that the society would take the 500 Jewish refugee children who were to come during the war. He sought the department's permission to publish details of the initiative: 'When publishing it we shall omit the word "Jewish". When we receive your permission we shall get in touch with the Jewish communty here in order to make arrangements for the reception and housing of the children.'[154]

Walshe sent a memorandum to de Valera on 5 April reviewing the background to Irish refugee policy and the willingness to accept 500 Jewish children. He also discussed the possibility of receiving a further 500 children after the war. Without any explanation, Walshe concluded his memorandum in the following vein:

> There is a great deal of pro-Jewish activity in Administration quarters in the United States at the present. For example, they have recently encouraged the new Zionist movement in favour of the restoration of Palestine as the Jewish homeland. The British reviews suggest that this phase is due to the approaching Elections.[155]

The formal decision to admit the first 500 Jewish children was taken the same day by de Valera; he told Walshe he would make a decision later on the admission of a further 500 Jewish refugee children after the war. Gray was informed of the decision and responded gratefully to the news.[156]

Ironically while the Irish government was being praised by Washington for its active policy on behalf of Jews in occupied Europe, a series of articles highly critical of Ireland appeared in a New York left-wing paper, *PM*. In the middle of March 1944, Michael Sayers, a graduate of Trinity College Dublin, wrote the first article entitled 'Truth about Nazi espionage in Eire – Irish terrorists work directly under Hitler's orders'.[157] The Irish consul in New York summarised the contents as follows:

> It states that Axis espionage has flourished on Irish soil since first days of war and de Valera's Government knows it. The article describes the German Legation as having spy courier system working across border, mentions Francis Stuart as broadcasting Nazi propaganda from Berlin.[158]

The following day he cabled Dublin again – in anticipation of what was likely to be in the other articles – suggesting 'you obtain urgently for publication here statement from Jewish leader and community in Ireland'.[159] Walshe consulted Colonel Dan Bryan at G2 in the meantime, and was able to inform the consul that Sayers had been born in Dublin, where he attended Trinity College in 1937 before going to England.[160]

Walshe met the leaders of the JRC, which issued a statement repudiating

> as false, irresponsible and mischievous any suggestion that the govern-
> ment of this country is anti-Semitic or that there is any organised
> anti-Semitic movement in Eire. The Jewish Community live and have
> always lived on terms of closest friendship with their fellow Irish citizens.
> Freedom to practise their religion is specifically guaranteed in the Irish
> Constitution. No Irish Government has ever discriminated between Jew
> and non-Jew.[161]

Robert Briscoe also issued a statement, drafted verbatim for him by Joseph
Walshe:

> As a member of the Irish Parliament and a practising adherent of the
> Jewish faith who has represented for seventeen years a Dublin
> constituency, 97 per cent Roman Catholics, I deny emphatically that the
> people of Ireland are or have ever been anti-Semitic. . . . I should like to
> add that the Jewish community in Eire are taking their full share in the
> Auxiliary Defence Forces of the country and that they whole heartedly
> support the government's policy of neutrality.[162]

Both statements were published in *PM* on 24 March, together with a comment:

> What P.M.'s article said, and what cannot be contradicted, is that the
> Germans have had some success in spreading the virus of anti-Semitism
> in Ireland with the help of such elements as General O'Duffy's Irish
> Fascist party which has adopted a Nazi-inspired 'Jewish peril' line, and of
> Fr Denis Fahey, author of anti-Semitic tracts taken partly from Nazi
> propaganda. . . . it is a fact, that the Dail has its Rankin element.[163]

By coincidence, in February 1944 a Jewish-owned premises in Grafton
Street, Dublin was defaced one night; 'JEWS' was painted in two-foot letters
and the words 'Perish Judah' were stuck on the windows.[164]

Within weeks of the *PM* episode, Chief Rabbi Herzog sent his next cable
on 5 April:

> EXTREMELY PERPLEXED. 235 JEWISH REFUGEE FAMILIES IN VITTEL VICHY
> FRANCE FOR WHOM YOU ONCE SUCCESSFULLY INTERCEDED ARE AGAIN
> THREATENED WITH DEPORTATION WHICH MEANS ALAS CERTAIN EXTERMINA-
> TION. PRAY MAKE IMMEDIATELY SUPREME EFFORTS SAVE DOOMED MOST
> RESPECTED FAMILIES. ANTICIPATORY THANKS BEHALF PEOPLE OF ISRAEL.
> GREETINGS.[165]

De Valera replied on 18 April, saying the Irish government was making a
further appeal on behalf of the Jewish families. Goodman, hearing the same
terrible news, sent a telegram which Walshe received on 16 April: 'Understand
position internees Vittel most grave. Deportation imminent. Earnestly ask
your immediate intervention.'[166] Walshe replied on 19 April pointing out that
they had so far failed to secure permission for the Vittel group to come to
Ireland and that the Irish representative had been instructed to make further
efforts. He understood that there was 'very little chance unless they have relatives here and even then very doubtful'.[167]

Walshe could afford to be emphatic because he had on file two recent, long reports from Con Cremin in Berlin which indicated that the fate of the Vittel Jews was already sealed. Cremin had been asked by the German authorities on 24 March why Ireland would want to receive Jews:

> If it was intended that these families should become Irish citizens the German authorities would, I was given to understand, 'gladly save us the inconvenience of having so many Jews'; if, on the other hand, it was proposed that these families should return to Europe after the end of the war it could be inferred that a German defeat was presupposed; if it was intended that they should later go to Palestine, the German government could not approve of an arrangement which would have for result to introduce further Jewish elements into an Arab territory; if finally any of the families in question had relatives in Ireland their case could, on receipt of information on that point, be examined individually.[168]

He concluded that no exit visas would be provided for Jews, even those with relatives in Ireland.[169] In another report three days later Cremin pointed out:

> You will probably not have overlooked one important element in connection with this question of the grant of Irish visas to Jews so as to alleviate the hardship of their situation, viz. that it would be necessary that they hold passports. It is doubtful whether a Jew, not authorised to emigrate, would now be granted a passport by the German authorities. Apparently only an infinitesimal fraction of the Jews who have entered Switzerland from France and Germany in the last three years have had visas.[170]

On 19 April Walshe requested Cremin to make a further intervention on behalf of the Vittel Jews. Replying that he was making representations as instructed, Cremin asked Walshe whether cognisance had been taken of his despatches of 24 and 27 March. Walshe replied that Irish motivation was 'purely humanitarian', and even if there was little hope he simply wanted Cremin to try again.[171] But unknown to Walshe, Cremin had been told by a German official that visas from Ireland or anywhere else would have no weight in preventing the possible deportation, as those likely to be deported were Jews whom the German government regarded as belonging to Germany. He said that those interned were not deported. Cremin told Dublin on 13 May that no decision had been reached and that 'measures for deportation of Jews involved [was] suspended pending final decision on our representation'.

Walshe sent a telegram the following day to both Herzog and Goodman informing them that the Vittel families would not be deported pending consideration of Irish representations.[172] That was a very sanguine reading of the situation, as was confirmed by Goodman on 27 May when he told Walshe that the Vittel internees had already been transferred to Drancy deportation camp, near Paris. On 12 June Cremin reported that the German Foreign Office had confirmed that there were Jews in Drancy but that it was not possible to say whether they were the ones in which the Irish were interested. Goodman was assured by Walshe on 19 June that he was continuing his representations. He sought further specific information, the names and addresses of the families; Goodman sent this information to Dublin on 22 June. When Cremin reported on 4 July, he had definite news that the Polish Jews at Vittel were in a camp in eastern Europe. Other Jews, including citizens of South American countries, were being kept for exchange against German civil internees. Cremin added that the official he spoke to said that the 'German authorities have been treating [our] application with all possible goodwill because it comes from Ireland instead of as would be done normally refusing it out of hand'.[173]

While Cremin continued to use his diplomatic skills in the macabre world of wartime Berlin, Herzog cabled de Valera and Walshe later in July:

> REFERENCE OUR COMMUNICATIONS MATTER JEWISH REFUGEES VITTEL ABOUT WHOM YOU WERE KIND ENOUGH MAKE INTERVENTION REGRET INFORM YOU THAT REPATRIATED REFUGEES FROM THAT CAMP JUST ARRIVED HERE STATE ALL EXCEPTION 29 SICK DEPORTED FROM VITTEL ON 18.4.44 AND 16.5.44 TO UNKNOWN DESTINATION. IT IS POSSIBLE THEY ARE IN CAMP BERGENBELSEN NEAR HANOVER. ON DAY OF DEPORTATION TERRIBLE SCENES TOOK PLACE. VIGOROUS EFFORTS BEING UNDERTAKEN ALLIED POWERS ARRANGE REPATRIATION THROUGH EXCHANGE BUT WE FEAR THAT COMPLETION NEGOTIATIONS FIND THEY HAVE ALREADY BEEN SENT TO DEATH CAMPS IN POLAND. MAY I ON BEHALF HOUSE ISRAEL WHILE THANKING ESTEEMED GOVERNMENT FOR PREVIOUS INTERVENTION APPEAL YOU MAKE CALL TO GERMAN GOVERNMENT HOLD UP DEPORTATION THESE PEOPLE. IN FACE CRUEL TRAGEDY WHICH WILL SHOCK HISTORY TILL END OF DAYS THE VOICE OF GOD AND CIVILISATION CALLS TO WHOLE HUMANITY NOT TO REST SAVE WHAT CAN BE SAVED SNATCH PRECIOUS [? BRANCHES] FROM FIRE. WARMEST THANKS GREETINGS YOURSELF TAOISEACH.[174]

De Valera cabled Herzog on 24 July: 'doing everything possible'. And he was.

Walshe cabled Cremin on 28 July relaying the contents of Herzog's telegram. On 2 August Cremin reported that he had raised the question of the Vittel Jews and hoped to get the information. Dublin did get some clarification in a letter from Goodman on 1 August. Quoting repatriated Vittel Jews, Goodman told Walshe that 'in the last few days the position there has become most grave with the Jews of South American nationality'. A newspaper clipping reported that 225 Vittel Jews were in Auschwitz, Silesia, where they faced extermination in the 'bath-houses'. Walshe cabled Cremin on 9 August with surnames and the number in the family, but all efforts proved futile. Goodman, in a cable received in Dublin on 14 August, stated that only thirty-four Jews remained in Vittel and again he urgently sought the help of the Irish government. Throughout the latter part of August came confirmation of the news that the Vittel Jews had gone to Bergen-Belsen. Based on Swiss sources, Cremin informed Dublin on 28 August that 163 of the Jews in Vittel had been removed in April and 129 in May, while some had escaped by committing suicide.[175] According to the historian Natan Eck, the families were sent to the extermination camp at Auschwitz where they were put to death.[176]

An eye-witness account of life in those last days at Vittel was provided in September 1944 by a nun from Northern Ireland, Sr Mary Ita Begley of the Congregation of Providence, Ruillé-sur-Loir. She had been interned for three and a half years in a camp of 4,000 British and American women. Vittel

Palace had been turned into a hospital which was staffed by nuns from various religious orders. Sr Mary described the arrival of Jews in the Vittel camp. They were 'very fine and good' families, she said, but the Germans treated them 'like dogs', selling them false passports for which they paid hundreds of pounds. The Jews, who were mainly Polish, thought they were buying US passports. She explained:

> Last May 400 to 500 Jews, men, women, and children, were taken away, and there were fifteen cases of suicide. They threw themselves out of the train and others threw themselves from windows, while some cut their veins. We did not know what became of the others. The Germans said they were taken to another camp in France.[177]

The Irish efforts must be set in context: between 75,000 and 83,000 Jews had been deported from France by the end of 1944 to be exterminated in Poland. The number of Jews who died during the war according to country of origin is as follows: Holland, 106,000; Belgium, 24,387; Luxembourg, 700; Italy, 8,000; Germany 160,000; Austria, 65,000; Poland, 3,000,000; and the Soviet Union, 1,000,000.[178]

Hungary, which came under direct German control on 19 March 1944, also became a focus of Irish diplomatic concern throughout the remainder of that year. About 750,000 Jews, once thought to be safe beyond the reach of the Nazis, found themselves likely candidates for deportation to the death camps. Two German requests to have the Jews in Hungary deported to greater Germany had been turned down in 1943. But within a few weeks of German occupation, plans were set in motion to carry out the deportations. The move began on 15 April 1944, with Jews first being driven from their villages and herded into ghettos and camps.[179] Deportations to Austria began on 15 May, and 289,357 had been sent there by mid-June. From his headquarters in Budapest, Adolf Eichmann, head of the Gestapo's Jewish affairs section, supervised the task of deporting tens of thousands to their deaths. The landing of the Allies in France on 6 June 1944 only led to the intensification of German efforts to get the remaining European Jews to the death camps. The final toll from Hungary was about 200,000.[180]

Goodman was one of the sources who kept de Valera informed of developments in Hungary. He cabled Walshe on 7 July 1944 urging him to take action. Walshe cabled Thomas J. Kiernan, Ireland's envoy at the Holy See, on 13 July stating that 'official action is not considered feasible but you might take occasion of informal conversation with Hungarian Minister to tell him of concern aroused here'. Kiernan reported two days later that the Hungarian minister and staff had resigned on arrival of the Allies in Rome in June 1944 and had formed an anti-German freedom movement. Also on 15 July, both the *Irish Press* and the *Irish Times* carried reports of the mass extermination of Hungarian Jews, while the dean of Christ Church Cathedral, E. H. Lewis-Crosby, wrote to de Valera requesting him to intervene and to seek to move the Hungarian and German authorities to ways of mercy. De Valera replied that 'you may rest assured that we will take advantage of every possibility of useful intervention which is now open to us'. Rabbi David Freilich, a native

Hungarian living in Ireland, wrote 'as a private individual' to de Valera drawing his attention to the 'mass murder of Jews now taking place in Hungary'. He wanted the Irish government to intervene: 'Even if all efforts prove fruitless, it will be a source of record that when our civilisation was stained with this blot, the voices of these nations were raised in protest.'[181] Kiernan again cabled Dublin on 23 July about reports which had been received by the Holy See from the papal nuncio in Budapest, stating that of the one million Jews in Hungary, about 400,000 were refugees without passports. The nuncio had told Rome that the anti-Jewish laws in Hungary had been applied with 'very great humanity'.[182] But that was flying in the face of the facts.

In London John Dulanty saw Harry Goodman on 1 August and was told that it was the intention of the British government to co-operate in the fullest possible manner with the Hungarian authorities in order to rescue as many Jews as possible. When Dulanty asked how the Irish government might co-operate Goodman suggested that a number of children might be granted temporary reception facilities in Ireland which would be supported fully by the chief rabbi of Great Britain.[183]

On 14 August Aaron S. Brown of the US legation in Dublin wrote to Walshe concerning Ireland's agreement in principle to accept 500 Jewish refugee children from France and requesting that the agreement be extended to Hungary.[184] The Irish government readily agreed. Walshe wrote to Brown on 21 August telling him that an independent approach had been made by Goodman's organisation in London, Aguda, to the Irish Red Cross concerning the evacuation of Jewish children from Hungary. 'Of course', he wrote, 'there is no possibility whatever of private organisations being able to effect any transfer of children to Ireland without the collaboration of the American or British Government.' It was best, Walshe thought, to prevent Aguda from taking an independent course which might cause confusion in US plans.[185] When the Irish Red Cross told Walshe by letter on 22 August that they were ready to receive the children from Hungary, Walshe replied that it would be advisable not to enter into any other commitments until the society had heard from the US authorities. 'Otherwise, there is a real danger of confusion', he wrote.[186] Walshe told US envoy David Gray of the situation, and the latter undertook to write to the US ambassador in London, John Winant. Gray explained the background of the Irish decision in the following way:

> In the course of our discussion with the Irish government it was agreed that in all existing circumstances five hundred was as many as the Jewish population in Eire could reasonably be expected to support and as many as the Irish economy could reasonably be expected to absorb. The quota is limited to children inasmuch as for security reasons it was considered undesirable both from the American and Irish viewpoint to permit the entrance of adult persons from Axis countries.[187]

Winant so advised Aguda, as did the Irish Red Cross. However, Aguda did not feel that it would be justified in withdrawing the request it had made to the Irish Red Cross. But it gave 'emphatic assurances' that in any further discussion between it and the Irish Red Cross the question of admitting additional Jews from Hungary would be taken up as an entirely separate arrangement so that it could not be construed as widening the scope of the existing agreement.[188] Goodman went further on 12 September and suggested to the US embassy in London that a limited number of adults should be allowed to accompany the children.[189] That was not the answer Walshe wanted to hear. It not only left room for further misunderstanding and friction between Goodman and the Irish authorities, but also had the potential of causing friction between Aguda and the leaders of the Jewish community in Dublin.

Oliver J. Flanagan, whose offensive anti-Semitic remarks on entering Dáil Éireann in 1943 have already been mentioned, made another unwelcome intervention in the proceedings. He put down a Dáil question concerning the request for Ireland to receive refugees or wounded from the war zones. Taoiseach Eamon de Valera replied on 20 September that no such request had been received: 'A proposal for the reception here of refugee children from Europe was made and was accepted. I cannot, however, at this stage give further information.' Flanagan replied in an offensive manner: 'I would much prefer to hear the Taoiseach giving the answer that he has given than telling this House a lie.' At that point, the ceann comhairle intervened and de Valera asked in anger: 'What did the Deputy mean by saying I told a lie?' Flanagan repeated his previous statement.[190]

On 9 September Walshe informed Con Cremin in Berlin that the Irish government had been asked to intervene with the Germans on behalf of Jews in Hungary; Dublin had heard that the Swiss and the Swedes had already done so. Cremin replied in a detailed cable giving the background to the Swedish intervention: 'The *démarche* made here about 6 weeks ago was informal, and Foreign Office at the time said that question is one for Hungarian authorities otherwise no reply has been received to date.'[191] Irish overtures concerning Hungarian Jews simply ran into the sands.

While the destruction of the Jews continued, Hitler's forces in Europe were in retreat. Goodman wrote to Walshe on 29 September stating his intention of coming to Dublin in a few weeks to renew 'the pleasant and fruitful relations' which he had initiated in April 1943. Walshe welcomed his proposed visit by letter on 5 October, but advised him to take 'no new step whatsoever without previous consultation with the American Embassy'. Walshe told Goodman that the US government would carry out the project of bringing the 500 children to Ireland and that he himself and the Irish Red Cross would consult with the local Jewish community at the appropriate moment.[192] Edwin Solomons of the Jewish Representative Council phoned Walshe on 16 October and told him he had heard that 'this fellow Goodman' was coming over. He was quite sure Walshe knew it already, but, in the opinion of the JRC, Goodman had no authority to come and talk to them or dictate to them. Agudas Israel was 'an extremist organisation, and the Jewish Council wanted to have nothing to do with it'. Walshe was told that 'The last time Goodman was over, he caused nothing but confusion.'[193]

Goodman visited Dublin and met Walshe on 18 October 1944. Walshe immediately explained that the transfer to Ireland of 500 Jewish refugee children had become exclusively an affair of the American and Irish governments. He told Goodman that it was particularly important for him to realise that any negotiations with the Jewish community in Dublin regarding the children would be carried on by the Irish government. Walshe continued in his report on their meeting:

> The Irish J. community did not feel too kindly towards an English Jew coming over here to advise them, or, still worse, to boss them or to admonish them, and he should be extremely careful in his relations with them.
> At this, Mr Goodman flared up and abused the Irish Jewish Council with great vigour, saying that he would report them to Agudas Israel and the World Council for being so selfish about helping their own people and hampering the good work which he was doing.[194]

Walshe told Goodman that the local Jewish community were extremely good people but they had their own interests to look after. They were not only good Irish citizens, but they were very charitable towards each other. They were a small community with relatively slender resources, and Goodman should not expect too much from them.[195] Walshe concluded that Goodman was a 'sincere worker and really wants to help his people'.[196] He then took Goodman to lunch and asked him if he was going to see the members of the JRC. Goodman said he was not going to meet them formally, but that some of his friends were organising a meeting for him that night.[197] Walshe ended his minute:

> While we should be ready to help Goodman as Secretary of Agudas Israel to secure every possible alleviation for suffering Jews in Europe, we should not accept him as in any way an intermediary between us and the Irish community of Jews.[198]

Goodman lunched with the US envoy, David Gray, on 19 October. He reported to Walshe that Gray promised to do his utmost to try to bring the 500 Jewish children to Ireland. Goodman hoped 'that on this occasion matters of communal prestige will not jeopardise the magnanimous offer of your government'. In conclusion, he wrote: 'We can do but little to alleviate the ocean of tears which the war has brought in its wake, but we must try not to leave that little undone.'[199]

The Goodman visit had its repercussions. He was reported as having said to a group of Jews in Dublin that the Irish high commissioner in London, John Dulanty, 'laid all the blame for trouble on the Dublin community'.[200] That indiscretion resurrected the old 1943 dispute and Walshe was again obliged to try to set the record straight with the local Jewish community. He told Edwin Solomons that what Dulanty had said was that the London people could do nothing without the consent and co-operation of the Dublin community.[201] The reception of the refugees was primarily a matter for the Irish government and the Dublin community. 'There is no use worrying about the past', Walshe wrote.[202] Edwin Solomons wrote to Walshe on 30 October saying that he had received a letter from Chief Rabbi Hertz in

Britain in which the chief rabbi wrote: 'I am indeed glad to learn that the statements freely made concerning the indifference of the Dublin community have no basis in fact.'[203] Further skirmishes ensued.

The pleas for help continued to reach the Department of External Affairs. On 26 October 1944, Goodman wired Walshe about deportations from Slovenia; he wanted the Irish government to make enquiries. The same day, Rabbis Rosenberg, Silver and Leventhal of the Union of the Orthodox Rabbis of the United States and Canada made an appeal to Dublin to find out about 12,000 Jews – including some well-known rabbis – deported from Kaunas, Lithuania.[204]

In Berlin Cremin made another futile journey to the German Foreign Office, where he was treated to yet another catalogue of naked lies. He reported on 27 October:

> The official concerned said that rumour of intention to exterminate Jews [was] being spread by various enemy sources but that as it is pure invention and lacks all foundation German authorities have no reason to make any statement on the subject. He added that he feels sure that if camps in question were to be abandoned their inmates would be evacuated and not killed as Germany would have no intention of losing their labour contributions. It is unlikely we will get any more formal declaration on this subject.[205]

There was no doubt at this time about the reality of the Holocaust. The horrors of Auschwitz, near Cracow, were confirmed on 13 November at the trial in Paris of a young French collaborator called Vernieres who had joined the Gestapo. He told the court that of the six camps in Auschwitz the worst was the Jewish camp: 'For the slightest sickness prisoners were sent to gas chambers.' He said 2,700 people had been killed there in a single day in April, but the German authorities had ordered a slowdown because the executions were causing labour shortages.[206]

Irish diplomatic missions abroad continued, nevertheless, to petition on behalf of Jews in the death camps. Thomas J. Kiernan had earlier requested the Vatican to intervene on behalf of Slovakian Jews; on 9 December Walshe instructed him to see the Slovakian and Hungarian representatives to the Holy See and to support Vatican representations. Kiernan was told by the Slovakian minister that all further intervention was useless as only Jews in hiding were left. The rest had been deported. The Slovakian minister spoke of 20,000 Jews hiding in the woods.

On 29 November Cremin reported from Berlin on his enquiries about the 12,000 Jews deported from Kaunas in Lithuania. The German Foreign Office official responsible for Ireland, with whom he was on most excellent relations, had told Cremin in informal conversation that the German authorities were anxious to help in every way that affected directly or indirectly Irish interests, but they found it difficult to understand how the question of Lithuanian Jews could affect Ireland particularly. Cremin sought instructions. He suggested he might argue that it was a matter of importance to Ireland because of the possible hostile propaganda if Dublin were seen to be indifferent in such cases. Walshe cabled support for that line on 7 December and added: 'You might also say that Jewish Community Dublin had asked us make enquiries.' Cremin got nowhere. On 13 December he told Walshe that he had seen the same Foreign Office official and followed instructions. But the official, who appeared to have talked to higher authorities, could not see that the question of Lithuanian Jews concerned Ireland at all, and he further indicated that

> German authorities regard *démarche* of this description by neutral governments as attributable to Jewish ruse and that Jews would consider German Government very naive if it were for instance to reply to our enquiry to effect that Jews in question had been in fact brought here.[207]

In the circumstances, Cremin did not see what further action he could take. Walshe minuted on the cable 'no action is fine' unless Goodman or the US Union of Orthodox Rabbis raised the matter again.

However, Cremin continued to press the case of the Jews. He maintained close contact with the Swiss legation in Berlin and was kept informed of their actions in this area. He cabled on 21 December that a memorandum he had prepared on Jewish refugees had been handed back to him by an official at the Foreign Office. There was no justification, he was told, for an intervention by the Irish; the persons concerned were not Irish and did not have any Irish connections. In a report to Dublin on 23 December Cremin reviewed his efforts over the previous weeks. He had been told by his contact at the German Foreign Office that he would, on personal grounds, try to find out about the Lithuanian Jews named by the Irish. Cremin had been told by the papal nuncio on 15 December that he had tried to intervene on behalf of Brazilian Jews in Bergen-Belsen but that his initiative had been rejected for the same reason as was that of the Irish.

As the enormity of Nazi crimes was being catalogued, Chief Rabbi Herzog cabled on 28 December:

> PRAY MAKE SUPREME EFFORT NOW SAVING BUDAPEST JEWS. IMMINENT EXTERMINATION. HEARTRENDING TRAGEDY. GREETINGS ANTICIPATORY THANKS.

Walshe replied to Herzog on 17 January 1945: 'Have been doing everything possible behalf Hungarian Jews.'[208] Walshe had kept in contact with US envoy David Gray about what could be done. 'This is just what we want', Gray told him on 19 January after Walshe had ordered yet another diplomatic intervention. The US War Refugee Board had Gray convey to 'the appropriate authorities in Eire its appreciation of their humanitarian initiative with regard to threatened Jewish internees of concentration camps in Germany'. They encouraged a further intervention in Berlin. David Gray was critical of the board's 'hardly tactful method of approach' but asked Walshe 'if in your own way you could suggest [to the German authorities] that the safety of the inmates of these camps were a matter of concern to your government'.[209] Walshe replied to Gray on 26 January that the Irish government had immediately wired Cremin in Berlin to approach the German authorities about Birkenau and Oswiecim (Auschwitz). Cremin reported on 1 February that the camps in question had been evacuated and the inmates transferred to another more central camp.[210] This news was immediately sent to David Gray.

Overtures were also made in mid-January 1945 to the Irish envoy in Washington, Robert Brennan, by Dr Jacob Hellmann and two other leaders of the World Jewish Congress. Brennan informed Walshe:

> I told the gentlemen that the ... request [to issue Irish documents to Jews in occupied territories] had been considered and had been found impracticable and that I doubted whether any representations from a neutral government at this time would be of any avail.[211]

The World Jewish Congress also sent a long cable to Dublin on 28 January which was shown to de Valera.[212]

In the context of the crying need to try to stop the mass slaughter of the Jews, the project to bring 500 orphaned Jewish children to Ireland lost its urgency. The German authorities were simply not prepared to allow this to happen. Nevertheless, Herman Good wrote to Walshe on 24 November 1944 on behalf of the Jewish Representative Council enquiring about the arrival of the 500 Jewish orphans; the fullest co-operation of the council was pledged for that undertaking.[213] Walshe, in reply, felt it might be better for Good or one of his colleagues to meet him about the children. There is no record of this meeting taking place. Goodman raised the matter on 13 February 1945 in a telegram to Walshe, who immediately replied that it would be better to leave the initiative to the US government. Goodman was in contact again with Dulanty in April, requesting an Irish intervention in Berlin on behalf of the Jews in Germany. 'No action possible at present', minuted Walshe on Dulanty's letter.[214] By then it was really too late to do anything. The Holocaust had claimed more victims.

What conclusions may be drawn from the evidence presented above? Firstly, de Valera responded positively to every overture to try to assist a specific group of Jews in danger of being deported to the death camps. Secondly, Ireland's diplomatic service was active in trying to save Jews. Thirdly, Ireland was prepared to receive two large groups of Jewish children as refugees. However, de Valera at no time introduced extraordinary measures to rescue Jews. He did not, for example, agree to a mass distribution of Irish passports to the Jewish refugees stranded in Vittel. Irish policy towards the Jews remained reactive rather than proactive throughout the war.

Finally, no evidence has been found to support the idea of the existence of an underground 'railway' for Jewish refugees into wartime Ireland. The US diplomat Harry Clinton Reed reported from Dublin in 1949:

> During the Hitler regime [Robert] Briscoe was instrumental in smuggling an undetermined number of Central European Jewish refugees into Ireland. When confronted by the Government authorities with proof that over 300 of these persons had illegally entered Ireland through his good offices, he staunchly denied it and has never admitted that he was engaged in this traffic.[215]

Suggestions of this kind have been flatly contradicted by Robert Briscoe's son, Ben.[216]

It remains very difficult to calculate the number of Jews allowed into Ireland during the war years.[217] Whatever the number – and it may have been as few as sixty – it was insignificant for the six years of war known officially in Ireland as 'the Emergency'. Many Irish people in the 1990s would have sympathy with Mona McCarthy, the teacher in Ita Daly's novel, *Unholy Ghosts*:

> I'd have said myself that an emergency is when you run out of drink on Christmas Day. Or when you've a burst mains and you can't find a plumber. Somehow when six million people are being slaughtered you'd think that there would be a more appropriate word for it than the Emergency.[218]

Irish witnesses to the Holocaust

The last five months of war in Europe witnessed a desperate attempt by the Germans, albeit faced by imminent defeat, to complete the work of the 'final solution'. Before the advancing Allied forces, many camp inmates were forced to go on what were to be called 'death marches'. Helen Lewis, a Czech who came to live in Belfast in 1947, was one of those who survived such an ordeal at Auschwitz:

> on 27 January 1945 our camp was evacuated and we embarked on what we hopefully thought would be a long, long way home. The term 'death march' was coined much later, and with hindsight.
>
> We were marched out of the camp in rows of five, leaving behind those who were not capable of walking. We knew from past experience what their fate would be and dared not talk, or even think, of them. ... We were escorted by the fiercest and most dreaded SS guards, who shouted their 'Schneller, schneller!' as if they wanted to hear the sound of their own voices. The SS women and a few officers travelled ahead in a horse-drawn cart. At night we were herded into an abandoned church, where we slept on the stones. It was very cold and we were terribly tired, but we still had our bread.

Other nights they were forced to sleep in the open. After a few days of wandering along icy roads and through hostile villages, her party began to realise that 'we were, in fact, going nowhere; we just kept walking in ever-decreasing circles'.[219]

Helen Lewis was rescued by the Soviet army. Her husband had died in the camps. She married for the second time in Czechoslovakia in 1947 and moved to Belfast. Helen Lewis rejects the idea that she survived because she was different in character to those who died. She simply survived.[220]

Soviet troops had entered Auschwitz-Birkenau on 27 January – the day Helen Lewis's camp was evacuated – as they pressed westwards towards Germany. On 15 April American troops entered Buchenwald, where 40,000 had died in the last years of the war. The same day the British liberated Belsen where they discovered 10,000 unburied bodies. Nordhausen also came under US control on 15 April, while Dachau was entered by the US army on 29 April.

The Irish journalist and playwright, Denis Johnston, was among the first to enter Buchenwald: 'As we entered the long hut the stench hit us in the face, and a queer wailing came to our ears' from the tier upon tier of shelves along each side of the shed. Living creatures were packed tightly side by side, like knives and forks in a drawer, he wrote later. At the sight of his uniform, Johnston said there came 'from their lips . . . that thin, unearthly noise' which he realised was meant to be cheering: 'We walked the length of the shed – and then through another one. From the shelves feeble arms rose and waved, like twigs in a breeze. Most of them were branded with numbers.'[221]

The Dublin doctor Robert Collis and Dutch translator Han Hogerzeil were among the first to enter Belsen with the British army. They have left this description of those moments:

> One man whose blue-striped pyjamas hung from him like a cloak, whose head was shaved and face mud coloured ran, or half ran, towards the leading tank, crying as he ran. A few paces off, he sank upon his knees and died.[222]

Han Hogerzeil, who later married Robert Collis and settled in Ireland, recalled how 'her work in Belsen changed her life and her outlook'.[223] As she spoke five languages, she took the case histories of victims who had been treated by the Nazis as 'if they had nothing to do with the human race'.[224] Belsen was a place where evil had triumphed, an evil she personally had seen in Hitler at the Olympic games in Berlin in 1936: 'It was like staring in a cobra's eye', she said of that occasion.[225] She had a vivid memory, too, of the day the huts in Belsen were burned – the thick black smoke symbolising the evil that had once inhabited the place.

She recalled how difficult it must have been for the prisoners to see themselves as human beings while still wearing the demeaning camp uniform. Then somebody got the idea to open a shop to distribute the clothes sent to Belsen and call it Harrods. People queued at one door in their hated prison uniforms and 'then they went shopping' for civilian clothes. There was a table with make-up at the end of the hut. 'You know what a bit of lipstick will do for a woman's morale', she added. Former inmates came out of the hut 'people again'.[226] A dance was held for the recovering internees in one of the squares between the blocks. Trees had been planted, flagpoles erected and coloured lights strung up. An RAF orchestra played:

> One very tall young Canadian Air Force sergeant danced with a tiny girl who came up only to his waist, holding her in his huge arms as he waltzed around with a great smile upon his boyish face. She looked so happy, it was hard for those who saw her not to smile or cry.[227]

Han Hogerzeil recalled that 'There was an awful lot of love in Belsen. I remember more about love and devotion than I do about hatred.'[228]

Helen Lewis wrote of her recovery period in hospital after liberation:

It was spring and each day I was allowed to spend some time in the garden. I sat under a tree, watching little birds hopping in the grass and listening to their excited song. I picked some flowers and held them in my hand and when I looked up I saw a blue sky without a trace of smoke.[229]

That contrasted with her earlier experience in Auschwitz, as evoked in Primo Levi's poem, 'Buna':

> Torn feet and crushed earth,
> The long line in the grey morning.
> The Buna smokes from a thousand chimneys,
> A day like every other day awaits us.[230]

In the post-war period, at least, a small number of Jews were permitted to rebuild their lives in Ireland under 'a blue sky without a trace of smoke', far away from the 'Buna' and the 'thousand chimneys'.

Writing of the international reaction to the refugee crisis, the historian David Wyman refers to the failure of the United States to save more Jews as a 'vast lost chance'.[231] He is referring, in particular, to the period between 1938 and 1941. Yet, between 1933 and 1945, about 250,000 refugees from Nazism had reached the United States. That compares with 150,000 who entered Palestine during the same period.[232] Ireland, in contrast, stands with Canada, Australia, New Zealand and the other dominions. 'Illiberal' may be a euphemism, but it describes their various policies towards refugees – and Jewish refugees in particular.[233] All could have done much more. It was for Ireland, as for other countries, a 'vast lost chance' to save many lives.

14. Harry Kernoff RHA

15. Estella Solomons (self-portrait)

16. A. J. (Con) Leventhal, academic and friend of
Samuel Beckett (portrait by Estella Solomons)

17. Stella Steyn

18. Jewish children on visit to Cork, 1959

19. Synagogue, South Terrace, Cork

20. Gerald Goldberg, at his home in Cork

21. Dedication of Jewish burial ground in Limerick, 1990 (left to right):
Most Rev. Jeremiah Newman, Bishop of Limerick; Judge H.C. Wine; Very Rev.
Ephraim Mirvis, the Chief Rabbi; Cllr Paddy Madden, Mayor of Limerick;
Rt Rev. Edward Darling, Bishop of Limerick and Killaloe; Denis Leonard,
Director of Limerick Civic Trust; Jack Higgins, Limerick City Manager

7

Ireland's post-war refugee policy

When President Franklin D. Roosevelt died on 12 April 1945 the Irish Jewish community, which had been well represented in the British forces and in the Irish defence forces throughout the war, mourned his loss, as did Dáil Éireann which was adjourned for a day as a mark of respect. At a meeting on 17 April, the Jewish Representative Council decided to organise a memorial service; Herman Good wrote that evening to the US envoy, David Gray, inviting him to attend a special service on 29 April for Roosevelt who, he said, would be 'remembered tenderly by Jews in Eire, as in every country throughout the world'.[1] The service was the result of the 'spontaneous desire' of the Jewish community, wrote Good, to remember 'a true friend of the Jewish cause' and a 'great American'.[2] Gray replied that he was unable to attend 'for I feel that, as this is a neutral country, it would be improper for the American legation to give official recognition to a memorial service to commemorate the commander in chief of the American Armies in time of war. I am sure you will understand my feelings in this matter.'[3] The commemorative ceremony took place in his absence.

Eamon de Valera had proved by his actions that he, too, was pro-Allied during the Second World War. Little wonder, then, that he, a profoundly anti-Axis political leader and a great admirer of Roosevelt, shocked Irish people and outraged the leaders of the Allied powers by visiting the German minister in Dublin, Edouard Hempel, on 2 May to express his condolences on the death of Adolf Hitler. News appeared in the press of de Valera's visit.[4] He had been accompanied by the secretary of the Department of External Affairs, Joseph Walshe. The assistant secretary of the department, Frederick Boland, is believed to have 'begged de Valera on bended knee not to go'.[5] A bad situation was made much worse when, the following day, a similar visit was made by Michael McDunphy, private secretary to the President of Ireland, Douglas Hyde.

The former Minister for Equality and Law Reform, Mervyn Taylor, who is

Jewish, said in 1996: 'I didn't, don't, and never will understand why de Valera did it.'[6] He explained that in May 1945 a demoralised and vulnerable Jewish community may not have been sufficiently confident to formulate a response. He said that the community would have found the action so inexplicable that a deputation would have been considered irrelevant. De Valera's visit, he said, still rankles with a community which continues to be upset by the painful memories of a restrictive wartime refugee policy.[7]

It is safe to assume, therefore, that the Jewish community reacted to the visit with justifiable incomprehension and anger. Many were all the more angry because a number of Dublin Jews had received anonymous threatening letters around that time. But it was the practice of the JRC to move with caution and diplomacy, so much so on that occasion that there is no record of any formal protest to de Valera.[8] That quietist style would be viewed with scepticism by Maurice Abrahamson and other leaders of the JRC in the 1950s and 1960s.[9] However, the virulence of international press reaction to de Valera's gaffe may have rendered protest from the Jewish community less urgent.[10] The Irish government also felt the chill of disapproval from London and Washington, a disapproval which narrowly stopped short of the withdrawal of envoys for consultation. The US envoy, David Gray, told his British counterpart, Sir John Maffey, on 5 May that de Valera's action had been a 'studied affront' to the United Nations by the Irish government.[11] The State Department told Gray on 16 May that Washington considered the personal calls made by de Valera and 'Dumphreys' to be 'most unfortunate even though greater courtesies were shown at time of President Roosevelt's death, namely adjournment of Dáil and resolutions of condolence passed by Dáil and Seanad'. The telegram went on to deplore the visit, though the phrase 'and will not be readily forgotten' was crossed out in a draft. No change, however, seemed necessary in the US policy of 'leaving Ireland severely alone'.[12]

Just how isolated de Valera must have felt in the first week of May may be judged by the fact that the only letter of support came from the British Union of Fascists. Writing from a clandestine address in England, it sent its congratulations to de Valera through the Irish high commissioner in London, John Dulanty:

> The British Union of Fascists, which is still in existence, although it had to go underground for the time being, have instructed me to write to your Excellency, and to express their deep appreciation of the news that the Secretary to the President of Eire has called on the German Minister in Dublin to express condolence on behalf of the President on the death of Adolf Hitler. The British Union of Fascists begs of your Excellency to convey its gratitude to the government of Eire for thus honouring the memory of the greatest German in history.

On receipt of this note, Dulanty forwarded it to Dublin together with the laconic minute: 'No Comment!'[13] With friends like that . . .

Celebrations took place in Dublin on 7 May following the unconditional surrender of Nazi Germany. The streets were thronged with people sharing in the victory festivities.[14] However, shortly after the BBC announced unconfirmed reports of a German surrender at 2 p.m., some fifty Trinity College students appeared on the university roof and staged an impromptu celebration; they waved the Union Jack and sang 'God Save the King', the 'Marseillaise' and 'It's a long way to Tipperary'. A little later, the Union Jack, the Hammer and Sickle, the Stars and Stripes and the Irish Tricolour were hoisted on the main flag-pole. A section of onlookers outside the gates of the college (including a future Taoiseach, Charles J. Haughey, who was a commerce student in University College Dublin at the time), took exception to the positioning of the Irish flag at the bottom of the pole and an effort was made to charge the gates. Tempers flared following a rumour that a group of Trinity College students had burned the Tricolour in protest. The attackers were driven back by gardaí with batons drawn.

The protesters were joined later by about sixty youths carrying Irish and Vatican flags. In a report of the incident to the Italian government, the newly arrived minister, Count Baron G. Vitaliano Confalonieri, wrote: 'During the demonstration many of the participants wore swastika badges in their button-holes and a few Nazi flags were waved around.'[15] Later a section of the mob attacked a well-known hotel in the capital shouting 'Give us the West Britons.' The windows of a fashionable restaurant, Jammet's, were smashed by a group singing 'The Soldier's Song'.[16] The protests did not constitute a serious threat to public order; however, in view of the affront to the Allies, protocol dictated that the Department of External Affairs call in both the British and US envoys to receive an official apology.[17] De Valera was always scrupulous about observing protocol to the letter of the law. Nevertheless, his international reputation suffered a severe setback as a result of his incomprehensible visit to express his condolences following the death of Hitler.

But if international opinion remained incensed, the Irish Jewish community could not afford the luxury of disturbing its harmonious relations with the government. The Jewish community in Dublin held a special service on 25 June in the Adelaide Road Synagogue to mark the occasion of the election of Seán T. O'Kelly to the presidency of Ireland. Rabbi Teddy Lewis paid tribute to O'Kelly's life-long work for a country that had always afforded peace, justice and freedom to the minorities inside its boundaries. 'At a time when the Jews had been so much persecuted and humiliated', he said, 'this small nation was one of the few places where the foul germs of anti-Semitism had found no fertile soil.'[18] De Valera, in the experience of the leaders of the Jewish community in Ireland, had helped consistently to eliminate those 'foul germs'. With that in mind, his visit to Hempel caused all the more puzzlement and even deeper hurt. But faced as the leaders of the Jewish community were with the enormity of the humanitarian tasks on the continent, there was no time for recrimination.

Defining post-war refugee policy

According to Michael Marrus,

> At the end of September [1945], the Western Allies cared for nearly seven
> million displaced persons; the Soviets claimed they took charge of an
> equal number. The largest group, in both cases, were Soviet citizens, over
> 7.2 million forced labourers and prisoners of war who had survived the
> ordeal of wartime Germany. Next came the French, with nearly two
> million, including 765,000 civilian workers; more than 1.6 million Poles,
> 700,000 Italians, 350,000 Czechs, over 300,000 Dutch, 300,000 Belgians
> and many others.[19]

When the first estimates of displaced persons were made in Germany,
between 50,000 and 100,000, or between 5 and 8 per cent, were Jews.
According to Marrus: 'On every scale of suffering, the Jews were invariably at
the uppermost registers, had been in captivity for the longest period, came
from the worst camps, and had the most ghastly appearance.'[20] Only 80,000
out of 3.3 million Polish Jews remained alive; 50,000 German Jews survived.
The figure overall, outside the Soviet Union, was about one million. Many of
these were orphaned children.[21] The United Nations Relief and Rehabilitation Agency, which had been founded in 1943, took the burden of organising
post-war relief.

The question of providing emergency relief for Europe did not present a
problem for the Irish government. The Irish gave generously. The government, the Irish Red Cross Society and the relief organisations of the various
churches all sought to play a role in helping to distribute humanitarian aid in
continental Europe. The work of rescuing Jewish refugees had also to
continue, and now with renewed determination.

The question of Ireland receiving large numbers of refugees – albeit on a
temporary basis – resulted in a vigorous interdepartmental policy debate. At
the request of the Department of Justice, a conference was held in the Department of External Affairs on 21 September 1945 to discuss the admission of
aliens. Assistant secretary Frederick Boland and T. J. Horan represented the
Department of External Affairs and Dan Costigan represented the Department
of Justice.[22] The government had been encouraged to review its refugee policy
as a matter of urgency because a request had been received from the president of University College Cork, Alfred O'Rahilly, to admit a number of Polish
third-level students. Moreover, Lady Listowel, who was Hungarian by birth
and whose husband was a member of the British cabinet, sought to gain
admission for about 150 displaced Hungarians.[23] Two days later, on de Valera's
instructions, Maurice Moynihan, secretary of the Department of the Taoiseach
met Frederick Boland and Dan Costigan to discuss the general question of
alien refugees. Costigan told the meeting that the Department of Justice
would favour the admission of about 250 refugees within the following twelve
months.[24] He reported to Minister for Justice, Gerald Boland: 'The view taken
at the conference was that, if any refugees are to be admitted to this country,
the persons admitted should be homeless persons from the Continent rather

than persons who have found refuge in Great Britain.'[25] Moynihan undertook to submit the views of the conference to de Valera. He minuted that, subject to the Taoiseach's approval and after consultation with the other departments concerned, the Department of Justice should make a submission to the government 'with a view to obtaining decisions on the lines of policy to be followed on the admission of refugees'.[26]

Costigan later received a telephone call from Moynihan stating that the Taoiseach approved generally of the conclusions reached at the conference on the admitting of refugees.[27] Costigan then prepared a draft memorandum for submission to the relevant departments, which he completed on 24 September. The following day he sent copies to his departmental secretary and assistant secretary, S. A. Roche and J. E. Duff. The draft text made express reference to Jews:

> It is the policy of the Department of Justice to restrict the immigration of Jews. The wealth and influence of the Jewish community in this country, and murmurs against Jewish wealth and influence are frequently heard. As Jews do not become assimilated with the native population, like other immigrants, there is a danger that any big increase in their numbers might create a social problem.[28]

In a covering note, Duff suggested to Roche that that paragraph be deleted.[29] Though the substance of the paragraph remained, the first sentence was changed to read: 'The immigration of Jews is generally discouraged.' That was a significant change as it removed direct responsibility for the anti-Jewish policy from the Department of Justice. The first draft represented the wartime reality. But it was not government policy: it was the policy of the Department of Justice.[30]

The Minister for Justice gave his approval to the amended memorandum, which was then sent to the Departments of External Affairs, Education, Industry and Commerce, and Local Government and Public Health. The memorandum outlined the context to the need for a policy on aliens:

> There are on the Continent at present millions of 'displaced' persons and it may be expected that in the near future numerous requests will be received for the admission of refugees into this country, and for the admission of people, other than refugees, who have suffered from the war, and who require a period of rest and recuperation.

The memorandum continued:

> The refugees who may be expected to seek admission are likely to be mainly Polish, Hungarian and perhaps Austrian Catholics of the 'upper classes' who are unwilling to live under the present regimes in those countries. The persons who may be expected to seek permission to come here for periods of rest and recuperation will be mainly French, Belgian, and Dutch, including relatives and friends of Jews resident here. There are, of course, more 'displaced' persons in Germany than in any other country, but it is unlikely that any Germans will be allowed to emigrate for some time.[31]

The Department of Justice then outlined its position in relation to differ-ent categories of aliens. 'Aliens coming on business visits are admitted freely, provided the Department is satisfied (after consultation with the Department of Industry and Commerce) that the business is not undesirable and that the aliens will be able to return to their own countries.'[32] Visas were granted freely to students provided the department could be satisfied that the students would leave on completion of their studies. In the case of aliens coming for permanent residence or asylum, the memorandum stated that applications from people married to Irish citizens 'receive sympathetic consideration'.[33] Applications from dependent relatives of aliens resident in Ireland were normally granted. Applications from persons such as distin-guished scholars also received sympathetic consideration, as did applications from aliens with special qualifications, provided they satisfied the Depart-ment of Industry and Commerce. The Department of Justice was not prepared to consider sympathetically 'applications from refugees, who have no special qualifications, but who wish to come here for temporary or perma-nent refuge'.[34] However, an exception would be made if 'the aliens have some connection with this country – e.g. the O'Rourke family of Poland'. It was in this context that the memorandum makes the point that 'an exception was made from this general rule, and approximately 150 "non-Aryan" refugees from Germany were admitted for temporary refuge'.[35] The department then outlined its position on Jewish immigration as quoted earlier.

The memorandum went on to summarise the various offers of relief made to date. It stressed that approximately 100 French children had been admit-ted and other groups were expected. The plan was to place the children in boarding schools, and after their studies had been completed they would be expected to return to France. The matter was in the hands of the Irish and French Red Cross. The memorandum also referred to the agreement by the Irish government in 1944 to admit 500 Jewish children at the end of the war; that offer had not been taken up, and it was unlikely that they would now come.[36]

All departments had returned their observations on the memorandum to the Department of Justice by 19 November. Only the Minister for Industry and Commerce, Seán Lemass, voiced opposition. He was opposed to any proposal 'which would have the effect of admitting even a limited number of refugees to this country while numbers of our own citizens remain un-employed'.[37] Lemass was prepared to consent to the admission of adult refugees only to the extent that they might in particular cases have special technical qualifications or business connections of value to the country.[38] That policy line had been taken consistently by Lemass since the 1930s. The Department of Industry and Commerce, Costigan learned, was preparing its own memorandum for government. Meanwhile, the Department of External Affairs was urging most strongly that more refugees be admitted into the country. Costigan revised his memorandum and suggested to Duff that it be submitted to government.[39]

Duff, writing to Minister Boland on 23 November, had 'considerable doubts as to the wisdom of taking on these refugees'. But in view of the attitude of the Department of External Affairs there seemed to be 'no alternative to submitting the matter to Government'. He felt that while the voluntary societies were initially full of enthusiasm, there was a tendency for their interest to flag and for them to leave the matter to government. Duff believed that there was going to be serious difficulty in supporting the refugees 'and in getting rid of those that prove undesirable'.[40] He noted the opposition of the Minister for Industry and Commerce, and he suggested to Boland that he 'should not urge too strongly the acceptance of the present proposals'. Duff added:

> Apart from the refugees who will be brought in by these Societies we are receiving large numbers of requests from persons here, mainly Jews, for sanctuary for their relatives on the Continent. Many of these are cases of such hardship that it would be impossible to refuse, but it all means that the number of aliens in the country is steadily increasing.[41]

Boland agreed to submit the memorandum to government.[42]

The Minister for Industry and Commerce also sent a memorandum to government. Dated 12 December, it cited the large numbers of unemployed in Ireland, pointing out that

> at present there are approximately 62,000 men and 8,000 women registered as unemployed, and that these numbers are likely to increase with the return from Great Britain and Northern Ireland of workers who had found temporary employment there during the war years. It may be mentioned that, since the year 1940, travel permits for employment outside the state were issued to 133,584 men and 58,776 women, a large proportion of whom may be expected to seek re-employment here according as their services elsewhere are no longer required. Army demobilisation may also be expected to add to the numbers of those looking for work.[43]

Lemass then restated the existing restrictions on admitting aliens. In the case of potential investors or employers, the Control of Manufactures Acts 1932 and 1934 were applied in an effort to ensure that business would be controlled by Irish nationals. In the case of foreigners entering into employment, they had to possess special qualifications which could be passed on to Irish nationals who would replace them in due course. Those seeking to engage in a business had to 'possess such special qualifications, knowledge, experience, or business connections as could be regarded as an asset to the country'.[44]

Despite these differing positions, progress was made at a cabinet meeting on 14 December. Maurice Moynihan recorded that de Valera opened by reading a memorandum from the Department of External Affairs. Drafted by Frederick Boland, it emphasised the need to liberalise refugee policy. Lemass intimated that he had no objection to the admission of persons with special qualifications or students coming to do university courses 'even if they were likely to remain there indefinitely after securing professional qualifications'. Moynihan minuted the views of the meeting in relation to students:

> There appeared to be a disposition among the members of the Government generally to agree to accept about 20 Poles as university students at

a cost to the state of say £250 a year for each student. It was suggested, however, by the Minister for Industry and Commerce that the courses which such students should take should be specified. As examples the Minister mentioned Engineering and Science. It was thought that the number of 20 should be regarded as a tentative figure and that this question should be examined.[45]

His conclusion succinctly captured the mood of the meeting: 'Generally, it was felt that a liberal attitude should be adopted. The Minister for Industry and Commerce said that he would be in favour of a liberal policy on a highly selective basis.'[46]

The following day, de Valera had further discussions with representatives from the Departments of External Affairs (Walshe and Boland), Industry and Commerce (W. Maguire) and Justice (Duff). Maurice Moynihan drafted the official minute of the meeting:

> The Taoiseach explained the attitude of the Government as being that our policy towards this problem should be liberal and generous, due regard being had to our own interests in regard to certain matters, such as employment, foreign relations and the necessity for excluding undesirable persons. Subject to the necessary safeguards in these respects we should be as helpful as possible and we should try positively to give asylum to aliens seeking refuge in existing circumstances.[47]

Summing up at the end of the conference, de Valera

> emphasised the necessity for a positive and liberal policy. Financial considerations should not be allowed to present an insuperable difficulty. He recognised that anything that might be done for the Poles might also have to be done for people of other nationalities. He would be prepared to contemplate the admission, ultimately, of at least 10,000 aliens.[48]

The policy line taken by de Valera was supported by Maguire of the Department of Industry and Commerce. He said that 'his Minister had instructed him to adopt a more liberal attitude than had previously been authorised'. With regard to the admission of people with special qualifications, de Valera said they would include scholars, technical experts, craftsmen and people with special business knowledge or experience likely to be of advantage to the country.[49] The Taoiseach stated that 'our attitude should be to seek positively to secure the admission of such persons provided that they were of the right types'. Frederick Boland suggested that a statement might be prepared indicating the types of people who would be suitable for admission. Maguire volunteered that his department would undertake the drafting of such a list 'on a tentative basis'. The statement 'would merely indicate the types of people whose services could probably be made use of here'.[50] No definite promises of employment could be given. Following further discussion, during which de Valera made clear the need to follow a liberal policy, he asked the representatives of the Departments of External Affairs, Justice, and Industry and Commerce to consult together on the practical steps which should be taken to implement government policy.[51]

A liberal refugee policy was thus laid down in the face of considerable
opposition from the Departments of Justice and Industry and Commerce.
But the modalities of implementing that policy had yet to be worked out.
That gave the conservative and obstructionist elements in the administration an opportunity to slow the pace of change. Although the Department of
Justice had lost the war of words, it was still in a position to engage in a form
of administrative guerrilla warfare. Dan Costigan wrote to Frederick Boland
on 8 January 1946 to find out whether the Department of External Affairs
intended to take the initiative.[52] Following a further exchange of letters
between these departments a conference was held on 5 February in the
Department of External Affairs; it was attended by Walshe, Boland and Horan
from the Department of External Affairs, Duff and Costigan from the Department of Justice, and Maguire from the Department of Industry and
Commerce. A number of applications from refugees were considered and in
practically all cases it was decided to authorise visas. Costigan minuted: 'The
general view taken at the conference was that all applications, other than
applications from Jews, should be dealt with sympathetically.'[53] In the
absence of the official minute of this meeting, the Costigan version must be
accepted as authoritative. Did that mean that the Department of Justice was
not alone in its opposition to the admission of Jews?

An example of the obtuseness of the Department of Justice was to be
found in the handling of the case of Rabbi Mendel Lew, a Palestinian
national who had been appointed acting headmaster at the Zion Schools,
Bloomfield Avenue in Dublin.[54] Leonard Abrahamson wrote to the department on behalf of the Jewish Representative Council in early January 1946
in support of the granting of residence to Rabbi Lew. To the astonishment of
Abrahamson, J. E. Duff replied to him on 15 January saying that 'the Minister regrets that he cannot see his way to permit ... Rabbi Mendel Law [*sic*]
to remain in this country'. Duff emphasised that the minister would have no
objection 'to the admission of any alien who is found suitable to take the
position of Assistant Minister to the United Hebrew Congregation and the
position of teacher in the Hebrew School which was vacated by Rabbi
Unterman'.[55] Duff then wrote to the Garda Síochána stating that the minister was no longer prepared to permit Lew to continue his residence in the
country; accordingly Lew should be instructed to arrange for his immediate
departure.[56] An incensed Abrahamson first met Duff and then wrote to him
on 22 January, on behalf of the JRC:

> The Minister's decision conveyed in your communication raised so grave
> an issue in regard to the spiritual welfare of the Jewish community, that it
> is being considered in all its implications. In the meantime, as it would
> appear from your letter and our interview that you have been misin-
> formed on certain essential particulars, I have been requested to state the
> facts. Rabbi Lew (not Law) was not appointed to the post in the Zion
> Schools vacated by Rabbi Unterman, as stated by you. Out of a number of
> candidates he was appointed acting headmaster and was to act for twelve
> months. If satisfactory, he would then receive the full post of Headmaster.
> He has thus been selected to replace Mr Shreider, who never acted as an
> official of any synagogue.[57]

The Minister for Justice reversed his decision.[58]

This was an example of the harshness of the Department of Justice to which the Departments of the Taoiseach and External Affairs continued to take exception. On one occasion, at least, this merited a rebuke from the Taoiseach. On 19 March 1947, Costigan minuted:

> The Minister [for Justice] informed me recently that the Taoiseach had mentioned to him that he thought the Department of Justice were too strict in refusing admission to aliens who were anxious to come here on account of conditions on the Continent. I suggested to Minister that all border line cases should be submitted to him in future, and he agreed with that suggestion.[59]

When it came to admitting members of the European radical right, the Department of Justice required no such reminder to be liberal.

Léon Degrelle

Léon Degrelle was the leader of the Belgian Rexist movement. Sentenced to death in his absence, he had gone to live in Franco's Spain.[60] Martin Conway has described Degrelle as a skilful tactician with a shrewd sense of political realities, 'but this ability was combined with an incorrigible tendency to fantasise his own importance. . . . His self-appointed role as architect of a historic understanding between Belgium and Nazi Germany was one which matched both Degrelle's personal vanity and his ideological ambitions and it was one which he would embrace with enthusiasm.'[61]

During 1946 rumours began to circulate that Degrelle might attempt to settle in Ireland. S. A. Roche, secretary of the Department of Justice, was strongly in favour of admitting him, while the Department of External Affairs was opposed. Frederick Boland, recently promoted to secretary of that department, told J. E. Duff of the Department of Justice on 3 September 1946 that 'it would be awkward for us to have a problem of this kind at the present juncture'. Boland suggested that if Degrelle turned up in Ireland, 'he should be put back on board and the vessel told to leave as soon as possible'.[62] Roche was not satisfied with Boland's proposed solution to the threatened visit of Degrelle. He wrote to Boland on 11 September:

> This man is a political refugee who was sentenced to death in his absence and it seems to me that it would be very difficult for us to refuse him asylum. I am sure that you have considered this aspect of the case already, but before definite instructions are issued, I should be glad to be assured that the Department of External Affairs are prepared to stand over a refusal of asylum in this case.[63]

Boland drafted a reply to Roche in which he pointed out that 'It is difficult for us to realise how strongly the Governments of the former Allied countries feel on this question of rounding up persons whom they regard as war criminals.'[64] He emphasised that they 'should not expose the country to the intense animosity' which a decision to admit Degrelle would entail. The distaste with which he held Roche's views was evident as he went on to outline Degrelle's record:

> This is a man who led a minority movement in his own country which relied on 'strong-arm' methods rather than on the ballot. . . . When his country was invaded, he donned the uniform of the invading forces (we have sent you a photograph of Degrelle in German uniform) and identified himself with the invader in his effort to make his occupation of the country effective.[65]

Boland then set forth his own understanding of the policy on granting asylum:

> Asylum, as you know, is not a right of the individual seeking it but of the Government according it – and whatever the theorists may say, the grant of asylum by a Government inevitably carries with it the implication that the individual concerned had, in at least natural law, the moral right to do as he did. Can even that be said as regards Degrelle?[66]

Despite rumours to the contrary, Degrelle did not come to Ireland.

Other lesser known Nazi sympathisers did take up residence in Ireland.[67] These included radical nationalists from the continent. One high-level ex-Nazi, Otto Strasser, sought to take up residence in Ireland in the late 1940s. He was refused residency but was allowed to visit a relative for a short holiday in 1955 at the Divine Word Missionary seminary, Donamon, Co. Roscommon.[68]

The Clonyn Castle children

During the later years of the war, Eamon de Valera had offered to admit groups of children for periods of rest and recuperation. There was agreement to admit 500 French children, 500 Jewish refugee children and an unspecified number of Dutch children. But the war frustrated any such development. By autumn 1945, however, 100 French children had arrived. Reviewing progress on 27 June 1947, Dáil Éireann was told that, for the period 1 January 1946 to mid-1947, the number of non-nationals – excluding tourists and exempted aliens – registered under the Aliens Order was 1,000. Of that number 462 were children, 421 of whom were of German nationality. The Irish Red Cross had taken responsibility for bringing in 403 of those children; the remaining eighteen had come to private families. Except for thirteen who were still in the Red Cross hostel at Glencree, Co. Wicklow, all had been taken in by families.[69]

This project, known as 'Operation Shamrock', had resulted from a public meeting in the Shelbourne Hotel, Dublin, on 16 October 1945. Dr Kathleen Murphy, a paediatrician, had taken the initiative, together with the Irish Red Cross and other interested parties. The Red Cross made arrangements to bring some hundreds of German children to the country in the latter part of 1946.[70] The *Irish Independent* reported on 19 November 1946 that the third group of German children to visit Ireland under Operation Shamrock were expected to arrive by mailboat on 20 November. The children, ranging in age from five to fifteen, came mainly from German Catholic families in the province of North Rhine Westphalia. They were first taken to St Kevin's, Glencree, and were then sent to foster homes. Many subsequently left Ireland. A large number of the 'children' and foster families engaged in Operation Shamrock had a joyful reunion in Glencree on 23 March 1997.[71]

Individual Irish families also took the initiative to foster children who had been orphaned by the war. Dr Robert Collis, who had worked in Belsen immediately after its liberation, returned to Ireland accompanied by a small number of children who had survived the camps. Among them were Zoltan and Edith Zinn. They were nursed back to health at Fairy Hill Hospital, on the Hill of Howth, north of Dublin. Dr Collis adopted both children. Another brother and sister who survived Belsen, Terry and Suzi (now Diamond), were also brought to Ireland by Dr Collis. They were adopted by the Samuels family in Dublin. Another Belsen survivor, Evelin Schwartz, was adopted by a Dublin family; she later moved to Australia.[72]

In the post-war period, Irish refugee policy on the admission of children was in general quite liberal. Nevertheless, the Department of Justice required some persuading in 1946 when Dr Solomon Schonfeld, on behalf of the chief rabbi of Great Britain's Religious Emergency Council, asked the Irish government to admit 100 orphaned Jewish children who were survivors of Bergen-Belsen. The Jewish organising group in Ireland had, with the help of money from Britain, acquired Clonyn Castle and 100 acres of land in Delvin, Co. Westmeath, where it was proposed to accommodate the refugees. Reviewing the case later, the Department of Justice recalled that the organisers

> stated that they would undertake entire responsibility for the transport of the children and their maintenance in this country. They stated that they 'would be prepared to follow the advice of the Eire authorities' in regard to the ultimate settlement of the children, mentioning that the children might remain in this country or that, alternatively, the [Religious Emergency] Council would undertake to make arrangements for their emigration after a specified period.[73]

Permission was refused, however, on the instruction of the Minister for Justice, Gerald Boland, in August 1946 on the grounds that 'It has always been the policy of the Minister for Justice to restrict the admission of Jewish aliens, for the reason that any substantial increase in our Jewish population might give rise to an anti-Semitic problem.'[74]

But the matter did not rest there. In September 1946, the chief rabbi of Palestine, Dr Isaac Herzog, visited Dublin and during separate meetings with the Taoiseach and the Minister for Justice he raised the issue of the 100 Jewish refugee children.[75] The Secretary of the Department of Justice, S. A. Roche, wrote on 25 October to Maurice Moynihan, his counterpart at the Department of the Taoiseach, outlining how Herzog had introduced the subject of the children while 'paying a courtesy call on the Minister'.[76] Roche was at pains to point out that the visit of the chief rabbi was not scheduled as a business call, and therefore Herzog was in breach of protocol in raising the matter. Herzog, Roche recorded, had promised that the children would come to Ireland only for temporary residence; the chief rabbi had said he had a guarantee from Mr La Guardia, formerly director general of the United Nations Relief and Rehabilitation Agency, that arrangements would be made for the admission of the children to the United States or, failing that, to Palestine. Roche was not convinced that it was possible for such promises to be kept: 'we doubt, however, not the good faith of these gentlemen but their power to implement their promises; it is clear that neither Dr Hertzog [sic] or Mr La Guardia has power to control immigration into the USA or into Palestine'. Roche then went on to invoke Gerald Boland's support:

> The Minister, whose freedom from racial and religious prejudice or whose desire to help people in distress will not be questioned, agrees that caution is necessary. We are inclined to take the line that we will agree to receive these children for a year or two years but only on a definite official guarantee that they will then be taken to and allowed into, some other state.

Roche concluded: 'We understand, however, that Dr Hertzog [sic] made approaches to the Taoiseach also. Would you oblige us by ascertaining whether this is so and whether the Taoiseach has any wishes in the matter?'[77]

Having consulted with de Valera, Moynihan replied to Roche on 31 October. He confirmed that the matter of admitting 100 children had been raised when Herzog saw de Valera: 'The Taoiseach I understand was noncommittal.' Moynihan added, however, that it was de Valera's view that permission 'should not be withheld' provided a guarantee that their stay would be of a definite, limited duration was given by a responsible organisation. De Valera would not press, Moynihan continued, 'for an official guarantee that they will in due course be allowed into another state'.[78]

So, despite its opposition, the Department of Justice was obliged in November 1946 to reverse its decision on the admission of the Jewish orphans

> on the understanding that they would be removed to some other country as soon as arrangements could be made, and that the Chief Rabbi's Religious Emergency Council would take full responsibility for the proper care and maintenance of the children while they remained in this country.[79]

The Department of Justice also reversed an earlier decision to refuse admission to a number of adult aliens to look after the children. The Irish high commissioner in London, John Dulanty, told Dr Solomon Schonfeld on 25 November of the decision to admit the children, and the chief rabbi in Britain wrote to Dulanty on 2 December accepting the conditions laid down by the government.[80]

Dulanty and Schonfeld remained in regular correspondence on the matter. Dulanty received a letter from Schonfeld on 12 August 1947 bringing him up to date on 'the plans for the temporary emigration into Ireland of the party of Jewish war orphans'. Then Dulanty sent Schonfeld, in accordance with his request, a statement concerning the authorised admission of the children. Dated 16 August 1947, it read:

> This is to confirm that the Government of Ireland has decided to admit to Ireland up to one hundred Jewish war orphans from Central and Eastern Europe selected by Rabbi Dr Solomon Schonfeld, Executive Director of the Chief Rabbi's Religious Emergency Council. The orphans are aged between 7 and 16 years. It has been agreed that all costs of this scheme will be borne by the above mentioned Chief Rabbi's council.[81]

Efforts to get the children from Czechoslovakia to England continued. Rabbi Schonfeld, in contact with the British Home Office, was given clearance on 1 January 1948 to bring them to England. The necessary instructions concerning 'the party of 100 children for Eire' had been issued to the British passport control officer in Prague. The British authorities noted that the children might have to remain in London for a few days: 'Provided their stay is confined to that period no objection will be raised.'[82] There was a communist *coup d'état* in Czechoslovakia between 21 and 25 February, and on 10 March Jan Masaryk, the former Czech Foreign Minister, died in Prague in mysterious circumstances. These events delayed the departure of the children.

Despite the uncertainties in Prague, plans to house the children in Ireland went ahead. Clonyn Castle, their appointed destination, was in very poor repair. Work began in early 1948 to make the premises habitable. Olga Eppel of Garville Road, Rathgar in Dublin was appointed organising secretary on 18 February.[83] Robert Briscoe was among the main organisers of the project, while others involved included Rabbi Zalman Alony and Rabbi Theodore Lewis. The burden of organising the repair of the castle fell on Eppel's shoulders. Rabbi Schonfeld came to Dublin in early March to discuss the project with Briscoe and Rabbi Alony. Margolis, a contractor from Manchester, was employed to do the work. His foreman was a Mr Mole, also from Manchester. The contractor employed a mixture of British and local staff. They employed a caretaker who also acted as night watchman and two gardeners. Another local man was employed to look after the generator.[84]

There was, however, a most unfortunate incident little over a month before the children finally came to Ireland. On 26 March Clonyn Castle was broken into and petrol was sprinkled on the floors of five rooms. An attempt was made to set fire to the floors but they did not catch light and the only damage done was a scorching of wood. A Department of Justice report stated:

> while numbers of the local people do not like the proposal to house Jewish children in the castle, there is not, as far as the police are aware, any local organised agitation against the admission of the children. A large number of workmen have been employed on renovation work at the castle for the past twelve months.[85]

Eppel wrote to Schonfeld on 29 March giving him information about the fire.

About two pints of petrol had been used, she had been told by the gardaí, who had 'absolutely no clue at all as to who could have done such a thing'. The intruders had broken in through a ground-floor window (the caretaker lived in a cottage half a mile away). They had removed their shoes and sprinkled a small quantity of petrol on the first floor and attempted to set it alight. They had then gone to the synagogue on the first floor and sprinkled petrol in front of the Covenant and on the doors of the Covenant. The damage done would only take about ten minutes to put right, she said. Eppel then speculated on who might have been responsible.

> My first thought was that the villagers [in Delvin] may have been jealous to see the electric lights on since they have no electricity, but I cannot really entertain this thought as I know the whole village are looking forward to the opening of the castle. It means employment for them and business to the shop keepers. Nor can I imagine it was anti-Semitism. You see that although one may hear an anti-Semitic remark in Eire now and again, there has never been a case of anything physical at all. The police say it is purely a case of vandalism, but not political or religious. They thought there may have been someone sacked or upset by the contractors, but this is not true. Mr Mole told me that he found the people of Delvin very obliging and kind and friendly. I too have found that since I started visiting Delvin.[86]

Eppel had heard indirectly that 'the same kind of fire had been attempted at the Roman Catholic Recreational Hall about a month ago'. She concluded that the fire was probably 'the work of some silly ass in the village'. Knowing how things were exaggerated in Ireland, Eppel felt it best not to make a fuss at all. But the fact that the matter had been reported to the gardaí meant that 'the whole village know of it'.[87]

Eppel also wrote to Ruth Lunzer of the chief rabbi's Religious Emergency Council in London and explained to her that she wanted the matter kept quiet. She assured her that there was no damage done and 'nor do I anticipate anything but a fade out of the story'. She had tried with the help of Robert Briscoe to have the story dropped. But the three national dailies had carried a short story on the fire and she enclosed cuttings about the incident from the *Irish Times*, the *Irish Press* and the *Irish Independent*. Eppel added: I do hope that the Rabbi will succeed in bringing some of the children over soon. The quicker they come, the less people will be running around in circles.'[88] Eppel had made the same plea to Schonfeld: 'Now that the place is nearing completion and people know about it all, it may be best to strike a "fait accompli" now and do the little jobs of work outstanding afterwards.'[89]

In subsequent letters, Eppel told Lunzer how pleased she was about the progress at the castle. Rabbi Alony and others continued to help get things ready. But she explained that there were many issues still to be resolved. They had been visited recently by Rabbi Konegishoeffer and another rabbi from Gateshead. Eppel was rather perturbed to learn that the former, who had been offered the position of spiritual leader at the castle, wanted a large number of rooms to house his wife and six children. Eppel raised a further question about the supply of milk to the castle. The rabbi from Gateshead said that milk would have to be got locally and that milking would have to be done under supervision. Eppel felt that this might prove awkward, as 'straight from the cow milk' in Ireland was not to be trusted. She explained that even Rabbi Alony used pasteurised milk in his own house. Eppel was scared of 'home milked' cows as there had been 'outbreaks of typhoid in Eire and it is not recommended to home milk the cows'. She added that the 'ordinary Eire farmer is not as hygienic as he might be, that is why all milk is pasteurised here'.[90]

Another matter arose in early April which really worried Eppel. The design on the front of the castle carried some crosses which were cut into the stone. 'These crosses are not Christian crosses, but a kind of designed cross showing round tops to the end of the crosses', she wrote.[91] The contractor had received instructions to fill them in. Eppel was told by the foreman that 'he would rather not fill them in until the very last moment, or, as he said "a hour before I leave Delvin"'. Eppel argued that

> in order to preserve the good feeling of the Catholics in Delvin we must not interfere with the crosses. The fact that they are not Christian crosses should be sufficient for us to ignore them. I would be very scared of awakening the anger of the people there and they are a very superstitious people and if anything happened in the village, such as sickness or so on, they would say 'We can't have any luck when the Jews took the crosses away.'[92]

Rabbi Alony, she said, agreed with her. It is probable that Eppel got her way.

Schonfeld finally went to Prague and returned on 22 April with 137 children from many different parts of central Europe. While the children were temporarily housed in the Jewish community's hostel in Sunderland, Schonfeld wrote to the Irish high commissioner in London, John Dulanty, on 26 April giving details. The Irish authorities were advised that the children would be arriving in the country within two weeks.[93]

Rabbi Theodore Lewis recalls that representatives of the Jewish community in Dublin met the children at the North Wall. They were taken in buses to Greenville Hall, South Circular Road, where they were given a nourishing meal.[94] Eppel wrote to Schonfeld on 9 May:

> You would have been indeed happy and proud, Dr Schonfeld, had you seen the Castle on Friday afternoon as I did. It was a glorious hot day and the children were all out playing football and the place looked as if they absolutely belonged there for years. I was so pleased.[95]

Eppel reported that the press had given them some good write-ups; Dorothy MacArdle, an author and strong supporter of Fianna Fáil, wanted to broadcast about the children on Radio Éireann on 18 May.[96]

Schonfeld wrote to Ms M. Wellstead at the Home Office the same day:

> I have just returned from Dublin after seeing eighty-four children safely and happily established in Clonyn Castle, and sixteen older ones in a home in Dublin. I enclose a list of the fifteen orphans whom our Council is keeping here. . . . You have thus once again been the cause of providing

a pleasant and promising life to youngsters deprived of their normal homes by the war and its sufferings. May God bless you.[97]

He also wrote to Dulanty on 23 May thanking him 'for the kind and sympathetic manner in which you facilitated this humanitarian undertaking'. Schonfeld was aware that since June 1946, when he had first approached him, the matter had taken up a good deal of Dulanty's attention, 'and in spite of its comparative smallness, you have always been ready to give it your own and your office's best attention'.[98]

The initial euphoria which followed the arrival of the children soon gave way to the practical challenge of trying to find funds to provide for the new charges. But there had already been indications of tension between Eppel and certain members of the Jewish Representative Council. As early as 23 March 1948, she wrote to Schonfeld:

> I am quite in agreement with your remarks concerning the Rep. Council here, but cannot help but know that in a small town like ours and with a clustered congregation, there is bound to be some talk, but, nevertheless, I do not attach much importance to it. The Rep. Council hold two meetings a year. At the moment they are having a meeting regarding the [price] of Pesach food. That is as far as their activities go in Dublin now. I think during the war they were representative somewhat of the congregation here, but since then they are not at all active.[99]

Eppel was very angry when she wrote to Schonfeld on 24 May. She had been to see Professor Leonard Abrahamson that day: 'He is annoyed with the Chief Rabbi's Council [in Britain] for not having consulted the Representative Council in Dublin regarding our children.' She reported that he was full of praise for the work of the Central Fund and for the Dublin Jewish Refugee Committee. Eppel asked Abrahamson how many Jewish refugees had come to Ireland and he told her they had brought in sixty refugees. 'I could not even answer him about that. 60 in 15 years', she wrote.[100]

When Eppel reported that conversation to her committee in Dublin, it was decided to continue working for the children without any contact with the JRC.[101] The simmering conflict between Eppel's committee and the JRC brought Schonfeld to Dublin in late May to act as a peacemaker. Despite these differences, the Delvin project was strongly supported by a very active committee in Dublin under its chairman, Erwin Goldwater. The Dublin community worked hard, through the Dublin Refugee Aid Committee, to bring about an improvement in conditions at the castle; one member of the community loaned his house in Kimmage to Eppel for the use of the children.[102] Olga Eppel herself did heroic work. The Minister for Health, Noël Browne, visited Clonyn Castle in early October 1948. The children read a message in English asking him to thank the government for providing such a home for them 'in this beautiful country where they hoped to grow up and play their part as citizens in a better world'.[103] The children sang a song of peace and cheered the minister as he left the castle.

Eppel, under the strain of trying to keep the work going, continued to be a stern critic of some sections of the Irish Jewish community. She wrote to a colleague of Schonfeld's in London on 28 December 1948:

> The collections from the Community this month slackened on account of Xmas. That may seem strange to you, but Dr Schonfeld will agree that the pleasure bound Jewry of Dublin are very unorthodox, and I am afraid Xmas comes before charity.

Asking for more money, Eppel added:

> In fact when I look at the overall contribution from your organisation to keep the children in Eire, I feel rather ashamed of my co-religionists here who could and should help more, nevertheless the children must eat . . .[104]

The children did eat. Fit and restored to good health, they left Ireland to find new homes and new lives abroad in Israel, Britain, Canada and the United States. One of the organisers of the project, Rabbi Theodore Lewis, also moved to the United States. He recalls an incident one Sabbath morning about 1970 when a young visitor was called to the reading of the Torah in the synagogue in Newport, Rhode Island. Coming down from the reading desk, he turned to Rabbi Lewis and said:

> Rabbi, I want to thank you for what you did, when I came to Dublin as a survivor of the Holocaust, and was later settled in Clonyn Castle. You will be happy to know that your efforts have borne fruit. I am now employed by the Federal Government in a position of authority.[105]

The inter-party government and refugee policy

De Valera, who had facilitated the admission of the Jewish children, was not in power during their stay in Ireland. Defeated in the February 1948 general election, his Fianna Fáil government was replaced by a five-party coalition, the inter-party government, made up principally of Fine Gael, Labour and the newly formed Clann na Poblachta. The new Taoiseach was John A. Costello of Fine Gael, and Seán MacBride, the leader of Clann na Poblachta, became Minister for External Affairs. De Valera had held both portfolios for sixteen years. The new Minister for Justice was Seán MacEoin of Fine Gael and the portfolio of Industry and Commerce was held by Labour's Seán Morrissey. During the three years that the inter-party government was in power, there were also changes in the senior staff of the Department of Justice. S. A. Roche retired and was replaced as secretary by J. E. Duff on 1 February 1949. Duff died the following August, and Thomas J. Coyne, chief wartime censor and assistant secretary at the Department of Justice since his return in 1946, became secretary; he held the post until 1961. Despite those senior personnel changes, the department's 'illiberal' ethos towards the admission of aliens and refugees remained unchanged.

The onset of the Cold War, however, had significantly changed the context of the refugee problem in Europe. Escape from behind 'the iron curtain', as Winston Churchill had called the frontier between East and West, was very difficult. Nevertheless, the International Refugee Organisation (IRO), taking over from the United Nations Relief and Rehabilitation Agency on 1 July 1947, had responsibility for the repatriation or resettlement of one and a half million people. Its work was eased by the foundation of the state of Israel on 15 May 1948, which provided a homeland for many Jewish refugees.[106] However, that historical development did not solve the international Jewish refugee problem.

Requests for admission to Ireland by refugees and aliens had slowed down considerably by the time the inter-party government came to power. Nevertheless, new guidelines were set down without delay to govern policy in those areas. It was decided to 'admit freely aliens of good character from countries to which they might be repatriated without difficulty'. Aliens from countries with which Ireland had visa agreements could take up residence provided they were in a position to maintain themselves and would not enter into employment or permanent business without advance permission.[107] Aliens 'of good character' from 'more remote countries' could be admitted provided 'it was decided that the purpose of the journey was not contrary to any Irish interest'. It was further decided to admit refugees, stateless aliens, displaced persons and east European nationals *only* if coming for permanent residence and after suitable scrutiny of credentials on security, character and economic grounds.[108] These guidelines presupposed that refugees would seek entry into Ireland in very small groups through recognised channels. They did not envisage the very different situation which developed in autumn 1949.

The *Victory*, with 385 refugees on board, was obliged to put in to Cobh, Co. Cork, on 30 September. The boat, which was destined for Canada, was overcrowded and unseaworthy. En route from Sweden, it had run aground and the captain had been forced to dock in Cobh for repairs. The refugees were from Estonia, Latvia, Lithuania, Finland, Hungary, Russia, Poland and Yugoslavia.[109] On eight occasions between 1946 and 1949, Swedish boats carrying refugees had called at Irish ports and the authorities had been left with seventeen refugees as a result.[110] The *Victory* was quite distinct from previous cases. Most of the refugees were undocumented and without Canadian entry permits. Dublin was informed by the acting Canadian high commissioner in London, David M. Johnson, that the Canadian authorities were sending an official to Cobh to warn the captain of the ship not to sail for Canada as only 141 of his passengers had visas.

The Irish authorities, on humanitarian grounds, transferred the refugees temporarily to an unoccupied army barracks at Rockgrove, five miles from Cork. The authorities faced the prospect of having to keep nearly 400 people in the short to medium term. According to a garda report of 27 October, a small number of the refugees had found employment. One Pole had been engaged to play the solo violin at the Cork Opera House while a Polish architect had been engaged by a firm in the city.[111]

On 19 October the cabinet referred the matter to a subcommittee comprising the Ministers for External Affairs, Justice, Defence, and Industry and Commerce.[112] The Minister for External Affairs, Seán MacBride, received a report from the Irish envoy in Stockholm, William Warnock, dated 21 October which emphasised the gravity of the situation. The envoy reported that the refugee problem was worsening. The Swedes, he said, were running out of patience with new waves of refugees coming to their country in small boats from the three former Baltic republics of Lithuania, Latvia and Estonia. Warnock explained that

> new types of illegal immigrants are now coming ... and they are not so sympathetically received – persons who leave their homes not as political refugees, but because they feel that economic conditions are so bad there that in order to better themselves it will be in their own interest to get away to Sweden or some other comparatively prosperous country in the hope of finding employment and a more settled outlook for the future. The influx of these new 'refugees' is now a cause of irritation and worry to the Aliens Commission, for they are now coming, mainly from Eastern Germany, in considerable numbers, several hundred a month.[113]

MacBride and his cabinet subcommittee had cause to view with growing concern the possibility that the *Victory* might be the first of a large influx of 'boat people', to use a present-day term.

The Canadian authorities took the case very seriously. David M. Johnson wrote to Seán MacBride on 26 October, stating that his government was not in a position to contribute to the transport costs of the refugees. He did offer to send a four-man immigration team to Cork to examine the refugees provided the Irish government would undertake not to allow those rejected to proceed to Canada. He also requested the Irish authorities to provide x-ray films of chests and radiologists' reports on applicants. The cabinet decided on 28 October to allow the Canadian team to come to Cork to interview the refugees.

An interdepartmental meeting on 12 November took the view that the state should not accept liability for the transport of the refugees to Canada unless it became clear that the refugees could not pay their own way and could not be absorbed into employment there. The Department of External Affairs put forward the view that those not admitted to Canada might be returned to Sweden even if they were not allowed to re-enter in order to discourage the influx of further refugees from that country.[114]

The Canadian immigration team arrived in Cork and carried out its investigations. In the end, only about fifty-eight were not allowed to enter Canada. Fifteen were refused entry on security grounds, though not on the grounds that they were communists but because they had collaborated with the Nazis; others were rejected on medical grounds.[115] On 15 December 1949, thirty-four left for Canada, leaving 349 in Cork. Local people tried to make the refugees feel welcome. Thanks to the work of the Irish Red Cross, those who remained at Rockgrove enjoyed a 'sumptuous Christmas' while a Polish priest studying at Maynooth, Jan Bogusz, was invited to celebrate Mass.[116] In the new year, the remaining refugees finally left for Canada or elsewhere.

The inter-party government continued to receive requests from various quarters for the admission of refugees, including the International Refugee Organisation, which was represented in Dublin by Professor John Dillon.[117]

The Vatican's representative to the IRO, Fr Edward J. Killion, told Archbishop John Charles McQuaid on 13 September 1948 that he was not in a position to give unqualified approval to the programme of that organisation; the archbishop in turn made those views known to the Department of the Taoiseach.[118] McQuaid himself became very active in securing places for invalided refugees and those in need of long-term hospital care. He was supported in his efforts by Killion, who visited Dublin in June 1950 and had an interview with the Minister for Justice, Seán MacEoin.[119] The priest explained his case for the admission of invalided refugees and the long-term ill. MacEoin wrote to Taoiseach John A. Costello:

> After consideration of the matter I think we should make an effort to assist. We have County Homes where the conditions are fairly good and it would be possible to ask each County Authority to adopt one or two of these people. There are 26 or 28 such County Homes and if each one adopted one or two it would give us a fairly decent number, and then homes might be got with ordinary people for some of their relatives.[120]

McQuaid gave the government further encouragement to act when he wrote to the Taoiseach on 2 September 1950 about finding a place for 'the hopeless hard-core of the refugees'. Both men met for a brief discussion on the matter which had been under active consideration by the government. [121] The Department of Justice prepared a memorandum for submission to government and its recommendations were broadly accepted at a cabinet meeting on 26 September.[122] Permission was given to accept incapacitated displaced persons for whom voluntary institutions in the country were willing to take responsibility. The voluntary institutions were to provide accommodation for the blind, the senile, the chronically ill, the disabled, and the mentally impaired. The cabinet decided to exclude tuberculosis cases (which was very prevalent in Ireland at the time) or other types of cases in which the caring organisations were already taxed to the full.[123] Applications for an employment permit from invalided refugees who were admitted to the country were to be considered on their merits, provided the offers of employment were for a minimum of twelve months.[124]

The government asked the Irish Red Cross Society to assume responsibility for the co-ordination of the work. The IRO representative, John Dillon, was advised on 29 September of the cabinet decision. Costello wrote personally to Archbishop McQuaid on 30 September to inform him of the decision; he also asked whether the archbishop might indicate how the placing of incapacitated displaced persons in voluntary institutions might best be carried out.[125] McQuaid's reply revealed the tension between himself and the IRO:

> I fear I must say that the situation has hitherto proved so complex, not to say, confusing, that I would prefer not to speak about the matter. Twice already I have personally approached the Institutions. The IRO has, without my knowledge I fear, also approached them.[126]

McQuaid informed Costello that the IRO was seeking a meeting with him and suggested that they themselves should meet to discuss the matter. A *modus operandi* was eventually worked out, as fifty refugees were admitted for institutional care.[127]

Reviewing the number of aliens and refugees admitted to Ireland since the end of the Second World War, a September 1950 Department of Justice memorandum provided the following figures:

> ... this country has admitted about 925 aliens from the Continent. Of these 355 are domestic servants, 170 are university students, most of whom are admitted on a temporary basis, and about 400 are children, dependent relatives of persons already resident here or aliens who have Irish relatives or some other connection with this country. Authorisations were given for the admission of an additional 450 aliens, but it is unlikely that these will now arrive.[128]

Despite the difficulties, the refugee policy of both the inter-party and the Fianna Fáil governments was not 'illiberal'; it could, however, have been much more generous.

Defeat for the Department of Justice

De Valera returned to power on 13 June 1951. Gerald Boland returned to the Department of Justice and Seán Lemass to the Department of Industry and Commerce; Frank Aiken was given the portfolio of External Affairs. The change of government did not indicate a change in refugee policy. Ireland acceded in November 1956 to the 1951 Convention relating to the Status of Refugees. The familiar battle lines of a restrictive Department of Justice seeking to hold the line in the face of pressure for a more generous attitude from both within government and outside agencies were clearly revealed in a case in 1953. Robert Briscoe, together with two members of the Paris-based Joint Distribution Committee which cared for Jewish refugees, met Boland on 12 February 1953. Briscoe wanted to find a home in Ireland for ten Jewish families, approximately twenty adults and twenty children. The official minute of the meeting recorded that the minister adopted 'a sympathetic attitude'. Briscoe, advised to put his request in writing, wrote to Boland the following day:

> As verbally explained, there is a small hurriedly constructed temporary camp to house 100 orthodox Jewish families who have escaped from behind the Iron Curtain into Austria. They are mostly of Hungarian or Czecho-Slovakian origin. Their position is very dangerous and the Joint Distribution Committee, which maintains these people, are fearful of the consequences which would flow to these people if by any chance or act they should again come under the power of the Communist authorities.[129]

The minister instructed one of his officials, Peter Berry, to prepare a memorandum for him on the subject. Berry told the departmental secretary, Thomas J. Coyne, on 16 February that Boland, who was going to speak about the matter to de Valera that afternoon, wanted the application examined as 'a matter of urgency'. Berry proceeded to outline his views on the subject:

I would strongly urge that if further refugees are to be admitted that they should not be selected on a racial or religious basis through the agency of a body such as the Joint Distribution Committee, a body of which we literally know nothing, but that selection of the most deserving cases should be left to the High Commissioner for Refugees who will be in a position to have the applicants cleared for security, character and health. I particularly don't like the bait thrown out that ample money will be forthcoming for the maintenance of these Jewish families if they are allowed to take their place at the head of the queue of thousands who have been waiting in fear and misery for an opportunity to start life anew in another country.[130]

He argued against the admission of the group as it 'would be contrary to established practice to admit aliens for temporary or permanent residence on racial or religious grounds'. The department had, he wrote,

refused literally hundreds of applications on behalf of refugees of good character of Catholic and Christian religions whose plight was no less pitiable than that of the group in question now. Some of the Catholic and Christian refugees were sponsored by persons of high standing such as bishops, professors in Universities, both here and abroad.[131]

Berry questioned the guarantees which had been given by Briscoe in good faith; it had been the experience of the department 'over many years that the Jews here are prepared to put forward any plea that would enable an alien co-religionist to get over an immediate difficulty'.[132] There was no evidence, he pointed out, that the refugees in question had clean health and security, and non-criminal records. There was also the question, he reminded Coyne, of the prevailing attitude towards Jews in Ireland:

There is a strong anti-Jewish feeling in this State which is particularly evident to the Aliens Section of the Department of Justice. Sympathy for the Jews has not been particularly excited at the recent news that some thousands are fleeing westwards because of the recent round-up of a number of communist Jews who had been prominent in Governments and Government service in Eastern European countries.[133]

Berry's thoughts on the case were sent to the Department of the Taoiseach and shown by Maurice Moynihan to de Valera the same evening. Moynihan minuted that de Valera was unable to examine the case in detail because of other pressing business.[134] De Valera, however, found time on 20 February to discuss the matter with Boland and his officials.[135]

Arising out of that discussion, Coyne – with Berry's assistance – prepared a memorandum for government. Dated 28 February, it continued to oppose the admission of the refugees: 'No reasons have been put forward why this Jewish group should take precedence over the thousands – even millions – of European refugees . . .'[136] Valuable statistical information on aliens and refugees was gathered in the preparation of the document. It was estimated that in February 1953 approximately 2,700 aliens were registered as permanently resident in the country; this did not include British subjects who were exempt from the application of the legislation on aliens.[137] Of that number,

620 were refugees and stateless persons, including about 170 university students who had a guarantee of readmission elsewhere on completion of their studies.[138] In addition to the 2,700 registered aliens, about 800 persons – exclusive of about 300 of British origin – had become Irish citizens by naturalisation; over 300 of these had formerly been refugees or stateless persons.

The memorandum was unable to produce any figures on aliens, displaced persons or naturalised Irish citizens who were of Jewish blood 'as official records were not kept on the basis of race or religion but observation from time to time seems to indicate that quite a number are Jewish'.[139] The Department of Justice followed this 'observation' with a clear statement of its position on Jewish refugees:

> In the administration of the alien laws it has always been recognised in the Departments of Justice, Industry and Commerce and External Affairs that the question of admission of aliens of Jewish blood presents a special problem and the alien laws have been administered less liberally in their case.[140]

The memorandum then went on to repeat familiar arguments:

> Although the Jewish community in Ireland is only 3,907 persons, according to the 1946 census, there is a fairly strong anti-Semitic feeling throughout the country based, perhaps, on historical reasons, the fact that the Jews have remained a separate community within the community and have not permitted themselves to be assimilated, and that for their numbers they appear to have disproportionate wealth and influence.[141]

The memorandum was circulated to the other departments in preparation for a cabinet meeting.

Briscoe's ministerial sources had kept him informed about the development of the case. He knew that the matter was very delicately balanced and had to be allowed to take its administrative course without unwelcome pressure from any lobby group. That did not happen. Charles Jordan, of the Joint Distribution Committee, had been in the delegation which had seen the Minister for Justice about the matter in early February. Impatient with the delay, he expressed his disappointment at the lack of development in a letter on 11 March to the chief rabbi of Ireland, Immanuel Jakobovits. He explained to Jakobovits that he had phoned Briscoe a number of times and had simply got 'the curt reply that nothing had happened yet'.[142] Jordan urged the chief rabbi to take action through the Jewish Representative Council.

Briscoe in turn received a curt note from Jakobovits: 'It is most disappointing that the impetus created by our visitors has not apparently been maintained and that this vital rescue work is experiencing such delays.'[143] The chief rabbi wanted Briscoe 'to ascertain the present attitude of the government' and inform Jordan accordingly. Jakobovits also said that he was contacting Herman Good of the JRC in the hope that all three of them might bring influence to bear on the responsible authorities. Briscoe told the chief rabbi on 19 March that a simple phone call to him would have enabled him to explain that 'the decision by the Government was delayed on account of the principle involved, which meant, also, the possibility of admitting East German Christian families equally destitute and deserving of refuge as Ireland is a Christian country'.[144] He added that he would also have been in a position to inform the chief rabbi of a favourable decision, news of which he had just conveyed to the JRC.

The cabinet decision on 13 March had indeed gone against the recommendations of the Department of Justice. The subtle wording of the minute revealed the delicacy of the situation in the cabinet: victory came to de Valera only after a struggle. The minute, which was drafted by the secretary to the cabinet, Maurice Moynihan, stated that the Minister for Justice, after consultation with the Minister for External Affairs, should submit proposals for the admission to the state, at the discretion of the Minister for Justice, of a limited number of refugees on the following conditions:

- that such refugees are of good character and are vouched for by a reputable organisation or by responsible persons;
- that satisfactory guarantees of provision for their maintenance while in Ireland are furnished;
- that assurances are given that they will leave Ireland within a limited period; and
- such other conditions as the Minister for Justice may consider it proper to recommend.

However, the government then ordered that,

subject to and in accordance with whatever decisions may be taken in respect of the proposals to be submitted by the Minister for Justice, five of the Jewish refugee families of Hungarian or Czech origin who recently arrived in Austria should be permitted to enter Ireland as refugees for a maximum period of two years.[145]

Briscoe, who had requested the admission of ten families, had to be content with five. This marked the end of the post-war struggle to admit Jewish refugees, and, most significantly, it ended in defeat for the Department of Justice. The actions of the Department of Justice had, in large measure, prevented a dramatic postwar increase in the Irish Jewish population. But the relative absence of new members did little to stifle the vitality of the intellectual debate inside the community. The foundation of the Dublin Jewish Progressive Congregation on 30 January 1946 by Larry Elyan, Rudi Neuman, Bethel Solomons, Con Leventhal and others displayed the desire among influential members of the community to identify with the principles and practices of Progressive Judaism. A graveyard was purchased at Woodtown, and a synagogue was opened at Leicester Road which continues to thrive in the 1990s with a congregation of roughly seventy-five households. Joan Finkel, who became the first woman president in 1987 (succeeding her husband, John), wrote that the creation in 1946 of the progressive congregation 'caused an unprecedented outbreak of bitter recrimination' in the wider community; although the community atmosphere is warmer forty years on, she wrote in 1986, 'there is still a sad lack of real understanding of us, our congregation and our Jewish way of life.'[146]

Epilogue

The Jewish community in
Ireland since the 1950s

'The smaller we get, the stronger we get', was how Alex Jaffe from Belfast, at the end of the 1980s, saw the future of a community in rapid decline.[1] That was trying to put a brave face on a bad situation. South of the border, the decline was steady but not quite as acute as in Northern Ireland. In 1946 the total Jewish population on the island was 5,381, with 3,907 in the South and 1,474 in the North. By 1961 the community had been reduced to 4,446 for the island, 3,255 in the Republic and 1,191 in the North. The figures for Northern Ireland then dropped steadily from 959 in 1971 to 517 in 1981. It was down to 410 in 1991, most of whom were over the age of fifty.[2] The drop in the Republic of Ireland was from 2,633 in 1971 to 2,127 in 1981 and to 1,581 in 1991. By the mid-1990s the number was between 1,000 and 1,200.[3] The annual average rate of decline, according to a study by J. J. Sexton and R. O'Leary, was 1.2 per cent in the period from 1946 to 1961. That rose to nearly 3 per cent in the intercensal period 1981–91.[4]

Jewish population in the South of Ireland, 1946–91

Year	Number	Annual average change in intercensal period (%)	% in Dublin
1946	3,907	+0.4	89.9
1961	3,255	−1.2	94.1
1971	2,633	−2.1	93.1
1981	2,127	−2.1	91.7
1991	1,581	−2.9	87.6

Source: Censuses of population[5]

The demographic decline may be illustrated more clearly by focusing on particular locations. There were 252 Jews living in Cork city and county in 1946; that figure dropped to 120 in 1961, to 75 in 1971 and 62 in 1981. In

Waterford city and county the drop was from 23 in 1946 to 6 in 1961 and 4 in 1971; there were no Jews returned as living there in 1981. Dublin, as the table shows, remained the most important centre of Jewish life. Writing in 1987, the historical geographer, Stanley Waterman, described the process of decline thus:

> Today, when one speaks of the Jewish community in Ireland, the reference is almost exclusively to Dublin. Over most of the past hundred years, Dublin has consistently accounted for 80 per cent or more of the Jews living in the twenty-six counties that constitute the Republic of Ireland, and, since 1936, over 90 per cent. Only Belfast, in Northern Ireland, had a community which came anywhere close to Dublin in numbers. Cork had, for many years, a community which reached a maximum size, in its heyday, of just under 500 persons. Earlier in the century, Limerick and Waterford too had small congregations. However, today, Belfast has dwindled to little over 300 persons and the Cork community is, to all intents and purposes, defunct.[6]

The ageing of the Jewish population is another indicator of decline. Sexton and O'Leary's study shows that only 3 per cent of the Jewish population in the South were over sixty-five years in 1926, compared with 25 per cent in 1991. Conversely, nearly 9 per cent were aged under five in 1926, compared with 4.5 per cent in 1991.[7]

Age profile of the Jewish population in the South of Ireland, 1926–91(%)

Age group	1926	1936	1946	1961	1981	1991
0–4 yrs	8.7	7.6	7.4	7.1	5.2	4.5
5–14	20.7	15.4	13.5	14.6	12.2	11.0
15–24	23.4	20.1	14.5	12.5	14.2	11.6
25–34	16.2	19.7	16.7	9.7	13.4	11.5
35–44	11.9	14.8	17.9	14.1	11.3	13.9
45–54	10.4	10.1	14.3	17.8	9.5	12.3
55–64	5.4	7.8	9.0	13.6	12.8	10.2
65+	3.3	4.5	6.7	10.6	21.4	25.0
Total	100.0	100.0	100.0	100.0	100.0	100.0

Source: Censuses of population[8]
Note: An age subdivision for the Jewish community is not available from the 1971 census.

The decline, according to Waterman, was more significant than a mere loss of numbers; it was

> something much more subtle, a metamorphosis of an immigrant community. For, during the fifty or sixty years or so that the modern community had been in existence, specific individuals or families had made specific community institutions their own personal fief. When they left the scene, the removal of what had often been a forceful personality with a lifelong involvement led to a qualitative decline too.[9]

The community had moved on since the 1950s when the chief rabbi, Immanuel Jakobovits, wrote about the Jewish communities in Ireland being modelled broadly on the Anglo-Jewish pattern, subject to four modifying factors.[10] Firstly, Ireland had been one of the few European countries not directly involved in the Second World War. Secondly, unlike the other two neutral states in Europe, Sweden and Switzerland, Ireland had hardly any influx of refugees before, during or after the war, with the result that Jewish life tended to be very conservative, as it remained uninfluenced by continental newcomers. (Over 80 per cent of Jewish households in the country, for example, used kosher meat.) Thirdly, the ratio of Jews to the rest of the population was very low, perhaps the lowest in any English-speaking country. Fourthly, Irish Jews lived in a staunchly Catholic environment, about 93 per cent of the population being Catholic. As a consequence of those factors, he concluded that Jewish life was marked by a relatively high degree of social isolation and self-containment.[11]

Jakobovits profiled the Irish Jewish community as leading a separate existence to that of the Jewish community in Britain, all the more so since the passage in 1949 of the External Relations Act had taken the Republic of Ireland out of the Commonwealth.[12] Links between the communities in Belfast and Dublin were quite strong up to the late 1960s. Marriage between members of the two communities was common, while tennis tournaments and other sporting and cultural events were organised.[13] Social contact, however, between Dublin and Belfast was significantly curtailed following the outbreak of conflict in Northern Ireland in the late 1960s.[14]

Belfast witnessed the gradual relocation of its Jewish community. In 1926 a Jewish Institute had been built in Ashfield Gardens, off Glandore Avenue. This two-storey building had a restaurant and tennis courts. It was the home of the Jewish Dramatic Society and the Junior Forum debating society. In the 1930s and 1940s some families moved out to the edge of the suburbs along Antrim Road, Donegall Park Avenue and Waterloo Road. By the 1950s about 25 per cent of the Belfast community lived in the Malone area. An attempt to open a synagogue in the area was discouraged by Rabbi Shacter. However, by the early 1960s a good many members of the community lived in the northern suburbs around the upper Antrim Road area. This was too far for the older people to walk to the synagogue in Carlisle Circus. The president of the community, Barnie Hurwitz, raised over £80,000 to build a new synagogue and community centre at Somerton Road; it was opened in 1964 and could seat 1,500. But the community's decline in the 1980s and 1990s necessitated the partitioning of the main synagogue to make it smaller and the selling off of some of the adjacent buildings.[15]

Originally, the Jewish community in Dublin had been concentrated on both sides of the River Liffey in the inner-city area. Over 20 per cent of Jewish households in 1941 were concentrated in a single 25-hectare square grid in the South Circular Road area.[16] The more prosperous members of the community had, by this time, moved to Blackrock, Dún Laoghaire or the Ballsbridge area. From the 1930s there was a significant shift in the Jewish population from 'Little Jerusalem' in the South Circular Road area southwards to an area between Harold's Cross and Terenure and also to the Rathmines/Rathgar area.[17] The Jewish community since the 1930s had been moving to Rathmines. As orthodox Jews walk to and from synagogue, it was decided to establish the Rathmines Hebrew Congregation in the mid-1930s. Services were held in the homes of B. Citron of Grosvenor Road and L. Epstein of Grosvenor Place. The Church of Ireland parochial hall on Leinster Road was made available to the community to conduct service on High Holy Day. A permanent synagogue was later acquired on Grosvenor Road. But as many members of the congregation were young couples with families living in the nearby suburb of Terenure, a site was purchased there by the members of the Grosvenor congregation. While funds were being raised for a new synagogue, services on the site were first conducted in a Nissen hut. The Terenure Hebrew Congregation Synagogue was opened in 1953. An arson attack in the mid-1960s did considerable damage to the building. Local Catholic and Protestant clergy offered the use of their halls for religious service, and the synagogue was reopened in 1966.

Terenure, with its new synagogue, thus replaced South Circular Road as the most important residential area for Dublin Jews. The synagogues were served by the chief rabbi and by Dayan (Judge) Zalman Alony.[18] By the 1980s, the seven conventicles in the South Circular Road area had disappeared. The Walworth Road Synagogue was converted into a Jewish museum which was opened by the President of Israel, Chaim Herzog, while on an official visit to Dublin in 1985.[19]

What remains of that once throbbing artery of Jewish life around the South Circular Road?, asks Asher Benson ruefully: 'the Adelaide Road synagogue, the Jewish Museum, a few Jewish-owned homes, two kosher butcher shops in Clanbrassil Street and one kosher bakery in Lennox Street owned by a non-Jew'.[20] Dublin had, by the 1960s, lost its 'Little Jerusalem'. By the end of the twentieth century, Ireland had a rapidly declining Jewish community.

Jews and Irish society in the 1950s

How did Chief Rabbi Jakobovits view the relationship between Jews and the Irish state in the post-war period?

> In so far as these relations are exemplified by the treatment of the small Jewish community in Ireland, they are certainly close and cordial. The rights of Jewish citizens as equals among the other denominational groups are expressly recognised in a special clause of the Irish constitution – probably the only Jewish community in the world to be constitutionally protected in this explicit manner. In practice, too, the Jews of Ireland have always felt free from discrimination. In fact, Ireland is one of the very few countries that has never blemished its record by any serious anti-Jewish outrages.[21]

Yet, anti-Semitism remained a peripheral subcurrent in Irish society. Certainly, upward social mobility partially explains the opening of a Jewish golf club at Edmondstown in Rathfarnham, Dublin.[22] But another reason was the prevalence of an anti-Jewish bias detected by members of the community who had been refused membership at other clubs for no good reason. The Jewish community in Belfast opened their own section in Fortwilliam golf club after similar experiences of discrimination. The US envoy in Dublin, Vinton Chapin, reported in 1949 that, although anti-Semitic feeling had not been common in Ireland, some prejudice had recently arisen because Jews 'are accumulating real estate and monopolies to a noticeable degree'. He claimed that Jews had purchased property so extensively in the once-fashionable summer resort of Bray in County Wicklow that the town was now termed 'Little Palestine'.[23] While Chapin's remarks were hardly rooted in serious sociological research, he was most probably recycling a prejudice fashionable in his Dublin milieu.

While Jewish leaders in Dublin could do little to combat such attitudes, they had no alternative but to confront the ideas put forward by the members of Maria Duce (Under the Leadership of Mary), a society founded in 1945 by Fr Denis Fahey. Its literature represented in tone and content the continuation of interwar anti-Jewish propaganda. It wrote about alleged Judaeo-Masonic control of the United States, the United Nations, the international press and cinema, and transnational business.[24] Its newspaper, *Fiat*, also attacked the Irish Association for Civil Liberties which was presided over by the writer Sean O'Faolain; the painter, Louis Le Brocquy, was also a member, as was Senator Owen Sheehy Skeffington.[25] According to the gardaí, elements from Maria Duce were responsible for the publication of an anti-Semitic news-sheet, *Saoirse* (Freedom) which appeared on 9 September 1950. The secretary of the Jewish Representative Council, Ernest Newman, accompanied by his father Arthur, called on the Taoiseach, John A. Costello, on 30 October. They were sent by him to the Department of Justice where they met two senior officials, Peter Berry and Dan Costigan. The latter told them that the government was most anxious to avoid 'any racial trouble in this country' and that the authorities could be expected to take any action within their power to prevent any encouragement of racial prejudice.[26]

After investigation, it was discovered that *Saoirse* had a negligible circulation. Published at irregular intervals, it was distributed outside the General Post Office in Dublin. A minute in the Department of Justice recorded: 'While it is anti-Jewish, it is mild in tone compared with a previous anti-Jewish publication called "Penapa".'[27] Its contents were not deemed to be subversive nor did any of the articles amount to criminal libel. The issue of *Saoirse* in the archives carries the headline: 'Communism is Jewish'.[28] The gardaí knew the man responsible for its publication and that it came from the offices of Aontas Náisiúnta in Pearse Street. The general advice from the gardaí to the Jewish community was to 'ignore the existence of this periodical'.[29] The IRA raided the *Saoirse* premises on 23 September 1950; no further issues of the paper appeared to trouble the leaders of the Jewish community. As for Maria Duce, it never attracted mass support; it declined steadily in influence during the latter part of the 1950s and disappeared, finally, in the 1960s.[30] There may have been incidents of general unpleasantness in the 1950s involving religious minorities in Ireland, but they differed radically in tone from the temper of the 1930s.[31]

Despite the need to defend their community, Jews in the 1950s – or indeed since the foundation of the state – did not show a willingness to play an active role in national politics. Jakobovits noted that, while 'Irish Jews suffer no civic or political disabilities, few are to be found in politics or the civil service'.[32] Fianna Fáil's Robert Briscoe was the exception. (Herman Good had been an unsuccessful candidate for the Labour Party in the 1944 general election.) Briscoe had been a TD since 1927, and it was a source of great pride in the community when, in 1956, he was elected lord mayor of Dublin. Chief Rabbi Jakobovits delivered a sermon on 8 July at Greenville Hall Synagogue:

> By his election, he has not only raised himself to a stature of world repute, to be the most prominent Jew ever born within these shores. He has also uplifted our standing, and turned the attention and regard of Jewish communities throughout the world to Irish Jewry. Not since my illustrious predecessor was called from Dublin to assume the highest spiritual office in Jewry as Chief Rabbi of the Holy Land has our community featured so conspicuously in the Jewish press in Israel, in the United States, in England, and in virtually every other land of our dispersion.[33]

Briscoe, who served in Dáil Éireann until 1965, was again elected lord mayor in 1961.[34] A small number of a later generation of Jews, in the 1970s and 1980s, would choose politics as their profession.

The Jewish community honours de Valera

De Valera retired from party political life in 1959 and became President of Ireland the same year. He held that position until 1973. De Valera, who had visited Israel in 1950, had not sanctioned de jure recognition of that country during his time as Taoiseach. Ireland had merely granted Israel de facto recognition in 1949. Irish policy was changed in 1963 from de facto to de jure recognition. Over ten years later, in December 1974, Ireland and Israel agreed to an exchange of diplomatic representatives. This was to be initially on a non-residential basis. At first, Ireland's representative in Switzerland was accredited to Israel. As a matter of convenience, that was changed in 1979 when it was decided that the Irish ambassador to Greece would be accredited to Israel. The Irish government gave approval for the establishment of an Israeli embassy in Dublin in 1993; Zvi Gabay presented his credentials on 22 July. An Israeli embassy was opened in Dublin in 1996.

In recognition of de Valera's contribution to public life, the Irish Jewish community decided in 1965 to honour him. It was proposed to plant a forest of 10,000 trees in Israel named after de Valera in recognition of his many years of devoted service in the cause of peace and freedom.[35] The site chosen for the forest was Kfar Kana, near Nazareth. All relevant matters regarding the proposed forest were administered by the Eamon de Valera Forest Committee under the chairmanship of Mervyn L. Abrahamson, Maurice's oldest brother.[36] It was also proposed to present him with a book in Celtic symbols based on the designs of the Book of Kells. E. A. O'Connor was commissioned to do the artwork.[37] A year later, the plan was realised.

De Valera wrote to Abrahamson on 26 July 1966, saying he understood that the latter was going to Israel to be present at the planting of the first tree in the forest which was to be given his name:

> I am deeply grateful to the Jewish community here for the honour that they are thus conferring upon me, and to the authorities in Israel for giving the necessary permission. Will you please thank the members of your community here and also the Government of Israel. I should like particularly to be remembered to Dr Ben Gurion, who showed me such kindness when I visited Israel some sixteen years ago, and to Dr J. Herzog, whose father I knew so well when he was Chief Rabbi here in Dublin.[38]

Abrahamson replied on 27 July:

> I know that the forest which will bear your name will be one of which you and Irish people will have every reason to be proud. When I return from Israel I hope to bring with me all the details of the forest itself and of the inaugural ceremony, which I will be most honoured to convey to you.[39]

The ceremonial planting of the first tree took place on 18 August.[40] The Israeli Prime Minister, Levi Eshkol, wrote to Abrahamson sending his greetings on the occasion:

> I see in the planting of trees in President de Valera's distinguished name a fitting expression of the traditional friendship between the Irish and the Jewish peoples, two nations that have so much in common of history and fulfilment.[41]

Eshkol hoped that the forest would serve in its green growth to strengthen and multiply the links of mutual regard and respect between Ireland and Israel.[42]

Jacob Herzog, the political director in Eshkol's office, also wrote to Abrahamson on 18 August. While the tone of the letter is appropriately celebratory, the text also contains evidence of the close relationship which continued to exist between de Valera and the Herzog family after Chief Rabbi Isaac Herzog's departure for Palestine in 1937:

> The name of Eamon de Valera is not only enshrined for all time on the tablets of Irish independence. His name is a by-word across the world as one of the pioneers of the present epoch in human history, a central theme of which is the emergence of small countries to independence, their assertion of their freedom and right to pursue their national destiny without external interference and to make their contribution on the international scene in equality.[43]

Herzog continued:

> Eamon de Valera's leadership, integrity, deep humanity and sense of purpose have for many decades now left their imprint on the international community. In Israel it is not forgotten that in the crucial years of struggle for independence, he evinced understanding and sympathy towards the

restoration of Israel in the land of its fathers. The forest which will rise in his name in the Galilee will, I have no doubt, be a lasting symbol of friendship between Ireland and Israel.[44]

He ended his letter on a personal note, recalling memories of 'this great figure' during his childhood in Dublin. He remembered the words of appreciation which he had heard so many years ago about de Valera, and he felt privileged to 'add today my humble tribute to that of his countless admirers in Ireland, in Israel and throughout the world'. Herzog said that, when meeting de Valera over the previous few years, he had been 'deeply moved by his understanding of the spiritual motive of Israel reborn'.[45]

Radio Israel covered the ceremony, and the commentary was given by the former actor and Irish civil servant, Cork-born Laurence Elyan, who had emigrated from Ireland some years before. The prayer recited at the ceremony was as follows:

> In the forest in honour of
> Eamon de Valera
> Make deep their roots and wide their crown
> Amongst all the trees of Israel,
> For good for beauty.

The Irish-born Israeli diplomat, Max Nurock, who was Abrahamson's uncle, spoke at the ceremony. He brought greetings from the Israeli Minister for Foreign Affairs and all the members of his ministry. Nurock recalled his meetings with de Valera going back to when he attended Harcourt Street School. De Valera, then a mathematics teacher at Blackrock College, used to swim with Nurock 'in the cold waters of the Irish Sea in Dublin Bay on many a chilly Irish summer afternoon'. Nurock told the assembly:

> Like a multitude of Jews, in a communion of national aspirations, I followed with eager if unspoken interest the onward and, at last, the successful march of the Irish people to renewed independence. It was an achievement parallel to Israel's own restoration to statehood – from the same alien dominion and, in large measure, by like action. There was the same dedication of leadership and rank and file, there were comparable sacrifices, the same unquenchable spirit flamed in each.[46]

Nurock then went on to find links of kinship between Ireland and Israel going back to ancient times:

> There are credible legends that link the first settlement of Ireland with mysterious voyages from the Land of Israel, almost as soon as Noah's Flood began to ebb. Designations of Irish tribes and princes strangely echo the syllables in the names of the great figures of the Bible's Book of Genesis. The Stone of Tara is claimed to be that whereon the patriarch Jacob reclined in his famous slumber. The Irish and the Jews alike are given to the elegiac note of poetry and to the minor key. Both are hospitable and affable to a fault. Both have prodigious memories, a quality that can at times embarrass.[47]

Nurock surpassed Herzog in his praise of de Valera:

> Among the countless public rewards and recognitions that he has merited
> by outstanding quality and performance as mathematician, soldier and
> statesman, indeed as one of the world's great minds, penetrating, compas-
> sionate and resolute, that distinguished Irishman has richly earned
> today's tribute in Israel by showing himself to be a constant and stalwart
> wellwisher of Jewry and of the Jewish State.[48]

The *Jewish Chronicle* later reported that de Valera was, according to the
chief rabbi of Ireland, Isaac Cohen, 'thrilled' at the honour that had been
accorded him by the dedication of the de Valera Forest at Kfar Kana.[49]

On 4 November 1966, de Valera was presented with the specially
commissioned hand-painted book at Áras an Uachtaráin in the presence of
leading members of the Jewish community.[50] The book carried a number of
tributes. Sarah Herzog, widow of Isaac Herzog, wrote: 'I consider the project
to inaugurate the Eamon de Valera Forest a well deserved tribute to a great
statesman – one who has won the esteem of all peace-loving peoples.' Arthur
Newman wrote: 'No man in my opinion is more deserving to be honoured by
our community than Eamon de Valera.'[51]

The tribute gave de Valera considerable pleasure as may be seen from
Abrahamson's response to a phone call from the President in January 1972:
'I am sorry I missed your kind phone call yesterday, but I am happy that the
thought of your forest in Israel continues to give you so much pleasure. As
you know, it has been a highlight of my life to have the privilege of planting
the first tree in the forest.'[52]

De Valera's closeness with the Herzog family was revealed in a letter he
received from the widow of Jacob Herzog, P'nina, on 20 April 1972, shortly
after the death of her husband:

> It is still only a few desolate weeks since Jacob died, and the anguish of
> my inexpressible loss is deep and enduring. But I find comfort in proud
> retrospect upon his life and works, and upon his manifold friendships. In
> those healing memories, I vividly and thankfully recall your own long
> and close friendship with him, marked as it was, by a very special
> approachability, a warm intimacy and a welcome regard. He spoke
> always of the inspiration and the knowledge with which his meetings
> with you, each time that he visited his birthplace in Ireland, were
> enriched. He felt for you the affection and admiring respect of a privi-
> leged disciple.[53]

P'nina Herzog asked de Valera to contribute a chapter to a book which was
being published in honour of her husband.[54] De Valera, because of his position as President, reluctantly felt obliged to refuse the invitation.

The gesture by the Irish Jewish community had a strong impact on those
who knew de Valera well. He had forged a deep friendship with leading
members of the Jewish community during the War of Independence and
afterwards. Those Irish Jews who knew the Fianna Fáil leader during the
interwar years remembered with gratitude his support during the time of the
Blueshirts and the period of Nazi triumph in Europe. But for all his closeness

to the Jewish community, de Valera's visit to the German minister following the death of Hitler in May 1945 was not, and never will be, forgotten.

Cearbhall Ó Dálaigh

Born and reared in Bray, Co. Wicklow, Cearbhall Ó Dálaigh – Irish scholar, journalist, attorney general, chief justice and later a member of the Court of Justice of the European Communities – was also known to be a lifelong friend of the Jewish community in Dublin. When asked by Gabriel Fallon in a letter on 20 February 1967 to become the first patron of the Ireland–Israel Friendship League, he wrote: 'Yes, it will be an honour to lend a hand. Yes.'[55] In 1971, he was invited to contribute the foreword to Louis Hyman's *The Jews of Ireland: From Earliest Times to the Year 1910*. He did so with great diffidence:

> Have you not, at some time or other, when sitting in a theatre, eagerly awaiting the beginning of the play, felt a sense of annoyance as an uncostumed non-actor has stepped brashly through the curtains and begun to chatter about something or other. The writer of a foreword is just such an uncostumed *non-actor*, and is, equally, a source of annoyance. . . . It is a privilege to be permitted to share a little, however unworthily, in the permanence which, I don't doubt, Louis Hyman's book will achieve.[56]

Ó Dálaigh became President of Ireland in 1974, his inauguration taking place at Dublin Castle on 19 December. He made time that evening to attend a special divine service in the Adelaide Road Synagogue in honour of the occasion, and he was the first President of Ireland to so mark his inauguration. He was conducted to a seat of honour by District Justice Herman Good, by Hubert Wine, chairman of the Jewish Representative Council, and by the council's honorary life president, Maurice Abrahamson. Chief Rabbi Isaac Cohen said in his address that the new President was no stranger to the Jewish community:

> Since his early youth he shared with many of our co-religionists the joys and the adventures, the anxieties and the hopes that have been experienced in our own Jewish life. His passionate love of learning, his breadth of humanity and his admiration of the achievements and hopes of the State of Israel have fashioned unbreakable ties of affection, esteem and honour in the hearts of the Jewish citizens of this great country.[57]

Cohen's remarks merely reflected the fact that Ó Dálaigh had many personal friends in the Irish Jewish community. He was to remain a good friend of that community throughout his short presidency. Resigning on 22 October 1976 following an incident in which the Minister for Defence spoke intemperately about him in his capacity as President, Ó Dálaigh retired to Sneem, Co. Kerry. He died suddenly at home as a result of a heart attack on 21 March 1978. The Jewish community was represented at his funeral in Sneem by Chief Rabbi Isaac Cohen. The chief rabbi angered some members of the Jewish community by standing outside the church, not being permitted by his priestly lineage to come within a certain distance of a dead body.[58] About two years later, the Irish Friends of the Hebrew University in Jerusalem endowed a lecture hall in the law faculty of that university on Mount Scopus, in memory of and as a tribute to Cearbhall Ó Dálaigh. His widow, Mrs Ó Dálaigh, was present at the ceremony, accompanied by the chairman of the JRC, Hubert Wine. The ceremony was attended by many Irish friends living in Israel.

Lingering anti-Semitism

The anti-Semitism which, as has been seen, lingered on in Irish society in the post-war decades was still evident in the 1970s to a perhaps surprising extent. In 1978 Micheál Mac Gréil published the results of a survey on prejudice and tolerance in Ireland, focusing particularly on Dublin. He concluded that the survey

> established the existence of a moderate degree of anti-Semitic prejudice in Dublin. The pattern of this prejudice is along classical lines, i.e., the negative monetary and religious myths are still believed by a significant percentage of Dublin adults.[59]

The table of findings on which Mac Gréil based this conclusion is worth reproducing in full.[60]

Findings of the Mac Gréil Survey, 1978
With regard to the Jews would you agree or disagree?

Statement	Agree (%)	Don't know (%)	Disagree (%)	P-score*	No.
1. That it would be good for the country to have many Jews in positions of responsibility in business	45.6	12.5	*41.9*	94.3	2,291
2. That Jews are a bad influence on Christian culture and civilization	*11.2*	5.6	83.2	28.0	2,290
3. That Jews have moral standards when dealing with each other but with Christians they are ruthless and unscrupulous	*22.2*	10.8	67.1	55.1	2,288
4. That it is wrong for Jews and Christians to intermarry	*27.7*	6.1	66.2	61.6	2,290
5. That golf clubs or similar organizations are justified in denying membership to a person because he or she is a Jew	*5.2*	2.0	92.8	12.5	2,290

	Agree	Don't know	Disagree	P-score*	No.
6. That Jews as a people are to blame for the crucifixion of Christ	15.8	8.5	75.7	40.0	2,283
7. That Jews do not take a proper interest in community problems and government	29.3	15.9	54.8	74.5	2,278
8. That Jewish power and control in money matters are far out of proportion to the number of Jews	57.3	17.6	25.1	132.2	2,289
9. That Jews are behind the money lending rackets in Dublin	49.2	22.8	28.0	121.3	2,291
10. That we should encourage Irish Jews just as much as anybody else to take up positions of importance in Irish life	84.6	4.1	*11.3*	26.7	2,290
Scale P-score				64.6	

*P-score = 100 (M-1)   *Note*: Negative scores are in bold italic.

The most negative responses were to items which had commercial or financial implications (See Nos. 1, 8 and 9). That was very much in line with the negative stereotypes of Jews. Nearly 60 per cent of those surveyed agreed that Jews were overrepresented in the control of money matters, while only 25 per cent disagreed with that view. The survey concludes that

> this exceptionally high percentage of agreement with an unsubstantiated allegation against the Jews, may be attributed to anti-Semitic prejudice and the acceptance by the vast majority of respondents of the common stereotypical view of the Jews as the controllers of money matters today.[61]

The results of the survey in relation to statement No. 9, where half of the sample agreed with the view that Jews were behind the money-lending rackets in Dublin while only 28 per cent disagreed, would support this conclusion.

The author of the survey felt that particular attention should also be paid to statement No. 6, where one-sixth of those polled agreed with the proposition that 'The Jews as a people are to blame for the crucifixion of Christ'. Mac Gréil wrote:

> For a minority . . . to be convicted of deicide, or the 'killing of Christ', is most serious in a society like Ireland. The evidence, then, of Item No. 6 above concerning the *ascription of blame* to the Jews as a people for the crucifixion of Christ merits serious attention.[62]

No question was asked on the Holocaust in this survey. But overall, its findings revealed a level of anti-Semitism which might not have been readily acknowledged in Irish society.

The survey, it is worth noting, was conducted over a decade after 2,221 Catholic bishops had, on 28 October 1965, added their signature to that of Pope Paul VI on the document *Nostra Aetate* ('In Our Time'), which was the Second Vatican Council's Declaration on the Relationship of the Church to Non-Christian Religions.[63] *Nostra Aetate* repudiated and deplored 'all hatreds, persecutions and displays of anti-Semitism directed against Jews at any time and from any source'. Pope John XXIII had acted earlier to remove some of the more blatant forms of the 'teaching of contempt' against Jews and Judaism which had found their way into the Roman rite. He had removed the phrase 'perfidious Jews' from the Good Friday prayer for Jews. Paul VI revised the prayer, which became one 'For the Jews' rather than 'For the conversion of the Jews'.[64] *Nostra Aetate* was implemented in Ireland in accordance with the 1974 Vatican guidelines for Catholic–Jewish relations.

Speaking to the Jewish leaders of Australia on 26 November 1986, Pope John Paul II said:

> For the Jewish people themselves, Catholics should have not only respect but also great fraternal love for it is the teaching of both the Hebrew and the Christian Scriptures that the Jews are beloved of God, who has called them with an irrevocable calling. No valid theological justification could ever be found for acts of discrimination or persecution against Jews. In fact such acts must be held to be sinful.

Earlier that year, while on a historic visit to the principal synagogue in Rome on 13 April, the Pope said:

> Today's visit is meant to make a decisive contribution to the consolidation of the good relations between our two communities, in imitation of the example of so many men and women who have worked and who are still working today, on both sides, to overcome old prejudices and to secure even wider and fuller recognition of that 'bond' and that 'common spiritual patrimony' that exists between Jews and Christians.

He declared that 'you are our dear beloved brothers and, in a certain way, it could be said that you are our elder brothers'. He continued:

> a considerable amount of time will still be needed, notwithstanding the great efforts already made on both sides, to remove all forms of prejudice, even subtle ones, to readjust every manner of self expression and there-fore to present always and everywhere to ourselves and to others, the true face of Jews and Judaism, as likewise of Christians and of Christianity, and this at every level of outlook, teaching and communication.

The Chief Rabbi of Italy, Elio Toaff, replied:

> Thus, we cannot forget the past, but today we wish to begin, with faith and hope, this new historical phase, which fruitfully points the way to

common understanding finally carried out in a plane of equality and mutual esteem in the interest of humanity.

The chief rabbi concluded: 'We have here a bond which, notwithstanding our differences, makes us brethren; it is an unfathomable mystery of grace which we dare to scrutinise in confidence, grateful to a God who grants us to contemplate together his plan of salvation.' The Holy See established formal diplomatic relations with Israel in 1994.

That spirit of dialogue has been embraced in Ireland by a group of highly dedicated religious and lay people. The Irish Council of Christians and Jews, in the tradition of the short-lived Pillar of Fire Society of the early 1940s, is helping to foster greater understanding in the Ireland of the 1990s. It demonstrates the lengths travelled since the inter-war deprecations of Fr Denis Fahey and those clerical voices in many parts of the Catholic world he so stridently represented.

Micheál Mac Gréil published a further study on prejudice in Irish society in 1996. The survey registered a relatively high level of prejudice towards Jews in the more rural areas of Ireland. A significant minority, 20 per cent, regarded Jews as being responsible for the crucifixion of Christ; this was 4 percentage points higher than the Dublin-based survey two decades earlier. The 'money matters' stereotype had declined since the 1970s. He concluded cautiously that 'on balance, the situation is moderately positive with room for improvement' on the question of anti-Semitism.[65]

Nevertheless, anti-Semitism continued to manifest itself in Ireland in the latter part of the century in the ranks of rightist Catholic groups and diminutive branches of British neo-fascist organisations. But these groups have been as unrepresentative as their actions have been inconsequential. The proximity of England meant that Dublin was sometimes seen as a convenient outpost in which to locate anti-Semitic printing operations. This was so in the 1970s in the case of the National Socialist Irish Workers' Party. Working out of a house in a poor area of Dublin, the party sought the 'repatriation' of Jews, Asians and Blacks, and stated that if that was not done the Irish would lose their distinctive culture.[66] An offshoot of a British neo-fascist organisation, its activities were closely observed by the gardaí. It attracted no more than a handful of followers in the capital. In the 1980s Cork also had a short-lived neo-fascist organisation, again working out of a house in one of the poorer parts of the city. But Ireland has not proved a fertile recruiting ground for international neo-fascist organisations.

Throughout the post-war period in Ireland, therefore, there was a need to address certain deficits in the civic culture concerning attitudes to minorities. However, where sensitivity developed in this area, it was substantially in reference to the crisis in Northern Ireland. From the 1960s onwards, Dr Garret FitzGerald and other leading politicians sought to emphasise the diversity of the Irish historical tradition and the growing pluralism of Irish society. The question of anti-Semitism is a matter which ought to receive greater reflection and action in the years to come.

Irish Jews and the wider community

Immanuel Jakobovits's comments on the diffidence of Irish Jews about becoming involved in politics were no longer applicable by the 1970s. For example, Gerald Goldberg, a distinguished member of the minuscule Jewish community in Cork, served as an independent member of Cork Corporation for eight years from 1967. He joined Fianna Fáil, and in 1977 he became the first Jewish lord mayor of Cork in the eight hundred years of the mayoralty; later, he commented sadly but accurately that he was also 'very likely its last'.[67] There were three Jewish members in the 27th Dáil which sat between 1991 and 1997. Ben Briscoe, son of Robert, was a member of Fianna Fáil. Mervyn Taylor, a lawyer and member of the Labour Party, was Minister for Equality and Law Reform.[68] Alan Shatter, also a lawyer, was a Fine Gael TD – the first in the history of the party. The Blueshirts of the 1930s cast a long shadow in the Irish Jewish community. Attracted by the ideas of the liberal wing of the party in the 1970s, Shatter broke with tradition.

A brief audit of the contributions of Jews to Irish life – many of which will already be familiar to the reader – reveals that the community has contributed disproportionately to its numbers. It should be emphasised that these examples are indicative rather than exhaustive. In the world of learning there were the contributions of Dr Jacob Weingreen, professor of Hebrew at Trinity College Dublin, and the literary criticism of A. J. (Con) Leventhal from the same university. The Solomons and Abrahamson families were very prominent in the medical profession. Bethel Solomons's son, Michael, was also a medical doctor and president of the Jewish Progressive Congregation. The Eppel and Freedman families were also associated with medicine. Michael Noyk and Bernard Shillman were distinguished members of the Irish legal profession. Herman Good, Hubert Wine and Henry Barron served in the judiciary. Hubert Wine and Mervyn Taylor both worked for a time in Herman Good's legal practice which had a large concentration of clients from very poor areas in the city.

Judge Hubert Wine retired in 1992 after sixteen years on the bench. He gave distinguished service for fourteen years as chairman of the Jewish Representative Council of Ireland, and was its honorary president in the 1990s. He will long be remembered for the manner in which he provided leadership for the Jewish community in Ireland from the 1960s. He will also be remembered as a strong humanitarian and a dedicated solicitor. If his grandfather had had his way, Hubert Wine would have entered the well-known family antique business in Dublin. But his early successes in court neutralised the scepticism of his grandfather, who took great pride in his grandson's chosen career.

Judge Wine's stand in 1989 which brought the issue of the inadequacy of care facilities for juvenile offenders to public notice deserves particular attention.[69] He refused to remand a 15-year-old girl to Mountjoy prison or allow the Director of Public Prosecutions (DPP) to withdraw charges against her of grievous bodily harm to another minor. The girl's foster mother, who was also the mother of the injured minor, had, as was her right, issued these proceedings; she had applied to the DPP, who agreed on the facts to prosecute the charge against the 15-year-old. It should be noted that the charges and proceedings could not be withdrawn by the DPP without the foster mother's consent. It appeared that although the foster mother had alleged that the 15-year-old had inflicted serious injuries to her son, nevertheless she loved her foster child and felt it was in the child's best interests to have the matter brought before the court. In view of the special circumstance of this case, and the evidence that was later adduced, she was correct, and courageous, in her decision.

Judge Wine insisted that the young girl be given a place in a suitable detention centre where she would have proper counselling. Unbelievably, no such centre for girls existed in the country at the time. The case proceeded and there were many remands. After two months, during which the unfortunate girl threatened, and attempted, to commit suicide on more than one occasion, counsel for the DPP applied to the court that a *nolle prosequi* be entered. In view of the foster mother's continued refusal, the judge refused the DPP's application, and counsel, on the instructions of the DPP, left the court and did not return.

During the next three months, and without a prosecutor, Judge Wine called many witnesses from the assessment team of twenty-four people including psychiatrists, psychologists, doctors, specialists, social workers and probation officers who were dealing with the accused's case. As a result of their sworn testimony, he made many pleas to the three ministers who had responsibility for the case (Justice, Education and Health), and, when unheeded, he referred publicly to 'passing the buck' from one minister to the other. The matter became so serious that it was raised in Dáil Éireann on several occasions. 'Eventually', he said, 'after much silence, many promises and commitments were made, but never kept.'

Following the intervention of the Taoiseach, Charles Haughey, the judge, with the consent of the foster mother and five months after the case had first commenced, withdrew the charges on 1 March 1990 on certain conditions being fulfilled. The conditions were that a house be provided for her immediately with psychiatrists, psychologists, probation officers, social welfare officers and doctors who would be on call twenty-four hours a day until she was well again. Cast-iron assurances were given in open court by the Eastern Health Board's solicitor.

Judge Wine thanked the Eastern Health Board, the fire brigade who had saved her on many occasions, the gardaí, and, particularly, the social welfare officers and probation officers, who, night after night, found a safe place for her over a lengthy period. Without their help, he said, this tragic problem would never have been resolved. 'Even if it were for one little soul who was saved it was worth it', he later recalled, adding 'I would do it again, but as I said at the time, "This is only the tip of the iceberg."' The Child Care Act, which addressed many of the issues raised by the case, became law in 1991.

In May 1996, Judge Wine spoke in three languages, Irish, Hebrew and English, at the Hebrew University, Mount Scopus, Jerusalem on the occasion of the endowment of a lecture room in his name in the law faculty. The plaque read: 'To an outstanding leader of the Dublin Jewish Community'.[70] The ceremony was attended by some 200 people including the former President of Israel, Chaim Herzog. Many messages were received at the function which followed, amongst which was one from President Mary Robinson:

> It gives me great pleasure to extend warm personal greetings to Judge Hubert Wine who is being honoured by the Irish Friends of the Hebrew University of Jerusalem. The endowment of a lecture room is ... an imaginative way of marking the dedicated contribution that Hubert Wine has made during his time as a solicitor and as a judge. ...[71]

The President of the Hebrew University, Professor Hanoch Gutfreund, said that Judge Wine's name had become 'a byword in Ireland for compassion and concern in the best tradition of the legal profession'.[72]

Mervyn Taylor was very much in the legal reform tradition of both Wine and Good; indeed Good's involvement in the Labour Party was largely instrumental in bringing Taylor into active politics. As Minister for Equality and Law Reform in successive coalitions in the mid-1990s – the Fianna Fáil/Labour government of 1993–4 and the Rainbow coalition of Fine Gael, Labour and Democratic Left, 1994–7 – Taylor's place in Irish political history is assured. Not only was he the first member of the Jewish community to hold ministerial office, he was also the first holder of the Equality and Law Reform portfolio, it being established in 1993 as part of the Labour Party's programme for government with Fianna Fáil. And the list of initiatives of this department under his stewardship is impressive. Mervyn Taylor was responsible, for instance, for having the report of the Commission on the Status of People with Disabilities completed in November 1996. A landmark report in a long-neglected area, it made 402 recommendations; an interdepartmental committee was then established to consider the implementation of the report. The Domestic Violence Act, which strengthens the power of the courts to make orders for the protection of persons in the home, came into force on 27 March 1996. The Council of Europe's Convention on the Exercise of Children's Rights was signed on 25 January 1996. His department was also responsible for the passage of the Civil Legal Aid Act, the Powers of Attorney Act, the Employment Equality Act and the Equal Status Act.[73] Taylor also had responsibility for overseeing the introduction of divorce in Ireland. He handled with great sensitivity the government's successful campaign to have the constitutional ban on divorce removed in the 1995 referendum, and he then prepared the legislation – the Family Law Divorce Act 1996 – which makes divorce legal in Ireland.

The contribution of members of the Jewish community to the world of arts and culture has been equally noteworthy. The late Victor Waddington was a gallery owner and promoter of the arts in Ireland. He was responsible for discovering and promoting Irish artists like Colin Middleton and George Campbell. The painter Gerald Davis runs a gallery in Dublin. Harry Kernoff, Estella Solomons and Stella Steyn were Jewish painters of distinction. The German graphic designer and calligrapher, Elizabeth Friedlander, who spent most of her life working in England, retired to Kinsale in County Cork and died in the home of her close friends, Sheila and Gerald Goldberg.[74] Dr Isaac Eppel was a pioneer of Irish cinema. The civil servant Laurence Elyan, who later went to live in Israel, was a creative and innovative force in Irish theatre, as was Carolyn Swift, a founder of the Pike Theatre in the 1950s.[75]

Hannah Berman was among the first novelists to emerge from the Jewish community in Dublin in the early years of the century. A few generations later, David Marcus, as literary editor of the *Irish Press*, played an important role in fostering young writers and poets through his justly renowned 'New Irish Writing' page. Marcus is also the author of a collection of short stories entitled *Who ever heard of an Irish Jew and other short stories* and the novel *A Land not Theirs*. His brother, Louis Marcus, is a distinguished film-maker, as is another member of the Jewish community, Louis Lentin. In the world of music, Dina Copeman and the concert pianist Estelle Wine, sister of Judge Hubert Wine, must be mentioned as might many others who have contributed to the intellectual, cultural and professional life of the country.

The Jewish community in Ireland has also contributed much to the sporting arena. For example, Bethel Solomons was capped ten times for Ireland in rugby, Louis Bookman played football for Ireland four times between 1914 and 1922, and Hubert Wine played table tennis for Ireland.[76] In all, no less than twenty-one Irish sportsmen of the Jewish faith have represented their country at cricket, fencing, golf and athletics as well as the sports already mentioned. Fr Michael O'Carroll, a Holy Ghost priest who himself has made a distinguished contribution to Jewish–Christian dialogue since the 1940s, has stated that the Jewish community has made a contribution to the life of the nation 'out of all proportion to its numbers'.[77]

Remembering the Holocaust

Mary Robinson, elected President of Ireland in 1990, continued the tradition of excellent relations between the Irish head of state and the Jewish community. She did much to demonstrate in a practical way her deep awareness of the suffering of Jews in the twentieth century. She visited Auschwitz-Birkenau on 23 June 1994 and laid a wreath at the Death Wall. Before leaving the camp, she wrote in the visitors' book:

> On my own behalf and of the people Ireland I have come to pay deep respect, to honour the victims, and to remember the terrible deeds in this place. We must always remember the inhumanity of man to men, to women and to children. Only if we remember will we remain eternally vigilant. Sadly, that vigilance is needed in our world today.[78]

Asked by a Polish journalist at Birkenau whether the concentration camps should not be destroyed completely rather than being preserved, she responded:

> I do not share that view. I believe that it is very important that not only the place would remain, but that it would remain as authentically as it remains at the moment. I know that it is difficult, and I know that for

some families in particular it must be almost too painful to come. We must come here. We must take on board what happened here. We must do it because it must not be allowed to recur. And yet, we know in our hearts that the ingredients of racism, of anti-Semitism, of ethnic hatred are there, and none of us can be complacent or feel that we don't need places like this. Yet we do. It is most important that you keep and you value as I do the opportunity – that is, to see at first hand the capacity for inhumanity that is with us – so that it may bring out the capacity for compassion, for tolerance, for reaching out to each other and for being open to each other.[79]

Her thoughts then turned to home: 'I know that this is a very special place for all Jewish communities, and I thought of our own Jewish community in Ireland, our small but beloved Jewish community. Some of them have lost relatives, close family, here.'[80] President Robinson said that it was important not just to remember, but to feel chastened, 'because this is not something that we can say comfortably, it is of the past, it is over'.[81] She went on:

Unfortunately, there can always be a resurgence of racism, of anti-Semitism, of ethnic violence. We see it in Europe, sadly. We see it elsewhere in the world. I am glad to come here as the first President of Ireland to visit Poland. It was important for me that I came here.[82]

Senior Irish politicians shared President Robinson's concern not to allow the fiftieth anniversary of the liberation of the death camps pass without showing Irish solidarity with the victims of the Holocaust; the Taoiseach, John Bruton, took steps to mark officially the liberation of Bergen-Belsen. Despite initial confusion caused by the choice of Saturday 15 April 1995 – the Jewish Sabbath and the first day of Passover – the date of the ceremony was rearranged.[83]

The Fine Gael TD, Alan Shatter, reviewed at that time the Irish government's wartime policy towards refugees and commented:

There has never been a State ceremony in Ireland to commemorate the 6 million Jews who were murdered in the Holocaust. There has never been any official expression of regret from any Irish government at the State's refusal to admit into Ireland the many Jews fleeing from Nazi terror.[84]

A joint commemoration of the liberation of Bergen-Belsen by the Jewish community and the Ireland–Israel Friendship League was announced for 26 April 1995. John Bruton was invited to attend the ceremony and to give an address. Included in the attendance were Holocaust survivors resident in Ireland, as well as the children and grandchildren of survivors. The congregation of 400 was drawn from all the churches, business and labour associations, and other civic groups.[85]

In his speech, the Taoiseach said: 'We in Ireland have not been immune from the bigotry and the indifference which manifested themselves in Europe this century.'[86] He acknowledged that official Irish archives had revealed that Ireland's doors 'were not freely open to those families and individuals fleeing from persecution and death'.[87] He said that some people did find refuge and comfort in Ireland, but their numbers were not very great. We must acknowledge the consequences of this indifference. As a society we have become more willing to accept our responsibility to respond to events beyond our shores. Tonight, on behalf of the Irish government and people I honour the memory of those millions of European Jews who died in the Holocaust.[88]

The Taoiseach stated that fifty years after the liberation of the death camps 'the recognition of the colossal evil enacted in these places is branded deep in the moral conscience of modern man'. He pointed out that the Holocaust did not take place in a far distant place or a far distant time: 'It was not the product of an alien culture. It happened in Europe in living memory. It was a product of intolerance, bigotry and a distorted concept of nationalism.' It was, he said,

first and foremost a crime against the Jewish people; more fundamentally it was a crime against all humanity. Its memory must always be kept alive. I would again quote Primo Levi when he said – 'It happened, therefore it can happen again.' Too much in today's world tells us that we have yet to grasp the full significance of this fact.[89]

Those sentiments, which are shared by all political parties in the country, have influenced two relevant pieces of legislation – the Prohibition of Incitement to Hatred Act 1989 and the Refugee Act 1997. (Ireland became a party to the 1967 New York protocol on refugees in November 1968.)

In the latter part of the 1990s, the refugee problem in Ireland has intensified in a manner reminiscent of the 1930s. The Irish Refugee Council records that the numbers seeking asylum in Ireland increased by 278 per cent between 1995 and 1996. There were 1,179 asylum seekers in 1996, compared with 39 in 1992.[90] The number had risen to 2,992 in September 1997. That new situation will – in a Europe where racism is on the increase – test the tolerance of Irish society in the twenty-first century. Leopold Bloom's words remain ever relevant: 'Force, hatred, history, all that. That's not life for men and women, insult and hatred.'[91]

This book ends where it began – in Lithuania. A niece of Gerald Goldberg, Adele Shillman and her husband, Lex Cohen, made a visit to Lithuania in August 1989 to retrace the steps of Adele's ancestors who fled persecution in Akmene (Akmijan) and in the surrounding area in the 1880s, travelled to Riga and then took ship downriver for the Baltic and freedom.[92] The industrial town of Akmene today is about twelve kilometres away from the old village which was once the home of Gerald Goldberg's family and of many of the Jews who came to Ireland in the 1880s and 1890s. There is a square in the village with a large church, which has a commemoration stone, 1557–1977. The villagers, mainly tradesmen and farm labourers, speak Lithuanian but no Russian. Once the Jewish community of Akmene lived in the houses clustered around that square. Once a synagogue, or possibly two, stood off the square. They were destroyed during one wave of anti-Semitism or another; pogroms conducted under the tsars, followed a few generations later by the Holocaust, have ensured that no visible remnants of Jewish culture are to be found in the village itself. On the outskirts of the village a madonna-like figure, carved from a tree trunk, stands at the entrance to the remains of what was once a thriving centre of Jewish culture. Nearby is the old Jewish cemetery with tombstones scattered among the trees. Adele recalled:

> . . . and as I stood beside Lex at the edge of the cemetery and he recited a *Kaddish* [prayer and blessing] for all of us, a quiet feeling of peace permeated my being. They, our forbears, slept quietly together as a *chevra* [group] having lived their lives with dignity and *yiddishkeit* [Jewishness] within a pale. They had taught their sons well and as I stood there . . . I said, 'Yes, we have freedom, we do not live within a pale; we have a life of dignity and affluence beyond anything you could have imagined and yes – you did well to let us go for we have not perished at the hands of the Litvaks nor been devoured by the teeth of the Holocaust – and yes the ways of *avinu malkenu* [Our Father, our King], the ways you taught, are with us and *mir Hashem* [God willing] will always be so.'[93]

Religion, culture and society throughout the island of Ireland have been enriched by the presence of Jews whose parents and grandparents – or many of them – found a haven of hope free from pogroms in the late nineteenth century. However, in the mid-twentieth century, Ireland failed to respond generously – even adequately – to the unprecedented humanitarian challenge posed by the rise of Nazism and by the Holocaust. Primo Levi's poem 'Shema', written on 10 January 1946, serves as a permanent reminder of the legacy of that failure and as an exhortation to do better next time:

> You who live secure
> In your warm houses,
> Who return at evening to find
> Hot food and friendly faces:
>
>> Consider whether this is a man,
>> Who labours in the mud
>> Who knows no peace
>> Who fights for a crust of bread
>> Who dies at a yes or a no.
>> Consider whether this is a woman,
>> Without hair or name
>> With no more strength to remember
>> Eyes empty and womb cold
>> As a frog in winter.
>
> Consider that this has been:
> I commend these words to you.
> Engrave them on your hearts
> When you are in your house, when you walk on your way,
> When you go to bed, when you rise.
> Repeat them to your children.
> Or may your house crumble,
> Disease render you powerless,
> Your offspring avert their faces from you.[94]

Notes and references

Introduction

1 Published by Blackstaff Press, Belfast, 1992.
2 I would like to pay tribute to these authors, on whom I have relied very heavily during the writing of this volume: see Louis Hyman, *The Jews of Ireland: From Earliest Times to the Year 1910* (Irish University Press, Shannon, 1972) and Bernard Shillman, *A Short History of the Jews in Ireland* (Eason, Dublin, 1945).

1: The Russian pogroms and the growth of the Jewish community in Ireland

1 P. L. S. Quinn, 'The Re-entry of the Jew into England and Ireland and His Re-establishment There' (PhD, University College Cork, 1966).
2 Louis Hyman, *The Jews of Ireland: From Earliest Times to the Year 1910* (Irish University Press, Shannon, 1972), p. 155.
3 Quinn, 'The Re-entry of the Jew into England and Ireland', p. 578; see also Hyman, *Jews of Ireland*, pp. 124–32.
4 See Bernard Shillman, *A Short History of the Jews in Ireland* (Eason, Dublin, 1945), p. 76.
5 The small community set about trying to raise funds. Some help was received from Sir Moses Montefiore, who was a frequent visitor to the synagogue. Money was also received from other sources in London. Quinn, 'The Re-entry of the Jew into England and Ireland', p. 582.
6 Hyman, *Jews of Ireland*, p. 155.
7 Quinn, 'The Re-entry of the Jew into England and Ireland', p. 576.
8 Shillman, *Jews in Ireland*, p. 75.
9 ibid.
10 Hyman, *Jews of Ireland*, p. 114.
11 Shillman, *Jews in Ireland*, p. 76.
12 Hyman, *Jews of Ireland*, p. 158.
13 David Cesarani, 'Great Britain', in David Wyman (ed.), *The World Reacts to the Holocaust* (Johns Hopkins University Press, Baltimore and London, 1996), p. 600.
14 Hyman, *Jews of Ireland*, pp. 120–1.

15   ibid., p. 122.
16   ibid., pp. 142–5.
17   ibid., pp. 145–6.
18   See Shillman, *Jews in Ireland*, pp. 90–1 and Hyman, *Jews of Ireland*, p. 110.
19   Hyman, *Jews of Ireland*, p. 147.
20   ibid., p. 148.
21   ibid. The libel case is discussed below in chapter 4. It may be of interest to note here that the leading member of the Irish Parliamentary Party, William O'Brien, married a Jew who converted to Catholicism. Her maiden name was Raffalovich. The mother of Charles Stewart Parnell was also of Jewish extraction. See Shillman, *Jews in Ireland*, p. 114.
22   Shillman, *Jews in Ireland*, p. 134.
23   Census of Ireland, 1891; I am grateful to Dr Caroline Windrum, Institute of Irish Studies, Queen's University Belfast, for providing me with this data.
24   Hyman, *Jews of Ireland*, pp. 204–5. Other founding members of the congregation were Julian Weimberg and Herman Boas, father of the Shakespearean scholar, Frederick Samuel. Julius Loewenthal and Max Veital were also prominent. Dr Joseph Chotzner of Cracow was the first minister of the congregation.
25   ibid., pp. 208–9.
26   Michael Davitt, *Within the Pale: The True Story of Anti-Semitic Persecutions in Russia* (Hurst and Blackett, London, 1903), pp. 26–9.
27   ibid., p. 29.
28   David Cesarani, *The Jewish Chronicle and Anglo-Jewry 1841–1991* (Cambridge University Press, Cambridge, 1994), p. 70; see also Nancy and Stuart Schoenburg, *Lithuanian Jewish Communities* (Garland Publishing, New York, 1991), p. 32.
29   Letter from Len Yodaiken, Kibbutz Kfar Hanasai, to Hubert Wine, 19 February 1993. Copy of letter in manuscript of Nurock and Abrahamson family history in possession of Maurice Abrahamson, Dublin.
30   ibid.
31   ibid.
32   ibid.; see also Schoenburg, *Lithuanian Jewish Communities*, pp. 401–17.
33   See CSORP, 1905/23538, NAI.
34   Interview with Frederick Rosehill, Cork, October 1996.
35   ibid.
36   Shillman, *Jews in Ireland*, p. 136.
37   Interviews with Gerald Goldberg, Cork, 1995–97.
38   This account is based on Des Ryan, 'Jewish Immigrants in Limerick – A Divided Community', in David Lee (ed.), *Limerick Remembered* (Limerick Civic Trust, Limerick, 1997), pp. 167–70.
39   See Indenture of Conveyance, 17 February 1902 by William Nunan and Hyman Graff; solicitor, James A. Doyle, 56 George Street, Limerick. This document was kindly supplied by Denis Leonard, Limerick Civic Trust. A plaque in the prayer house carries the names in Hebrew in the following order, Moshe Yakov Blond, Dovid Tzvi Krofman, Moshe Yosef Grenfeld, Lev Tovye Klein, Chaim Shalom Krofman, Boruch Bnedet Shochat, Shrage Dov Grif, Dov Guld, Yitzkak Aranoff, Rabbi Eli Dov Levin, Chaim Meir Graf, Yeheskel Dov Graf, Shaul Zerom, Mordechai Lev Yaffe, Chaim Zeev Meisel, Boruch Yaffe, Zeev Toohey, Shrage Mordechai Toohey, Binzion Moshe Meizel and Aaron Shabbtai Yaffe. The inscription is: For posterity may the names of the founders be remembered for good – O you who dwell in the shelter of the most high.
40   Information kindly supplied to me by Limerick Civic Trust.

41 Gerald Goldberg, 'Note on the Jewish Community in Cork', in Shillman, *Jews in Ireland*, p. 141.

42 ibid.

43 John Crowley, 'Narrative and Place: A Cultural History of the South Parish' (MA, University College Cork, 1993), p. 80.

44 Interview with Gerald Goldberg, Cork, December 1995. Fully intending to emigrate to the United States, Louis Goldberg set out with his family on two occasions to take the boat at Cobh. He changed his mind the first time and returned to the city. The next time his daughter required medical attention after she got her hand caught in a door at the station. This he took as an omen to remain in Cork. He did so, and Cork was the richer for that decision. He died on 22 December 1932.

45 ibid.

46 Hyman, *Jews of Ireland*, p. 218.

47 Interview with Frederick Rosehill, Cork, October 1996; Gerald Goldberg opened a footbridge across the River Lee when he was lord mayor of Cork. Close to the synagogue, it was named Holy Trinity bridge, but quickly became known as the 'passover'.

48 Hyman, *Jews of Ireland*, p. 218.

49 Gerald Goldberg in Shillman, *Jews in Ireland*, p. 142.

50 Shillman, *Jews in Ireland*, p. 95.

51 ibid.

52 Hyman, *Jews of Ireland*, pp. 164–5.

53 ibid., p. 165.

54 ibid., p. 209.

55 ibid., p. 195.

56 With accommodation for 300 male worshippers in the body and over 150 women in the gallery, this fine edifice had been built for a total cost of £5,000. An adjoining area contained a number of schoolrooms which could hold up to 200 students.

57 Quoted in Ira B. Nadel, *Joyce and the Jews: Culture and Texts* (University Press of Florida, Gainesville, 1996), p. 186.

58 Hyman, *Jews of Ireland*, p. 210. No satisfactory explanation has been provided for this outbreak of violence. Hyman speculates that a maid-servant in the household observed the ritual slaughter of a fowl, and anti-Jewish rumours spread in the community.

59 ibid., p. 211; *Cork Examiner*, quoted in *Jewish Chronicle*, 25 April 1884.

60 Hyman, *Jews of Ireland*, p. 211.

61 ibid., pp. 218–20.

62 ibid., p. 221.

63 ibid., p. 222; Another member of the Irish Parliamentary Party, Justin McCarthy, wrote on 9 May that the reports of attacks on the homes of Jews in Cork had filled him with surprise and regret: 'The Irish people are in strong political sympathy with the Jews.' He referred to Thomas Moore's frequent comparison between the Irish race and that of the 'Sad One of Zion'. McCarthy stated that the ill-treatment of Jews 'is regarded with utter detestation by every Irish nationalist'. See ibid.

64 Quoted in ibid., pp. 161–2.

65 'Ireland and the Jews', letter to the editor from Michael Davitt, *Freeman's Journal*, 13 July 1893.

66 ibid.

67 ibid.

68 ibid.

69   ibid.
70   'The Jew in Ireland', *Lyceum*, Vol. VI, No. 70 (July 1893), pp. 215–18. Fr
     Thomas Finlay, the Jesuit social reformer and promoter of the co-operative
     movement, wrote a series of articles in the *Lyceum* in 1892–93; in these he did
     not express his opposition to Jews on grounds of race, religion or nationality
     but rather on their alleged involvement in moneylending. See Fr Thomas
     Finlay, 'The Jew Amongst Us', *Lyceum*, Vol. VI, No. 71, p. 235, which refers to
     the use of Christian blood in the making of Jewish ceremonial bread; *Lyceum*,
     June, July, August/September 1892, Vol. V, Nos. 58, 59, 60, pp. 195, 221 and
     256 respectively. See also Thomas Finlay, 'A Model Masonic Government', Vol.
     VI, No. 67, p. 153. Reference supplied by Fr Brian Murphy, Glenstal Abbey,
     County Limerick. Fr Tom Morrissey confirms that a copy of the *Lyceum* in the
     Jesuit library in Dublin had the name of Fr Finlay written on it.
71   'The Jew in Ireland', pp. 215–16.
72   ibid., pp. 216–17.
73   ibid., p. 217.
74   ibid., pp. 217–18.
75   ibid., p. 218.
76   ibid.
77   See Eugen Weber, *Action Française: Royalism and Reaction in Twentieth-
     Century France* (Stanford University Press, Stanford, 1962), pp. 1–7.
78   Fear of 'Jewish power' was particularly prevalent in 'Catholic' France at the turn
     of the century where the Radical ministry of E. Combes began on 2 June 1902.
     On 18 March 1903 many Catholic religious orders were dissolved. The French
     ambassador was withdrawn from the Vatican on 17 May 1904, and church and
     state were separated on 6 December 1905.
79   Quoted by John Hellman, 'The Jews in the "New Middle Ages": Jacques Mari-
     tain's Anti-Semitism in its Times', in Robert Royal (ed.), *Jacques Maritain and
     the Jews* (American Maritain Association, Indiana, 1994), p. 90. See also Eugen
     Weber, *Action Française,* p. 33.
80   Eugen Weber, *The Nationalist Revival in France, 1905–1914* (University of
     California Press, Berkeley and Los Angeles, 1968), pp. 1–68.
81   I am cautious about attributing all the anti-Semitic content in the paper to the
     personal pen of Griffith, but as editior he took overall responsibility for the
     content of his paper.
82   *United Irishman*, 23 September 1899.
83   ibid.
84   An editorial in *La Croix* stated: 'On every side, people demand a strong man, a
     man ready to risk his life to wrest France from the traitors, the factious, and the
     imbeciles who are handing it over to the foreigner . . . And who will deliver us
     from this gang of hoodlums.' Eugen Weber, *Action Française*, p. 33.
85   *United Irishman*, 5 August 1899.
86   ibid. Another article, on 19 August, opined that 'two thirds of the foreign jour-
     nalists, who are not English or Yankee, are Jews'.
87   Jean-Denis Bredin, *The Affair: The Case of Alfred Dreyfus* (George Braziller,
     New York, 1986), pp. 402–51.
88   *United Irishman*, 16 September 1899.
89   *United Irishman*, 26 August 1899. For background on Frederick Ryan, who
     was the first national secretary of the Socialist Party of Ireland, see Manus
     O'Riordan (ed.), *Socialism, Democracy and the Church* (Labour History
     Workshop, Dublin, 1984), p. 69; Manus O'Riordan (ed.), *Sinn Féin and Reac-
     tion, articles by Frederick Ryan with obituaries by Jim Larkin, Arthur
     Griffith and F. Sheehy Skeffington* (Labour History Workshop, Dublin, 1984),

p. 51. I am very grateful to Manus O'Riordan for supplying me with copies of these publications.

90 Instructions to RIC and DMP, 2 February 1903, CSORP, 1905/23538, NAI.

91 CSORP, 1905/23538, NAI.

92 CSORP, 1905/23538, NAI.

93 Jews in Ireland, Summary of Reports of County Inspectors, 23 February 1903, CSORP, 1905/23538, NAI.

94 RIC report, Belfast City, 13 February 1903, CSORP, 1905/23538, NAI.

95 RIC report, County Cork, East Riding, 13 February 1903, CSORP, 1905/23538, NAI.

96 ibid. The report also stated that there were no 'Jew tea-dealers in Cork and no instance has come under notice of Jews collecting tea-leaves at Hotels etc. for the purpose stated'.

97 RIC report, County Cork, West Riding, 13 February 1903, CSORP, 1905/23538, NAI.

98 ibid.

99 ibid.

100 RIC report, Limerick, 12 February 1903, CSORP, 1905/23538, NAI.

101 ibid.

102 RIC report, County Kilkenny, 17 February 1903, CSORP, 1905/23538, NAI.

103 Chamberlain to Under Secretary, 23 February 1903, CSORP, 1905/23538, NAI.

104 ibid.

105 ibid. The letter stated that samples of tea taken in County Limerick were in the hands of the county analyst. Reports from other areas were also being examined. It would appear that none of those reports proved positive. In the case of moneylending, police enquiries turned up seven cases (four in Cork and one each in Laois, Louth and Waterford) where Jews secured court judgments during 1902 against farmers. In none of the cases did the moneylenders, all with offices in Dublin (named Liebe Levin, Joseph Levin in four of the cases and William Allaun in two), obtain any hold on the farms of their debtors.

106 Irish pawnbrokers, for example, must not have been pleased to face competition from Jewish traders prepared to sell on a weekly credit system to the poorest sectors of society.

A bizarre event took place in summer 1899 which did not endear Jewry to members of the Royal Irish Academy and to Irish archaeologists. British Israelites unsuccessfully excavated the Rath of the Synods at the Hill of Tara in search of the Ark of the Covenant. See G. F. Mitchell, 'Antiquities', in T. Ó Raifeartaigh (ed.), *The Royal Irish Academy: A Bicentennial History 1785–1985* (Royal Irish Academy, Dublin, 1985), p. 151. R. A. S. Macalister, in a paper read to the Royal Irish Academy on 28 January 1919, said that the rath had been 'almost wholly devastated' in the excavation: 'had the Anglo-Israelites even done as much to record what they actually did find we might have partly forgiven them. But they did not even make this small compensation for their offence against science and against reason.' See *Proceedings of the Royal Irish Academy*, Vol. XXXIV, 1917–19, pp. 252–3. For background to this excavation, see the Tara Committee's report, in the *Royal Society of Antiquaries of Ireland Journal*, Series 5, Vol. XIII, 1903, pp. 102–4. It concluded: 'the condition in which the Rath of the Synods has been left is deplorable'. For further details, see Seán P. Ó Riordáin, *Tara: The Monument on the Hill* (Dundalgan Press, Dundalk, 1954), p. 22; see also Peter C. Woodman, 'Who Possesses Tara?': Politics in Archaeology in Ireland', in *Theory in Archaeology: A World Perspective* (Routledge, London, 1995), pp. 278–97.

2: The Limerick 'pogrom', 1904

1   O'Riordan was published by Kegan Paul, London; Plunkett was published by John Murray, London.

2   For his pains, he was repeatedly attacked in the columns of the *United Irishman*. On 30 September 1899, his social radicalism and his defence of Jews were held up to ridicule during the Dreyfus affair: 'The fusion of New Tipperary in the New Jerusalem has happened, accordingly, at a time when the Anglo-Jew Conspiracy against France will have need of all its recruits.'

3   He travelled to Russia as a journalist in 1903 and reported for the papers of William R. Hearst.

4   Michael Davitt, *Within the Pale: The True Story of Anti-Semitic Persecutions in Russia* (Hurst and Blackett, London, 1903).

5   This was pointed out to me by Gerald Goldberg whose family lived there in 1904 and were obliged to leave the city as a consequence of the disturbances.

6   Born in Thomondgate on 19 August 1870, Creagh was from a middle-class family. His mother died when he was eight. His father removed him from the Christian Brothers' School to the diocesan seminary where the future bishop of Limerick, Dr Edward Thomas O'Dwyer, was rector. He returned to the Christian Brothers when the school closed. He entered the Redemptorists at the age of fourteen. He studied for three years in the juvenate with the order before going to Liverpool, where he did his novitiate. He then moved to South Devon and was professed on 18 October 1888. He was ordained on 1 September 1895. He spent five years as a professor of scripture and theology in England. He was sent to Belfast and then he was moved to Esker, Athenry, Co. Galway. From there he was transferred to Limerick. See 'Father Creagh – His voyage to the Philippines', undated press cutting in the Holy Family Chronicles, 1900–42 (Part 1), Redemptorist Archives, Redemptorist House, Limerick (hereafter cited as Holy Family Chronicles, Limerick). See also Creagh's curriculum vitae, written in Liverpool in 1887 while he was in the novitiate. My thanks to Fr Brendan Mc Convery, archivist, Marianella, Dublin.

7   Interview with Creagh, 'Catholic and Jew, Father Creagh in Belfast, his version of the crusade', *Northern Whig*, 8 February 1904.

8   Samuel J. Boland, 'Fr John Creagh in the Kimberleys', *Old Limerick Journal*, No. 23 (Spring 1988), p. 152. Creagh spent much of his later life in Australia; Boland wrote:

> He embarrassed the [Australian] government by speaking about the grant of one shilling a year to the Sisters' mission ... He enraged the pearling companies by describing, with an abundance of vivid detail, the exploitation of crews and divers, most of them Asiatics, living for years in exile to support impoverished families.

9   Creagh declared his fear about undertaking his new position, but trusted in the goodness of God to help him to continue the splendid work of the arch-confraternity. Undated press cuttings in Holy Family Chronicles, Limerick.

10   ibid.

11   Creagh's stepmother died on 6 January 1904 and he officiated at the funeral. Her remains were removed from St. Munchin's Church the following day and taken by rail to Miltown Malbay, Co. Clare, where she was buried at Killarin cemetery. See *Limerick Leader*, 7 January 1904, quoted in Des Ryan, 'The Jews of Limerick' (Part 2), *Old Limerick Journal*, No. 18 (Winter 1985), p. 36.

12   Cutting from the *Limerick Journal*, 13 January 1904 in Holy Family Chronicles, Limerick.

13   ibid.

14   ibid.

15   See Ryan, 'The Jews of Limerick', p. 36. Creagh said:
      Just a few minutes ago I was handed a copy of the Chronicle with an
      account of a Jewish wedding. Listen to what it says: 'At the Synagogue,
      inside and out, were large crowds and the difference between them being
      that whereas those outside (most of them) wore poverty's motley, those
      inside were clad in fine broadcloth, and silks and satins goodly to look
      upon. From the outside to the door of the Synagogue itself, choice decora-
      tions were displayed, and the feet of the maiden trod as dainty a carpet as
      ever was laid down in the most "fashionable" edifice in the country.' Mark
      the words 'those outside (most of them) wore poverty's motley'. This
      certainly tells its own tale.
16   Cutting from the *Limerick Journal*, 13 January 1904 in Holy Family Chroni-
      cles, Limerick.
17   ibid.
18   ibid. Creagh contrasted the rates of interest charged by Jews with those of other
      lending institutions:
      The Jews lend money in time of need, but at what rates of interest? Let me
      enter into a few figures. If you want £5 you get not the 5 but 4.1s.3d. or
      18s.9d. less, which means 75 per cent at the end of the year. In the Perry
      Jubilee office you are only charged 4d. in the pound. In the banks the
      charge is 5 per cent, so you only pay 5.5s.0d. at the end of the year,
      whereas you have to pay something like double the amount borrowed from
      the Jews. Is not this robbery?
19   ibid.
20   ibid. This sermon was delivered again the following night. It may even have
      been given on the Wednesday evening.
21   ibid.
22   ibid.
23   The letter was published on 18 January. Cutting in Holy Family Chronicles,
      Limerick.
24   ibid.
25   ibid.
26   ibid.
27   ibid. Davitt said that Limerick had a 'Bishop of splendid intellectual powers,
      who is a great Churchman, whatever faults some of us occasionally find with
      him in relation to other questions'. He said that a mind as clear as that of
      Bishop O'Dwyer's 'will not allow the fair name of Catholic Ireland to be sullied
      through an anti-Jewish crusade, under his spiritual jurisdiction, to the injury
      and shame of a city of which every Irish man is historically proud'.
      A letter from 'a Limerick Confraternity man', dated 20 January 1904,
      attacked Davitt for his defence of Jews:
      Limerickmen love their native land, and its grand traditions, many of
      which are immortalised in song and story, but which we well know would
      not improve by affinity with aliens to our Faith and Fatherland, aye, not
      only aliens but avowed enemies. One tradition I would especially draw
      attention to as sung by Tom Moore, viz. – 'Rich and rare were the gems she
      wore' – as testifying to the purity of the Irish character. How many such are
      to be found in the mishna? Or I wonder how long would those precious
      gems remain unsullied in the midst of a Jewish population. This strikes me
      all the more forcefully, as while I write a matter comes to hand which
      informs me that an old Jew – grey and decrepid – standing in his doorway
      a few evenings ago, invites into his parlour some young women passing by,
      offering as a gift a new dress. One came on who no sooner heard the invita-

tion than like a true daughter of Limerick hurled the old wretch from his battlement with the same old weapons as of yore.

Davitt was also attacked in the letters columns of the *Limerick Echo* and the *Munster News* but he was defended in the London *Times* on 23 January 1904. See also Louis Hyman, *The Jews of Ireland: From Earliest Times to the Year 1910* (Irish University Press, Shannon, 1972), p. 216 and Bernard Shillman, *A Short History of the Jews in Ireland* (Eason, Dublin, 1945), p. 137. For a brief description of Davitt's views on the persecution of the Jews, see T .W. Moody, *Davitt and Irish Revolution 1848–82* (Clarendon Press, Oxford, 1982).

28   Holy Family Chronicles, Limerick.
29   Levin to Hayes, 13 January 1904, CSORP, 1905/23538, NAI. Emphasis added by RIC.
30   ibid.
31   O'Hara Report, 16 January 1904, CSORP, 1905/23538, NAI.
32   County Inspector Thomas Hayes to Dublin Castle, 27 January 1904, CSORP, 1905/23538, NAI.
33   ibid.
34   ibid.
35   ibid.
36   O'Hara report, 18 January 1904, CSORP, 1905/23538, NAI. Emphasis added by Dublin Castle. These events were fully reported in 'Excitement in the city', *Limerick Chronicle*, 19 January 1904.
37   District Inspector O'Hara also forwarded cuttings from the *Freeman's Journal* which contained correspondence on Limerick, including the letter from Michael Davitt. O'Hara report, 18 January 1904, CSORP, 1905/23538, NAI.
38   ibid. Emphasis added by Dublin Castle.
39   ibid. Emphasis added by Dublin Castle. He confirmed again that special measures had been taken to protect the houses in the Jewish quarters.
40   Ryan, 'The Jews of Limerick', p. 37.
41   'Hear all sides', *Limerick Leader*, 18 January 1904.
42   See 'A Limerick priest's attack on the Jews', *Jewish Chronicle*, 22 January 1904, quoted in Ryan, 'The Jews of Limerick', p. 37.
43   Cutting from *Jewish Chronicle*, 22 January 1904, Holy Family Chronicles, Limerick; the article is date-lined 17 January, but there can be little doubt that it was sent on the evening of the 18th after the intimidation and the threats of violence, and in fact the report refers to 'today' as Monday.
44   ibid.
45   'Mischief-making in Limerick', *Jewish Chronicle*, 22 January 1904.
46   Among those who criticised Creagh were I. Julian Grande, director of the Irish Mission to Jews. At a meeting in Dublin he said he was sorry to find that a strong feeling of anti-Semitism had made itself felt in Limerick. A resolution was unanimously passed condemning the unjust and unchristian attacks made on the Jewish community in Limerick. Undated cutting from the *Limerick Journal*, probably 19 January 1904, in Holy Family Chronicles, Limerick.
47   Ryan 'The Jews of Limerick', p. 37.
48   'Jewish trade in Limerick – reply by the Rev. Father Creagh, C.SS.R.', *Limerick Echo*, 19 January 1904, cutting in Holy Family Chronicles, Limerick.
49   ibid.
50   ibid.
51   ibid.
52   ibid.

53 On this issue Creagh based his arguments on a very uncritical reading of the anti-Semitic work of l'Abbé Rene F. Rohrbacher, *Histoire universelle de l'eglise catholique,* 5 vols. (no publisher, 1842). The later edition of 1856 has 29 volumes. Both editions are in the Library of Congress, Washington DC. See also reference in press cutting, Holy Family Chronicles, Limerick.

54 Cutting from *Limerick Echo,* 19 January 1904, in Holy Family Chronicles, Limerick.

55 ibid.

56 O'Hara report, 19 January 1904, CSORP, 1905/23538, NAI.

57 Considine minute, 19 January 1904, CSORP, 1905/23538, NAI.

58 Considine minute, 21 January 1904, CSORP, 1905/23538, NAI.

59 O'Hara report, 22 January 1904, CSORP, 1905/23538, NAI; for full report of the petty sessions, see *Limerick Weekly Echo,* 23 January 1904.

60 Undated cutting from the *Limerick Journal* in Holy Family Chronicles, Limerick.

61 Ryan, 'The Jews of Limerick', p. 37.

62 A file marked 'Jews' containing two letters from David Alexander, president of the London Committee of Deputies of British Jews, is what remains in the archives. See File 35, Edward Thomas O'Dwyer papers, Limerick Diocesan Archives. I am grateful to Bishop Donal Murray for giving me access to the O'Dwyer papers.

63 The Redemptorist Holy Family Chronicle is not particularly helpful in this regard while the Domestic Chronicle merely recorded the following at the time:

> Rev. J. Creagh denounced the Jews of Limerick at the Confraternity meeting for their extortions. Mr Davitt replied by an angry and abusive letter in the *Freeman's Journal.* At the next meeting the men clapped their hands when Fr Creagh appeared in the pulpit. A meeting was held to protest against Davitt's letter and letters were published in the city newspapers attacking him. Assaults were made in some places on the Jews, and some of those who did so were fined heavily by the Magistrates.

Mt St Alphonsus, Domestic Chronicle, Vol. 3 (1899–1911), Redemptorist Archives, Redemptorist House, Limerick.

64 Two-page excerpt entitled 'an Extract from the Provincial Chronicles 1904', in Holy Family Chronicles, Limerick. It began:

> Fr Creagh preached many sermons to the Confraternity at Limerick on the Jews; showing how extortionate they were: giving details of their evil deeds in every country in Europe from the earliest times. Soon afterwards the Jews were assaulted in the streets and Jewish families were reduced to such distress that they had to leave Limerick. The Jews were doing great harm by their extortions and the sale of immoral pictures. However their defence was taken up by the Protestants of Limerick and violent attacks were made on Fr Creagh. Some English newspapers published most violent attacks both on Fr Creagh and the Catholics of Limerick. 'The Times' had leading articles on the subject in which they defended the Jews and attacked the Catholic Church. At the Protestant Synod of Bishops in Dublin Dr Bunbury the Protestant Bishop of Limerick spoke strongly against Fr Creagh and expressed his astonishment that he was not silenced by his Superiors. He was called a *pulpit firebrand* and an *ecclesiastical incendery* [sic].

65 ibid.

66 This is speculation on my part, but it would appear that O'Dwyer was angry at having his diocese a centre of anti-Semitic outbursts which would be an indirect criticism of his handling of affairs.

67 Two-page excerpt entitled 'an Extract from the Provincial Chronicles 1904', in Holy Family Chronicles, Limerick.

68 Alexander to Logue, 8 April 1904, File 35, Edward Thomas O'Dwyer papers, Limerick Diocesan Archives.

69 Alexander to O'Dwyer, 25 April 1904 (enclosing a copy of his letter to Logue), File 35, Edward Thomas O'Dwyer papers, Limerick Diocesan Archives.

70 Fr Brendan Mc Convery to author, 3 May 1997. Fr Mc Convery, who has written on the history of the Redemptorists in Ireland, gave me generous assistance in the writing of this chapter. He recounts a saying among Redemptorists of an earlier generation about the three superior generals whose rule spanned the late nineteenth and early twentieth centuries: 'Mauron was all head, Raus was all heart, Murray was neither head nor heart.'

71 Mt St Alphonsus, Domestic Chronicle, Vol. 3 (1899–1911), Redemptorist Archives, Redemptorist House, Limerick.

72 ibid.

73 Address to Raus by the Hebrew Congregation of Limerick, Synagogue Chambers, 63 Colooney Street. Original kept in Holy Family Chronicles, Limerick.

74 Two-page excerpt entitled 'an Extract from the Provincial Chronicles 1904', in Holy Family Chronicles, Limerick.

75 Letter from P. Hayes, secretary of the Mechanics' Institute, Bank Place, 22 January 1904, in Holy Family Chronicles, Limerick.

76 'The Jews – action by archconfraternity', *Limerick Leader*, 25 January 1904.

77 ibid.

78 Undated press cutting in Holy Family Chronicles, Limerick.

79 See *Northern Whig*, 8 February 1904, republished in the *Limerick Leader*, 17 February 1904 and quoted in Ryan, 'The Jews of Limerick', p. 38.

80 ibid. The same interview was the subject of an editorial in the *Derry Journal*, 12 February 1904.

81 Holy Family Chronicles, Limerick.

82 Two-page excerpt entitled 'an Extract from the Provincial Chronicles 1904', in Holy Family Chronicles, Limerick.

83 Cutting from the London *Times* and from the *Cork Examiner*, 6 April 1904, in Holy Family Chronicles, Limerick.

84 *United Irishman*, 23 April 1904.

85 ibid.

86 ibid.

87 *United Irishman*.

88 ibid.

89 Cutting in Holy Family Chronicles, Limerick. Jaffe went on to explain an incident which occurred in Killaloe, Co. Clare, about six or seven years before. A missioner gave such a fiery sermon on the crucifixion that the following day Jews who had come to the town to trade were shunned like lepers and in other cases beset by a wild and infuriated mob. Jaffe sent a letter to the local bishop and that had the effect of restoring peace.

90 Church of Ireland clergyman E. H. Lewis-Crosby had a critical letter in the London *Times* on 11 April 1904. There were further critical reports in the *Irish Times*, 13 April 1904 and in the *Northern Mail*, 15 April 1904. The London *Times*, carrying many letters critical of the priest in its correspondence columns, condemned the attacks on the Limerick Jews in an editorial on 5 April. An article in the *Birmingham Post* of 15 March 1904 was critical of the outbreak of intolerance and intimidation in Limerick.

91 Ryan, 'The Jews of Limerick', p. 38.

92 County Inspector Thomas Hayes to Dublin Castle, 28 January 1904, CSORP, 1905/23538, NAI. Emphasis added by Dublin Castle.
93 List of allegations investigated by the police, January–March 1904, CSORP, 1905/23538, NAI.
94 ibid.
95 ibid.
96 Statement by Isaac Sandler, 25 March 1904, CSORP, 1905/23538, NAI.
97 Statement by Norah Keeffe, Kilbradran, 29 March 1904, CSORP, 1905/23538, NAI.
98 Statement by Isaac Sandler, 25 March 1904, CSORP, 1905/23538, NAI.
99 Report by Sergeant William McEvoy, 29 March 1904, CSORP, 1905/23538, NAI.
100 ibid.
101 ibid.
102 Considine minute, 8 April 1904, CSORP, 1905/23538, NAI.
103 Dublin Castle minute, 9 April 1904, CSORP 1905/23538, NAI.
104 Draft letter to London Committee of Deputies of British Jews (undated but probably late March 1904), CSORP, 1905/23538, NAI. The reply had been toned down considerably. An earlier draft had phrases such as: 'that however reprehensible the language attributed to the Revd Mr Creagh may be there is not available evidence sufficient to bring home to him the commission of any crime'.
105 Dublin Castle minute (undated) and copy of letter, 5 April 1904, from Charles H. Emanuel, secretary, London Committee of Deputies of British Jews, CSORP, 1905/23538, NAI.
106 I. Julian Grande, letter 'The Jews in Limerick', *Irish Times*, 1 April 1904.
107 *Daily Express*, 1 April 1904.
108 ibid.
109 Considine minute, 9 April 1904, CSORP, 1905/23538, NAI.
110 O'Hara report, 7 April 1904, CSORP, 1905/23538, NAI.
111 O'Hara report, 13 April 1904, CSORP, 1905/23538, NAI. Emphasis added by Dublin Castle.
112 ibid.
113 Considine minute, 14 April 1904, CSORP, 1905/23538, NAI.
114 Cutting of House of Commons debate, 14 April 1904, CSORP, 1905/23538, NAI.
115 'The Jewish troubles – boy sent to jail', *Limerick Leader*, 15 April 1904.
116 'A new Irish industry – the manufacture of "intolerance"', editorial in *Limerick Leader*, 15 April 1904.
117 'The Jewish question – action of the corporation', *Limerick Chronicle*, 21 April 1904.
118 O'Hara report, 14 May 1904, CSORP, 1905/23538, NAI.
119 'The Jewish trouble – release of the boy Raleigh', *Limerick Leader*, 13 May 1904.
120 ibid.
121 *Irish Times*, 16 April 1904.
122 ibid.
123 ibid.
124 ibid.
125 ibid.
126 *Freeman's Journal*, 16 April 1904.
127 O'Hara report, 22 April 1904, CSORP, 1905/23538, NAI.
128 'The Jewish question – action of the corporation', *Limerick Chronicle*, 21 April 1904.
129 ibid.

130 'Dr Bunbury's speech', editorial in *Munster News*, 20 April 1904. The relationship between Protestants and Catholics lies outside the scope of this study. But Dr John Long was a controversial figure. In Limerick since 1897, he ran a free medical clinic. He suffered intimidation from those who objected to his attempts to make converts to Protestantism. Reference to his activities may be found in Ryan, 'The Jews of Limerick', p. 38. See also Anon. (An Irishman), *Intolerance in Ireland – Facts not Fiction* (Simpkin Marshall, Hamilton, Kent and Co., London, 1913), pp. 36–49.

131 William J. Moloney, 'The libel of Limerick', *Leader*, 30 April 1904, p. 148.

132 ibid.

133 William J. Moloney, 'Limerick and the Jews', *Leader*, 7 May 1904, p. 71.

134 William J. Moloney, 'The libel of Limerick', *Leader*, 30 April 1904, p. 150.

135 Hyman, *Jews of Ireland*, pp. 216–17.

136 Ryan, 'The Jews of Limerick', p. 39.

137 *Limerick Echo*, 1 October 1904.

138 ibid.

139 Dublin Castle minute, 6 October 1904, CSORP, 1905/23538, NAI.

140 Hayes report, 12 March 1905, CSORP, 1905/23538, NAI.

141 Dublin Castle report, 13 March 1905, CSORP, 1905/23538, NAI.

142 ibid. District Inspector O'Hara had filed a very detailed report on this topic on 12 March 1905. Of the total of 49 who had left, 16 were men, 8 were women and there were 25 children. The three families who left for private reasons were that of 'Rabbi Goldberg' (possibly a reference to Louis Goldberg, who was not a rabbi but who did have a synagogue in his house during the split), who left owing to the settlement of 'an inter-Jewish schism during the prevalence of which two Rabbis were employed in Limerick', and two families called Weinronk who left to join the heads of that family in South Africa. Of the 26 families that remained, 18 were in 'poor circumstances'. Their trade in the city as pedlars and traders was 'gone' and not likely to return. O'Hara said that the statement that the Jews were left severely alone was true in general, but people still dealt with a dentist called Jaffe and a furniture dealer called Tuohy.

143 Cutting from House of Commons debate, 4 July 1905, CSORP, 1905/23538, NAI.

144 Levin to Long, 11 July 1905, CSORP, 1905/23538, NAI.

145 Hyman, *Jews of Ireland*, p. 217.

146 See copy of article by Asher Benson, 'Storm before the Storm', about the divisions within the Jewish community in Limerick over the purchase of a Jewish burial ground. There is also correspondence between Benson and one of Levin's sons, Salmond, in Box 39, Irish Jewish Museum Archives, Dublin.

147 O'Hara report, 12 March 1905, CSORP, 1905/23538, NAI.

148 See press cutting circa November 1905, Holy Family Chronicles, Limerick. As director of the arch-confraternity, he was also expected to play a role as mediator in trade disputes. On 19 March 1906, for example, he received the text of a resolution from the secretary of the Mechanics' Institute, J. Hayes, thanking him for 'the noble and businesslike way he brought to a close the protracted dispute in the mason trade'.

149 'A loss to Limerick', editorial in *Limerick Echo*, 24 April 1906.

150 Undated and unidentified cutting in Holy Family Chronicles, Limerick.

151 'Father Creagh's departure', editorial in *Limerick Leader*, 27 April 1906.

152 'Rev. Father Creagh', editorial in *Munster News*, 9 May 1906.

153 ibid.

154 Undated and unidentified cutting in Holy Family Chronicles, Limerick.

155 ibid.

156 ibid.
157 After the Philippines, Creagh worked in Northern Australia and in New Zealand, all the time in the service of poorer sections of those societies. Wherever he went, controversy dogged him. In any future study, it would be worth attempting to place Creagh in his wider intellectual and cultural context by examining his family background, his formation in the seminary, the ethos of the Redemptorist order at the time, the links through his order with French Catholicism, the place of the order in the contemporary debate on anti-Semitism, and the nature and structure of Limerick society at the turn of the century. This wider study may reveal Creagh to be at once villain and victim – the prey of the intellectual anti-Semitism of his church and of his time.
158 Interview with Richard Haslam, Cork, November 1997.
159 ibid.
160 Information kindly supplied by Denis Leonard, Limerick Civic Trust.
161 See invitation card, Limerick Civic Trust archives, Limerick.
162 *Irish Times*, 15 November 1990.
163 *Limerick Leader*, 17 November 1990.
164 *Irish Times*, 15 November 1990.

3: Leopold Bloom, the Jewish community and independent Ireland

1   One of the future leaders of the 1916 Rising, James Connolly, had an appeal issued on his behalf in Yiddish during his campaign in 1902 for election to Dublin Corporation. He was standing for Wood Quay Ward where Jews were in the majority in a number of streets. See Manus O'Riordan, 'Connolly, Socialism and the Jewish Worker', *Saothar,* Vol. 13 (1988), pp. 120–30.
2   See *Leader*, 16 July 1904. An earlier edition of the *Leader*, 25 June 1904 (p. 275), refers to the refusal of the *Evening Telegraph* and the *Evening Herald* to publish an advertisement from the Dublin tailor John S. Kelly Ltd which included the words: 'No connection with Jews'.
3   William Bulfin, *Rambles in Eirinn* (Gill & Son, Dublin, 1907), pp. 307–8.
4   ibid., p. 308.
5   ibid., p. 309.
6   Oliver St John Gogarty, 'Ugly England', *Sinn Féin*, 24 November 1906.
7   Oliver St John Gogarty, 'Ugly England', *Sinn Féin*, 1 December 1906.
8   Michael Noyk, 'Statement Regarding 1910–1921 Period' given to the Military History Bureau, Dublin. See MS 18,975, NLI.
9   'United Irishman' entry in Robert Welch (ed.), *The Oxford Companion to Irish Literature* (Oxford University Press, Oxford, 1996), p. 580.
10 Richard Ellman, *James Joyce* (Oxford University Press, Oxford, 1983), p. 373.
11 ibid., p. 144.
12 ibid., p. 156; Joyce's chance meeting with his future wife Nora Barnacle walking down Nassau Street on 10 June 1904 may be described as a defining moment in the personal life of that artist. They walked together for the first time on 16 June at Ringsend. He set the entire action of *Ulysses* on that date.
13 Louis Hyman argues that Joyce was misled by his brother, Stanislaus, into believing that Hunter was a Jew. See Louis Hyman, *The Jews of Ireland: From Earliest Times to the Year 1910* (Irish University Press, Shannon, 1972), p. 169.
14 'Ulysses' entry in Welch (ed.), *Oxford Companion to Irish Literature*, p. 577.
15 Ira B. Nadel, *Joyce and the Jews: Culture and Texts* (University Press of Florida, Gainesville, 1996), p. 139.
16 Ellman, *James Joyce*, p. 373.
17 James Joyce, *Ulysses*, annotated students' edition (Penguin, London, 1992), p. 798.

18   ibid.
19   Hugh Kenner, *Ulysses*, revised edn (Johns Hopkins University Press, Baltimore and London, 1993), p. 43.
20   Joyce, *Ulysses*, p. 417.
21   ibid., p. 432.
22   ibid., p. 377.
23   ibid., pp. 419–20.
24   ibid., p. 421.
25   ibid., p. 430.
26   ibid., pp. 432–3.
27   ibid., p. 438.
28   ibid., pp. 444–5.
29   ibid., pp. 428–9.
30   In Gogarty's first 'Ugly England' article, he makes reference to the death of twelve Zulus 'murdered to intimidate others and justify Jewry'. See *Sinn Féin*, 24 November 1906. There are resonances of this in *Ulysses*, where there are references to a Zulu chief and his entourage who were visiting Manchester. See ibid., pp. 433–44.
31   ibid., p. 41.
32   ibid.
33   ibid., pp. 44–5.
34   The place of Bloom in Irish history is sensitively reviewed in Gerald Y. Goldberg's 'Ireland is the only country . . . Joyce and the Jewish Dimension', *Crane Bag* Vol. 6, No. 1 (1982), pp. 5–11.
35   Bloom's final end also resides in a world between fact and fiction. Asher Benson recalls the story of his visit to the Bleeding Horse bar, in Camden Street, Dublin, 'some years ago'. There he met 'Sniffer' Cohen who, after lowering four pints, told Asher about Bloom's death.
     In 1942 Cohen was called to the dying Bloom's bedside in a Bishop Street tenement. Wearing a faded prayer shawl (property of Greenville Hall Synagogue was written on it), he had a grease-stained skull cap (embroidered with the word 'Jerusalem') on his head and a tattered Hebrew prayer book upside down in his lap. 'Promise me', he urged 'Sniffer' Cohen, 'to bury me in the Jewish cemetery in Dolphin's Barn.' Bloom then took a jug of porter, blew off the froth, drank the contents in one uninterrupted swallow and expired cursing James Joyce and saying he would settle with 'Jimmy' in Hell.
     When Bloom was denied burial by the cemetery committee, 'Sniffer' and his friends took the corpse on a barrow to Aughavanagh Road on the perimeter of the cemetery. There Bloom was buried with his head and shoulders under the wall of the Jewish cemetery and the rest of him in undergrowth at the side of Aughavanagh Road. The unorthodox burial party had brought a piece of wood on which was written, 'Leopold Bloom, 16 June 1942. His head was Jewish even if the rest of him wasn't. May he rest in peace.' This was thrown over the wall and found many years later by Asher Benson, or so the story goes. See Asher Benson, 'Jewish Genealogy in Ireland', in *Aspects of Irish Genealogy: Proceedings of the First Irish Genealogical Congress* (First Irish Genealogical Congress Committee, 1993), pp. 26–7.
36   Sr Katherine Butler, 'Rosa Solomons', paper read to the Old Dublin Society, 2 February 1977. I am grateful to Sr Katherine for supplying me with a copy of her paper.
37   Bethel Solomons, *One Doctor in His Time* (Christopher Johnson, London, 1956), pp. 18–19.
38   ibid.

39 See *Portraits of Patriots* (Dublin, 1966).

40 Solomons, *One Doctor in His Time*, pp. 12–13.

41 ibid., p. 17.

42 ibid., pp. 47–8.

43 ibid., p. 25. Delighted to be picked for the school rugby team for the first time, he told his father who dumbfounded him by saying that he could not play sport on a Saturday, the Sabbath. But his mother, who was much more religious than his father, reasoned with her husband: 'We are living in a Christian country, wait until we get to Palestine, then we shall not allow games on Saturday. But he can play.'

44 ibid., p. 169.

45 He also subscribed to a suffrage journal, *The Egoist*. His memoirs contain a very acute observation on the role of women in Irish society:
> Although universities were beginning to open their doors, the average woman seemed to have little chance of a career outside marriage. I am sure that many married without love, for security and a home. The alternatives were ill-paid and ill-regarded. Some became governesses, a position of equivocal status, involving a good deal of hard work. Nurses received only a pittance and conditions were bad. The hours of shop assistants were long and those who sought posts as companions might well find themselves acting as 'scivvies'. Domestic service in a good household must have had compensations, but in a place where the girl was exploited it was sheer hell.
>
> ibid., pp. 47–8.

46 ibid., pp. 157–8.

47 Bethel Solomons took a liberal attitude towards inter-marriage, but his father was almost unrepentantly hostile:
> My father, in common with many of his friends and relations, regarded a mixed marriage as about the worst thing that could happen to anyone. He refused to be friendly with those relatives who married out of the Faith. In theory, I believe it is better for husbands and wives to belong to the same religion, but love is strong and many mixed marriages turn out well. . . . Father had even put in his will that any child marrying out of the Faith was not to share in his property. I may say at this stage that, when he was eighty, I got him to delete this clause and he was 'big' enough to do so.
>
> I had a feeling that my sister Estella would marry a non-Jew, which she did. ibid., pp. 12–13.

48 Many of those who contributed to the development of the Jewish community in early twentieth-century Dublin were associated with the Adelaide Road Synagogue; they included: Arthur Newman, N. Levin, Selig Dundon, Israel Ellis, Henry Fridberg, W. Goldfath, Maurice Jackson, Jack Myers, H. Sherowitz, Hoseas Weiner, O. White, Louis and Harry Wine. Other families active in the Jewish community were Landau, Tomkin, Isaacson, Hesselberg, Ginsberg, Levy, Hyman, Horwich, Stein, Cowan, Clein, Davis, Taylor, Price, Carby, Zolkie, Noyek, Eppel, Green, Levi, Marcus, Jackson and Woolfson.

49 Melisande Zlotover, *Zlotover Story: A Dublin Story with a Difference* (Hely Thom, Dublin, 1966), p. 45.

50 See Con Leventhal entry, in Welch (ed.), *Oxford Companion to Irish Literature*, p. 308. Leventhal's mother, Rosa, was a poet, a lifelong Zionist activist and a founder member of the Women's Zionist Society.

51 A. J. Leventhal, 'What it means to be a Jew', *Bell*, Vol. 10, No. 3 (June 1945), pp. 207–8.

52 ibid., p. 208.

53 ibid.

54 ibid.
55 ibid., p. 210.
56 ibid., p. 209.
57 ibid., pp. 209–10.
58 ibid., p. 209.
59 ibid., p. 210.
60 ibid., pp. 212–13.
61 Anon., *Saul Harris Wigoder* (no publisher listed, Dublin, 1933), p. 7.
62 ibid., p. 8.
63 ibid., p. 9.
64 ibid.
65 ibid., p. 12.
66 ibid. They sublet part of the house and also carried on their frame-making business there. There Harry devoted himself entirely to the framing business, making for firms in the city. On one occasion, he made 144 frames in one day. He also started a small business offering pictures for sale on a weekly repayment basis.
67 ibid., pp. 17–18.
68 ibid.
69 His brother Philip, who was nearing the end of his school days, decided he wanted to become a dentist. Myer Joel's brother, George, was in practice in Dublin and he helped Philip to pay his tuition fees in order to take the preliminary exams at the Royal College of Surgeons. He did so in 1903 and then went to South Africa to live with another uncle. There he earned enough money to return three years later to start his university course. Another sister, Sarah, studied medicine and took part of her final examination. She then married.
70 Bernard Shillman, *A Short History of the Jews in Ireland* (Eason, Dublin, 1945), p. 119.
71 Solomons, *One Doctor in His Time*, p. 63.
72 Solomons to Shillman, 11 October 1933, Box 38, Irish Jewish Museum Archives, Dublin.
73 Shillman to Brother Meers, 28 January 1964, Box 38, Irish Jewish Museum Archives, Dublin. Shillman seemed to recall that Eamon de Valera gave him extra classes on a Saturday in the school. Brother Meers was unable to confirm whether or not that was true.
74 ibid.
75 Hannah Berman published two remarkable Russian novels, one a translation from Yiddish and the other an original novel by herself. See *Dublin Herald*, 28 March 1914. She was interviewed by the *Jewish Chronicle* on 29 May 1914.
76 Nurock was elected First Classical Scholar in 1912 when still only a Freshman. In 1913 he was awarded the Vice-Chancellor's Latin Medal, the first Berkeley Gold Medal in Greek, the Ferrar Memorial Prize in Philology and Greek and the Composition Prize in Classics. In 1915 he was awarded the Wray prize in Philosophy and became editor of the college magazine, *TCD*. Nurock also won a classical studentship, worth £500, in his final year, *Official Gazette*, 3 January 1932. Cutting in Nurock/Abrahamson family scrapbook kindly made available to me by Maurice Abrahamson, Dublin.
77 Nurock/Abrahamson family scrapbook.
78 Newspaper cutting in Irish, dated simply 1914, signed by Leonard Mac Abram in Nurock/Abrahamson family scrapbook.
79 He too was the first of the firsts for many years, winning the Hutchinson Setwart Scholarship as well as prizes in Celtic languages and Hebrew. He represented Trinity College in the Irish inter-university debate in 1914. As a medical

student he secured first place in the second and third professional examinations, and in all branches of the final examinations. He was awarded the Fitzpatrick Prize, the Medical Travelling Prize and the Banks Medal. He later studied in London and in Paris. He became professor of pharmacology at the Royal College of Surgeons. See press cutting in Nurock/Abrahamson family scrapbook.

80   See undated newspaper cutting in Nurock/Abrahamson family scrapbook.
81   See newspaper cutting, 11 August 1914, in Nurock/Abrahamson family scrapbook.
82   See undated newspaper cutting in Nurock/Abrahamson family scrapbook.
83   This account is taken from material put together by Nelson McCausland, Belfast and supplied to me by Dr Caroline Windrum, Institute of Irish Studies, Queen's University, Belfast.
84   I have no evidence to support this theory. But it seems likely that in the working-class districts of Irish towns which supplied the cannon-fodder for the trenches feelings against the local Jewish 'Germans' would have run high.
85   See *Jewish Chronicle*, 24 September 1915.
86   Interview with Maurice Abrahamson, Dublin, October 1996.
87   Zlotover, *Zlotover Story*, p. 46.
88   Thomas Burbage, 'Ritual murder among the Jews', *Catholic Bulletin*, Vol. 6, No. 6 (May–June 1916), pp. 309–14.
89   The charge of ritual murder against the Jews had been exposed as a lie by Michael Davitt in 1903. There was a further infamous case in 1913 which arose out of charges of alleged ritual murder in Russia and which was covered in the Irish national press. A boy named Yusheninsky was found dead with a number of stab wounds on his body. Mendel Beiliss, a clerk and a Jew by birth, was accused of ritual murder. The state prosecution built a case around the 'certain' belief that it was part of the Jewish religion to kill Christian children in order to use their blood for purposes of ritual. The murder trial at Kieff found the accused not guilty in November 1913. An editorial in the *Irish Times* commented: 'Even the most violent of pagan bigots would recoil in horror from the idea of putting forward a similar accusation against any civilised race or religion.' The entire state action was, according to the *Irish Times*, 'proof of the survival of barbarism in that country'. Editorial 'The murder trial at Kieff', *Irish Times*, 11 November 1913; see also editorial 'Blood ritual', *Dublin Evening Mail*, 11 November 1913.
90   Burbage, 'Ritual murder among the Jews', p. 309.
91   Elyan to Walsh, 10 and 23 June 1916, William Walsh papers, Dublin Archdiocesan Archives. I am grateful to Fr Brian Murphy, Glenstal Abbey, Limerick, for material outlining the background to these events.
92   Sherlock to Walsh, 12 June 1916, William Walsh papers, Dublin Archdiocesan Archives.
93   Reference kindly supplied by Fr Brian Murphy.
94   ibid.
95   See James O'Connor to Chief Secretary, 25 August 1916; reference supplied by Fr Brian Murphy.
96   See *Catholic Bulletin*, Vol. 6, No. 9 (September 1916), p. 466; reference supplied by Fr Brian Murphy.
97   Thomas Burbage, 'What is freemasonry?', *Catholic Bulletin*, Vol. 7, No. 2 (February 1917) and 'Masonic crimes and terrorism', *Catholic Bulletin*, Vol. 7, No. 6 (June 1917), pp. 376–84. He cited as his source the articles in the *Lyceum* by Fr Thomas Finlay quoted in chapter 1.
98   David Marcus, *A Land not Theirs* (Corgi, Reading, 1986).

99   ibid., p. 64.

100   ibid.

101   ibid., p. 108.

102   ibid., p. 152.

103   ibid., p. 114.

104   ibid., p. 116.

105   Michael Noyk, 'Statement Regarding 1910–1921 period', MS 18,975, NLI, p. 12.

106   ibid., p. 82.

107   ibid., p. 24.

108   Piaras Béaslaí, *Michael Collins: Soldier and Statesman* (Talbot Press, Dublin and Cork, 1937), p. 264.

109   ibid., p. 136.

110   ibid.

111   ibid., p. 264.

112   Noyk remained close to Irish political leaders during the 1920s and 1930s. He was a lifelong friend of the Cumann na nGaedheal TD, Gearóid O'Sullivan, who was a veteran of the 1916 Rising and a former aide-de-camp to Michael Collins. Noyk was later a very strong supporter of Shamrock Rovers Football Club and patron of Irish football. I am grateful to Fr Gearóid Ó Súilleabháin, St Vincents, Sunday's Well, Cork, for this information.

113   Béaslaí, *Michael Collins*, p. 136. See above n. 8, where reference was made to Noyk's friendship with Griffith.

114   See Sr Katherine Butler, 'Centenary of a Synagogue: Adelaide Road 1892–1992', *Dublin Historical Record,* Vol. 48, No. 1 (Spring 1994), pp. 46–55.

115   Robert Briscoe (with Alden Hatch), *For the Life of Me* (Little, Brown & Co., Boston, 1958), pp. 3–81.

116   See obituary of Bewley in *Irish Times*, 3 February 1969.

117   Mervyn O'Driscoll, 'Irish–German Relations, 1922–1939' (MA, University College Cork, 1992), pp. 8–9.

118   See Brian P. Murphy, *John Chartres: Mystery Man of the Treaty* (Irish Academic Press, Dublin, 1995), in particular, pp. 99, 100, 106–8.

119   Briscoe to Chartres, 21 January 1922, Germany Subject File 1922, D/FA D/PG/IFS Berlin 1922–24, quoted in O'Driscoll, 'Irish–German Relations', pp. 24–5.

120   Briscoe, *For the Life of Me*, p. 259.

121   O'Driscoll, 'Irish–German Relations', p. 26.

122   ibid.

123   ibid. Though the letter was unsigned and undated, Bewley was undoubtedly the author.

124   ibid., p. 28.

125   ibid., p. 30.

126   ibid.

127   ibid., p. 31.

128   ibid., pp. 31–2.

129   ibid., p. 33.

130   Hilaire Belloc, *The Jews* (Constable, London, 1922). It was reprinted the same year and again in 1927 and 1937.

131   Arthur Clery, 'Belloc on Christians and Others', *Studies*, Vol. 11 (December 1922), p. 648.

132   ibid., pp. 648–9.

133   ibid., pp. 649–50.

134   Interview with Gerald Goldberg, Cork, July 1997.

135   Isaac Herzog was born in Lomza, Poland, in 1889. His father was Rabbi Joel Leib Herzog, who was in turn the son of Rabbi Nafthali Hirsch Herzog. (The

Nazis obliterated the 10,000 Jews of Lomza and destroyed the synagogue in the town square.) Herzog's father moved to Worcester, Massachusetts, then to Leeds and finally to Paris shortly before the outbreak of the First World War. Isaac was acknowledged in his youth to be an outstanding Talmudist. He studied Oriental languages at the Sorbonne and read classics and mathematics at the University of London where he was awarded a doctorate. He was also a marine biologist. See Chaim Herzog, *Living History: A Memoir* (Pantheon Books, New York, 1996), pp. 6–7.

According to his entry in *Encyclopedia Judaica* (Jerusalem, 1971), Herzog was soon 'recognised as one of the great rabbinical scholars of his time, besides being a linguist and jurist and at home in mathematics and natural sciences . . . the charm of his personality, which combined ascetic unworldliness with conversational wit and diplomatic talents, made a great impression'.

136   She was born in 1899 in Rega, Latvia. Her father had been a rabbi in Berezino, Belarus, and later moved with his two children to London.

137   Zlotover, *Zlotover Story*, p. 50.

138   A committee under the chairmanship of Jacob Elyan, consisting of the representatives of the various congregations, invited Herzog to take up the position in Dublin.

The idea of attracting him from Belfast had first been planted when Joseph Zlotover visited London shortly after the end of the First World War. He asked Rabbi Samuel Isaac Hillman his advice about securing a spiritual leader for the Jewish community in Dublin. This had been a 'burning question' in the community there and everyone had been 'on the lookout for the right man'. Hillman replied to Zlotover: 'Would you consider my son-in-law? He is young but is already a great and learned Rabbi?' ibid.

139   Jacob took his doctorate in international law in Canada. See Herzog, *Living History*, p. 15.

140   ibid., p. 12.

141   Interview with Brian Quinn, chairman of the Ireland–Israel Friendship League, October 1996. Brian has that on good authority from his father who was the political editor of the *Sunday Independent* for many years.

142   Herzog, *Living History*, pp. 11–12.

143   Interview with Hubert Wine, Dublin, April 1997.

144   Minute in the Department of Foreign Affairs, 17 May 1922, D/J H33A, NAI.

145   D/J H33A, NAI.

146   D/J H33A, NAI.

147   Upon transmission of those particulars to the Department of External Affairs, the Department of Home Affairs (later Justice) would be notified and make enquiries from the references and from the police of the locality where the alien had formerly resided. In suitable cases a permit would then be issued by the Department of Home Affairs to the foreign representative who would then be authorised to issue a passport. That only applied to cases where aliens were coming direct to Ireland without passing through England. There would also be some special cases, such as those of diplomatic personages, where Irish references would not be required. Minute in the Department of External Affairs, 17 May 1922, D/J H33A, NAI.

148   I am not allowed to use the names cited in the files of the Department of Justice, and therefore I will deal with the cases anonymously.

149   D/J 33/276, NAI.

150   ibid.

151   Another case involving a Jew who had lived in Ireland was referred to the Dublin Metropolitan Police (DMP) for their assessment. A reply came on 26

November 1923. The case involved a Jew who had served in the British army during the First World War. He was born in Wexna, Kovno in 1883 and had come with his parents to Dublin as a child. In May 1907 he joined the artillery, and was invalided during the war. His wife, who was also born in Kovno, had come as a child with her parents to Dublin and became a naturalised British subject. The couple had married in 1919 and, according to the DMP, the wife had become an alien on that date and should have registered. She did not do so. Neither did the husband, who had been told that he was, as a consequence of serving in the army, a British citizen. They conducted a small grocery business at 38 Lennox Street. The man in question applied for registration as an Irish citizen and on 29 November 1923, the secretary of the Department of Home Affairs stated that as the two 'appeared to have a claim to Irish citizenship, no proceedings should be instituted against them for failure to register'. D/J 33/274, NAI.

152 D/J 33/251, NAI.

153 His wife was a painter of distinction who had work exhibited by the Royal Hibernian Academy.

154 William T. Cosgrave was approached in August 1930 by the Labour leader, William O'Brien, to grant asylum to Leon Trotsky, who had been deported from Russia in 1929. Residing in Turkey since his exile, Trotsky had failed to win admission to any western European country, including Britain. Cosgrave, refusing his request on security and religious grounds, recorded the following exchange with O'Brien: 'I asked his nationality. Reply Jew. They were against religion.' See Doireann Fitzgerald, 'How Leon Trotsky was refused admission to the Irish Free State', *Slainte: UCD History Review*, Vol. 7 (1993), p. 11. Fitzgerald shows how further representations made on behalf of Trotsky to de Valera also failed in 1934.

155 Interview with Fr Michael O'Carroll, Blackrock College, Dublin, 1996.

156 Herzog, *Living History*, pp. 13–14.

157 ibid., p. 9.

158 Solomons, *One Doctor in His Time*, pp. 12–13.

159 ibid. Solomons continued:
    People calling themselves Christians are often anti-Semites, forgetting that in having these sentiments they are acting against the first principles of the teaching of Christ. 'How odd of God to choose the Jews', said Belloc. 'But not so odd as those who chose a Jewish God and spurn the Jews', is one of the many answers.

160 Interviews with Gerald Goldberg, Cork, March 1996 and Frederick Rosehill, Cork, October 1996.

161 Quoted in Patrick Maume, *Life that is Exile* (Institute of Irish Studies, Belfast, 1993), p. 284.

162 See Richard Devane, 'Indecent Literature: Some Legal Remedies', *Irish Ecclesiastical Record*, February 1925, quoted in Susan O'Shea, 'The Politics of Irish Culture, 1922–1939' (M Phil, University College Cork, 1995), chapter 1. See also Richard S. Devane SJ, 'Suggested Tariff on Imported Newspapers and Magazines', *Studies*, Vol. 16 (December 1927), pp. 544–69 and 'The Menace of the British Press Combines', *Studies*, Vol. 19 (March 1930), pp. 54–69.

163 See O'Shea, 'Politics of Irish Culture', chapter 1.

164 John Horgan, 'Saving us from Ourselves: Contraception, Censorship and the "Evil Literature" Controversy of 1926', *Irish Communications Review*, Vol. 5 (1995), p. 62.

165 ibid.

166 The Dance Hall Act, which provided that a licence from a district court was

needed to hold a public dance, was passed in 1935. The Criminal Law Amendment Act, banning the importation for sale of contraceptives, also became law in 1935.

167   Herzog, *Living History*, p. 15.

168   See Leventhal file, Box 2, Irish Jewish Museum Archives, Dublin.

169   Laurence K. Emery (A. J. Leventhal), 'The Ulysses of Mr James Joyce', *Klaxon*, 1923, p. 16.

170   ibid.

171   ibid., p. 20.

172   ibid.

173   See Leventhal file, Box 2, Irish Jewish Museum Archives, Dublin. After moving to Paris in 1963, Leventhal acted as Beckett's literary assistant.

174   See Welch (ed.), *Oxford Companion to Irish Literature*, p. 564.

175   Kevin Rockett, Luke Gibbon and John Hill, *Cinema in Ireland* (Syracuse University Press, Syracuse, 1988), pp. 42–4.

176   ibid.

177   See the National Gallery of Ireland and the Douglas Hyde Galleries, *Irish Women Artists: From the Eighteenth Century to the Present Day* (Dublin, 1987), p. 187.

178   Brian Kennedy, *Irish Art and Modernism 1880–1950* (Institute of Irish Studies, Belfast, 1991), pp. 44–6.

179   Stella Steyn, 'An Autobiographical Memoir', in S. B. Kennedy (ed.), *Stella Steyn 1907–1987* (Gorry Gallery Exhibition Catalogue, Dublin, 1995), p. 12.

180   Representatives of the congregations in Camden Street, St Kevin's Parade, Lennox Street and Oakfield met that year in the home of Joseph Zlotover. They decided to work in unison to build 'a house of learning and prayer'. They instituted a scheme of house-to-house penny collections. In 1913 they purchased Greenville House and grounds. The First World War interfered with the completion of the project. However, the foundation stone of the hall was laid in April 1916 – the month of the Rising – and the building was completed by September. Meanwhile, Greenville House had been converted into a temporary synagogue and the smaller communities in the city were invited to join the congregation. The Camden Street community accepted the invitation.

181   Zlotover, *Zlotover Story*, p. 50; see also Shillman, *Jews in Ireland*, p. 121.

182   Shillman, *Jews in Ireland*, pp. 110–15.

183   ibid.

184   Archbishop John Charles McQuaid, who knew Edwin Solomons very well, regarded him as being 'a very honourable man, having for acquaintances and friends all his life, Dublin Catholics'. McQuaid to Gino Paro [nunciature, Dublin], 13 June 1949, Department of Foreign Affairs folder, Box 1 (Government), John Charles McQuaid papers, Dublin Archdiocesan Archives.

185   See Butler, 'Rosa Solomons'. The chief rabbi of the British Empire, J. H. Hertz, preached at the Adelaide Road Synagogue on 2 January 1926.

186   Clipping from the *Jewish Chronicle*, 26 June 1925, Nurock/Abrahamson family scrapbook.

4: Irish society and the culture of fear, 1932–37

1   Robert Briscoe (with Alden Hatch), *For the Life of Me* (Little, Brown & Co., Boston, 1958), p. 235. He shared the constituency with future Taoiseach Seán Lemass.

2   ibid., pp. 230–1.

3   ibid., p. 231.

4   Some years later, de Valera took Briscoe to one side apologetically to explain

why. Briscoe, who greatly respected de Valera, accepted the situation without question.

5   Briscoe, *For the Life of Me*, p. 247.

6   ibid.

7   *Dáil Éireann Debates*, Vol. 28, col. 679 (20 February 1929). Briscoe explained (col. 681) the case of somebody who borrowed £5. They got into their hands £3 15s in cash, 5s in the pound being charged as interest. That was immediately deducted from the total amount. But the £3 15s was repayable plus the £1 5s charged as interest at the rate of 5s per week. Briscoe claimed that that type of moneylender wanted the client to borrow more in order to be able to meet the repayments and in that way get deeper and deeper into debt.

8   ibid.

9   *Minutes of Evidence taken before the Select Committee on the Moneylenders Bill, 1929*, 28 May 1930, p. 32.

10   ibid., p. 56.

11   ibid., p. 33.

12   ibid., p. 32.

13   *Dáil Éireann Debates*, Vol. 49, col. 330 (20 July 1933).

14   Bernard Shillman, *A Short History of the Jews in Ireland* (Eason, Dublin, 1945), pp. 127–8

15   'Chief Rabbi Herzog – Outstanding Scholar and Leader', Obituary, *Jewish Chronicle*, 31 July 1959.

16   Sokolow was accompanied by his daughter, Selina. See cuttings in Nurock/Abrahamson family scrapbook in the possession of Maurice Abrahamson, Dublin.

17   ibid.

18   ibid.

19   ibid.

20   ibid.

21   Interview with Ben Briscoe TD, Dublin, 1996.

22   Interview with Maurice Abrahamson, Dublin, April 1997.

23   United States Holocaust Memorial Museum, *Historical Atlas of the Holocaust* (Macmillan, New York, 1996), pp. 13–14.

24   While his extremism may have rubbed off on a small number of the seminarians in his classes, there was a general antipathy to his anti-Semitic ideas among his pupils. He took great offence when opposition was expressed to his world view. This assessment is based on interviews with members of the Holy Ghost order who were educated by Fahey.

25   At first, he led a rather charmed life as a publicist and his enthusiasm was indulged briefly after 1941 by the new archbishop of Dublin, the Holy Ghost priest, John Charles McQuaid. But the archbishop felt obliged to lift his protection in the 1940s. See Denis Fahey, *The Rulers of Russia* (Dublin, 1938); *The Social Rights of Our Divine Lord Jesus Christ, the King* (Dublin, 1932); *The Church and Farming* (Cork, 1953); *The Kingship of Christ and the Conversion of the Jewish Nation* (Dublin, 1953); *Money Manipulation and Social Order* (Dublin, 1944); *The Mystical Body of Christ in the Modern World* (Dublin, 1935); *The Mystical Body of Christ and the Reorganisation of Society* (Cork, 1944). Fahey also contributed extensively to many popular Catholic journals.

26   Mary Christine Athans, *The Coughlin–Fahey Connection: Fr Charles E. Coughlin, Fr Denis Fahey, C.S. Sp., and Religious Anti-Semitism in the United States, 1938–1954* (P. Lang, New York, 1991).

27   See unsigned article, 'The Fahey Theories', *Ballintrillick Review*, No. 28 (1990), pp. 6ff.

28 Denis Fahey, *The Mystical Body of Christ in the Modern World* (Dublin, 1935), pp. 193–4.

29 ibid., p. 175.

30 ibid., p. 169.

31 ibid.

32 See Edward Cahill papers, Jesuit Archives, Dublin.

33 Finín O'Driscoll, 'The Search for the Christian State: Irish Social Catholicism, 1913–1939' (MA, University College Cork, 1994), p. 158.

34 Edward Cahill, *The Framework of a Christian State* (Gill & Son, Dublin, 1932).

35 O'Driscoll, 'The Search for the Christian State', p. 144.

36 Edward Cahill, *Freemasonry and the Anti-Christian Movement* (Gill & Son, Dublin, 1929) and *Ireland's Peril* (Gill & Son, Dublin, 1930).

37 Cahill, *Ireland's Peril*, pp. 28–9.

38 Cahill, *The Framework of a Christian State*, pp. 185–6.

39 ibid., pp. 240–1.

40 Cahill's prayers were apparently answered with the arrival in power of Eamon de Valera in 1932. He wrote to de Valera:

> I thank God from my heart that the ten year 'nightmare' is over and I thank God too that you have been spared to take charge of the helm again. I have great hopes that the good God will utilise you to do great things for His glory in building the destinies of the country you love so well and have served so faithfully. You have suffered calumny as few men have; and, as far as I know, have borne it with remarkable Christian patience. All this I look upon as an earnest of the blessings with which God will crown the work which is now before you.

Cahill to de Valera, 22 March 1932, Eamon de Valera papers, 1095/1, Franciscan Archives, Killiney, Co. Dublin.

41 See Maurice Manning, *The Blueshirts* (Gill & Macmillan, Dublin, 1970).

42 An influential section of Catholic Ireland in the 1930s often politically identified with Fine Gael, was much more interested in the vocationalist movement – a form of corporatism inspired by the papal encyclicals which had Salazar's Portugal as one of its models. The 'success' of Mussolini's fascist Italy was also admired. This strain sought to reorganise Irish society along lines laid down in recent papal encyclicals and held many attractions. But intellectually it drew upon right-wing continental Catholicism for its inspiration. Therefore, there was a risk that those espousing vocationalist views might also be influenced by the anti-Semitism which usually accompanied such ideas and movements in France, Belgium, Holland, Austria and other European countries.

43 K.C.C., 'Ireland for the Irish', *Blueshirt*, 8 June 1935.

44 ibid. At least one member of the Jewish community in Ireland proved that a Jew was not welcome. A young Gerald Goldberg presented himself at Blueshirt offices in Cork only to be told that he could not become a member as it was confined to Christians. Interview with Gerald Goldberg, Cork, December 1995.

45 Blythe to Newman, 29 October 1934, Box 1, Irish Jewish Museum Archives, Dublin.

46 ibid.

47 ibid.

48 The Fianna Fáil government, refusing to underestimate the threat posed by O'Duffy, had taken a very strong law-and-order stand from the outset. De Valera's government proscribed a march to Leinster House planned by O'Duffy and his Blueshirts for 13 August 1933 to commemorate the anniversary of the deaths eleven years before of the founding fathers of the state, Arthur Griffith and Michael Collins. O'Duffy called off at the last minute his Mussolini-style tactic.

49 Attributed to a Dr Moody, the publisher sought to make it clear in the preface
    We have no desire to say one word in defence of the Jewish pornographist,
    the Jewish usurer, the Jewish receiver of stolen property, or the Jewish
    clean-up and clear-off shopkeeper. The machinery of law and order should
    be set in vigorous motion against all wrong-doers, Jew or Gentile. The
    Jewish Community themselves, we have no doubt, will welcome such steps
    as will foil their own unscrupulous minority; but even when society can no
    longer find fault with the Jew for the dubious dealings of his less reputable
    brother, there will remain the Jewish problem.
    Doctor Moody, *Why are the Jews Persecuted?* (Catholic Truth Society, Dublin,
    24 November 1938), p. 1.

50 ibid., p. 28.

51 ibid.

52 ibid.

53 ibid., pp. 25–6.

54 The source given in support of the argument is *Secret Powers Behind the Revolution*, by Vicomte Leon de Poneins. See *Cross*, Vol. 25 (May 1934).

55 ibid.

56 Herzog to the editor of the *Cross* (undated); copy in Edward Byrne papers,
    Dublin Archdiocesan Archives.

57 ibid.

58 ibid.

59 He also enclosed a copy of his letter to the editor of the *Cross*.

60 Herzog–Byrne correspondence, in Edward Byrne papers, Dublin Archdiocesan
    Archives.

61 ibid.

62 The *Cross*, reply from editor, contained in ibid.

63 ibid.

64 A query was put to the Department of Justice as to whether or not the correspondence should be destroyed. It remains on file in the archives in the 1990s.
    See D/J D 48/35, NAI.

65 The role of Axis diplomats in fomenting anti-Semitic ideas in Ireland has yet to
    be researched. But there is evidence that the Italian consul and later minister,
    Lodi Fe, harboured anti-Semitic feelings and expressed them in his reports, as
    did his successor, Vincenzo Berardis. The situation is less clear regarding the
    German legation. It is my view that at least one official there during the war
    was responsible for encouraging the spread of anti-Semitism in Ireland.

66 Given Bewley's earlier performance in Germany in 1921–22, he would appear
    to have been a most unlikely candidate for the position of envoy extraordinary
    and minister plenipotentiary to Berlin. But he confounded his critics and was
    moved by the President of the Executive Council, Eamon de Valera, to Berlin in
    July 1933 from the Holy See where he had served for three years.

67 *Allgemeine Zeitung*, 20 August 1933, in D/FA 217/28, NAI; quoted in Mervyn
    O'Driscoll, 'Irish–German Relations 1922–39' (MA, University College Cork,
    1992), p. 145.

68 ibid. Daniel Binchy had criticised National Socialism in two articles: 'Heinrich
    Bruning', *Studies*, Vol. 21 (September 1932), pp. 385–403 and 'Adolf Hitler',
    Studies, Vol. 22 (March 1933), pp. 29–47.

69 O'Driscoll, 'Irish–German Relations', p. 145.

70 ibid., p. 154.

71 ibid.

72 Charles Bewley, *Memoirs of a Wild Goose* (Lilliput Press, Dublin, 1990), p. 165.
    Bewley has not left a very full record of his time in Berlin. It is instructive to

contrast the memoirs with the content of his written reports from Berlin between 1933 and 1939.

73 Frick was giving a lecture to the diplomatic corps and the foreign press in a series organised by the Foreign Department of the Nazi Party.

74 Confidential Reports, 19 February 1934, D/FA 19/50, NAI.

75 ibid.

76 ibid.

77 ibid.

78 ibid.

79 ibid. Bewley was told that the greatest difficulty facing his informant was the problem created by Jews who had returned from abroad with French or Czech passports.

80 ibid. Bewley was told that the German authorities 'could not believe in the sincerity of the Jews, having regard to the experiences which not only Germany but Spain and other countries had had in the past of Jews reverting to their former religion when the advantages of renouncing it had passed'.

81 Charles Bewley, *Hermann Göring and the Third Reich* (Devin-Adair, USA, 1962).

82 Confidential Reports, 11 May 1934, D/FA 19/50, NAI.

83 ibid.

84 Confidential Reports, 6 June 1934, D/FA 19/50, NAI.

85 ibid.

86 ibid.

87 ibid.

88 ibid.

89 He cited General Krasnoff, *The Largo of Haendel*, to support the views on ritual murder.

90 Confidential Reports, 6 June 1934 D/FA 19/50, NAI.

91 ibid.

92 Martin Gilbert, *Atlas of the Holocaust: The Complete History* (Dent, London, 1993), p. 17.

93 Confidential Reports, 19 July 1935, D/FA 19/50, NAI.

94 Confidential Reports, 26 July 1935, D/FA 19/50, NAI.

95 O'Driscoll, 'Irish–German Relations', pp. 194–6.

96 Confidential Reports, 17 September 1935, D/FA 19/50, NAI.

97 ibid.

98 *Irish Press*, 16 September 1935.

99 *Irish Times*, 12 September 1935.

100 E. Bachellery, 'Julius Pokorny (1887–1970)', *Études Celtique*,Vol. 14 (1974), pp. 283–5; see also Diarmuid Breathnach and Máire Ní Murchú (eds.), Beathaisnéis, Vol III, pp. 144–5.

101 Pokorny to Best, 5 May 1933, MS 11,996 (2), Richard Irvine Best papers, NLI.

102 ibid.

103 ibid.

104 Pokorny to Best, 4 May 1933, MS 11,003 (B), Richard Irvine Best papers, NLI. He also had given the following names as references to McCauley in Berlin: Bergin, Michael Buckley, Michael O'Brien, Joseph O'Neill and Eoin MacNeill.

105 Pokorny to Best, (?) 14 October 1933, MS 11,003 (B), Richard Irvine Best papers, NLI.

106 ibid.

107 Pokorny to Best, 27 December 1933, MS 11,003, Richard Irvine Best papers, NLI.

108 Pokorny to Best, 21 October 1935, MS 11,003, Richard Irvine Best papers, NLI.

109 Pokorny to Best, undated letter, MS 11,003, Richard Irvine Best papers, NLI. He explained in the letter how Muhlhausen, with whom he had always been on the best of terms, 'did at once everything in order to get my post!!' Pokorny explained that the 'danger was grave, he being an old S.A. man'. Only the fact that he had done 'practically nothing in all these 20 years has saved me, the authorities in Prussia being a little bit more broad-minded than in the smaller states'.

110 Pokorny to Best, 27 April 1935, MS 11,003, Richard Irvine Best papers, NLI.

111 Pokorny to Best, 21 October 1935, MS 11,003, Richard Irvine Best papers, NLI.

112 ibid.

113 Pokorny to Best, 1 May 1936, MS 11,003, Richard Irvine Best papers, NLI.

114 ibid.

115 Boland minute, 20 August 1945, D/T S6631B, NAI.

116 Undated Bryan minute (? early 1939), Adolf Mahr file, G2/0130, Irish Military Archives, Dublin.

117 Boland minute, 20 August 1945, D/T S6631B, NAI.

118 Brase was born on 4 May 1875 at Egestorf, near Hanover. He attained a leading position among the bandmasters of the imperial German army. In October 1922, he was asked to set up an Irish Army School of Music. Brase was given the rank of colonel. He died in Dublin in 1940. (Biography supplied by Commandant Peter Young, Director, Irish Military Archives.)

119 Brase to Adjutant General, Department of Defence, 14 May 1935, G2/2/37672, Irish Military Archives, Dublin.

120 Brase's German assistant in the Army School of Music, Captain Christian Sauerzweig, did not share his superior's political ideas. He was a strong opponent of Hitler.

121 From G2 profile of Mahr, 25 January 1943 (almost certainly compiled by Bryan), G2/0130, Irish Military Archives, Dublin.

122 Boland minute, 20 August 1945, D/T S6631B, NAI.

123 From G2 report on Mahr, 1939, G2/0130, Irish Military Archives, Dublin.

124 Bryan minute, 19 December 1945, G2/0130, Irish Military Archives, Dublin.

125 Dermot Keogh, *Ireland and Europe 1919–1989* (Hibernian University Press, Cork and Dublin, 1989), p. 90.

126 See Count Tomacelli file, G2/0222, Irish Military Archives, Dublin.

127 ibid.

128 The *Irish Independent* adopted a blatantly pro-Franco stance in its reporting of the Spanish Civil War. Both the *Irish Times* and the *Irish Press* took a less partisan position. The popular reaction to the war in the country was closer to the line of the *Irish Independent*. For example the Oblate pilgrimage to Lourdes had made the primary intention of their Mass at the grotto 'the triumph of the Catholic Church in Spain'.

129 *Irish Independent*, 31 August 1936.

130 *The Irish Christian Front* (Dublin, 1936), pp. 1–5.

131 *Dáil Éireann Debates*, Vol. 59, col. 522 (6 November 1935).

132 *Irish Independent*, 30 December 1936.

133 *Irish Press*, 30 December 1936; quoted in O'Driscoll, 'Irish–German Relations', p. 242.

134 *Irish Independent*, 30 December 1936. *The Irish Press* carried a report but did not mention some of the more extreme statements made by Rollins or quote the Belton letter.

135 Herzog to Byrne, 1 January 1937, Edward Byrne papers, Dublin Archdiocesan Archives.

136 ibid.

137   See Manus O'Riordan, 'Irish and Jewish Volunteers in the Spanish Anti-Fascist War', a 50th anniversary lecture given at the Irish Jewish Museum, 15 November 1987.
138   Keogh, *Ireland and Europe*, pp. 63–97.
139   Belton to MacRory, 17 February 1937, Joseph MacRory papers, Armagh Archdiocesan Archives.
140   Belton to MacRory, 29 December 1937, Joseph MacRory papers, Armagh Archdiocesan Archives.
141   *Irish Press*, 9 October 1936.
142   ibid.
143   ibid.
144   The first in his five-volume study on the institutions of Jewish law had recently appeared. See Isaac Herzog, *The Main Institutions of Jewish Law*, Vol. 1 (Soncino Press, London, 1936).
145   Chaim Herzog, *Living History: A Memoir* (Pantheon Books, New York, 1996), p. 27.
146   Interview with Asher Benson, Dublin, November 1995.
147   Dermot Keogh, 'The Constitutional Revolution: An Analysis of the Making of the Constitution', *Administration*, Vol. 35, No. 4 (1987), p. 69.
148   Interview with Asher Benson, Dublin, November 1995.
149   Bunreacht na hÉireann, Article 44.1.3; see also Dermot Keogh, *The Vatican, the Bishops and Irish Politics, 1919–1939* (Cambridge University Press, Cambridge, 1986). The constitution was amended in 1972 and subsections 2 and 3 of Article 44.1 were deleted. The concern at the time was to remove the clause which stated that 'the State recognises the special position of the Holy Catholic Apostolic and Roman Church as the guardian of the Faith professed by the great majority of the citizens'. When it was decided that that section should be taken out, it followed that the other section also had to be deleted.
150   See Keogh, 'The Constitutional Revolution', pp. 4–84.
151   There is evidence of an organised attempt to intimidate the Jewish community in Dublin towards the end of 1937. An article in *Labour News* on 11 December 1937 quoted one provincial paper as stating that an anti-Jewish campaign had been going on in Dublin for many months. Some prominent Jews had been warned to leave the city without delay. The houses of individual Jewish families had been placed under garda protection. See 'Jews' in *Labour News*, 11 December 1937. (My thanks to Sandra McAvoy for bringing this article to my attention.)
152   *Irish Times*, 6 April 1937.
153   ibid.
154   ibid.
155   J. B. Lyons, *Oliver St John Gogarty* (Blackwater, Dublin, 1980), pp. 182–5.
156   Quoted in Louis Hyman, *The Jews of Ireland: From Earliest Times to the Year 1910* (Irish University Press, Shannon, 1972), pp. 148–9.
157   See High Court file, 300 P/1937, NAI.
158   Lyons, *Oliver St John Gogarty*, p. 186.
159   See High Court file, 300 P/1937, NAI.
160   ibid.
161   ibid.
162   See James Knowlson, *Damned to Fame: The Life of Samuel Beckett* (Bloomsbury, London, 1996), pp. 279ff. See also Deirdre Bair, *Samuel Beckett: A Biography* (Jonathan Cape, London, 1978), pp. 265ff.; Lyons, *Oliver St John Gogarty*, pp. 182–94.
163   Knowlson, *Damned to Fame*, p. 279.

164   Lyons, *Oliver St John Gogarty*, p. 194.
165   The lord mayor of Dublin, Alfie Byrne, was in attendance together with the Fine
      Gael TD, Gearóid O'Sullivan, the Labour TD, Luke Duffy, and the Fianna Fáil
      TD, Robert Briscoe; Mr Zlotover represented the Rabbinate Committee and Dr
      Joshua Baker represented the organising committee.
              Those on the platform, in addition to the speakers, included: E. M.
      Solomons, Bethel Solomons, R. M. Smyllie, M. Ellis, W. Leon, P. Toohey, R.
      Segal, Rev. Mr Roith, Rev. Mr Garb, A. Benson, B. Eppel, M. W. Robinson, M.
      Jacobson, S. White, M. Golding, I. Maslin, L. Levinson, D. Kantor, M. Josephs, M.
      Leventhal, H. Wiener, J. Mirrelson, M. Green, S. Green and J. Marcus. *Irish
      Press*, 9 April 1937.
166   ibid.
167   ibid.
168   ibid.
169   ibid.
170   ibid.
171   *Irish Times*, 10 April 1937.
172   Both the *Irish Times* report and the *Irish Press* report quoted above attribute
      this comment to Herzog; perhaps the editorial writer was mistaken in attribut-
      ing it to Abrahamson.
173   *Irish Times*, 10 April 1937.
174   *Irish Press*, 12 April 1937.
175   Chaim Herzog had gone to Jerusalem to study in May 1935. See Herzog, *Living
      History*, p. 29.
176   ibid.
177   ibid.
178   De Valera is so described by Shulamit Eliash in 'The "Rescue" Policy of the
      Chief Rabbinate of Palestine before and during World War II', *Modern Judaism*,
      October 1983, p. 298; I am grateful to Professor Eliash for sending me copies of
      her article.

5: Irish refugee policy, anti-Semitism and the approach of the Second World War

1   'Ireland' entry in *Encyclopedia Judaica* (Jerusalem, 1971).
2   Herzog's obituary in the *Jewish Chronicle* in 1959 commented that his 'prac-
    tical achievement for the development of Dublin Jewish life and institutions was
    as valuable for the local community as was his scholastic output for wider
    Jewish circles'. See 'Chief Rabbi Herzog – Outstanding Scholar and Leader',
    Jewish Chronicle, 31 July 1959.
3   Undated cutting in Nurock/Abrahamson family scrapbook (2) in the possession
    of Maurice Abrahamson, Dublin.
4   William Nurock obituary, in the *Jewish Chronicle* (undated), Nurock/Abra-
    hamson family scrapbook.
5   Nurock had been a vice-president and a treasurer of the Dublin Hebrew Congre-
    gation, a treasurer of the Keren Hayesod and Zionist foundation funds. He was
    described by a correspondent for the *Jewish Chronicle* as 'a gentle soul' who, in
    his life, 'made not an enemy and never lost a friend'. Nurock/Abrahamson
    family scrapbook.
6   William Nurock obituary, in the *Jewish Chronicle* (undated), Nurock/Abra-
    hamson family scrapbook.
7   Bernard Shillman, *A Short History of the Jews in Ireland* (Eason, Dublin,
    1945), p. 133. The JRC was reconstituted in 1941 and a new constitution was
    drawn up.

8   ibid.

9   See Colette Mary Cotter, 'Anti-Semitism and Irish Political Culture, 1932–1945' (M Phil, University College Cork, 1996), chapter 2.

10 Under the Unemployment Insurance Acts 1920 and 1933, aliens employed in the country were treated equally with nationals for all purposes of those Acts, including the payment of contributions and the receipt of unemployment benefit. However, the benefits under the Unemployment Assistance Acts 1933 and 1935 only applied to nationals. ibid.

11 ibid.

12 The following is the number of certificates of naturalisation granted during each of the years 1936 to 1946: 1936, 42; 1937, 52; 1938, 76; 1939, 67; 1940, 23; 1941, 13; 1942, 13; 1943, 7; 1944, 16; 1945, 22 and 1946, 167. Information kindly supplied to me by G. McConnell, Department of Justice, January 1997.

13 The Act provides:

> (1) The Minister may, if and whenever he thinks proper, do by order . . . any of the following things in respect . . . of all aliens of a particular nationality. . . .
>
> > (e) make provision for the deportation and exclusion of such aliens from Saorstát Éireann and provide for and authorise the making by the Minister of orders for that purpose;
> >
> > (f) require such aliens to reside or remain in particular districts or places in Saorstát Éireann;
> >
> > (g) prohibit such aliens from residing or remaining in particular districts or places in Saorstát Éireann.
>
> (2) An aliens order may contain certain provisions for all or any of the following purposes, that is to say: . . .
>
> > (b) conferring on the Minister and on officers of the Minister, officers of customs and excise and the military and police forces of the State all such powers (including powers of arrest and detention) as are, in the opinion of the Minister, necessary for giving full effect to or enforcing compliance with such order.

Quoted in Cotter, 'Anti-Semitism and Irish Political Culture', p. 54. Articles 8 and 9 outlined the restrictions on a change of name by aliens. This was to have direct application to Jewish refugees in particular.

14 Leydon to Walshe, 22 May 1937, D/FA (General) S13/3, NAI.

15 ibid.

16 My mother, Maureen O'Sullivan, was a junior executive officer in the department from 1932 until the marriage bar obliged her to leave in 1944. She worked in the aliens section and in the accounts branch.

17 Interview with Tom Woulfe, Dublin, December 1996.

18 For a general survey of Ireland's position at Geneva see Michael Kennedy, *Ireland and the League of Nations 1919–1946* (Irish Academic Press, Dublin, 1996).

19 Murphy to Cremins, 15 May 1936, D/FA (General) S13/3, NAI.

20 ibid.

21 ibid.

22 Michael R. Marrus, *The Unwanted: European Refugees in the Twentieth Century* (Oxford University Press, Oxford and New York, 1985), pp. 164–5.

23 ibid.

24 Leydon to Walshe, 22 May 1937, D/FA (General) S13/3, NAI.

25 ibid.

26 Rynne to Cremins, Geneva, 5 June 1937, D/FA (General), S13/3, NAI.

27 ibid.

28   Marrus, *The Unwanted*, p. 165.
29   ibid., pp. 167–8.
30   *Irish Press*, 14 March 1938.
31   ibid.
32   Marrus, *The Unwanted*, p. 168.
33   Bruce F. Pauley, *From Prejudice to Persecution: A History of Austrian Anti-Semitism* (University of North Carolina Press, Chapel Hill and London, 1992), p. 275ff.
34   Marrus, *The Unwanted*, p. 168.
35   ibid.
36   ibid., pp. 172–3.
37   ibid., p. 170.
38   ibid.
39   For an excellent review of the proceedings, see Paul R. Bartrop, 'The Dominions and the Evian Conference, 1938: A Lost Chance or a Golden Opportunity?', in Paul R. Bartrop (ed.), *False Havens: The British Empire and the Holocaust*, Studies in the Shoah, Vol. X (University Press of America, Lanham, Maryland, 1995), pp. 53–78.
40   Murphy to Cremins, 12 July 1938, relaying de Valera's instruction, D/FA S13/3/2, NAI.
41   Official Report of Plenary Session of Evian Conference, July 1938, 36, Myron Taylor papers (2), US National Archives and Records Administration, Franklin D. Roosevelt Library, Hyde Park, New York.
42   ibid. Given the country's high emigration, this may have appeared a convincing argument. But Ireland was far from being overpopulated. There were areas in the country where an industrious and scientifically trained farmer could have survived without constituting a threat to the existing community. For a general discussion of Irish population density, see J. J. Lee, *Ireland 1912–1985: Politics and Society* (Cambridge University Press, Cambridge, 1989), pp. 511–13.
43   Official Report of Plenary Session of Evian Conference.
44   Statement by the Irish Delegation, Intergovernmental Committee, Evian, 11 July 1939 (Technical Subcommittee), Index of Conference Proceedings, Myron Taylor papers (2), US National Archives and Records Administration, Franklin D. Roosevelt Library, Hyde Park, New York.
45   Hubert Butler, 'The Kagran Gruppe', in *The Children of Drancy* (Lilliput Press, Mullingar, 1988), p. 198.
46   Tony Kushner, *The Holocaust and the Liberal Imagination: A Social and Cultural History* (Blackwell, Oxford, 1994), p. 50.
47   Marrus, *The Unwanted*, pp. 169–70.
48   See Bartrop, 'The Dominions and the Evian Conference', pp. 59–61. A short consultation took place between the dominions on 6 July – the day the conference opened. What followed brought no comfort to refugees in general and Jewish refugees in particular. Michael Marrus describes how 'one delegation after another read statements into the record, justifying existing restrictive policies and congratulating themselves on how much had already been accomplished for refugees'. Marrus, *The Unwanted*, pp. 170–1.
     The Canadians made the following statement:
     Unfortunately, the continuance of serious unemployment and of economic uncertainty and disturbance still limits, severely, Canadian power to absorb any considerable number of immigrants.
     The Australian delegate at Evian said much the same:
     Under the circumstances, Australia cannot do more, for it will be appreciated that in a young country man power from the source from which most

of its citizens have come is preferred, while undue privileges cannot be given to one particular class of non-British subject without prejudice to others. It will no doubt be appreciated also that, as we have no real racial problems, we are not desirous of importing one by encouraging any scheme of large-scale foreign migration.

Bartrop, 'The Dominions and the Evian Conference', pp. 64, 66.

49 The statistics in this passage and the following table were supplied to the Department of Justice by the Garda Síochána. See D/J 69/4983, NAI.

50 D/J 69/2585, NAI.

51 D/J 69/682, NAI.

52 D/J 69/323, NAI.

53 D/J 69/484, NAI.

54 D/J 69/32, NAI.

55 See Adolf Nussenblatt to Dublin, 21 November 1938, D/FA 102/571, NAI; quoted in Mervyn O'Driscoll, 'Irish–German Relations, 1922–1939' (MA, University College Cork, 1992), p. 222.

56 Memorandum, 14 November 1938, D/T S11007A, NAI.

57 ibid.

58 Duff or Roche minute, 23 March 1938, D/J 69/2538, NAI.

59 ibid. On line one of the minute Gudansky was referred to as the 'Chief Rabbi'; the word 'rabbi' was crossed out and 'minister' inserted. The same correction presumably was overlooked in the phrase 'and the Chief Rabbi approved of the appointment'.

60 ibid. The Department of Justice had previous experience of the appointment of an alien as first reader and cantor of the Lennox Street congregation. In August 1931 David Garbarz, who had previously been employed as a singer in the Folies Bergere theatre in Brussels according to Department of Justice sources, had been granted a visa to come to Ireland on a holiday visit to see his brother Wolf Garbarz, the first reader of the Dolphin's Barn Hebrew congregation. When the three months were up, his brother asked for an extension in order to teach him the religious rites and a better knowledge of English. The application for an extension was refused. He then sent in a medical certificate to the department and was given a further two months.

David Garbarz was appointed on 7 February 1932 reader and cantor of the Lennox Street congregation at a salary of £1. Despite the appointment being approved by the chief rabbi, the Department of Justice refused him permission to remain. He returned to the continent on 11 April 1932. Following special representations, Garbarz was allowed to take up the appointment in the Lennox Street Synagogue in July 1932. He held the post for six months before going to Waterford as cantor of the Hebrew congregation. He left to take up an appointment in England in July 1934. (The 1938 minute gives the file reference to the Garbarz case as D/J 221/1649.)

61 Duff or Roche minute, 23 March 1938, D/J 69/2538, NAI.

62 ibid.

63 ibid.

64 Frankel to Briscoe, 19 August 1937, Robert Briscoe papers in the possession of Ben Briscoe TD.

65 Dr Joshua Baker to Briscoe, 30 August 1937, Robert Briscoe papers.

66 Robert Briscoe papers.

67 Briscoe to Ruttledge, 22 April 1938, Robert Briscoe papers.

68 Roche memorandum, 11 March 1938, D/J 69/1919, NAI. A report from the detective branch of the Garda Síochána, dated 15 March 1938, reported that Frankel was working on Hebrew manuscripts in Trinity College library and the

National Library. He had conducted services at Ormond Quay and given lectures at the synagogue in Rathmines. But the detective who investigated the case, Michael S. Mehigan, expressed the opinion that 'his services are availed of [in Ormond Quay] solely for the purpose of allowing him to remain in this country'. He recommended, in the circumstances, that 'no further facilities be afforded him'. See D/J 69/1919, NAI.

69 Duff minute, 31 March 1938, D/J 69/2495, NAI.
70 Roche minute, 1 April 1938, D/J 69/2495, NAI.
71 Ruttledge stressed that nothing was known 'unfavourable to the character of either alien or of their friends here, but [the decision had been taken] on more general grounds of policy'. See Ruttledge to Briscoe, 11 April 1938, Robert Briscoe papers.
72 ibid.
73 ibid.
74 ibid.
75 ibid. Ruttledge argued that the plea would be open to the criticism of the dependence of the Jewish community on non-Irish elements; he wrote: 'We have always to take into account the danger . . . that men admitted for religious purposes may be found afterwards engaged in trade or labour and that it may then be impossible, in practice, to send them out of the country.'
76 Briscoe to Ruttledge, 22 April 1938, Robert Briscoe papers.
77 ibid.
78 ibid.
79 ibid.
80 Roche to Briscoe, (no day given) May 1938, Robert Briscoe papers. The secretary of the Department of Justice stated further that in the case of the orphaned girl the minister had been advised that Briscoe was under a misapprehension in thinking that she could be brought into the country and kept there for three years without any permit.
81 ibid.
82 ibid.
83 ibid.
84 ibid.
85 ibid.
86 D/J 69/2495, NAI.
87 Walshe to Roche, 7 September 1938, D/FA 102/438, NAI; quoted in O'Driscoll, 'Irish–German Relations', pp. 235–6.
88 Quoted in O'Driscoll, 'Irish–German Relations', p. 236.
89 See Garda report, 23 May 1938, D/J 69/2830, NAI.
90 Walshe to Leydon, 16 August 1938, D/J 69/3002, NAI.
91 ibid.
92 ibid. Walshe added that de Valera was in entire agreement with statements in a report from Bewley 'as to the undesirability of and the necessity for checking assertions as to Jews being allowed to settle in Ireland and influence to that effect having been brought to bear on the Taoiseach'.
93 Duff to Leydon, 23 August 1938, D/J 69/3002, NAI.
94 ibid.
95 Marrus, *The Unwanted*, p. 168.
96 Patrick Kavanagh, 'Epic', in *Collected Poems* (MacGibbon and Key, London, 1968), p. 136.
97 *Irish Press*, 10 October 1938.
98 ibid.
99 See Marrus, *The Unwanted*, pp. 173–6.

100   Bewley report, 6 October 1938, D/J 69/4109, NAI.
101   ibid.
102   ibid.
103   Duff circular, 12 October 1938, D/J 69/4109, NAI.
104   Roche to Leydon, 19 October 1938, D/J 69/4109, NAI.
105   Bewley report, 27 October 1938, D/J 69/4109, NAI.
106   Duff to Boland, 26 November 1938, D/J 69/4109, NAI.
107   ibid.
108   Duff to Leydon, 20 January 1939, D/J 69/4109, NAI.
109   ibid.
110   Leydon to Roche, 1 February 1939, D/J 69/4109, NAI.
111   Bewley report, 25 October 1938, D/J 69/4109, NAI.
112   ibid.
113   Bewley to Walshe, 2 November 1938, D/FA 102/520, NAI; quoted in O'Driscoll, 'Irish–German Relations', pp. 232–3.
114   I have no evidence that this report was circulated to the Department of Justice by the Department of External Affairs.
115   See Bewley to Walshe, 9 December 1938, Confidential Reports, D/FA 202/63, NAI.
116   ibid.
117   ibid.
118   ibid.
119   ibid.
120   ibid.
121   ibid.
122   ibid.
123   ibid.
124   ibid.
125   ibid. The second half of this quotation, from 'Naturally . . .', was highlighted on the original by either Walshe or Boland in the Department of External Affairs.
126   ibid. Bewley ended his thirteen-page report by stating that it was 'impossible to give even a summary of the *Jewish problem* [my emphasis] except in a very insufficient form'. He stated that the official German position was contained in an official publication of some 400 pages. There is no evidence that Walshe requested him to send the document on to Dublin.
127   Frederick Boland, the assistant secretary of the department, drew up a memorandum on 20 December 1938 accusing Bewley of having failed to make regular returns of the Berlin accounts. Boland regarded his actions as 'contumacy, and wilful disregard of his responsibilities as sub-accounting officer'. I am grateful to Frank Sheridan, Department of Foreign Affairs, Dublin, who made this material available to me.
128   Walshe to Bewley, 26 January 1939, Confidential Reports, D/FA 219/4, NAI.
129   Bewley to de Valera, 2 August 1939, Confidential Reports, D/FA 219/4, NAI.
130   Bewley had no supporters in the Department of External Affairs. He was succeeded in Berlin by a young diplomat, William Warnock. Bewley lived mainly in Rome during the Second World War where he worked as a journalist for a pro-Nazi Swedish newspaper and travelled to and from Germany on a forged Irish diplomatic passport.
     Three important conclusions may be drawn concerning Bewley's time in Berlin. Firstly, the Irish government – and de Valera as Minister for External Affairs – had laboured under a considerable disadvantage because of Bewley's propensity to 'go native'. Ireland, therefore, paid a very high opportunity cost for keeping Bewley in Berlin for so long. Secondly, Bewley seized every

opportunity to warn about the 'Jewish problem' – as he termed it – and, despite his deteriorating professional standing in the department, his ideas influenced policy decisions. Finally, he was invested with even greater decision-making powers in his last year in Berlin over whether or not individuals should be admitted to the country, and that at a time when he had lost his professional credibility.

131   See list of factories in Ireland owned by aliens, D/J 69/4083, NAI; see also George Clare, *Last Waltz in Vienna: The Destruction of a Family, 1842–1942* (Macmillan, London, 1980), p. 204.

Another factory, Les Modes Modernes, had been opened in Galway in 1938 with great publicity. The Minister for Industry and Commerce, Seán Lemass, had first suggested that a subsidiary of this Paris-based business be opened in Ireland while on a visit to the French capital in 1935. The Irish factory was run by Marcus Witztum, a Jew from Poland who had come to Ireland in the mid-1930s via Argentina to set up a number of enterprises. His manager in Galway was also Jewish, Serge (Szulim) Philipson (sometimes spelled Phillipsohn).

There were other related concerns: Western Cloths Ltd, Wings Ltd, Plunder and Pollak (Ireland) Ltd, Malbay Manufacturing Co. Ltd and Irish Milanese Ltd. See list of factories, D/J 69/4083, NAI.

132   See Clare, *Last Waltz in Vienna*, pp. 228ff.

133   George Clare, *Berlin Days, 1946–47* (Pan Books, London, 1989), pp. 5–7.

134   See Clare, *Last Waltz in Vienna*, p. 210.

135   ibid.

136   ibid.

137   ibid., p. 212.

138   Clare, *Berlin Days*, pp. 5–7.

139   The Kristallnacht was sparked by the assassination of a German diplomat in Paris. The killer was a German-born Jew, Herschl Grynszpan, who was living as a refugee in Paris. The expulsion of Polish Jews from Germany had forced his family to cross the border into Poland. See Karl Dietrich Bracher, *The German Dictatorship: The Origins, Structure and Consequences of National Socialism* (Penguin, London, 1970), pp. 455–6.

140   Marrus, *The Unwanted*, p. 177.

141   Pokorny to Best, (undated) 1938, MS 11,003, Richard Irvine Best papers, NLI.

142   Clare, *Berlin Days*, p. 6.

143   Clare, *Last Waltz in Vienna*, p. 229.

144   These details are taken from a Garda report on the movements of the Clares and their associates. See G2/0252, Irish Military Archives, Dublin.

145   Clare to his parents, 18 January 1941, G2/0252, Irish Military Archives, Dublin.

146   Information kindly supplied by Tadhg O'Sullivan, postgraduate student in the Department of History, University College Cork. See Laurence Darton, *An account of the Friends' Committee for Refugees and Aliens, first known as the German Emergency Committee of the Society of Friends 1933–1950*, issued by the Friends Committee for Refugees and Aliens, Dublin, 1954.

147   Lucy O. Kingston, *Emerging from the Shadows: Based on Personal Diaries, 1883–1969*, compiled by Daisy Swanton (Attic Press, Dublin, 1994), p. 128. She trained as a midwife in the Rotunda and worked in Dublin throughout the war.

148   Interview with Betty Pearson (conducted by Tadhg O'Sullivan), Dublin, February 1997.

149   Interview with Maurice Abrahamson, Dublin, April 1997.

150   The honorary treasurers were M. Ellis and D. Vard. The honorary secretary was R. Kahan.

151 The Society of Vincent de Paul had received £1,000 from the Holy See to help settle refugees in the country. The Secretary of State, Cardinal Eugenio Pacelli, had expressed the hope that 'the act of paternal generosity on the part of the august Pontiff might stimulate the magnanimous hearts of Irish Catholics to do their utmost to help the Catholic refugees from Germany'. *Bulletin of the Society of St Vincent de Paul*, November 1938; quoted in T. W. T. Dillon, 'The Refugee Problem', *Studies*, Vol. 28 (1939), p. 414.

152 Herzog to de Valera, 9 October 1938, D/FA 131/143, NAI.

153 Dillon to de Valera, 10 November 1938, D/T S11007, NAI.

154 Memorandum outlining work of the Co-ordinating Committee, 14 November 1938, D/T S11007/B1, NAI.

   Dillon outlined the guiding philosophy of the committee in an article in *Studies*. Their rescue initiative would concentrate on Christian Jews rather than on Jews. He argued:

   It is certainly worse to be a Christian Jew in Germany to-day than to be a Jew *tout court* The Jew has a better chance of emigrating and is sure of a good reception in any foreign country from the local Jewish Community. The Christian, and in particular the Catholic, Jew is in an even more unhappy state inside Germany and is less sure of a welcome from his co-religionists outside. . . . There are then a large body of Catholics – some thousands – who are to-day treated as pariahs in Germany and Austria.

   Dillon, 'The Refugee Problem', pp. 407–8.

155 Memorandum outlining work of the Co-ordinating Committee, 14 November 1938, D/T S11007/B1, NAI.

   The medical profession vetoed the entry of a number of Austrian Catholic doctors. The papal nuncio, Paschal Robinson, had been instructed by his superiors in Rome to raise the cases of a group of doctors who were Jewish converts to Catholicism. On 8 April 1939, the Minister for Justice, Patrick Ruttledge, replied to Rome that the medical profession in Ireland was controlled by an independent body and he felt that it would object strongly to the admission of foreign medical practitioners. He also added that Ireland could not provide employment for its own medical graduates each year. Therefore, he had to refuse the request from the Holy See. Dermot Keogh, *Ireland and Europe, 1919–1989* (Hibernian University Press, Cork and Dublin, 1989), pp. 109–10.

   Among the appeals for intervention came one from the British Labour MP, Fenner Brockway. He wrote to de Valera on 9 April 1938 about the case of Walther Simon, 'a very dear comrade of ours and in imminent risk of losing his life in Vienna'. Brockway reminded de Valera: 'You perhaps remember me in the old prison days', presumably a reference to when they had been in jail together after the First World War. Brockway to de Valera, 9 April 1938, D/FA 127/121, NAI.

156 Memorandum outlining work of the Co-ordinating Committee, 14 November 1938, D/T S11007/B1, NAI.

157 ibid.

158 *Irish Press*, 5 December 1938.

159 ibid. Sir Joseph Glynn and R. J. Kidney were made joint honorary treasurers and Dr R. W. Ditchburn was honorary secretary. The other members of the committee were: Senator J. Douglas, E. H. Lewis-Crosby, S. Kyle, F. J. Meyrick and Conrad A. Pim.

160 ibid.

161 ibid.

162 ibid.

163 ibid.

164   ibid.
165   The signatories were drawn from among the most distinguished citizens in the
       country: Cardinal MacRory, the Catholic archbishops of Dublin (Edward
       Byrne), Cashel (John M. Harty) and Tuam (Thomas P. Gilmartin), Canon P.
       Boylan, Rev. R. K. Hanna, Rev. J. M. Ailry, Senator R. F. Browne, Prof.
       D. J.Coffey, James Dillon TD, Senator J. G. Douglas, Frank Duff, F. Fahy TD
       (ceann comhairle), Hugo V. Flynn TD (parliamentary secretary), Senator
       Maurice Hayes, Senator Sir John Keane, Samuel Kyle, Sir John Lumsden, T. S.
       Martin, F. J. Meryrick, Dr Lombard Murphy, Conrad A. Pim, Prof. J. M.
       O'Sullivan TD, Senator E. J. Rowlette MD and Sir J. M. Glynn. Among the other
       signatories to the appeal were: archbishop of Dublin, John Allen Fitzgerald
       Gregg; the bishop of Cashel, Emly, Lismore, Waterford and Tramore, Thomas
       Harvey; the dean of Christ Church Cathedral, Dublin, E. H. Lewis-Crosby; the
       lord mayor of Dublin, Alfred Byrne TD; Rev. Patrick Sexton, Canon T. W. Drury,
       Clive Brooks, Miss Helen Chenin, Prof. A. W. Conway, Prof. T. W. T. Dillon, H. M.
       Dockrell TD, T. P. Dowdall TD, J. Eason, Senator Prof. R. P. Farnan, F. Jacob,
       Henry Kennedy, P. J. Little TD, Martin Maguire KC, Senator Frank MacDermot,
       W. Norton, R. Lloyd Praeger, the Provost of Trinity College, W. E. Thrift and
       Major J. H. de W. Waller.
166   Butler, 'The Kagran Gruppe', pp. 197–8.
167   Lorna Siggins, 'An escape from hell remembered', *Irish Times*, 17 December
       1988.
168   Interview with Betty Pearson (conducted by Tadhg O'Sullivan), Dublin, Febru-
       ary 1997.
169   ibid.
170   This information is contained in a loose sheet in the Society of Friends
       Archives, Dublin. It is entitled 'Friends' work with Jewish refugees brought to
       Ireland before Second World War'. But, in the opinion of Betty Pearson, the
       information dates from the post-war period. Edwin B. Jacob, Tramore, Co.
       Waterford, went regularly to Rosslare and Cobh to meet refugees off the boat.
       Charles S. Jacob, Waterford, was also very active in relief work. Interview with
       Betty Pearson (conducted by Tadhg O'Sullivan), Dublin, February 1997.
171   Dillon, 'The Refugee Problem', p. 412.
172   ibid.
173   ibid.
174   ibid.
175   In the light of the experience of late 1938 and early 1939, a decision was taken
       to reorganise Catholic refugee work. A new group, he said, was formed called
       the Irish Catholic Council for Refugees. The proposal was to set up local
       committees throughout the country to fulfil the dual task of maintaining indi-
       vidual refugees and collecting funds to cover the cost of emigration. ibid., pp.
       413–14.
176   Bennington Cooper to de Valera, 10 December 1938, D/J 69/80, NAI.
177   ibid. She told de Valera that one of her friends was a world-renowned veteri-
       nary surgeon.
178   Boland to Roche, 16 December 1938, D/J 69/80, NAI.
179   D/J 69/80, NAI.
180   D/J 69/80, NAI.
181   On 8 December 1938, Duff wrote to an enquirer living in Blackrock: 'I am
       directed by the Minister for Justice to state that any application for a visa which
       is made by the Irish Co-ordinating Committee for Refugees will receive sympa-
       thetic consideration.' D/J 69/80, NAI.
           A letter by J. E. Duff to Boland, 15 March 1939, illustrates the self-percep-

tion of primacy exhibited by the Department of Justice in this area:

> I am directed by the Minister for Justice to suggest that the Chamber of Commerce should be informed that aliens are permitted to reside in this country at the discretion of the Minister for Justice; that the Minister grants permission to reside here to aliens who are in employment, only if the aliens obtain employment permits from the Minister for Industry and Commerce, and that the Minister is prepared to allow aliens to engage in professions in this country only if it is shown that there is some special need for their services.

> D/J 69/80, NAI.

182 D/J 69/80, NAI.
183 D/J 69/80, NAI.
184 *Irish Times*, 2 December 1983.
185 ibid.
186 ibid.
187 Interview with Gerald Goldberg, Cork, December 1995.
188 Duff minute, 23 March 1939, D/J 69/4182, NAI.
189 ibid.
190 ibid.
191 Frank Gallagher papers, MS 10058/116, Trinity College Dublin (TCD).
192 Frank Gallagher papers, MS 10058/117, TCD.
193 Frank Gallagher papers, MS 10058/118, TCD.
194 ibid.
195 ibid.
196 Frank Gallagher papers, MS 10058/119, TCD.
197 ibid.
198 Frank Gallagher papers, MS 10058/127, TCD.
199 ibid.
200 Frank Gallagher papers, MS 10058/128, TCD.
201 Frank Gallagher papers, MS 10058/130, TCD.
202 ibid.
203 Frank Gallagher papers, MS 10058/131, TCD.
204 Frank Gallagher papers, MS 10058/132, 133, 140, 142 and 144, TCD.
205 Frank Gallagher papers, MS 10058/134, TCD.
206 Frank Gallagher papers, MS 10058/136, TCD.
207 Frank Gallagher papers, MS 10058/150, TCD; interview with Ann Gallagher, Dublin, 1996.
208 Edouard Hempel to German Foreign Ministry, 7 December 1938, Records of the German Foreign Office received by the Department of State, microfilm K834/K214845-849, National Archives, Washington DC. I am grateful to Professor Matthew MacNamara for translating this document for me from German.
209 Ó Braonáin to de Valera, 21 November 1938, D/FA 102/568, NAI.
210 *Irish Times*, 23 February 1939, in D/FA 227/24, NAI.
211 ibid.
212 ibid.
213 ibid.
214 Translated and reported to Dublin by William Warnock, 28 February 1939, D/FA 227/24, NAI.
215 ibid.
216 ibid.
217 Herman Good was the younger son of Rev. Abraham Gudansky. He entered Trinity College Dublin in 1925, and graduated with the degree of LLB and a moderatorship in legal and political science. He was auditor of the Solicitors'

Apprentices Debating Society of Ireland, by whom he was awarded the gold medal for oratory, legal debate and impromptu speaking. He was a member of the Jewish Debating Society between 1927 and 1929. He was also closely connected with Dublin dramatic circles. He married Sybil Wine, daughter of Mr and Mrs Frank Wine of Manchester. See *Belfast Gazette*, January 1933, cutting in Nurock/Abrahamson family scrapbook.

218   *Irish Times*, 1 March 1939.

219   ibid.

220   D/T S6631A, NAI.

221   He wrote further: 'The Party rules strictly forbid any interference with matters political abroad and prescribe a codex of honesty and straightforwardness also in private matters, which is wholly praiseworthy and contains nothing sinister or detrimental to mutual goodwill amongst decent men'; he claimed he had been able to obtain Humboldt studentships for fifteen Irish students at German expense, amounting to £1,500. ibid.

222   He commented:

> I have already held the opinion and I cling to it, that in occupying this posi-tion I have undertaken nothing which even in the slightest degree, ever could be incompatible with the oath of allegiance which binds me as a civil servant of this country, a country which has honoured me significantly by entrusting me with the custodianship of its national treasures.

ibid.

223   Mahr concluded:

> I beg to acknowledge gratefully that the government was punctiliously fair towards my natural national feelings in never having raised the matter. For this I tender my most sincere thanks. It confirms my conviction that the incompatibility does not exist as far as fair-minded people are concerned. I beg of you to notify An Taoiseach of my resolution, in his capacity as Minis-ter for External Affairs, and naturally, I would be grateful if you would bring this letter also before the Minister for Education.

ibid.

224   Profile of Mahr, 25 January 1943, G2/0130, Irish Military Archives, Dublin.

225   ibid.

226   Menche to Mecking, 6 June 1939, Heinz Mecking file, Irish Military Archives, Dublin.

227   Minutes of meeting in the Department of Education, 23 March 1939, G2/0130, Irish Military Archives, Dublin.

228   Draft memorandum for government, 21 September 1945, D/T S6631B, NAI.

229   Another intercepted letter by G2 states: 'I don't see much of Mahr – he turned into a drunkard.' On 7 May 1940, he wrote to Hempel that he was going on a lecture tour of Hungary and Switzerland. By November 1941, he had moved to Berlin. Minute by Bryan, based on intercepted Kunstler/Crinion correspon-dence, in profile of Mahr, 25 January 1943, G2/0130, Irish Military Archives, Dublin.

230   Hempel had once told Boland that 'he blamed Mahr's influence for the fact that the German Foreign Office failed on occasions to act on the counsels of prudence he [Hempel] constantly gave them' as regards Ireland. Boland minute, 20 August 1945, D/T S6631B, NAI.

231   After the war Mahr sought to return to Ireland to take up his position as direc-tor of the National Museum. De Valera's government discussed his request without reaching a decision on 21 September 1945 and 9 July 1946. On both occasions, the item was withdrawn. It fell to the inter-party government to reach the conclusion on 5 November 1948 that 'Dr Adolf Mahr, Director and

Senior Keeper, National Museum of Ireland, should be retired from the Civil Service, and that such award of superannuation should be made in his case as might, after consultation between the Ministers for Education and Finance, be determined to be appropriate'. He retired with a pension from the Irish state. Cabinet minutes, 5 November 1945, Item 6, G.C. 5/45. Copy on D/T S6631B, NAI.

232 See litärgeographische Angaben über Irland, Süd– und Ostküste (Von Mizen Head bis Malin Head); Text und Bildheft mit Kartenanlagen, Abgeschlossen am 31 Mai 1941 (Generalstab des Heeres, Abteilung fur Kriegskarten und Vermessumgswesen (IV. Mil. – Geo.), Berlin 1941; This also carried the stricture: Nur für den Dienstgebrauch! I am grateful to Colonel Maurice Walsh for drawing this source to my attention; see also Dan Harvey and Gerry White, *The Barracks – A History of Victoria/Collins Barracks, Cork* (Mercier Press, Cork, 1997), pp. 145–51.

233 Briscoe to Ziff, Miami Beach, Florida, 22 September 1939, Robert Briscoe papers. Robert Briscoe supported the New Zionist Organisation. Its founder, Vladimir (Ze'en) Jabotinsky, was accused by David Ben-Gurion, who became the first Prime Minister of Israel in 1948, and the Zionist left of espousing the cause of extreme nationalism and of imitating fascist methods. For a study of his early life, see Shmuel Katz, *Lone Wolf: A Biography of Vladimir (Ze'ev) Jabotinsky*, 2 vols. (Barricade, New York, 1996). See also Leni Yahil, *The Holocaust: The Fate of European Jewry, 1932–1945* (Oxford University Press, Oxford, 1990), p. 188.

6: Ireland, the Second World War and the Holocaust

1 The card was probably made in 1944. Nurock/Abrahamson family scrapbook (2) in the possession of Maurice Abrahamson, Dublin.

2 Under the terms of the Anglo-Irish Treaty of 1921 Britain had the right to use the naval bases at Berehaven and Cobh in County Cork and at Lough Swilly in County Donegal – the 'Treaty ports'; that right was forfeited under the 1938 Anglo-Irish Agreement. Dermot Keogh, *Ireland and Europe, 1919–1989* (Hibernian University Press, Cork and Dublin, 1989), pp. 121–64.

3 The chief of staff of the IRA, Seán Russell, had travelled to Berlin in 1940 to receive instruction in the latest bomb-making techniques. Abwehr spies enjoyed indifferent success in Ireland during the early years of the war. News of arrests, particularly in the case of the German spy and IRA sympathiser Stephen Held on 24 May 1940, demonstrated the malfeasance of the German regime. Abwehr's special adviser on Ireland, Dr Edmund Vessenmayer, had already developed a strategy involving the IRA in a central subversive role. To that end, he had arranged for the 'escape' of a leading Irish republican, Frank Ryan, from Burgos jail in July 1940. (Ryan had been captured and imprisoned by Franco's forces during the Spanish Civil War.) That was part of his plan to prepare a 'Quisling' cadre in the country in anticipation of a German invasion. For details on this plan, see Keogh, *Ireland and Europe*, pp. 149–55. See also Seán Cronin, *Frank Ryan: The Search for the Republic* (Repsol Press, Dublin, 1980); and Robert Fisk, *In Time of War: Ireland, Ulster and the Price of Neutrality 1939–45* (André Deutsch, London, 1983), pp. 292–5.

4 See Dermot Keogh, *Twentieth-Century Ireland: Nation and State* (Gill & Macmillian, Dublin, 1994), pp. 108–56.

5 Arno J. Mayer, *Why Did the Heavens not Darken?* (Verso, London, 1990), pp. 279–312. State functionaries, party officials and SS officers were present. The meeting was chaired, in the absence of Heinrich Himmler, by Reinhard Heydrich.

6   Martin Gilbert, *Atlas of the Holocaust: The Complete History*, 2nd edn (Dent & Co., London, 1993), pp. 99–100.

7   Despite knowing the pitiless intention of the Nazis, mercifully we will never know who, if anyone, might have emerged as the Celtic Pétain or Quisling. We will never know if Irish men and women would have collaborated in the transporting of their Jewish compatriots in coffin ships to the continent. But it is probable, if not certain, that neither de Valera nor Cosgrave would have taken on the mantle of a Pétain. There is convincing evidence to show that de Valera's Fianna Fáil government did not intend to collaborate with Nazi invaders. The Irish army was under orders to put up strong resistance until the arrival of Allied forces from Northern Ireland and from across the channel. De Valera and his ministers would disperse to 'safe houses' and carry on the government of the country in much the same clandestine manner as Dáil Éireann had done between 1919 and 1921. A tier of regional governors had been selected from the ranks of the higher civil service to take over in the event of a breakdown of central government.

8   Leo Goldberger (ed.), *The Rescue of the Danish Jews: Moral Courage under Stress* (New York University Press, New York and London, 1987), pp. 1–74.

9   For the situation in France, see Michael R. Marrus and Robert O. Paxton, *Vichy France and the Jews* (Basic Books, New York, 1984) and Frances Malino and Bernard Wasserstein (eds.), *The Jews in Modern France* (Brandeis University Press, Hanover and London, 1985); for the Netherlands, see Bob Moore, *Refugees from Nazi Germany in the Netherlands 1933–1940* (Nijhoff, Dordrecht, Boston and Lancaster) – I am grateful to Dr Hans Leydekkers, Schagen, for this reference; for Austria, see Bruce F. Pauley, *From Prejudice to Persecution: A History of Austrian Anti-Semitism* (University of North Carolina Press, Chapel Hill and London, 1992); for Hungary, see Randolph L. Braham, *The Politics of Genocide: The Holocaust in Hungary*, 2 vols. (Columbia University Press, New York, 1981); for Poland, see Chimen Abramsky, Maciej Jachimczyk and Antony Polonsky (eds.), *The Jews in Poland* (Basil Blackwell, Oxford, 1986).

10 Mary Rose Doorly, *Hidden Memories: The Personal Recollections of Survivors and Witnesses to the Holocaust Living in Ireland* (Blackwater Press, Dublin, 1994), p. 10.

11 ibid.

12 ibid.

13 He made those remarks at a memorial service for the writer Sean O'Faolain in in 1991 where he also quoted the editorial in the first edition of the *Bell* in October 1940: 'Whoever you are then, O reader, Gentile or Jew, Protestant or Catholic, priest or layman, Big House or small house, the *Bell* is yours.' The words 'Gentile or Jew', Cruise O'Brien emphasised, took on a special significance in the context of 1940–41. He also argued that the Gaelic League had fallen under 'some sinister influence in those days'. An editorial in the *Bell* in 1942 quoted from a Gaelic League pamphlet: 'From certain Continental movements we have much to learn. As a fact, the temper of our movement, and the energy and daring of it, have more in common with them than with those nearer home.' Cruise O'Brien also cited another Gaelic League pamphlet of the same year: 'We cannot allow film-making to remain in the hands of the Jews, the eternal enemies of Christianity.' See Conor Cruise O'Brien, Sean O'Faolain memorial address, in Seán Dunne (ed.), *The Cork Review*, 1991, pp. 95–6.

14 Interview with Gerald Goldberg, Cork, December 1995.

15 Interview with Michael Solomons, Dublin, November 1995.

16 A. J. Leventhal 'What it means to be a Jew', *Bell*, Vol. 10, No. 3 (June 1945), pp. 212–13.

17 Interviewed on my behalf by Dr Caroline Windrum, Institute of Irish Studies, Queen's University Belfast, 1996–7.

18 ibid.

19 ibid. In 1942, Rada, who was a medical student at Queen's University, married Herbert Smith from Johannesburg whom she met in Belfast while he was on leave.

20 Czeslaw Milosz, *Facing the River* (Ecco Press, New Jersey, 1995), p. 34.

21 Roche to Minister for Justice, 5 September 1939, D/J 69/4785, NAI.

22 ibid. The people who would be stopped at Dún Laoghaire could simply travel to Belfast and come south by land.

23 ibid. It was argued that it was not practical to impose delays and restrictions upon such people for the purpose of stopping 'the comparatively few undesirables'.

24 ibid.

25 ibid.

26 ibid.

27 See Department of Justice memorandum to government, dated September 1939, D/J 69/4855, NAI.

28 (?) Garda authorities to Roche, 13 September 1939, D/J 69/4785, NAI. J. E. Duff, in a letter dated 15 June 1940, commented upon the letter of 13 September 1939:

> To date, however, recommendations have been made by the Garda Síochána for the deportation of only approximately 70 British subjects. It has been represented to the Minister that a large number of Jews and other undesirable persons who fled to this country from Great Britain since the 1st of August last are still residing here.

29 See Department of Justice memorandum to government, September 1939, D/J 69/4855, NAI.

30 ibid.

31 ibid. They were not obliged to register up to that point until they had been in the country for three months. The minister also wanted the power, on a trial basis, to have hotel and boarding house registers made known to the police.

32 ibid.

33 There was a further reason why the government appeared to be reluctant to support draconian restrictions on entry from Britain. The Revenue Commissioners had expressed the fear that the emergency order, as drafted by the Department of Justice, might deter wealthy people from visiting the country with a consequent loss to Irish revenue of an estimated £150,000. Roche to Revenue Commissioners, 5 December 1939, D/J 69/4855, NAI.

34 ibid.

35 Department of Justice to Dan Bryan, Military Intelligence, 25 May 1940, D/J 69/4083, NAI.

36 Roche to Moynihan, 25 October 1946, D/T S11007B/1, NAI.

37 I am grateful to Mr Joe Briscoe for providing me with this information. He sent me copies of correspondence in the possession of Rachel Levy, daughter of Serge Philipson, which included a letter from J. E. Duff, assistant secretary at the Department of Justice, to Philipson's secretary, dated 29 December 1939:

> I am directed by the Minister for Justice to refer to your letter of the 20th instant, and to state that the Minister is not prepared to permit Abraham Philipson, Hanna S. Philipson, Sola Siemion and Myrian Siemion, Polish nationals, to enter this country.

38 See S. Phillipsohn file, G2/1800, Irish Military Archives, Dublin.
39 Archer to John Belton, Department of External Affairs, 23 July 1940, G2/2631, Irish Military Archives, Dublin.
40 Archer to Roche, 23 July 1940, G2/2631, Irish Military Archives, Dublin.
41 Siev to Minister for Justice, 14 October 1939, D/J 69/4849, NAI.
42 Minister for Justice to Bisko, 26 September 1939, D/J 69/4849, NAI.
43 Siev to Minister for Justice, 14 October 1939, D/J 69/4849, NAI. Emphasis added by Department of Justice official.
44 ibid.
45 D/J 69/4849, NAI.
46 Roche to secretary, JRC, 12 July 1940, D/J 69/5490, NAI.
47 ibid.
48 R. Kahan to Minister for Justice, 6 September 1940, D/J 69/5490, NAI.
49 ibid.
50 Roche to Minister for Justice, 9 September 1940, D/J 69/5490, NAI.
51 Ira B. Nadel, *Joyce and the Jews: Culture and Texts* (University of Florida Press, Gainesville, 1996), pp. 226–30; see also James Knowlson, *Damned to Fame: The Life of Samuel Beckett* (Bloomsbury, London, 1996), p. 304.
52 Richard Ellman, *James Joyce* (Oxford University Press, Oxford, 1983), pp. 732–4.
53 ibid., p. 734
54 Knowlson, *Damned to Fame*, p. 304.
55 ibid., p. 304.
56 See Cian Ó hÉigeartaigh, 'Léon's last letters', *Irish Times*, 4 April 1992.
57 ibid.
58 Damien McHugh, 'The Dublin woman who was gassed at Auschwitz', *Evening Press*, 27 April 1995.
59 'Refugees at Millisle, 70 acres of land leased', *Newtownards Chronicle*, 20 May 1939.
60 Robert Sugar, 'Millisle Farm', *Jewish Monthly*, October 1990, pp. 26–9.
61 ibid. The children had prayers in the morning followed by breakfast. They then had English lessons followed by recreation. They were given half a crown pocket money a week and were allowed to visit Donaghadee where they could go to the cinema at a reduced rate. See Martin Gilbert, *The Boys: Triumph over Adversity* (Weidenfeld and Nicolson, London, 1996), p. 327.
62 Gilbert, *The Boys*, p. 327.
63 (?) Egan to JRC, 9 May 1941, JRC correspondence, Box 40, Irish Jewish Museum Archives, Dublin.
64 ibid.
65 Egan to Newman, 14 May 1941, JRC correspondence, Box 40, Irish Jewish Museum Archives, Dublin.
66 Newman to Gudansky, 15 May 1941, JRC correspondence, Box 40, Irish Jewish Museum Archives, Dublin.
67 McQuaid to Jakobovits, 26 May 1949, D/FA 305/62/1, NAI.
68 Fisk, *In Time of War*, pp. 432–6.
69 This is a hypothesis based on interviews I have done over the past twenty years with Irish intelligence and military personnel who served during the Second World War.
70 See Donal Ó Drisceoil, 'Censorship in Ireland during the Second World War', (PhD, University College Cork, 1994), pp. 177–8; Donal Ó Drisceoil, *Censorship in Ireland 1939–1945* (Cork University Press, Cork, 1996), pp. 186–7; *Penapa*, Vol. 1, No. 2 (January 1941), Irish Military Archives, Dublin.
71 *Penapa*, Vol. 1, No. 2 (January 1941), p. 3.

72   ibid., p. 7.

73   Ó Drisceoil, 'Censorship in Ireland during the Second World War', p. 279.

74   JRC to Superintendent McGloin, 10 December 1941, JRC correspondence, Box 40, Irish Jewish Museum Archives, Dublin.

75   Superintendent McGloin to JRC, 13 December 1941, JRC correspondence, Box 40, Irish Jewish Museum Archives, Dublin.

76   Solomons to Weingreen, 29 June 1942, JRC correspondence, Box 40, Irish Jewish Museum Archives, Dublin.

77   Keogh, *Ireland and Europe*, pp. 177–8.

78   ibid.

79   ibid., p. 177.

80   ibid.

81   ibid., p. 178.

82   ibid.

83   Fahey purported to set out where Jews controlled key supplies. One Jew allegedly had a monopoly of wood for making chairs and furniture; 'Wood and clothing are very Jewish in London, I think', he wrote. Another had a monopoly on bandages, cotton-wool and surgical supplies. Yet another controlled smelting and was the government agent for the purchase of gold. Another member of the Jewish community had got the contract to produce the 1916 commemorative medal. 'The Galway Hat Factory, I am told, is run by Jews.' He also wrote that Jews were opening chemists' shops and asked: 'Is there a monopoly of supplies being planned?' Fahey to Cosgrave, 20 October 1941, Denis Fahey papers, (correspondence files), Holy Ghost Fathers Archives, Provincial House, Dublin.

84   ibid.

85   Interview with Fr Michael O'Carroll, Dublin, July 1996.

86   Ó Broin to Elyan, 25 September 1942, JRC correspondence, Box 40, Irish Jewish Museum Archives, Dublin.

87   ibid.

88   ibid.

89   Legion of Mary box, John Charles McQuaid papers, Dublin Archdiocesan Archives. My thanks to Mr David Sheehy, archivist, Dublin Archdiocesan Archives for drawing this source to my attention.

90   Interview with Leon Ó Broin, Dublin, 1986.

91   León Ó Broin, *Frank Duff: A Biography* (Gill & Macmillan, Dublin, 1982), pp. 62–3.

92   Interview with Fr Michael O'Carroll, Dublin, July 1996. Fr O'Carroll was also a founder member of the Mercier Society.

93   Flanagan to Fahey, 26 May 1943, Denis Fahey papers (correspondence files), Holy Ghost Fathers Archives, Provincial House, Dublin. Flanagan offered to set up guilds all over his constituency where they could spread the message of Fahey's book, *The Rulers of Russia* (Dublin, 1938). He said he would visit Fahey after the election to plan 'for future education of the plain people on this Bid and Christian and Holy Cause'. Flanagan concluded: 'With trust in God *we cannot fail.*'

94   Flanagan joined Fine Gael in 1952 and rose to the rank of Minister for Defence in the Fine Gael–Labour coalition in the mid-1970s.

95   *Dáil Éireann Debates*, Vol. 91, col. 569 (9 July 1943), quoted in part in Joseph T. Carroll, *Ireland in the War Years* (David and Charles, Newton Abbot, 1975), p. 137. See also G. M. Golding, *George Gavan Duffy, 1882–1951: A Legal Biography* (Irish Academic Press, Dublin, 1982), p. 131.

96   Golding, *George Gavan Duffy*, p. 131.

97   J. Smyth, deputy chairman, Longford County Council, 6 August 1943, D/T S13310A, NAI.
98   Anonymous letter, address, Rathgar, Dublin, 18 June 1943, D/T S 13310A, NAI. Brian Boru was a high king of Ireland who was killed, as every Irish school child used to know, at the Battle of Clontarf in 1014.
99   Tony Kushner, *The Holocaust and the Liberal Imagination: A Social and Cultural History* (Blackwell, Oxford, 1994), pp. 131–2.
100 Marrus and Paxton, *Vichy France and the Jews,* p. 343.
101 D/FA 419/44 NAI. This file contains details of all the correspondence between the Department of Foreign Affairs and individual Jews and Jewish organisations.
102 ibid.
103 ibid.
104 ibid.
105 Born in east London, Goodman was throughout his life 'an energetic defender of Orthodox practice'. His obituary in the *Jewish Chronicle* also spoke about his 'earnestness and extremity of opinion'. Goodman was a strong and persistent critic of 'those Zionist leaders who set out to establish a Jewish state without ensuring that it was based on traditional Judaism'. During the war, he worked as an adviser to the BBC's European division and also worked at the British Ministry of Information where he edited the *Jewish Bulletin*, a paper which was distributed abroad by the ministry. Obituary in the *Jewish Chronicle*, undated clipping in file of Agudas correspondence kindly supplied to me by Professor David Kranzler, New York (hereafter cited as Goodman papers).
106 D/FA 419/44, NAI.
107 ibid.
108 ibid.
109 ibid.
110 ibid.
111 Goodman memorandum on trip to Dublin, 16 May 1943, Goodman papers.
112 Goodman to Walshe, 5 May 1943, Goodman papers.
113 D/FA 419/44, NAI.
114 Marcus Retter, 'The Setting', in David Kranzler and Gertrude Hirschler (eds.), *Solomon Schonfeld: His Page in History* (Judaica Press, New York, 1982), p. 41.
115 Goodman memorandum on trip to Dublin, 16 May 1943, Goodman papers.
116 The United States and Britain refused to take any radical steps to secure the release of Jews in Europe. There was an emphasis on the plight of the 6,000 Jewish refugees in Spain. See David Wyman, *The Abandonment of the Jews: America and the Holocaust 1941–1945* (Pantheon Books, New York, 1985), pp. 119–21; for reaction in Britain, see Kushner, *The Holocaust and the Liberal Imagination*, pp. 181–3.
117 Goodman to Dulanty, 20 May 1943, D/FA 419/44, NAI.
118 Randall to Dulanty, 21 May 1943, D/FA 419/44, NAI.
119 Dulanty to Walshe, 7 June 1943, D/FA 419/44, NAI.
120 Goodman to Walshe, 23 July 1943, D/FA 419/44, NAI.
121 The text is quoted in ibid.
122 ibid.
123 Goodman to Walshe, 9 August 1943, D/FA 419/44, NAI.
124 Goodman to Walshe, 24 November 1943, D/FA 419/44, NAI.
125 D/FA, 419/44, NAI.
126 D/FA, 419/44, NAI.
127 D/FA, 419/44, NAI.
128 D/FA, 419/44, NAI.
129 Walshe to Briscoe, 10 August 1943, D/FA 419/44, NAI.

130 Cremin to Walshe, 3 September 1943, D/FA 419/44, NAI.
131 ibid.
132 Pokorny to Best, 30 August 1945, MS 11,003, Richard Irvine Best papers, NLI.
133 On 13 May 1943 Goodman sent Walshe a copy of a pamphlet by Eleanor F. Rathbone MP entitled *Rescue the Perishing*. This 25-page pamphlet was issued by the National Committee for Rescue from Nazi Terror in London.
134 Walshe to Murphy, 25 August 1943, D/FA 419/44.
135 Dulanty to Goodman, 7 September 1943, Goodman papers.
136 Goodman to Dulanty, 17 September 1943, D/FA 419/44, NAI.
137 Goodman to Dulanty, 20 October 1943, D/FA 419/44, NAI.
138 ibid.
139 Dulanty to Walshe, 27 October 1943, D/FA 419/44, NAI.
140 ibid.
141 Walshe to Cremin, 1 November 1943, D/FA 419/44, NAI.
142 Cremin to Walshe, 18 November 1943, D/FA 419/44, NAI.
143 Cremins to Walshe, 10 November 1943, D/FA 419/44, NAI.
144 Murphy to Walshe, 14 December 1943, D/FA 419/44, NAI. Murphy also stated that the Swiss were the only country to make any effort to repatriate their Jewish nationals. They did so with a collective visa and in two convoys.
145 Herzog to de Valera, 15 December 1943, D/FA 419/44, NAI.
146 Walshe to Murphy, 18 December 1943, D/FA 419/44, NAI.
147 Murphy to Walshe, 29 December 1943, D/FA 419/44, NAI. Goodman wrote to Dulanty on 29 December stating that Herzog had cabled him to ask for his personal intervention in Dublin in the matter of the Jewish refugees in France who held Paraguayan passports. He added: 'My past experience has not been too happy and I am not quite sure what I should do in this instance.' He asked Dulanty to supply him with some information as he was obliged to cable Herzog. Goodman to Dulanty, 29 December 1943, Goodman papers.
148 Walshe to Cremin, 4 January 1944, D/FA 419/44, NAI.
149 Cremin to Walshe, 11 January 1944, D/FA 419/44, NAI.
150 Cremin to Walshe, 17 March 1944, D/FA 419/44, NAI.
151 Goodman to Dulanty, 17 March 1944, D/FA 419/44, NAI.
152 Dulanty to Walshe, 28 March 1944, D/FA 419/44, NAI.
153 Gray to Walshe, 22 March 1944, D/FA 419/44, NAI.
154 Secretary, Irish Red Cross to Walshe, 1 April 1944, D/FA 419/44, NAI
155 Walshe to de Valera, 5 April 1944, D/FA 419/44, NAI.
156 Gray to Walshe, 8 April 1944, D/FA 419/44, NAI.
157 Cable from Irish New York Consulate General, 14 March 1944, Secretary's files, D/FA P90, NAI.
158 ibid.
159 Cable from Irish New York Consulate General, 15 March 1944, Secretary's files, D/FA P90, NAI.
160 Cable from Department of External Affairs to Consul General, 16 March 1944, Secretary's files, D/FA P90, NAI.
161 Among the people who signed the JRC statement were: Edwin Solomons, president (stockbroker); Leonard Abrahamson, vice-president (consultant physician and professor at Royal College of Surgeons, Dublin); Joshua Baker (lawyer); Maurice Ellis (businessman); Charles Spiro (lawyer); Jacob Jaffey (businessman); Ernest Newman (company director); Laurence Elyan (prominent actor); Carl Feldman (businessman); and Herman Good, honorary secretary (lawyer).
162 Secretary's files, D/FA P90, NAI.
163 Secretary's files, D/FA P90, NAI.

164 A delegate at the January 1944 Fine Gael annual conference stated that it seemed impossible to get a Jew convicted in the Special Criminal Court. The same person also stated that criminals fleeing justice in central Europe were setting themselves up in businesses in Ireland and employing slave labour. The report of this incident was held back by the censor. Department of Justice, Press Censorship Monthly Reports, January and February, 1944; quoted in Donal Ó Drisceoil, 'Censorship in Ireland during the Second World War', pp. 279–80.

165 D/FA 419/44, NAI.

166 Goodman telegram, received in Dublin on 16 April 1944, Goodman papers.

167 Walshe to Goodman, 19 April 1944, D/FA 419/44, NAI.

168 Cremin to Walshe, 24 March 1944, D/FA 419/44, NAI.

169 ibid. Cremin explained that the official with whom he dealt was a member of the SS who was a fully accredited member of the Foreign Office. Cremin said that the case revealed how the SS always had to be consulted when exit visas were sought for Jews.

170 Cremin to Walshe, 27 March 1944, D/FA 419/44, NAI.

171 Walshe to Cremin 29 April 1944, D/FA 419/44, NAI.

172 D/FA 419/44, NAI.

173 Cremin to Walshe, 4 July 1944, D/FA 419/44, NAI.

174 D/FA 419/44, NAI.

175 Cremin to Walshe, 28 August 1944, D/FA 419/44, NAI.

176 Natan Eck wrote to the Department of Foreign Affairs on 10 June 1958 requesting copies of the documents which Cremin had submitted to the German Foreign Office. He wrote that on 6 January 1944 the Irish embassy in Berlin sent an *aide mémoire* to the German Foreign Office stating that various 'Jewish Organisations' had contacted the Irish government requesting that it consent to allow the immigration of 200 Polish Jewish families who were being held in Vittel, France. The *aide mémoire* went on to say that the Irish government was prepared to grant entry visas to them for a limited time, and enquired whether they would be given exit permits by the German authorities. Eck concluded: 'That Aide Memoire was merely the first in a series of attempts made by the Charge d'Affaires Cremin orally and in writing to intervene on behalf of the foregoing families, unfortunately to no avail.' See D/FA 419/44, NAI.

177 'Repatriates return home – stories of internment conditions under the Nazis', *Manchester Guardian*, 11 September 1944.

178 Gilbert, *Atlas of the Holocaust*, p. 316.

179 ibid., pp. 185–6.

180 ibid., p. 244.

181 Freilich to de Valera [no date], D/FA 419/44, NAI.

182 Kiernan to Walshe, 23 July 1944, D/FA 419/44, NAI.

183 Dulanty to Walshe, 1 August 1944, D/FA 419/44, NAI.

184 Brown to Walshe, 14 August 1944, D/FA 419/44, NAI.

185 Walshe to Brown, 21 August 1944, D/FA 419/44, NAI; M.R. Springer, Agudas, London to Irish Red Cross Society, 6 August 1944, D/FA 419/44, NAI.

186 Walshe to M. MacNamara, 22 August 1944, D/FA 419/44, NAI.

187 Gray to Winant, 23 August 1944, D/FA 419/44, NAI.

188 See Winant to Gray, 29 August and 8 September 1944; US legation for Winant to Agudas, 29 August 1944, D/FA 419/44, NAI.

189 Goodman to Sidney H. Browne, US embassy, London, 12 September 1944, D/FA 419/44, NAI.

190 *Dáil Éireann Debates*, Vol. 94, cols. 1649–50 (20 September 1944).

191 Details of the Swedish initiative may be found in Steven Koblik, *The Stones Cry*

Out: Sweden's Response to the Persecution of the Jews 1933–1945 (Holocaust Library, New York, 1988), pp. 245ff.

192   Goodman to Walshe, 29 September 1944, Walshe to Goodman, 5 October 1944, D/FA 419/44, NAI.

193   Walshe minute on Goodman interview, 18 October 1944, D/FA 419/44, NAI.

194   ibid.

195   ibid.

196   ibid. Goodman was an orthodox Jew, Walshe minuted, who held 'very strongly that, if the Jews are to go back to Palestine, it must be for the purpose of reviving and practising the old religion there'. He was 'entirely opposed to Jewish secularism and materialism as manifested in several of the modern Jewish settlements in Palestine'.

197   ibid.

198   ibid.

199   Goodman to Walshe, 20 October 1944, D/FA 419/44, NAI.

200   Walshe minute, 26 October 1944, D/FA 419/44, NAI.

201   Walshe to Solomons, 29 November 1944, D/FA 419/44, NAI. Walshe told Solomons that Dulanty had informed him most positively that he never expressed the views attributed to him. Dulanty told Walshe that he had always made a point of praising what he knew to be the praiseworthy attitude of the Dublin community in the matter of helping refugees as well as in relation to all charitable works.

202   Walshe to Solomons, 26 October 1944, D/FA 419/44, NAI.

203   Solomons to Walshe, 30 October 1944, D/FA 419/44, NAI.

204   See cable dated 26 October 1944, D/FA 419/44, NAI.

205   Cremin to Walshe, 27 October 1944, D/FA 419/44, NAI. The same day, Walshe told Robert Briscoe of the content of Cremin's cable.

206   Jewish Telegraphic Agency report, Paris, 13 November 1944, D/FA 419/44, NAI.

207   Cremin to Walshe, 13 December 1944, D/FA 419/44, NAI.

208   Walshe to Herzog, 17 January 1945, D/FA 419/44, NAI.

209   D/FA 419/44, NAI.

210   Cremin to Walshe, 1 February 1945, D/FA 419/44, NAI.

211   Brennan to Walshe, 18 January 1945, D/FA 419/44, NAI.

212   D/FA 419/44, NAI. Dr N. Barou of the European division of the World Jewish Congress wrote to John Dulanty on 5 February to request the Irish government to make representations to the Holy See to intervene with the German authorities. Barou also wanted Dublin to make representations to the German authorities to stop the massacre of the remaining Jews. Dulanty, in his covering note on 7 February 1945, wrote: 'I formed the impression that Dr Barou did not think Mr Goodman's Organisation one of leading importance.' D/FA 419/44, NAI.

213   Good to Walshe, 24 November 1944, D/FA 419/44, NAI.

214   Goodman again pressed for the admission of Jewish children to Ireland in mid-May and received the same answer from Walshe. D/FA 419/44, NAI.

215   Harry Clinton Reed to State Department, 17 May 1949, G 84, Ireland, National Archives, Washington DC.

216   This was confirmed to me by Mr Ben Briscoe TD in January 1996.

217   A memorandum from the Department of Justice in 1953 stated that there was no record of the number of aliens, displaced persons or naturalised Irish citizens that were of Jewish blood as official records were not kept on the basis of race or religion but observation from time to time 'seems to indicate that quite a number are Jews'. Memorandum submitted to government by Minister for Justice, 28 February 1953, D/T S11007/B2, NAI.

218 Ita Daly, *Unholy Ghosts* (Bloomsbury, London, 1996), p. 81.
219 Helen Lewis, *A Time to Speak* (Blackstaff Press, Belfast, 1992), pp. 96–8.
220 Interview with Helen Lewis, Belfast, August 1996.
221 Denis Johnston, *Nine Rivers from Jordan: The Chronicle of a Journey and a Search* (Derek Verschoyle, London, 1953), pp. 395–6.
222 Robert Collis and Han Hogerzeil, *Straight On* (Methuen, London, 1947), pp. 50–1.
223 Interview with Dr Han Hogerzeil, Newtownmountkennedy, Co. Wicklow, August 1996. Born in Arnhem, Han Hogerzeil came from a family which had been associated with the medical profession for generations. One of her ancestors had been William of Orange's doctor at the Battle of the Boyne where he had successfully tended to a life-threatening wound suffered by the king in battle.
     Han had been to a state school where she had studied with Jews, though she did not know their religion; Holland was a very tolerant country, she said. At one point, a young rabbi came to their town with his family. He was fleeing persecution in Germany. If two children in the school agreed to study Hebrew, he would be employed. Han studied Hebrew. She later learned to speak Yiddish.
     Her family was very much aware of what was happening in Germany. Her mother had a close school friend, a German, whom she had met at finishing school in Switzerland. The woman used to visit them in Holland and write every Christmas. Her letters showed how she moved from a position of hostility to Hitler and Nazism in 1933 to being a full-blown Nazi by 1937–38. Following the occupation, Han and her family did not know initially what was happening to Jews. They were being sent to labour camps. But she noticed that none of them ever came back. Her family provided a safe house for Jews throughout the war; she hid seven Jews in her own house for most of the war. Her family home was destroyed in the Allied bombing raids. Among the items lost was a tooth of William of Orange, which her ancestor had extracted.
     In 1944, Han crossed the Rhine and made her way into the Canadian sector. She joined the Red Cross as a translator, met Robert Collis and his team of Irish doctors, and went with them to Belsen as a translator.
224 ibid. Han Hogerzeil explained to me how she later attended the trial at Lüneburg of the camp male and female commandants, Kramer and Irma Greese. Asked did he believe in God, he replied 'Ja'. Asked why he had personally turned on the gas one day in Auschwitz, he replied: 'I had a chit from Herr Himmler for fifty corpses.' Irma Greese, the daughter of anti-Nazi parents, shared Kramer's fate. They were both hanged. For another account see Robert Collis, *To Be a Pilgrim* (Secker and Warburg, London, 1975), pp. 117–20.
225 Interview with Dr Han Hogerzeil, Newtownmountkennedy, Co. Wicklow August 1996.
226 ibid.
227 Collis and Hogerzeil, *Straight On*, p. 74.
228 Interview with Dr Han Hogerzeil, Newtownmountkennedy, Co. Wicklow, August 1996. Professor Jacob Weingreen and his wife Bertha, both of whom held the rank of lieutenant colonel in the British army, also helped in Belsen to strengthen hope in the survivors of the Holocaust. Rabbi Simon Harris, 'Professor Jacob and Bertha Weingreen, a tribute on their diamond wedding anniversary', *Irish Jewish Year Book*, 1994–95, pp. 59–60.
229 Lewis, *A Time to Speak*, p. 117.
230 Primo Levi, *Collected Poems* (Faber and Faber, London and Boston, 1988), p. 5.
231 David Wyman, *Paper Walls: America and the Refugee Crisis 1938–1941* (Pantheon Books, New York, 1985), p. 209.
232 ibid.

233 See the relevant chapters in Paul R. Bartrop (ed.), *False Havens: The British Empire and the Holocaust* (University Press of America, Lanham, Maryland, 1995).

7: Ireland's post-war refugee policy

1 JRC to Gray, 17 April 1945, JRC correspondence, Box 40, Irish Jewish Museum Archives, Dublin.

2 ibid.

3 Gray to Good, 29 April 1945, JRC correspondence, Box 40, Irish Jewish Museum Archives, Dublin.

4 The *Irish Press* put the notice under the heading 'People and Places', the *Irish Times* used the headline 'Condolence', and the *Irish Independent* used 'Herr Hitler's Death'.

5 This version of events was given to me by T. Desmond Williams, who was a close friend of Boland. Boland himself was somewhat reluctant to speak about the episode when I spoke to him but he did confirm that he had been opposed to the visit. Mrs Boland also confirmed that her husband had been opposed to the visit. Con Cremin, Ireland's envoy in Berlin at the time, while stressing that he had not been in the country, told me that he had also heard the same version of events.

6 Interview with Mervyn Taylor TD, Dublin, December 1996.

7 ibid.

8 The practice of the Jewish community in the 1930s and during the war years had been, where possible, to eschew public protest. There is one letter in the records of the JRC which indicates that there was a demand for action. On 8 May, Herman Good received a note from a member of the JRC regarding a recommendation by that body to send a deputation to de Valera on the question of anti-Semitism. As 'such important issues' had been raised by the resolution, Good counselled that further discussion should take place before a decision was finally made. It is probable that a deputation went to see de Valera. See member of JRC to Herman Good, 8 May 1945, JRC correspondence, Box 40, Irish Jewish Museum Archives, Dublin.

9 Interview with Maurice Abrahamson, Dublin, April 1997.

10 Cuttings on Secretary's files, D/FA P98, NAI. The *New York Times* had a front-page item on 3 May headed 'De Valera proffers sympathy to Reich'. The *Herald Tribune,* on page 3, carried a two-column heading 'De Valera at German legation offers condolences on Hitler'. The *Washington Post* had a front-page headline 'De Valera expressed condolence for Hitler'. Another US paper's front-page headline read 'De Valera extends sympathy to Nazis'. On 4 May, the *New York Times* had an item entitled: 'Mr de Valera's regrets'. The headline on a *Herald Tribune* editorial read: 'Neutrality gone mad'. On 5 May, the *Washington Post* had an editorial entitled 'Moral myopia' which attacked the visit, linking Ireland and authoritarian Portugal. De Valera also made front-page headlines in most of the major newspapers in Britain and in the Commonwealth countries. The *Yorkshire Post* felt that Ireland had taken refuge in neutrality 'which penalised the friends of liberty and abetted its enemies. It is an ignominious history to which this last gesture is a fitting climax.' The *Sunday Express* headlined 'Herr de Valera annoys Canada' and quoted the *Toronto Telegram*: 'De Valera has demonstrated that had the war gone differently he might have been another Laval. To retain a High Commissioner at Dublin is as derogatory to Canada's honour as it is to maintain an Ambassador at Vichy.'

11 Gray noted that nobody representing the President had called to the US legation upon the death of Roosevelt.

12 State Department to Gray, 16 May 1945, RG 84, State Department Records, Ireland, Confidential Report Records, 711.41D/5-545, National Archives, Washington DC.

13 The British Union of Fascists then said that they had had 'wonderful news from our comrades in Norway'. They had learned that the 'Fuehrer is not dead' but had left with some leading Nazis in a submarine. Secretary of the British Union of Fascists (no name or address) to Dulanty, May 1945, D/FA P12/14 (2), NAI.

14 The neutrality policy of the government had not prevented between 70,000 and 80,000 Irishmen from fighting on the side of the Allies. See Nicholas Mansergh, 'Ireland, the Republic outside the Commonwealth', *International Affairs*, Vol. 28, No. 3 (July 1952), p. 186. There is considerable confusion and controversy about the exact number of Irishmen who fought in the British forces during the war.

15 Count Confalonieri to Italian Minister of Foreign Affairs, 10 May 1945. Telegram number 364/100, Political Affairs file, Ireland and Italy, 1945, Italian Department of Foreign Affairs, Rome.

16 *Irish Times*, 8 May 1945.

17 With the trauma of the German legation visit very much to the fore, Walshe found it necessary to try to smooth over another embarrassing problem. This time it was the Italian minister, Count Confalonieri, who was directly involved. On 7 May, the *Irish Independent* carried a notice of 'a political manifestation which some Italians and Irish sympathisers meant to make by having a Mass celebrated for the repose of the soul of Benito Mussolini'. Confalonieri complained to Walshe that while the censor passed this news item, 'it was not even thought advisable to let the communiqué of the Italian government drawing the attention of the public to the execution of hostages and the crimes committed in Northern Italy [by the Germans] to be published'. Walshe condemned the idea of a Mass for Mussolini and promised to look into the matter. (Confalonieri to Walshe, 11 May 1945, Political Affairs file, Ireland and Italy, 1945, Italian Department of Foreign Affairs, Rome.)

Walshe later reported to Confalonieri that the ecclesiastical authorities had no knowledge of the Mass which was celebrated in good faith by a Franciscan priest.

Some other charitable souls in Dublin organised a Mass to be said on 3 June 1945 in the Church of the Visitation, Fairview, for 'the repose of the soul of Herr Hitler and the welfare of the German nation'. The circular, which was unsigned, came into the possession of the Department of External Affairs. Joseph Walshe minuted on 30 May: 'Informed Fr O'Connell the A[rch] B[ishop]'s secretary about this matter. He told me he would inform His G[race] immediately.' McQuaid took immediate action. On 1 June, a Department of External Affairs minute noted: 'His Grace told Secy. that he had stopped the Mass.' See Dermot Keogh, *Ireland and Europe, 1918–1989* (Hibernian University Press, Cork and Dublin, 1989), pp. 197–8.

18 The service concluded with the singing of the national anthem. Among those present were R. Briscoe, Prof. Abrahamson, Prof. J. Weingreen, Dr C. Spiro, Dr J. Baker, L. Lapidus, E. Newman, A. Benson, A. Newman, S. Crivon, M. L. Gordon, B. Shillman, H. Good, Dr L. Elyan, Rabbi H. Medalie, Rabbi Alony, Rev. Cantor Frielich, Rev. Roith, Rev. Hollander, E. M. Solomons, M. Ellis, S. White, M. Jacobson, G. R. Morris and W. A. Freedman. *Irish Press*, 26 June 1945.

19 Michael R. Marrus, *The Unwanted: European Refugees in the Twentieth Century* (Oxford University Press, Oxford and New York, 1985), p. 299.

20 ibid., p. 309.

21 ibid.
22 Costigan draft memorandum, 24 September 1945, D/J 69/8027, NAI.
23 ibid.
24 Costigan to Minister for Justice, 25 September 1945, DJ 69/8027, NAI.
25 ibid.
26 Moynihan minute, 26 September 1945, D/T S11007A, NAI.
27 Costigan to Roche, 25 September 1945, D/J 69/8027, NAI.
28 Costigan draft memorandum, 24 September 1945, D/J 69/8027, NAI.
29 Duff to Roche, 25 September 1945, D/J 69/8027, NAI.
30 In parenthesis, attention might also be drawn to a conversation on 9 October
    1945 between Joseph Walshe of the Department of External Affairs and Sir
    Basil Newton of the British Foreign Office; Newton reported Walshe as saying
    that

    > there were 5,000 Jews in Dublin and that the ostentatious behaviour of
    > some of them was not making them popular. He evidently did not wish to
    > see any considerable immigration of Jews into Eire and, after mentioning a
    > visit he had made some time ago to Tel Aviv and the Middle East, showed
    > no great sympathy for Jewish aspirations in Palestine.

    Memorandum prepared by Sir Basil Newton, Foreign Office, on his conversa-
    tion with Joseph Walshe in London on 9 October 1945, FO 371/50364, Public
    Record Office, London. I am grateful to Aengus Nolan for providing me with this
    reference.
31 Department of Justice memorandum, September 1945, D/T S11007A, NAI.
32 ibid.
33 ibid.
34 ibid.
35 ibid.
36 ibid.
37 Costigan minute, 19 November 1945, D/J 69/8027, NAI.
38 ibid.
39 ibid.
40 Duff to Minister for Justice, 23 November 1945, D/J 69/8027, NAI.
41 ibid.
42 Department of Justice memorandum, 30 November 1945, D/T S11007A, NAI.
43 Department of Industry and Commerce memorandum, 12 December 1945, D/T
    S11007A, NAI.
44 ibid.
45 Moynihan minute, 15 December 1945, D/T S11007A; see also CAB, 14 Decem-
    ber 1945, G.C. 4/12 Item 4, NAI.
46 ibid.
47 Moynihan memorandum, 21 December 1945, D/T S11007A, NAI.
48 ibid.
49 ibid.
50 ibid.
51 ibid.
52 Costigan to Frederick H. Boland, 8 January 1946, D/J 69/8027, NAI.
53 Costigan minute, 7 February 1946, D/J 69/8027, NAI.
54 D/J 69/80/518, NAI.
55 ibid.
56 ibid.
57 ibid.
58 ibid.
59 Costigan minute, 19 March 1947, D/J 69/8027, NAI.

60   As background to the Rexist leader see Martin Conway, *Collaboration in Belgium: Léon Degrelle and the Rexist Movement* (Yale University Press, New Haven and London, 1993).

61   ibid., p. 20.

62   Frederick H. Boland to Duff, 3 September 1946, D/FA P253, NAI.

63   Roche to Frederick H. Boland, 11 September 1946, D/FA P253, NAI.

64   Draft Boland letter to Roche, undated and no note of it having been sent, D/FA P253, NAI.

65   ibid.

66   ibid.

67   The leader of the British Union of Fascists, Oswald Mosley, took up residence in Galway for a short time after the war, which he was entitled to do as a British citizen.

68   D/FA P253, NAI.

69   *Dáil Éireann Debates*, Vol. 47, No. 2, col. 163 (25 June 1947).

70   The Red Cross had also been asked to arrange a holiday in Ireland for about 250 Polish youths between the ages of sixteen and nineteen. The youths were orphans and apprentices to trades in the Polish air force in Britain. They were in Ireland between 25 July and 14 August 1946.

71   Roisin Ingle, 'A piece of Irish history to be proud of', *Irish Times*, 22 March 1997; see also *Irish Times*, 24 March 1997.

72   Interview with Dr Han Hogerzeil, Newtownmountkennedy, Co. Wicklow, August 1996. See also Mary Rose Doorly, *Hidden Memories: The Personal Recollections of Survivors and Witnesses to the Holocaust Living in Ireland* (Blackwater Press, Dublin, 1994), p. 18; Robert Collis, *To Be a Pilgrim* (Secker and Warburg, London, 1975), pp. 121–3.

73   Department of Justice memorandum, 'Admission of One Hundred Jewish Children', 28 April 1948, D/T S11007B/1, NAI.

74   ibid.

75   ibid.

76   Roche to Moynihan, 25 October 1946, D/T S11007B/1, NAI.

77   ibid.

78   Moynihan to Roche, 31 October 1946, D/T S11007B/1, NAI.

79   Department of Justice memorandum, 28 April 1948, D/T S11007B/1, NAI.

80   Dulanty to Schonfeld, 5 December 1946, Folder 1, 183/302, Solomon Schonfeld papers, Parks Library, University of Southampton (hereafter cited as SS/P).

81   Dulanty to Schonfeld, 16 August 1947, Folder 1, 183/302, SS/P. This letter was meant to act as a note which Schonfeld could present to governments in Europe; it was addressed – 'To whom it may concern'.

82   M. Wellstead, British Home Office to Schonfeld, 1 January 1948, Folder 1, 183/302, SS/P.

83   Schonfeld to Eppel, 18 February 1948, Folder 1, 183/302, SS/P.

84   Eppel to Schonfeld, 27 April 1948, Folder 1, 183/302, SS/P.

85   Department of Justice memorandum, 28 April 1948, D/T S11007B/1, NAI.

86   Eppel to Schonfeld, 29 March 1948, Folder 1, 183/302, SS/P.

87   ibid.

88   Eppel to Lumser [Lunzer], 30 March 1948, Folder 1, 183/302, SS/P.

89   Eppel to Schonfeld, 29 March 1948, Folder 1, 183/302, SS/P.

90   Eppel to Lunzer, 7 April 1948, Folder 1, 183/302, SS/P.

91   Eppel to Lunzer, 13 April 1948, Folder 1, 183/302, SS/P.

92   ibid.

93   Schonfeld to Dulanty, 26 April 1948, Folder 1, 183/302, SS/P.

94   Rabbi Theodore Lewis to author, 4 August 1996.

95   Eppel to Schonfeld, 9 May 1948, Folder 1, 183/302, SS/P.
96   ibid.
97   Schonfeld to M. Wellstead, 9 May 1948, Folder 1, 183/302, SS/P.
98   Schonfeld to Dulanty, 23 May 1948, Folder 1, 183/302, SS/P.
99   Eppel to Schonfeld, 23 March 1948, Folder 1, 183/302, SS/P.
100   Eppel to Schonfeld, 24 May 1948, Folder 1, 183/302, SS/P. In an earlier letter of the same date, she said she had met one of Professor Abrahamson's family who had told her that he was 'rather peeved at not having been consulted before'.
101   Eppel to Schonfeld, 31 May 1948, Folder 1, 183/302, SS/P.
102   Eppel to Schonfeld, 10 June 1948, Folder 1, 183/302, SS/P.
103   Paper cutting in letter, Eppel to Schonfeld, 11 October 1948, Folder 2, 183/302, SS/P.
104   Eppel to Pels, 28 December 1948, Folder 2, 183/302, SS/P.
105   Rabbi Theodore Lewis to author, 4 August 1996.
106   See draft article by author on 'Ireland and the Recognition of the State of Israel' (forthcoming).
107   Those countries were Belgium, Denmark, France and Saar, Iceland, Italy, Liechtenstein, Luxembourg, Norway, Sweden, the Netherlands and the USA.
108   Department of Justice memorandum, 28 February 1953, D/T S11007B/2, NAI.
109   *Irish Independent*, 6 October 1949.
110   D/J 69/15871, NAI.
111   D/J 69/15871, NAI.
112   See D/T S11007B, NAI.
113   ibid.
114   ibid.
115   ibid.
116   *Irish Independent*, 29 December 1949.
117   Correspondence between Dillon and Moynihan, 13 September and 29 September 1950, D/T S11007B/1, NAI.
118   D/T S11007B, NAI.
119   MacEoin to Costello, 12 June 1950, D/T S11007B, NAI.
120   ibid.
121   McQuaid to Costello, 2 September 1950, D/T S11007B/1, NAI. The archbishop had been approached by Fr Killion, at Geneva, anxiously enquiring if anything had yet been agreed about such people. He wondered if any Irish institutions would be willing to take even a few.
122   Extract from CAB, G.C. 5/206, Item 6, 26 September 1950, D/T S11007B/1, NAI.
123   ibid.
124   ibid.
125   Costello to McQuaid, 30 September 1950, D/T S11007B/1, NAI.
126   McQuaid to Costello, 2 October 1950, D/T S11007B/1, NAI.
127   Department of Justice memorandum, 28 February 1953, D/T S11007B/2, NAI.
128   Department of Justice memorandum, 4 September 1950, D/T S11007B/1, NAI.
129   As quoted in draft Department of Justice memorandum, February 1953, D/T S11007B/2, NAI.
130   Berry to Coyne, 16 February 1953, D/T S11007B/2, NAI.
131   ibid.
132   ibid.
133   ibid.
134   Moynihan minute, 16 February 1953, D/T S11007B/2, NAI.
135   D/T S11007B/2, NAI.
136   Department of Justice memorandum, 28 February 1953, D/T S11007B/2, NAI.

137   ibid. None of the following were subject to registration: children under sixteen years of age, aliens who were wives or widows of Irish citizens, and aliens in the country for less than a three-month period. The corresponding figure in 1948 was 1,465.
138   ibid.
139   ibid.
140   ibid.
141   ibid. The memorandum further recorded that Ireland had admitted close to 1,000 refugee children, including 500 Germans, over 200 Poles and over 200 Austrians. They were first admitted for temporary care in selected centres or in the homes of suitable persons and they included 100 Jewish children. 'Almost all of the 1,000 alien children', the memorandum recorded, 'have since left but a small number have been informally adopted.'
142   Jordan to Jakobovits, 11 March 1953, Robert Briscoe papers in the possession of Ben Briscoe TD, Dublin.
143   Jakobivits to Briscoe, 13 March 1953, Robert Briscoe papers.
144   Briscoe to Jakobovits, 19 March 1953, Robert Briscoe papers.
145   D/T S11007B/2, NAI.
146   Maurice Ryan, *Another Ireland* (Stranmillis College, Belfast 1996), pp. 9–13; *Menorah* (Golden Jubilee, 1996) kindly supplied to the author by Mrs Joan Finkel.

Epilogue: The Jewish community in Ireland since the 1950s

1   Mark Lieberman, 'The Jews of Northern Ireland: Living in Peace in a Troubled Land', *Jewish Monthly*, March 1989, p. 19.
2   *Census of Population of Northern Ireland, 1991*; figures kindly supplied by Dr Caroline Windrum, Institute of Irish Studies, Queen's University Belfast.
3   Andy Pollak, 'Dublin's Jewish community "is here for the long haul" despite its decline', *Irish Times*, 7 March 1995.
4   J. J. Sexton and R. O'Leary, 'Factors Affecting Population Decline in Minority Religious Communities in the Republic of Ireland', in *Building Trust in Ireland: Studies Commissioned by the Forum for Peace and Reconciliation* (Blackstaff Press, Belfast, 1996), pp. 307–9.
5   ibid.
6   Stanley Waterman, 'On the South Side of the Liffey', *Jewish Quarterly*, Spring 1987, p. 28.
7   Sexton and O'Leary, 'Factors Affecting Population Decline', pp. 307–9.
8   ibid.
9   Waterman, 'On the South Side of the Liffey', p. 30.
10   Immanuel Jakobovits, *Journal of a Rabbi* (W. H. Allen, London, 1967), pp. 57–60.
11   ibid., p. 54.
12   The areas of exception were Zionist organisation and youth work. ibid., p. 55.
13   Information based on interviews conducted on my behalf in 1996–97 by Dr Caroline Windrum, Institute of Irish Studies, Queen's University Belfast.
14   ibid.
15   Information supplied to me by Dr Caroline Windrum, Institute of Irish Studies, Queen's University Belfast.
16   Stanley Waterman, 'Changing Residential Patterns of the Dublin Jewish Community', *Irish Geography*, Vol. 14 (1981), pp. 43–4.
17   ibid., p. 44.
18   Jakobovits, *Journal of a Rabbi*, pp. 57–60.
19   Asher Benson, 'Jewish Genealogy in Ireland', *Aspects of Irish Genealogy: Proceedings of the First Irish Genealogical Congress* (First Irish Genealogical Congress Committee, 1993), p. 21. Four out of every five Jewish children of school age, of whom there were about 500 in the 1950s, received regular Jewish

instruction, according to Jakobovits (*Journal of a Rabbi*, pp. 57–60). There was a strong attendance at Zion Schools. There were fifteen Jewish youth organisations in Dublin during that decade. Members of the Jewish community going on to third-level education usually attended Trinity College Dublin.

20 Benson, 'Jewish Genealogy in Ireland', p. 21.

21 Jakobovits, *Journal of a Rabbi*, p. 64.

22 The Dublin Maccabi opened its own sports grounds on 25 May 1952. ibid., pp. 57–60.

23 He also stated that the Elliman family had recently secured a controlling interest in the Royal, Metropole, Gaiety and Savoy theatres in Dublin as well as having theatrical interests in Cork and Limerick. Vinton Chapin to State Department, 17 May 1949, G 84, State Department, Ireland (security segregated records), National Archives, Washington DC.

24 Dermot Keogh, 'The Role of the Catholic Church in the Republic of Ireland 1922–1995', in *Building Trust in Ireland: Studies Commissioned by the Forum for Peace and Reconciliation* (Blackstaff Press, Belfast, 1996), p. 137.

25 Andrée Sheehy Skeffington, *Skeff: A Life of Owen Sheehy Skeffington 1909–1970* (Lilliput Press, Dublin, 1991), pp. 141–62.

26 See D/J S13/50/1, NAI.

27 ibid.

28 ibid.

29 ibid.

30 Keogh, 'The Role of the Catholic Church in the Republic of Ireland 1922–1995', pp. 134–42.

31 The Fethard-on-Sea case, involving the children of a mixed marriage in County Wexford, provided negative headlines for a short time in 1957. ibid., pp. 142–9.

32 Jakobovits, *Journal of a Rabbi*, p. 270.

33 ibid.

34 His son, Ben, succeeded him in the Dáil in 1965; he too became lord mayor of Dublin, on 5 July 1988. See Ted Nealon, *Nealon's Guide to the 27th Dáil and Seanad: Election 1992* (Gill & Macmillan, Dublin, 1993).

35 'Eamon de Valera and Israel', File 844, Eamon de Valera papers, Franciscan Archives, Killiney, Co. Dublin.

36 *Lusk Leader*, 15 May 1965; cutting in File 844, Eamon de Valera papers, Franciscan Archives, Killiney, Co. Dublin.

37 The Eamon de Valera Forest Committee was listed in the book as follows: chairman, M. L. Abrahamson; vice-chairmen, N. Mendell, R. Black, G. Y. Goldberg; treasurers, D. Newman, L. O'Shea; secretary, M. Fridberg; and committee H. S. Elliott, E. Sampson, M. Green, H. Bridberg, N. Jameson, R. Briscoe, A. Cowan, H. A. Leon, J. Marcus, G. Davis, H. Simmons, R. Watchman, A. Diamond, L. Watson, C. Esses, J. White, H. Davis. File 844, Eamon de Valera papers, Franciscan Archives, Killiney, Co. Dublin.

38 De Valera to Abrahamson, 26 July 1966, File 844, Eamon de Valera papers, Franciscan Archives, Killiney, Co. Dublin.

39 Abrahamson to de Valera, 27 July 1966, File 844, Eamon de Valera papers, Franciscan Archives, Killiney, Co. Dublin.

40 *Irish Press*, 17 August 1966.

41 Eshkol to Abrahamson, 18 August 1966, File 844, Eamon de Valera papers, Franciscan Archives, Killiney, Co. Dublin.

42 ibid.

43 Herzog to Abrahamson, 18 August 1966, File 844, Eamon de Valera papers, Franciscan Archives, Killiney, Co. Dublin.

44 ibid.

45 ibid.
46 Max Nurock speech, 18 August 1966, File 844, Eamon de Valera papers, Franciscan Archives, Killiney, Co. Dublin.
47 ibid.
48 ibid.
49 *Jewish Chronicle*, 14 September 1966; cutting in File 844, Eamon de Valera papers, Franciscan Archives, Killiney, Co. Dublin.
50 *Irish Press*, 5 November 1966; cutting in File 844, Eamon de Valera papers, Franciscan Archives, Killiney, Co. Dublin.
51 Book dedicated to de Valera, File 844, Eamon de Valera papers, Franciscan Archives, Killiney, Co. Dublin.
52 Abrahamson to de Valera, 10 January 1972, File 844, Eamon de Valera papers, Franciscan Archives, Killiney, Co. Dublin.
53 Herzog to de Valera, 20 April 1972, File 844, Eamon de Valera papers, Franciscan Archives, Killiney, Co. Dublin.
54 ibid.
55 See correspondence in Cearbhall Ó Dálaigh file, Box 25, Irish Jewish Museum Archives, Dublin.
56 Cearbhall Ó Dálaigh, 'Foreword', in Louis Hyman, *The Jews of Ireland: From Earliest Times to the Year 1910* (Irish University Press, Shannon, 1972), p. xv.
57 'Jewish Community honours President', *Irish Times*, 20 December 1974. Isaac Cohen was the third chief rabbi of Ireland and, with a tenure of twenty years, the longest-serving one to date. The list of chief rabbis of Ireland is: Isaac Herzog (1919–37), Immanuel Jakobovits (1949–59), Isaac Cohen (1959–79), David Rosen (1979–84), Ephraim Mirvis (1984–92), Simon Harris (1993–4), Gavin Broder (1996–).
58 See photograph and caption, p. 1, *Irish Times*, 23 March 1978. The view was strongly expressed to me by a leading member of the Jewish community that he might have allowed the community to be represented by somebody else who would have joined the funeral service inside the church.
59 Micheál Mac Gréil, *Prejudice and Tolerance in Ireland: Based on a Survey of Intergroup Attitudes of Dublin Adults and Other Sources* (no publisher listed, 1978), p. 525.
60 ibid., p. 333.
61 ibid.
62 ibid.
63 Eugene J. Fisher, 'Nostra Aetate, for Our Times and for the Future', in Eugene J. Fisher et al. (eds.), *Twenty Years of Jewish–Catholic Relations* (Paulist Press, New York, 1986), p. 1.
64 Eugene J. Fisher, 'The Roman Liturgy and Catholic–Jewish Relations since the Second Vatican Council', in Eugene J. Fisher et al. (eds.), *Twenty Years of Jewish–Catholic Relations* (Paulist Press, New York, 1986), pp. 135–8.
65 Micheál Mac Gréil, *Prejudice in Ireland Revisited* (Survey Research Unit, Maynooth, 1996), p. 223.
66 'Irish Nazis: Why Dublin is a Fascist Haven', *In Dublin*, 24 July, No. 259, pp. 24–7.
67 Gerald Y. Goldberg, 'The Freeman of Cork', *Cork Review* (special issue on Sean O'Faolain 1900–1991), 1991, pp. 58–9.
68 Herman Good, as mentioned earlier, stood unsuccessfully for the Labour Party in the 1944 general election.
69 The following account is based on papers and press cuttings in the possession of Hubert Wine and an interview with Hubert Wine, Dublin, April 1997. See also Padraig Yeates, 'Judge renews criticism of youth care facilities', *Irish Times*, 13 November 1992.
70 Cutting from *Jewish Chronicle*, 21 June 1996, in Hubert Wine papers.

71   Hubert Wine papers.

72   Gutfreund to Wine, May 1996, Hubert Wine papers.

73   See *Activities of Government Departments: Reports from Departmental Press Officers* (Government Information Services, Dublin, 1997), pp. 62–4.

74   Joe Burns, 'Visually speaking', *Cork Examiner*, 29 February 1988. Elizabeth Friedlander was also a skilled wood engraver. She designed book jackets for Penguin. See Friedlander collection, Boole Library, University College Cork (donated by Gerald and Sheila Goldberg).

75   See Gerald Davis, 'On being a Jew in Ireland', *Everyman*, No. 1, 1968, pp. 109–10.

76   Hubert Wine won the Irish table tennis championship and represented his country in the world championships at Wembley, getting to the fourth round. He is also a former captain of Edmondstown Golf Club, and was chairman for many years of Dublin's Maccabi Association Sports Club.

77   Interview with Fr Michael O'Carroll, Dublin, July 1996.

78   *Irish Times*, 24 June 1994.

79   ibid.

80   ibid. President Robinson mentioned that an Irish government minister, Mervyn Taylor, had lost family members there.

81   ibid.

82   ibid.

83   His office felt it appropriate to choose the anniversary of the actual day of liberation, 15 April. On the personal initiative of the Taoiseach, invitations to a short ceremony at the War Memorial in Islandbridge, Dublin, were sent out. This was to be followed by a reception in the Royal Hospital Kilmainham. The Taoiseach was very quick to change the date. His office said that he had consulted a 'senior member of the Jewish community' before doing so. That may have been his cabinet colleague, Minister for Equality and Law Reform, Mervyn Taylor. Bruton's party colleague, Alan Shatter, who is also Jewish, said that he was disappointed the Taoiseach did not contact him beforehand and that the embarrassment could have been avoided. See Geraldine Kennedy, 'Ceremony changed after Passover clash revealed – Belsen to be commemorated', *Irish Times*, 8 April 1995.

84   *Irish Times*, 21 April 1995.

85   See *The Ireland–Israel Friendship League Newsletter*, Vol. 1, No. 2 (September 1995).

86   Text of John Bruton's speech, 26 April 1995, kindly supplied by the Government Information Services.

87   ibid.

88   ibid. Bruton also said: 'I also recall the gypsies and homosexual community who were marked down for extermination and all those who were persecuted for resisting the Nazi tyranny . . . I am also humbled to be here when we have with us some of those who have borne witness personally to the horror and reality of the Holocaust.'

89   ibid.

90   Martin Wall, '£20 million cost to maintain refugees', *Sunday Tribune*, 20 April 1997.

91   James Joyce, *Ulysses*, annotated students' edition (Penguin, London, 1992), pp. 432–3.

92   Adele (Shillman) and Lex Cohen, 'A Memoir of a Journey to Riga and old Akmene, August 1989'; I am grateful to Gerald Goldberg, who has the manuscript, for permission to cite this very valuable source.

93   ibid.

94   Primo Levi, *Collected Poems* (Faber and Faber, London, 1988), p. 9.

Bibliography

Primary Sources

National Archives, Dublin

Department of the Taoiseach
    Cabinet minutes
    S files
Department of External Affairs
    Confidential Reports from Irish missions abroad: London, Berlin, Paris, Rome, the
        Holy See, Lisbon, Madrid, Ottawa, Washington and Canberra.
    Files of embassies to the Holy See and France
    Secretary's files
    League of Nations files
    General Registry files
Department of Finance
    General files
Department of Justice
    General files for the period from 1922 to 1955
    Case files, aliens section
Chief Secretary's files, Dublin Castle
    Limerick, 1890s to 1905 CSORP 1905/23538

Public Record Office, Belfast

Ministry of Commerce 'E' files
Com/23, concerning applications for residence in the United Kingdom from 1945
    onwards
Com/63, various commercial development files relating to the post-1945 period
Com/87, files relating to applications for naturalisation
HA/32/1, files relating to national defence and the employment of aliens in Northern
    Ireland
HA/5/795, files relating to an application to bring in from Belgium a person who would
    be employed as reader in the local synagogue
Lab.5/1, files relating to requests to bring forty Jewish boys, aged fifteen, to Northern

Ireland to train in rudiments of agriculture

Public Record Office, Kew, London

Foreign Office files
Dominions Office files

National Archives, Washington DC and Maryland

State Department (RG 59)
    Ireland: US embassy files, Dublin
    Confidential Records, US embassy, Dublin
Military Branch, files relating to Ireland

National Library of Ireland

Richard Irvine Best papers
Robert Briscoe papers
Frank Gallagher papers
Harry Kernoff papers
Micheal Noyk papers
William O'Brien papers

Maurice Abrahamson family archives, Dublin

Four scrapbooks tracing the history of the Nurock and Abrahamson families from the
    late nineteenth century

Armagh Archdiocesan Archives

Michael Logue papers
Patrick O'Donnell papers
Joseph MacRory papers

Robert Briscoe papers

The bulk of this large collection is in the Jabotinsky Centre, Israel. Ben Briscoe
    generously made available to me copies of relevant sections

Dublin Archdiocesan Archives

Edward Byrne papers
William Walsh papers
John Charles McQuaid papers

Franciscan Archives, Killiney, Co. Dublin

Eamon de Valera papers
    Files relating to de Valera's relationship with the Jewish community in Ireland
    Correspondence with the Herzog family, Israel
    Files on the drafting of the 1937 constitution

Holocaust Museum, Washington DC

Books and holdings on the Holocaust

Holy Ghost Fathers Archives, Dublin

Denis Fahey papers

Irish Jewish Museum Archives, Dublin
Various files and materials relating to the history of the Jewish community in Ireland

Irish Military Archives, Dublin
General records
G2 files (Irish military intelligence)

Jesuit Archives, Dublin
Edward Cahill papers

Redemptorist House, Limerick
Holy Family Chronicles, 1900–42

Society of Friends, Dublin
Archives relating to the reception of refugees during the 1930s and 1940s

Trinity College Dublin (Manuscripts Collection)
Frederick H. Boland papers
Michael Davitt papers
Frank Gallagher papers
Con Leventhal papers
Seumas O'Sullivan papers

University College Cork
Oral History Project, interviews with Dr Gerald Goldberg conducted by Dr Damien
  Bracken
William O'Brien papers
Alfred O'Rahilly papers

University College Dublin
Ernest Blythe papers
Dan Bryan papers
Desmond FitzGerald papers
Seán MacEntee papers
Patrick McGilligan papers
James Ryan papers

University of Southampton, Parks and Hartley Library
Solomon Schonfeld papers

Correspondence
The author received correspondence conveying information relevant to the study
from the following: Ben Briscoe TD, Joe Briscoe, Mary Fleming, Noel Henry, Professor
John Horgan, Rabbi Theodore Lewis, Fr Tom Morrissey

Interviews
The author conducted interviews with the following: Maurice Abrahamson, Dublin;
Asher Benson, Dublin; Ben Briscoe TD, Dublin; Dr Gerald Goldberg, Cork; Dr Han
Hogerzeil, Wickow; John Horgan, Dublin; Dr Bill Hyland, Cork; Helen Lewis, Belfast;
Fr Michael O'Carroll, Dublin; Brian Quinn, Dublin; Frederick Rosehill, Cork; Alan

Shatter TD, Dublin; Raphael Siev, Dublin; Michael Solomons, Dublin; Mervyn Taylor TD, Dublin; Judge Hubert Wine, Dublin; Tom Woulfe, Dublin.

Interviews were conducted on my behalf by Dr Caroline Windrum, Institute of Irish Studies, Belfast with the following: Louis Fredlander (Friedlander), Belfast; June and Alex Jaffe, Belfast; Rada Smith (née Hyman), Belfast; Dr David Warm, University of Ulster, Jordanstown

Interviews conducted on my behalf by Mr Tadhg O'Sullivan, postgraduate student, Department of History, University College Cork: Dr David O'Donoghue, Dublin; Betty Pearson, Dublin; Daisy Swanton, Cobh, Co. Cork

Secondary Sources

Abrahamsen, Samuel, *Norway's Response to the Holocaust* (Holocaust Library, New York, 1991)

Abramsky, Chimen, Maciej Jachimczyk and Antony Polonsky (eds.), *The Jews in Poland* (Basil Blackwell, Oxford, 1986)

Adams, Michael, *Censorship: The Irish Experience* (University of Alabama Press, Alabama, 1968)

Alderman, Geoffrey, 'The Jew as Scapegoat? The Settlement and Reception of Jews in South Wales before 1914', *Transactions of the Jewish Historical Society of England*, Vol. 26 (1979), pp. 62–70

Anon., 'After the Holocaust – 50 years on survivors in Ireland recall the horror', *Sunday Tribune*, 22 January 1995

Anon., 'Dr Isaac Herzog appointed – twenty years' service in Dublin', *Irish Times*, 2 December 1936

Anon., *Educational Jewish Aspects of James Joyce's Ulysses* (Irish Jewish Museum, Dublin, 1992)

Anon., 'Hill of Tara, County Meath', *Proceedings of the Royal Society of Antiquaries of Ireland*, 5th Series, Vol. 13 (1903), pp. 102–3

Anon. [An Irishman], *Intolerance in Ireland: Facts not Fiction* (Simpkin Marshall, Hamilton, Kent and Co., London, 1913)

Anon., *The Irish Christian Front* (Dublin, 1936)

Anon., 'The Jews in Ireland', *Lyceum*, Vol. 6, No. 70 (July 1893), pp. 215–18

Anon., 'Obituary of Chief Rabbi Herzog – outstanding scholar and leader', *Jewish Chronicle*, 31 July 1959

Anon., *Saul Harris Wigoder* (no publisher listed, Dublin, 1933)

Arnold, Bruce, *What Kind of Country: Modern Irish Politics, 1968–1983* (Jonathan Cape, London, 1984)

  Irish Art (Thames and Hudson, London, 1989)

  Mainie Jellett and the Modern Movement in Ireland (Yale University Press, London and New Haven, 1991)

Bachellery, E., 'Julius Pokorny (1887–1970)', *Études Celtiques*, Vol. 14 (1974), pp. 283–5

Bair, Deirdre, *Samuel Beckett: A Biography* (Jonathan Cape, London, 1978)

Bardon, Jonathan, *A History of Ulster* (Blackstaff Press, Belfast, 1992)

Barrington, Ruth, *Health, Medicine and Politics in Ireland, 1900–1970* (Institute of Public Administration, Dublin, 1987)

Barton, Brian, *The Blitz: Belfast in the War Years* (Blackstaff Press, Belfast, 1989)

  Northern Ireland in the Second World War (Ulster Historical Foundation, Belfast, 1995)

Bartrop, Paul R., 'The Dominions and the Evian Conference, 1938: A Lost Chance or a Golden Opportunity?', in Paul R. Bartrop (ed.), *False Havens: The British*

Empire and the Holocaust, Studies in the Shoah, Vol. X (University Press of America, Lanham, Maryland, 1995), pp. 53–78

Bauer, Yehuda, *From Diplomacy to Resistance* (Jewish Publication Society, Philadelphia, 1970)

My Brother's Keeper (Jewish Publication Society, Philadelphia, 1974)

The Holocaust in Historical Perspective (Washington University Press, Seattle, 1978)

American Jewry and the Holocaust: The American Jewish Joint Distribution Committee, 1939–1945 (Wayne State University Press, Detroit, 1982)

Jews for Sale: Nazi–Jewish Negotiations, 1933–1945 (Yale University Press, New Haven and London, 1994)

Béaslaí, Piaras, *Michael Collins: Soldier and Statesman* (Talbot Press, Dublin and Cork, 1937)

Belloc, Hilaire, *The Jews* (Constable, London, 1937)

Benson, Asher, 'Jewish Genealogy in Ireland', in *Aspects of Irish Genealogy: Proceedings of the First Irish Genealogical Congress* (Irish Genealogical Congress Committee, 1993), pp. 17–27

Berman, Hannah (updated by Melisande Zlotover), *Zlotover Story: A Dublin Story with a Difference – A Social Survey of Jewish Dublin of Approximately the First Six Decades of the Twentieth Century* (Hely Thom, Dublin, 1966)

Bew, Paul, Peter Gibbon and Henry Patterson, *The State in Northern Ireland 1921–1972: Political Forces and Social Classes* (Manchester University Press, Manchester, 1979)

Bew, Paul and Henry Patterson, *Seán Lemass and the Making of Modern Ireland, 1945–66* (Gill & Macmillan, Dublin, 1982)

Bewley, Charles, *Hermann Göring and the Third Reich* (Devin-Adair, USA, 1962)

Memoirs of a Wild Goose (Lilliput Press, Dublin, 1990)

Bielenberg, Christabel, *The Past is Myself* (Ward River Press, Dublin, 1982)

Binchy, D. A., 'Heinrich Bruning', *Studies*, Vol. 21 (September 1932), pp. 385–403

'Adolf Hitler', *Studies*, Vol. 22 (March 1933), pp. 29–47

'Paul von Hindenburgh', *Studies*, Vol. 26 (1937), pp. 223–42

Blamires, Harry, *The New Bloomsday Book: A Guide Through Joyce*, 3rd edn (Routledge, London and New York, 1996)

Boland, Thomas P., 'Fr John Creagh of the Kimberleys', *Old Limerick Journal*, No. 23 (Spring 1988), pp. 151–5

Bolchover, Richard, *British Jewry and the Holocaust* (Cambridge University Press, Cambridge, 1993)

Bolster, Evelyn, *The Knights of Saint Columbanus* (Gill & Macmillan, Dublin, 1979)

Bonhoffer, Dietrich, *Letters and Papers from Prison* (Collier Books, New York, 1972)

Bosworth, R. J. B., *Explaining Auschwitz and Hiroshima: History Writing and the Second World War 1945–90* (Routledge, London, 1993)

Bowman, John, *De Valera and the Ulster Question, 1917–73* (Clarendon Press, Oxford, 1982)

Bracher, Karl Dietrich, *The German Dictatorship: The Origins, Structure and Consequences of National Socialism* (Penguin, London, 1970)

Brady, Conor, *Guardians of the Peace* (Gill & Macmillan, Dublin, 1974)

Braham, Randolph L., *The Politics of Genocide: The Holocaust in Hungary*, 2 vols. (Columbia University Press, New York, 1981),

Breathnach, Diarmuid and Máire Ní Murchú (eds.), 'Julius Pokorny', *Beathaisnéis*, Vol. III, pp. 144–5

Bredin, Jean-Denis, *The Affair: The Case of Alfred Dreyfus* (George Braziller, New York, 1986)

Briscoe, Robert (with Alden Hatch), *For the Life of Me* (Little, Brown & Co., Boston, 1958)

Brown, Terence, *Ireland: A Social and Cultural History 1922–79* (Fontana, London, 1981)

'Religious Minorities in the Irish Free State and the Republic of Ireland 1922–1995', *Building Trust in Ireland: Studies Commissioned by the Forum for Peace and Reconciliation* (Blackstaff Press, Belfast, 1996), pp. 215–54

Browne, Alan (ed.), *Masters, Midwives and Ladies-in-Waiting: The Rotunda Hospital 1745–1995* (A. and A. Farmar, Dublin, 1995)

Browne, Noël, *Against the Tide* (Gill & Macmillan, Dublin, 1986)

Browning, Christopher R., *Ordinary Men: Reserve Police Battalion 101 and the Final Solution in Poland* (HarperPerennial, New York, 1992)

The Path to Genocide (Cambridge University Press, Cambridge and New York, 1992)

Bulfin, William, *Rambles in Eirinn* (Gill & Son, Dublin, 1907)

Burbage, Thomas, 'Ritual Murder among the Jews', *Catholic Bulletin*, Vol. 6, No. 6 (May–June 1916), pp. 309–14

'What is Freemasonry?', *Catholic Bulletin*, Vol. 7, No. 2 (February 1917), pp. 93–8

'Masonic Crimes and Terrorism', *Catholic Bulletin*, Vol. 7, No. 6 (June 1917), pp. 376–84

Butler, Hubert, *The Children of Drancy* (Lilliput Press, Mullingar, 1988)

Butler, Sr Katherine, 'Synagogues of Old Dublin', *Dublin Historical Record*, Vol. 27, No. 4 (September 1974), pp. 118–30

'Rosa Solomons', paper read to the Old Dublin Society, 2 February 1977

'Centenary of a Synagogue: Adelaide Road 1892–1992', *Dublin Historical Record*, Vol. 48, No. 1 (Spring 1994), pp. 46–55

Cahill, Edward, *Freemasonry and the Anti-Christian Movement* (Gill & Son, Dublin, 1930)

Ireland's Peril (Gill & Son, Dublin, 1930)

The Framework of a Christian State (Gill & Macmillan, Dublin, 1932)

Carlson, Julia (ed.), *Banned in Ireland: Censorship and the Irish Writer* (Routledge, London, 1990)

Carmody, Fiona and Margaret Daly, 'Irish Jews and anti-Semitism in the Early Twentieth Century', *Retrospect: Journal of the Irish History Students' Association*, 1984, pp. 46–50

Carroll, Joseph T., *Ireland in the War Years* (David and Charles, Newton Abbot, 1975)

Carter, Carolle J., *The Shamrock and the Swastika: German Espionage in Ireland in World War II* (Pacific Books, Palo Alto, Calif., 1977)

Casey, Dan, 'Bei mir bistu Sean – from Dublin's 1 Zion Road to Cork, Ireland's 2,644 Jews are at home', *Jewish Monthly*, April 1987, pp. 44–9

Celan, Paul, *Collected Prose* (P.N. Review, Carcanet, 1986)

Selected Poems (Penguin Books, London, 1990)

Cesarani, David, 'Great Britain', in David Wyman (ed.), *The World Reacts to the Holocaust* (Johns Hopkins University Press, Baltimore and London, 1996), pp. 599–641

The Final Solution: Origins and Implementation (Routledge, London, 1996)

Chalk, Frank and Kurt Jonassohn, *Genocide: The History and Sociology of Genocide* (Yale University Press, New Haven and London, 1990)

Chaplin, Charles, *My Autobiography* (Penguin, London, 1974)

Chubb, Basil, *The Government and Politics of Ireland*, 2nd edn (Longman, London, 1982)

Clare, George, *Last Waltz in Vienna: The Destruction of a Family, 1842–1942* (Macmillan, London, 1980)

Berlin Days 1946–47 (Pan Books, London, 1989)

Clein, Michael A., *The Clein Family* (Judaic Studies Program, University of Miami, 1989)

Clery, Arthur, 'Belloc on Christians and Others', *Studies*, Vol. 11 (December 1922), pp. 648–50

Cohen, Adele (Shillman) and Lex, 'A Memoir of a Journey to Riga and old Akmene, August 1989', unpublished manuscript

Cohen, Isaac, 'Community Spirit', in Aidan Carl Mathews (ed.), *Immediate Man: Cuimhní ar Chearbhall Ó Dálaigh* (Dolmen Press, Portlaoise, 1983), pp. 59–62

Cohn-Sherbok, Dan, *Holocaust Theology* (Lamp Press, London, 1989)

Coleman, Sheelagh and Tessa, *Full Circle* (Town House, Dublin, 1995)

Collis, Robert, *To Be a Pilgrim* (Secker and Warburg, London, 1975)

Collis, Robert and Han Hogerzeil, *Straight On* (Methuen, London, 1947)

Connolly, P. (ed.), *Literature and the Changing Ireland* (Colin Smythe, Gerrard's Cross, Bucks., 1982)

Conway, Martin, *Collaboration in Belgium: Léon Degrelle and the Rexist Movement* (Yale University Press, New Haven and London, 1993)

Coogan, T. P., *The IRA* (Pall Mall Press, London, 1980)

Michael Collins: A Biography (Arrow, London, 1991)

Cooper, Leo, *Genocide: Its Political Use in the Twentieth Century* (Yale University Press, New Haven and London, 1981)

Costello, Peter, *Leopold Bloom: A Biography* (Gill & Macmillan, Dublin, 1981)

Corish, P. J., *The Irish Catholic Experience: A Historical Survey* (Gill & Macmillan, Dublin, 1985)

Cotter, Colette Mary, 'Anti-Semitism and Irish Political Culture, 1932–1945' (MPhil, University College Cork, 1996)

Cronin, Anthony, *Samuel Beckett: The Last Modernist* (HarperCollins, London, 1996)

Cronin, Seán, *Frank Ryan: The Search for the Republic* (Repsol Press, Dublin, 1980)

Washington's Irish Policy, 1916–1986 (Anvil, Dublin, 1987)

Crowley, John, 'Narrative and Place: A Cultural History of the South Parish' (MA, University College Cork, 1993)

Cruise O'Brien, Conor, *To Katanga and Back* (Simon and Schuster, New York, 1962)

Herod: Reflections on Political Violence (Hutchinson, London, 1978)

God Land: Reflections on Religion and Nationalism (Harvard University Press, Cambridge, Mass., 1988)

'Ireland in International Affairs', in Owen Dudley Edwards (ed.), *Conor Cruise O'Brien Introduces Ireland* (McGraw Hill, New York, 1969), pp. 104–34

Daly, Ita, *Unholy Ghosts* (Bloomsbury, London, 1996)

Daly, Mary E., 'An Irish-Ireland for Business?: The Control of Manufactures Acts, 1932 and 1934', *Irish Historical Studies*, Vol. 24 (November 1984), pp. 246–72

Davis, Gerald, 'On being a Jew in Ireland', *Everyman*, No. 1, 1968, pp. 109–10

Davitt, Michael, *Within the Pale: The True Story of Anti-Semitic Persecution in Russia* (Hurst and Blackett, London, 1903)

Dawidowicz, Lucy S., *The War against the Jews 1933–45* (Penguin, London, 1987)

Deane, Séamus, *A Short History of Irish Literature* (Hutchinson, London, 1986)

de Vere White, Terence, *Kevin O'Higgins* (Methuen, London, 1948)

Devane, Richard, S., 'Suggested Tariff on Imported Newspapers and Magazines', *Studies*, Vol. 16 (December 1927), pp. 544–69

'The Menace of the British Press Combines', *Studies*, Vol. 19 (March 1930), pp. 55–69

Dillon, T. W. T., 'The Refugee Problem', *Studies*, Vol. 28 (1939), pp. 402–14

Dinnerstein, Leonard, *Anti-Semitism in America* (Oxford University Press, New York and Oxford, 1994)

Donoghue, Denis, *Warrenpoint* (Jonathan Cape, London, 1991)

Doorly, Mary Rose, *Hidden Memories: The Personal Recollections of Survivors and Witnesses to the Holocaust Living in Ireland* (Blackwater Press, Dublin, 1994)

Dudley Edwards, Owen, *Eamon de Valera* (GPC Books, Cardiff, 1987)

Dudley Edwards, Ruth, *An Atlas of Irish History*, 2nd edn (Methuen, London and New York, 1986)

Duggan, J. P., *Neutral Ireland and the Third Reich* (Lilliput Press, Dublin, 1989)
    A History of the Irish Army (Gill & Macmillan, Dublin, 1991)

Dunne, Seán, *In my Father's House* (Anna Livia Press, Dublin, 1991)

Elborn, Geoffrey, *Francis Stuart: A Life* (Raven Arts Press, Dublin, 1990)

Eliash, Shulamit, 'The "Rescue" Policy of the Chief Rabbinate of Palestine Before and During World War II', *Modern Judaism*, October 1983, pp. 291–308

Ellman, Richard, *James Joyce* (Oxford University Press, Oxford, 1983)

Ericksen, Robert P., *Theologians under Hitler* (Yale University Press, New Haven and London, 1985)

Evens, Richard J., *In Hitler's Shadow: West German Historians and the Attempt to Escape from the Nazi Past* (Pantheon Books, New York, 1989)

Fahey, Denis, *The Kingship of Christ, According to the Principles of St Thomas* (Dublin, 1931)
    The Social Rights of Our Divine Lord Jesus Christ, the King (Dublin, 1932)
    The Mystical Body of Christ in the Modern World (Dublin, 1935)
    The Rulers of Russia (Dublin, 1938)
    Money, Manipulation and Social Order (Dublin, 1944)
    The Mystical Body of Christ and the Reorganisation of Society (Cork, 1944)
    The Church and Farming (Cork, 1953)
    The Kingship of Christ and the Conversion of the Jewish Nation (Dublin, 1953)

Fanning, Ronan, *The Irish Department of Finance 1922–1958* (Institute of Public Administration, Dublin, 1978)
    Independent Ireland (Helicon, Dublin, 1983)
    'Neutral Ireland?', *An Cosantóir*, September 1989, pp. 45–8
    'The Dublin link', *Sunday Independent*, 6 January 1991

Farrell, Brian, *Seán Lemass* (Gill & Macmillan, Dublin, 1983)

Farrell, Brian (ed.), *Communications and Community in Ireland* (Mercier Press, Dublin and Cork, 1984)

Feeney, J., *John Charles McQuaid* (Mercier Press, Dublin and Cork, 1974)

Feingold, Henry L., *Bearing Witness: How America and its Jews Responded to the Holocaust* (Syracuse University Press, Syracuse, 1995)

Felstiner, John, *Paul Celan, Poet, Survivor, Jew* (Yale University Press, New Haven and London, 1995)

Fennell, Desmond (ed.), *The Changing Face of Catholic Ireland* (Geoffrey Chapman, London, 1968)

Finlay, Fergus, *Mary Robinson: A President with a Purpose* (O'Brien Press, Dublin, 1990)

Fisher, Eugene J. et al. (eds.), *Twenty Years of Jewish–Catholic Relations* (Paulist Press, New York, 1986)

Fisk, Robert, *In Time of War: Ireland, Ulster and the Price of Neutrality 1939–45* (André Deutsch, London, 1983)

FitzGerald, Garret, *All in a Life* (Gill & Macmillan, Dublin, 1992)

Fleming, Gerald, *Hitler and the Final Solution* (Oxford University Press, Oxford, 1986)

Fogelman, Eva, *Conscience and Courage: Rescuers of Jews During the Holocaust* (Cassell, London, 1995)

Foot, M. R. D., *Resistance* (Paladin, London, 1976)

Frankl, Viktor, *Man's Search for Meaning: An Introduction to Logotherapy* (Touchstone Books, New York, 1984)

Friedlander, Saul, *Nazi Germany and the Jews: The Years of Persecution 1933–1939*, Vol. 1 (HarperCollins, New York, 1997)

Friedman, Philip, *Their Brothers' Keepers* (Holocaust Library, New York)

Gallagher, M., *Political Parties in the Republic of Ireland* (Gill & Macmillan, Dublin, 1985)

Garvin, Tom, *The Evolution of Irish Nationalist Politics* (Gill & Macmillan, Dublin, 1972)

Nationalist Revolutionaries in Ireland 1858–1928 (Clarendon Press, Oxford, 1987)

1922: The Birth of Irish Democracy (Gill & Macmillan, Dublin, 1996)

Gibbons, Luke, *Transformations in Irish Culture* (Cork University Press, Cork, 1996)

Gies, Miep (with Alison Leslie Gold), *Ann Frank Remembered: The Story of the Woman who Helped to Hide the Frank Family* (Simon and Schuster, New York, 1987)

Gilbert, Martin, *The Holocaust: The Jewish Tragedy* (Fontana Collins, London, 1986)

Atlas of the Holocaust: The Complete History, 2nd edn (Dent and Co., London, 1993)

The Boys: Triumph over Adversity (Weidenfeld and Nicolson, London, 1996)

Gill, Anton, *The Journey Back from Hell* (Grafton Books, London, 1988)

Gogarty, Oliver St John, *As I Was Going Down Sackville Street* (London, 1937)

'Ugly England', *Sinn Féin*, 24 November 1906

'Ugly England', *Sinn Féin*, 1 December 1906

Goldberg, Gerald Y., 'Note on the Jewish Community in Cork', in Bernard Shillman, *A Short History of the Jews in Ireland* (Eason, Dublin, 1945)

'Ireland is the only country . . . Joyce and the Jewish Dimension', *Crane Bag*, Vol. 6, No. 1 (1982), pp. 5–11

'The Freeman of Cork', *Cork Review* (special issue on Sean O'Faolain 1900–1991), 1991, pp. 58–9

Goldberger, Leo (ed.), *The Rescue of the Danish Jews: Moral Courage under Stress* (New York University Press, New York and London, 1987)

Goldhagen, Daniel Jonah, *Hitler's Willing Executioners: Ordinary Germans and the Holocaust* (Little, Brown & Co., New York, 1996)

Golding, G. M., *George Gavan Duffy, 1882–1951: A Legal Biography* (Irish Academic Press, Dublin, 1982)

Gordon, Lois, *The World of Samuel Beckett 1906–1946* (Yale University Press, New Haven and London, 1996)

Harkness, David W., *The Restless Dominion: The Irish Free State and the British Commonwealth of Nations* (Macmillan, London, 1969)

Northern Ireland since 1920 (Helicon, Dublin, 1983)

'Patrick McGilligan: Man of Commonwealth', *Journal of Imperial and Common-wealth History*, Vol. 8, No. 1 (October 1979), pp. 117–35

Harlow, Barbara, *Resistance Literature* (Methuen, New York and London, 1987)

Harris, Mary, *The Catholic Church and the Foundation of the Northern Irish State* (Cork University Press, Cork, 1993)

Harris, Simon, 'Professor Jacob and Bertha Weingreen, a tribute on their diamond wedding anniversary', *Irish Jewish Year Book, 1994–95*

Heaney, Seamus, *North* (Faber and Faber, London, 1975)

Hellman, John, 'The Jews in the "New Middle Ages": Jacques Maritain's anti-Semitism in its Times', in Robert Royal (ed.), *Jacques Maritain and the Jews* (American Maritain Association, Indiana, 1994)

Herzog, Chaim, *Living History: A Memoir* (Pantheon Books, New York, 1996)

Herzog, Isaac, *The Main Institutions of Jewish Law*, Vol. 1 (Soncino Press, London, 1936)

Hesketh, Tom, *The Second Partitioning of Ireland: The Abortion Referendum of 1983* (Brandsma Books, Dublin, 1990)

Hilberg, Raul, *The Destruction of the European Jews* (Holmes and Meier, New York and London, 1985)

    Perpetrators, Victims, Bystanders: The Jewish Catastrophe 1939–1945 (Harper-Perennial, New York, 1992)

Hobsbawm, Eric, *Age of Extremes* (Michael Joseph, London, 1994)

Hogan, James, *Could Ireland become Communist?: The Facts of the Case* (Cork University Press, Cork, c. 1935)

Hollis, Christopher, 'The Mystery of Jewish Survival', *Studies*, Vol. 30 (1941), pp. 205–18

Hopkinson, Michael, *Green against Green: The Irish Civil War* (Gill & Macmillan, Dublin, 1988)

Horgan, John, 'Saving us from Ourselves: Contraception, Censorship and the "Evil Literature" Controversy of 1926', *Irish Communications Review*, Vol. 5 (1995), pp. 61–7

Hyman, Louis, *The Jews of Ireland: From Earliest Times to the Year 1910* (Irish University Press, Shannon, 1972)

Jacobs, Louis, *The Jewish Religion: A Companion* (Oxford University Press, Oxford, 1995)

Jakobovits, Immanuel, *Journal of a Rabbi* (W. H. Allen, London, 1967)

Jeffares, A. Norman, 'Oliver St John Gogarty', *Proceedings of the British Academy*, Vol. 46 (1960), pp. 73–96.

Joannon, Pierre (ed.), *De Gaulle and Ireland* (Institue of Public Administration, Dublin, 1991)

Johnston, Denis, *Nine Rivers from Jordan: The Chronicle of a Journey and a Search* (Derek Verschoyle, London, 1953)

Joyce, James, *Ulysses,* annotated students' edition with introduction by Declan Kiberd (Penguin, London, 1992)

Katz, Stephen T., *Post-Holocaust Dialogue: Critical Studies in Modern Jewish Thought* (New York University Press, New York and London, 1985)

Kavanagh, Patrick, *Collected Poems* (MacGibbon and Kee, London, 1968)

Keatinge, Patrick, *The Formulation of Irish Foreign Policy* (Institute of Public Administration, Dublin, 1973)

    A Place Among the Nations: Issues of Irish Foreign Policy (Dublin, 1978)

Kee, Robert, *The Green Flag: A History of Irish Nationalism* (Weidenfeld and Nicolson, London, 1972)

Keneally, Thomas, *Schindler's Ark* (Hemisphere Publishing, London, 1982)

Kenna, Colm, 'Irish religious freedom praised at induction of chief rabbi', *Irish Times*, 17 February 1997

    'The Rising Fascist Tide: Irish Nazis', *In Dublin,* No. 259 (24 July/6 August) [no year given]

Kennedy, Brian P., *Dreams and Responsibilities: The State and the Arts in Independent Ireland* (Arts Council, Dublin, 1990)

Kennedy, Geraldine, 'Ceremony changed after Passover clash revealed', *Irish Times*, 8 April 1995

Kennedy, Michael, *Ireland and the League of Nations 1919–1946* (Irish Academic Press, Dublin, 1996)

Kennedy, S. Brian, *Irish Art and Modernism 1880–1950* (Institute of Irish Studies, Belfast, 1991)

Kennedy, S. Brian (ed.), *Stella Steyn 1907–1987* (Gorry Gallery Exhibition Catalogue, Dublin, 1995)

Kenner, Hugh, *Ulysses*, revised edn (Johns Hopkins University Press, Baltimore and London, 1993)

Keogh, Dermot, *The Rise of the Irish Working Class: The Dublin Trade Union Movement and Labour Leadership 1890–1914* (Appletree Press, Belfast, 1982)

The Vatican, the Bishops and Irish Politics, 1919–1939 (Cambridge University Press, Cambridge, 1986)

Ireland and Europe, 1919–1948 (Gill & Macmillan, Dublin, 1988), revised and extended edition: *Ireland and Europe 1919–1989* (Hibernian University Press, Cork and Dublin, 1989)

Twentieth-Century Ireland: Nation and State (Gill & Macmillan, Dublin, 1994)

Ireland and the Vatican: The Politics and Diplomacy of Church–State Relations, 1922–1960 (Cork University Press, Cork, 1995)

'Irish Department of Foreign Affairs', in Zara Steiner (ed.), *The Times Survey of Foreign Ministries of the World* (Times Books, London, 1982), pp. 276–96

'De Valera, the Bishops and the Red Scare', in J. P. O'Carroll and John A. Murphy (eds.), *De Valera and his Times* (Cork University Press, Cork, 1983), pp. 134–59

'The Irish Constitutional Revolution: An Analysis of the Making of the Constitution', *Administration*, Vol. 35, No. 4. (1987), pp. 4–84

'Church, State and Society', in Brian Farrell (ed.), *De Valera: His Constitution and Ours* (Gill & Macmillan, Dublin, 1988), pp. 103–22

'Jewish Refugees and Irish Government Policy in the 1930s and 1940s', in *Remembering for the Future*, Proceedings of Conference, Oxford, July 1988 (Pergamon Press, Oxford, 1988), Conference Pre-print, Vol. 1, pp. 395–403

'Eamon de Valera and Hitler: An Analysis of International Reaction to the Visit to the German Minister, May 1945', *Irish Studies in International Affairs*, Vol. 3, No. 1 (1989), pp. 69–92

'The Jesuits and the 1937 Constitution', *Studies*, Vol. 78, No. 309 (Spring 1989), pp. 82–95

'Church and State in Europe', in Adrian Hastings (ed.), *Directory of Vatican II after 25 Years* (SCM Press, London, 1990), pp. 289–302

'Profile of Joseph Walshe, Secretary of the Department of Foreign Affairs 1922–46', *Irish Studies in International Affairs*, Vol. 3, No. 2 (1990), pp. 59–80

'Democracy gone Dotty: Sean O'Faolain and the Professorship of English at University College Cork', *Cork Review* (special issue on Seán Ó Faolain, 1900–1991), 1991, pp. 29–33

'Ireland, de Gaulle and World War II', in Pierre Joannon (ed.), *De Gaulle and Ireland* (Institute of Public Administration, Dublin, 1991), pp. 23–52

'Ireland, the Vatican and the Cold War', *Irish Studies in International Affairs*, Vol. 3, No. 3 (1991), pp. 67–114

'Ireland, the Vatican and the Cold War: The Case of Italy, 1948', *Historical Journal*, Vol. 34, No. 4 (1991), pp. 931–52

'Mannix, de Valera and Irish Nationalism', in John O'Brien and Pauric Travers (eds.), *The Irish Emigrant Experience in Australia* (Poolbeg Press, Dublin, 1991), pp. 196–225

'Episcopal Decision-making in Ireland', in Maurice O'Connell (ed.), *Education, Church and State: Proceedings of the Second Annual Daniel O'Connell Workshop* (Institute of Public Administration, Dublin, 1992), pp. 1–18

'The Catholic Church and the Modern Irish State', *Renaissance and Modern Studies*, Vol. 36 (1993), pp. 70–92

'The Catholic Church and Politics in Ireland', in Maurice O'Connell (ed.), *People Power: Proceedings of the Third Annual Daniel O'Connell Workshop* (Institute of Public Administration, Dublin, 1993), pp. 57–79

'Jack Lynch', in Seán Dunne (ed.), *The Cork Anthology* (Cork University Press, Cork, 1993), pp. 334–41

'The Catholic Church and Politics in Ireland', *A and E: Anglistik und Englischun-terricht: Ireland: Literature, Culture, Politics* (Band 52, Heidelberg, 1994), pp. 147–68

'An Eye Witness to History: Fr Alexander J. McCabe and the Spanish Civil War, 1936–1939', *Breifne: Journal of Cumann Seanchais Bhreifne,* Cavan, 1994, pp. 445–88

'Ireland and the Vatican 1921–1949', in Peter C. Kent and John F. Pollard (eds.), *Papal Diplomacy in the Modern Age* (Praeger, New York, 1994), pp. 87–104

'Church, State and Pressure Groups', in Bernard Treacy and Gerry Whyte (eds.), *Religion, Morality and Public Policy: A Doctrine and Life Special* (Dominican Publications, Dublin, 1995), pp. 42–61

'The Irish Free State and the Refugee Crisis, 1933–1945', in Paul R. Bartrop (ed.), *False Havens: The British Empire and the Holocaust* (University Press of America, Lanham, Maryland, 1995), pp. 211–38

'Ireland and 'Emergency' Culture, 1922–1961', in *Ireland: A Journal of History and Society* (first issue, 'Irish Democracy and the Right to Freedom of Information'), Summer 1995, pp. 4–43

'Ireland', in David Wyman (ed.), *The World Reacts to the Holocaust* (Johns Hopkins University Press, Baltimore, 1996), pp. 642–69

'Liam Cosgrave', in Brian H. Murphy (ed.), *Nos Autem: Castleknock College and its Contribution* (Gill & Macmillan, Dublin, 1996), pp. 157–70

'The Role of the Catholic Church in the Republic of Ireland 1922–1995', in *Building Trust in Ireland: Studies Commissioned by the Forum for Peace and Reconcili-ation* (Blackstaff Press, Belfast, 1996), pp. 85–214

'The Catholic Church and the Godless Colleges: A Study of the History of Theology in the Irish Universities' (Dominican Publications, Dublin, forthcoming, 1997)

Keogh, Dermot and Finín O'Driscoll, 'Ireland', in Tom Buchanan and Martin Conway (eds.), *Popular Catholicism in Europe 1918–1965* (Clarendon Press, Oxford, 1996), pp. 270–300

Keogh, Dermot and Joe Mulholland (eds.), *Emigration, Employment and Enterprise* (Patrick MacGill Summer School, Hibernian University Press, Cork and Dublin, 1989)

Keogh, Dermot and Michael Haltzel (eds.), *Northern Ireland and the Politics of Recon-ciliation* (Cambridge University Press, Cambridge and New York, 1993)

Kiberd, Declan, *Inventing Ireland* (Jonathan Cape, London, 1995)

Kilbride-Jones, Howard, 'A visit to Galway', *Archaeology Ireland*, Vol 9, No. 4 (Winter 1995), pp. 22–3

Kingston, Lucy O., *Emerging from the Shadows: Based on Personal Diaries, 1883–1969,* compiled by Daisy Swanton (Attic Press, Dublin, 1994)

Knowlson, James, *Damned to Fame: The Life of Samuel Beckett* (Bloomsbury, London, 1996)

Koblik, Steven, *The Stones Cry Out: Sweden's Response to the Persecution of the Jews 1933–1945* (Holocaust Library, New York, 1988)

Kranzler, David and Gertrude Hirschler (eds.), *Solomon Schonfeld: His Page in History* (Judaica Press, New York, 1982)

Kritzman, Lawrence D., *Auschwitz and After: Race, Culture and 'the Jewish Ques-tion' in France* (Routledge, New York and London, 1995)

Kushner, Tony, *The Persistence of Prejudice: Anti-Semitism in British Society during the Second World War* (Manchester University Press, Manchester, 1989)

The Holocaust and the Liberal Imagination: A Social and Cultural History (Black-well, Oxford, 1994)

Laffan, Michael, *The Partition of Ireland, 1911–1925* (Dundalgan Press, Dundalk, 1983)

Laqueur, Walter, *The Terrible Secret: Suppression of the Truth about Hitler's Final Solution* (Little, Brown & Co., Boston and Toronto, 1980)

Lee, J. J., *Ireland 1912–1985: Politics and Society* (Cambridge University Press, Cambridge, 1989)

'Aspects of Corporatist Thought in Ireland: The Commission on Vocational Organisation, 1939–43', in Art Cosgrove and Donal McCartney (eds.), *Studies in Irish History Presented to R. Dudley Edwards* (University College Dublin, Dublin, 1979), pp. 324–46

Lee, J. J. (ed.), *Ireland 1945–70* (Gill & Macmillan, Dublin, 1979)

Ireland: Towards a Sense of Place (Cork University Press, Cork, 1985)

Leventhal, Con (using the alias, Laurence K. Emery), 'The Ulysses of Mr James Joyce', in *Klaxon* (single issue journal), 1923, pp. 14–20

Leventhal, Con, 'What it means to be a Jew', *Bell*, Vol. 10, No. 3 (June 1945), pp. 207–16

Levi, Primo, *Collected Poems* (Faber and Faber, London, 1988)

Lewis, Helen, *A Time to Speak* (Blackstaff Press, Belfast, 1992)

Lieberman, Mark, 'The Jews of Northern Ireland: Living in Peace in a Troubled Land', *Jewish Monthly,* March 1989, pp. 10–19

Lifton, Robert Jay, *The Nazi Doctors: Medical Killing and the Psychology of Genocide* (Basic Books, New York, 1986)

Lipschitz, Chaim U., *Franco, Spain, the Jews, and the Holocaust* (Ktav Publishing House, New York, 1984)

Lipstadt, Deborah E., *Beyond Belief: The American Press and the Coming of the Holocaust* (Free Press, New York, 1986)

Denying the Holocaust: The Growing Assault on Truth and Memory (Plume Books, New York, 1994)

Litton, Frank (ed.), *The Constitution of Ireland 1937–1987* (Institute of Public Administration, Dublin, 1988)

Longford, Lord and T. P. O'Neill, *Eamon de Valera* (Arrow Books, London, 1970)

Lottman, Herbert R., *Pétain: Hero or Traitor? The Untold Story* (Viking, London, 1985)

Lynch, Patrick and James Meenan (eds.), *Essays in Memory of Alexis FitzGerald* (Gill & Macmillan, Dublin 1987)

Lyons, F. S. L., *Ireland since the Famine* (Weidenfeld and Nicolson, London, 1971)

Lyons, J. B., *Oliver St John Gogarty* (Blackwater, Dublin, 1980)

McConkey, Kenneth, *A Free Spirit: Irish Art 1860–1960* (Antique Collectors' Club, London, 1990)

MacCurtain, Margaret and Donncha Ó Corráin (eds.), *Women in Irish Society: The Historical Dimension* (Arlen House, Dublin, 1978)

MacDonald, Malcolm, *Titans and Others* (Collins, London, 1972)

Mac Gréil, Micheál, *Prejudice and Tolerance in Ireland: Based on a Survey of Intergroup attitudes of Dublin Adults and Other Sources* (no publisher listed, 1978)

Prejudice in Ireland Revisited (Survey Research Unit, Maynooth, 1996)

McHugh, Damien, 'The Dublin woman who was gassed at Auschwitz', *Evening Press,* 27 April 1995

McKee, Eamonn C., 'From Precepts to Praxis: Irish Governments and Economic Policy, 1939 to 1952' (PhD, University College Dublin, 1987)

'Church–State Relations and the Development of Irish Health Policy: The Mother-and-Child Scheme, 1944–53', *Irish Historical Studies*, Vol. 25, No. 98 (November 1986), pp. 159–94

MacManus, M. J., *Eamon de Valera* (Talbot Press, Dublin, 1945)

McMahon, Deirdre, *Republicans and Imperialists: Anglo-Irish Relations in the 1930s* (Yale University Press, New Haven and London, 1984)

'Ireland, the Dominions and the Munich Crisis', *Irish Studies in International Relations*, Vol. 1, No. 1 (1979), pp. 30–7

Maier, Charles S., *The Unmasterable Past* (Harvard University Press, Cambridge, Mass. and London, 1988)

Malino, Frances and Bernard Wasserstein (eds.), *The Jews in Modern France* (Brandeis University Press, Hanover and London, 1985)

Manning, Maurice, *The Blueshirts* (Gill & Macmillan, Dublin, 1970)

Mansergh, Nicholas, *The Irish Free State: Its Government and Politics* (Allen and Unwin, London, 1934)

   The Unresolved Question: The Anglo-Irish Settlement and its Undoing 1912–1972 (Yale University Press, New Haven and London, 1991)

Marcus, David, *A Land not Theirs* (Corgi Books, London, 1986)

   Who ever heard of an Irish Jew and other short stories (Bantam, London, 1988)

Marcus, Louis, 'The Ireland of the Sixties', in Bernard Harris and Grattan Freyer (eds.), *Integrating Tradition: The Achievements of Seán Ó Riada* (Irish Humanities Center and Keohanes, Ballina and Dufour Editions, Chester Springs, Pennsylvania, 1981)

Marrus, Michael R., *The Unwanted: European Refugees in the Twentieth Century* (Oxford University Press, Oxford and New York, 1985)

   The Holocaust in History (University Press of New England, Hanover and London, 1987)

   'The History of the Holocaust: A Survey of Recent Literature', *Journal of Modern History*, Vol. 59, No. 1 (March 1987), pp. 114–60

Marrus, Michael R. and Robert O. Paxton, *Vichy France and the Jews* (Basic Books, New York, 1984)

Martin, Augustine (ed.), *James Joyce: The Artist and the Labyrinth* (Ryan Publishing, London, 1990)

Marton, Kati, *Wallenberg* (Random House, New York, 1982)

Maume, Patrick, *Life that is Exile* (Institute of Irish Studies, Belfast, 1993)

Mayer, Arno J., *Why Did the Heavens not Darken?* (Verso, London, 1990)

Michaelis, Meir, *Mussolini and the Jews: German–Italian Relations and the Jewish Question in Italy 1932–1945* (Clarendon Press, Oxford, 1978)

Mills, Michael, 'Fighting world slump of the thirties: rise and decline of the Blueshirts', *Irish Press*, 24 January 1969

Minerbi, Sergio I., 'The Vatican and Israel', in Peter Kent and John Pollard (eds.), *Papal Diplomacy in the Modern Age* (Prager, Westport and London, 1994)

Mitchell, A. and P. Ó Snodaigh (eds.), *Irish Political Documents 1916–1949* (Irish Academic Press, Dublin, 1985)

Mitchell, G. F., 'Antiquities', in T. Ó Raifeartaigh (ed.), *The Royal Irish Academy: A Bicentennial History 1785–1985* (Royal Irish Academy, Dublin, 1985)

Moody, Doctor, *Why are the Jews Persecuted?* (Catholic Truth Society, Dublin, 24 November 1938)

Moody, T. W., *Davitt and Irish Revolution 1848–82* (Clarendon Press, Oxford, 1982)

Moore, Bob, *Refugees from Nazi Germany in the Netherlands 1933–1940* (Nijhoff, Dordrecht, Boston and Lancaster)

Moriarty, Nigel, 'Ireland's Reaction to the Cold War: Aspects of Emergency Planning, 1947–1963' (MA, University College Cork, 1995)

Morris, Benny, *The Birth of the Palestinian Refugee Problem, 1947–1949* (Cambridge University Press, Cambridge, 1987)

Mosse, George L., *Towards a Final Solution: A History of European Racism* (University of Wisconsin Press, Madison, 1985)

Muller-Hill, Benno, *Murderous Sciences: Elimination by Scientific Selection of Jews, Gypsies and others in Germany 1933–1945* (Oxford University Press, New York, 1988)

Murphy, Brian P., *John Chartres: Mystery Man of the Treaty* (Irish Academic Press, Dublin, 1995)

Murphy, J. A., *Ireland in the Twentieth Century* (Gill & Macmillan, Dublin, 1975)

Nadel, Ira B., *Joyce and the Jews: Culture and Texts* (University Press of Florida, Gainesville, 1996)

National Gallery of Ireland and the Douglas Hyde Galleries, *Irish Women Artists: From the Eighteenth Century to the Present Day* (Dublin, 1987)

Neuberger, Julia, *On being a Jew* (Heinemann, London, 1995)

Newton, Verne W. (ed.), *FDR and the Holocaust* (St Martin's Press, New York, 1996)

Ní Dhonnchadha, Máirín and Theo Dorgan (eds.), *Revising the Rising* (Field Day, Derry, 1991)

Nowlan, Kevin B. and T. Desmond Williams, *Ireland in the War Years and After, 1939–51* (Gill & Macmillan, Dublin, 1969)

Ó Broin, Leon, *Michael Collins* (Gill & Macmillan, Dublin, 1980)

Frank Duff: A Biography (Gill & Macmillan, Dublin, 1982)

Just Like Yesterday (Gill & Macmillan, Dublin, n.d.)

Ó Broin, Leon (ed.), *In Great Haste: The Letters of Michael Collins and Kitty Kiernan* (Gill & Macmillan, Dublin, 1983)

Ó Buachalla, Séamus, *Education Policy in Twentieth-Century Ireland* (Wolfhound Press, Dublin, 1988)

O'Callaghan, Orlaith, 'Theatre and the Modern Irish State: A Case Study of the Pike Theatre Club' (MA, University College Cork, 1995)

O'Carroll, J. P. and John A. Murphy, *De Valera and his Times* (Cork University Press, Cork, 1983)

O'Carroll, Michael, *Pius XII: Greatness Dishonoured, a Documentary Study* (Laetere Press, Dublin, 1980)

Ó Dálaigh, Cearbhall, 'Foreword', in Louis Hyman, *The Jews of Ireland: From Earliest Times to the Year 1910* (Irish University Press, Shannon, 1972), p. xv

O'Donnell, Peadar, 'The Clergy and Me', *Doctrine and Life*, Vol. 24, No. 10 (October 1974), pp. 539–44

Ó Drisceoil, Donal, *Censorship in Ireland 1939–1945* (Cork University Press, Cork, 1996)

O'Driscoll, Finín, 'The Search for the Christian State: Irish Social Catholicism, 1913–1939' (MA, University College Cork, 1994)

O'Driscoll, Mervyn, 'Irish–German Relations, 1922–1939' (MA, University College Cork, 1992)

O'Duffy, Eoin, *Crusade in Spain* (Browne and Nolan, Dublin, 1938)

O'Faolain, Sean, *The Life Story of Eamon de Valera* (Talbot Press, Dublin and Cork, 1933)

De Valera: a New Biography (Penguin, London, 1939)

O'Farrell, Padraic, *The Burning of Brinsley MacNamara* (Lilliput Press, Dublin, 1990)

Ó Giolláin, Diarmaid, 'An Cultúr Coiteann agus Léann an Bhéaloidis', *Leachtaí Cholm Cille*, Vol. 26 (1996), pp. 137–58

O'Halloran, Clare, *Partition and the Limits of Irish Nationalism* (Gill & Macmillan, Dublin, 1987)

Ó hÉigeartaigh, Cian, 'Léon's last letters', *Irish Times*, 4 April 1992

Ó hEithir, Breandán, *The Begrudger's Guide to Irish Politics* (Gill & Macmillan, Dublin, 1986)

O'Leary, Con, *Irish Elections 1918–1977* (Gill & Macmillan, Dublin, 1979)

318   *Bibliography*

O'Malley, Padraig, *Biting at the Grave: The Irish Hunger Strikes and the Politics of Despair* (Blackstaff Press, Belfast, 1990)
O'Riordan, Manus, 'Anti-Semitism in Irish Politics', *The Jewish Year Book, 1984–85*, pp. 15–27
    'Irish and Jewish Volunteers in the Spanish anti-Fascist War: A 50th Anniversary Lecture and Record Recital', 15 November 1987, manuscript, 36 pp.
    'Connolly, Socialism and the Jewish Worker', *Saothar: Journal of the Irish Labour History Society*, Vol. 13 (1988), pp. 120–30
    'Communism in Dublin in the 1930s: The Struggle against Fascism', manuscript, 18 pp.
O'Riordan, Manus (ed.), *Articles by Frederick Ryan, First National Secretary of the Socialist Party of Ireland (1909)* (Labour History Workshop, Dublin, 1984), 69 pp.
    Articles by Frederick Ryan: Sinn Féin and Reaction (Labour History Workshop, Dublin, 1984), 51 pp.
    The Rise and Fall of Anti-Semitism, containing articles by Pat Feeley on 'The 1904 Campaign' and by Manus O'Riordan on 'The Sinn Féin Tradition' (Labour History Workshop, Dublin, 1984), 36 pp.
O'Riordan, Michael, *The Connolly Column: The Story of the Irishmen who fought for the Spanish Republic 1936–1939* (New Books, Dublin, 1979)
Ó Riordáin, Seán P., *Tara, the Monument on the Hill* (Dundalgan Press, Dundalk, 1954)
O'Shea, Susan, 'The Politics of Irish Culture, 1922–1939' (MPhil, University College Cork, 1995)
O'Sullivan, Donal, *The Irish Free State and its Senate* (Faber and Faber, London, 1940)
O'Toole, Fintan, 'Provincial thinking and the Holocaust', *Irish Times*, 2 September 1992
Ó Tuathaigh, M. A. G., 'The Land Question, Politics and Irish Society, 1922–1960s', in P. J. Drudy (ed.), *Ireland: Land, Politics and Society*, Irish Studies, 2 (Cambridge University Press, Cambridge, 1982)
    'Religion, Nationality and a Sense of Community in Modern Ireland', in M. A. G. Ó Tuathaigh (ed.), *Community, Culture and Conflict* (Galway, 1986)
Ó Tuathaigh, M. A. G. and Joe Lee, *The Age of de Valera* (Ward River Press, Dublin, 1982)
Paldiel, Mordecai, *The Path of the Righteous: Gentile Rescuers of Jews during the Holocaust* (KTAV Publishing House, New Jersey, 1993)
Palumbo, Michael, *The Waldheim Files* (Faber and Faber, London and Boston, 1988)
Patterson, Henry, *The Politics of Illusion: Republicanism and Socialism in Modern Ireland* (Hutchinson, London, 1989)
Patterson, Robert J., 'Ireland and France: An Analysis of Diplomatic Relations 1929–1950' (MA, University College Cork, 1993)
Pauley, Bruce F., *From Prejudice to Persecution: A History of Austrian Anti-Semitism* (University of North Carolina Press, Chapel Hill and London, 1992)
Paxton, Robert O., *Vichy France: Old Guard and New Order 1940–1944* (Columbia University Press, New York, 1972)
Peck, John, *Dublin from Downing St* (Gill & Macmillan, Dublin, 1978)
Pollak, Andy, 'Dublin's Jewish community "is here for the long haul" despite its decline', *Irish Times*, 7 March 1995
    'Dublin's closed door on Jewish refugees', *Irish Times*, 14–15 April 1995
Prager, Geoffrey, *Building Democracy in Ireland: Political Order and Cultural Integration in a Newly Independent Nation* (Cambridge University Press, Cambridge, 1986)

Pulzer, Peter G. J., *The Rise of Political Anti-Semitism in Germany and Austria* (John Wiley and Sons, New York, London and Sidney, 1974)

Quinn, P. L. S., 'The Re-entry of the Jew into England and Ireland and His Re-establishment There (PhD, University College Cork, 1966)

Raymond, R. J., 'De Valera, Lemass and Irish Economic Development: 1933–1948', in J. P. O'Carroll and John A. Murphy (eds.), *De Valera and his Times* (Cork University Press, Cork, 1983)

'David Gray, the Aiken Mission and Irish Neutrality, 1940–41', *Diplomatic History*, Vol. 9 (1985), pp. 55–71

Reich, William, *The Mass Psychology of Fascism* (Pelican, London, 1975)

Rockett, Kevin, Luke Gibbon and John Hill, *Cinema in Ireland* (Syracuse University Press, Syracuse, 1988)

Rosenberg, J. L., 'The 1941 Mission of Frank Aiken to the United States: An American Perspective', *Irish Historical Studies*, Vol. 22, No. 86 (September 1980), pp. 162–77

Roskies, David G., *Against the Apocalypse: Responses to Catastrophe in Modern Jewish Culture* (Harvard University Press, Cambridge, Mass. and London, 1984)

Rothery, Seán, *Ireland and the New Architecture 1900–1940* (Lilliput Press, Dublin, 1991)

Rothfels, Hans, *The Political Legacy of the German Resistance Movement* (Inter Nationes, Bad Godesberg, 1969)

Rousso, Henry, *The Vichy Syndrome: History and Memory in France since 1944* (Harvard University Press, Cambridge, Mass. and London, 1991)

Ryan, Des, 'The Jews of Limerick (Part 2)', *Old Limerick Journal*, No. 18 (Winter 1985)

'Jewish Immigrants in Limerick: A Divided Community', in David Lee (ed.), *Remembering Limerick* (Limerick Civic Trust, Limerick, 1997), pp. 166–76

Ryle Dwyer, T., *Irish Neutrality and the USA 1939–47* (Gill & Macmillan, Dublin, 1977)

Rynne, Xavier, *Letters from Vatican City* (Faber and Faber, London, 1963)

Salmon, Trevor, *Unneutral Ireland: An Ambivalent and Unique Security Policy* (Clarendon Press, Oxford, 1989)

Schloss, Eva, *Eva's Story* (W. H. Allen, London, 1989)

Sereny, Gitta, *Into that Darkness: The Mind of a Mass Murderer* (Picador, London, 1977)

Sexton, Brendan, *Ireland and the Crown 1922–1936: The Governor-Generalship of the Irish Free State* (Irish Academic Press, Dublin, 1989)

Sexton, J. J. and R. O'Leary, 'Factors Affecting Population Decline in Minority Religious Communities in the Republic of Ireland', in *Building Trust in Ireland: Studies Commissioned by the Forum for Peace and Reconciliation* (Blackstaff Press, Belfast, 1996), pp. 255–332

Shatter, Alan, 'Lethal racism influenced government policy to exclude fugitive Jews', *Irish Times*, 21 April 1995

Sherman, A. J., *Island Refugees: Britain and Refugees from the Third Reich 1933–1939* (Cass, London, 1994)

Shillman, Bernard, *A Short History of the Jews in Ireland* (Eason, Dublin, 1945)

Siggins, Lorna, 'Erwin Strunz: an escape from hell remembered', *Irish Times*, 17 December 1988

Solomons, Bethel, *One Doctor in His Time* (Christopher Johnson, London, 1956)

Solomons, Michael, *Pro-Life? The Irish Question* (Lilliput Press, Dublin, 1992)

Steinberg, Jonathan, *All or Nothing: The Axis and the Holocaust 1941–1943* (Routledge, London and New York, 1991)

Steinberg, Lucien, *Jews against Hitler* (Gordon and Cremonsi, London, 1974)

Stephan, Enno, *Spies in Ireland* (Stackpoke, Harrisburg, 1969)

Sugar, Robert, 'Millisle Farm – Once Upon a Farm: A Refugee Tale', *Jewish Monthly*, October 1990, pp. 26–9

Tenenbaum, Joseph, *Underground: The Story of a People* (Philosophical Library, New York, 1952)

United States Holocaust Memorial Museum, *Historical Atlas of the Holocaust* (Macmillan, New York, 1996)

Valiulis, Maryann Gialanella, *Almost a Rebellion: The Army Mutiny of 1924* (Tower Books, Cork, 1985)

    Portrait of a Revolutionary: General Richard Mulcahy and the Foundation of the Irish State (Irish Academic Press, Dublin, 1992)

Walsh, Dick, *The Party: Inside Fianna Fáil* (Gill & Macmillan, Dublin, 1986)

Ward, Stephen, 'Why the BBC ignored the Holocaust', *Independent on Sunday*, 22 August 1993

Wasserstein, Bernard, *Britain and the Jews of Europe 1939–45* (Oxford University Press, Oxford, 1988)

Waterman, Stanley, 'Changing Residential Patterns of the Dublin Jewish Community', *Irish Geography*, Vol. 14 (1981), pp. 41–50

    'Neighbourhood, Community and Residential Change Decisions in the Dublin Jewish Community', *Irish Geography*, Vol. 6 (1973), pp. 55–66

    'A Note on the Migration of Jews from Dublin', *Jewish Journal of Sociology*, Vol. 27, No. 1 (June 1985), pp. 23–7

    'On the South Side of the Liffey', *Jewish Quarterly*, Spring 1987, pp. 28–30

Weafer, John A., 'Change and Continuity in Irish Religion, 1974–1984', *Doctrine and Life,* Vol. 36, No. 10 (December 1986), pp. 508–17

Weber, Eugen, *Action Française: Royalism and Reaction in Twentieth-Century France* (Stanford University Press, Stanford, 1962)

    The Nationalist Revival in France, 1905–1914 (University of California Press, Berkeley and Los Angeles, 1968)

Webster, Paul, *Pétain's Crime: The Full Story of French Collaboration in the Holocaust* (Papermac, London, 1990)

Welch, Robert (ed.), *The Oxford Companion to Irish Literature* (Oxford University Press, Oxford, 1996)

Werblowsky, R. J. Zwi and Geoffrey Wigoder (eds.), *The Oxford Dictionary of the Jewish Religion* (Oxford University Press, Oxford, 1997)

Whyte, J. H., *Church and State in Modern Ireland, 1923–79',* 2nd edn (Gill & Macmillan, Dublin, 1984)

Wiesel, Elie, *Night* (MacGibbon and Kee, New York, 1982)

Williams, T. Desmond, 'From the Treaty to the Civil War', in T. Desmond Williams (ed.), *The Irish Struggle 1916–1926* (Routledge and Kegan Paul, London, 1966)

    'Ireland and the War', in K. B. Nowlan and T. D. Williams (eds.), *Ireland in the War Years and After, 1939–51* (Gill & Macmillan, Dublin, 1969)

Woodman, K., *Media Control in Ireland 1923–1983* (Galway, 1986)

Wyman, David, *The Abandonment of the Jews: America and the Holocaust 1941–1945* (Pantheon Books, New York, 1985)

    Paper Walls: America and the Refugee Crisis 1938–1941 (Pantheon Books, New York, 1985)

Wyman, David (ed.), *The World Reacts to the Holocaust* (Johns Hopkins University Press, Baltimore and London, 1996)

Yahil, Leni, *The Holocaust: The Fate of European Jewry, 1932–1945* (Oxford University Press, Oxford, 1990)

Zahn, Gordon C., *I cattolici tedeschi e le guerre di Hitler* (Vallecchi, Firenze, 1973)

Zlotover, Melisande, see under Hannah Berman

Zuccotti, Susan, *The Italians and the Holocaust* (Peter Halban, London, 1987)

Index